# Lecture Notes in Computer Science          11418

*Commenced Publication in 1973*
Founding and Former Series Editors:
Gerhard Goos, Juris Hartmanis, and Jan van Leeuwen

More information about this series at http://www.springer.com/series/7412

Shoji Tominaga · Raimondo Schettini
Alain Trémeau · Takahiko Horiuchi (Eds.)

# Computational Color Imaging

7th International Workshop, CCIW 2019
Chiba, Japan, March 27–29, 2019
Proceedings

 Springer

*Editors*
Shoji Tominaga
Norwegian University of Science
and Technology
Gjøvik, Norway

Raimondo Schettini ⓘ
University of Milano Bicocca
Milan, Italy

Alain Trémeau
University Jean Monnet
Saint-Etienne, France

Takahiko Horiuchi ⓘ
Chiba University
Chiba, Japan

ISSN 0302-9743          ISSN 1611-3349   (electronic)
Lecture Notes in Computer Science
ISBN 978-3-030-13939-1          ISBN 978-3-030-13940-7   (eBook)
https://doi.org/10.1007/978-3-030-13940-7

Library of Congress Control Number: 2019931872

LNCS Sublibrary: SL6 – Image Processing, Computer Vision, Pattern Recognition, and Graphics

This Springer imprint is published by the registered company Springer Nature Switzerland AG
The registered company address is: Gewerbestrasse 11, 6330 Cham, Switzerland

# Preface

We would like to welcome you to the proceedings of CCIW 2019, the Computational Color Imaging Workshop, held in Chiba, Japan, March 27–29, 2019.

This event, the seventh CCIW, was organized by Chiba University, Institute for Global Prominent Research at Chiba University, and Next Generation Research Incubator "Creation of Imaging Science and Technology for Material Appearance" at Chiba University with the endorsement of the International Association for Pattern Recognition (IAPR), the Color Science Association of Japan (CSAJ), the Groupe Français de l'Imagerie Numérique Couleur (GFNIC), Associazione Italiana per la ricerca in Computer Vision, Pattern recognition e machine Learning (CVPL) affiliated with IAPR, and the Special Interest Group on Foundations of Visual Information (SigFVI) affiliated with CSAJ.

Since the first Computational Color Imaging Workshop was organized in 2007 in Modena, Italy, CCIW has been held every other year in Italy, France, and Japan.

The aim of the workshop was to bring together engineers and scientists of various imaging companies and technical communities from all over the world to discuss diverse aspects of their latest work, ranging from theoretical developments to practical applications in the field of computational color imaging, including multispectral imaging, appearance modeling, and color image processing. The field is based on knowledge not only of computer science but also of human vision and perception, neuroscience, and optics.

There were many excellent submissions of high scientific level, and each paper was peer-reviewed. However, because of the time slot constraint, only the best 22 papers were selected for the presentation at the workshop. The final decision of which paper to be chosen was based on the criticisms and recommendations of the reviewers, and the content relevance of the particular paper to the goal of the workshop. Only 64% of the papers submitted were accepted for inclusion in the program.

Seven different sessions were organized to present an overview of current research directions:

- Computational Color Imaging
- Multispectral Imaging
- Perceptual Model and Application
- Color Image Evaluation
- Color Image Filtering
- Color Image Applications
- Color Imaging for Material Appearance

In addition to the contributed papers, eight distinguished researchers were invited to this seventh CCIW to deliver keynote speeches on current hot research directions of the topics on computational color imaging:

Tutorials

- Shin'ya Nishida, on "Image Features for Human Material Perception"
- Roland W. Fleming, on "Visual Perception of Materials and Their Properties"
- Ming Ronnier Luo, on "Status Quo of Color Appearance Modeling"
- Ko Nishino, on "Freeing Computer Vision from Its Fundamental Limits"

Invited talks

- Takayuki Okatani, on "Improving Generalization Ability of Deep Neural Networks for Visual Recognition Tasks"
- Mathieu Hébert, on "How Microarrangement of Colored Materials Influences the Macroscopic Color of a Surface"
- Daisuke Iwai, on "Computational Imaging in Projection Mapping"
- Jon Y. Hardeberg, on "On the Acquisition and Reproduction of Material Appearance"

There are many organizations and people who have helped us in the planning of this meeting. Among them, we are pleased to acknowledge the generous support of the University of Milano-Bicocca, Italy, the University Jean Monnet at Saint Etienne, and the Laboratoire Hubert Curien, France, and Chiba University, Japan.

March 2019

Shoji Tominaga
Raimondo Schettini
Alain Trémeau
Takahiko Horiuchi

# Organization

CCIW 2019 was organized by Chiba University, Japan, in cooperation with the University of Milano-Bicocca, Italy, and the University of Saint Etienne, France.

## Executive Committee

### Conference Chairs

| | |
|---|---|
| Shoji Tominaga | NTNU, Norway/Nagano University, Japan |
| Raimondo Schettini | University of Milano-Bicocca, Milan, Italy |
| Alain Trémeau | Université Jean Monnet, Saint-Etienne, France |
| Takahiko Horiuchi | Chiba University, Japan |

## Program Committee

| | |
|---|---|
| Sebastiano Battiato | Università di Catania, Italy |
| Eva M. Valero Benito | University of Granada, Spain |
| Simone Bianco | University of Milano Bicocca, Italy |
| M. Emre Celebi | University of Central Arkansas, USA |
| Silvia Corchs | University of Milano Bicocca, Italy |
| Brian Funt | Simon Fraser University, Canada |
| Francesca Gasparini | University of Milano Bicocca, Italy |
| Yeong-Ho Ha | Kyungpook National University, Korea |
| Jon Ynge Hardeberg | NTNU, Norway |
| Markku Hauta-Kasari | University of Eastern Finland, Finland |
| Mathieu Hébert | Université Jean Monnet, France |
| Javier Hernández-Andrés | University of Granada, Spain |
| Keigo Hirakawa | University of Dayton, USA |
| Francisco Imai | Canon USA, Inc., USA |
| Hiroaki Kotera | Kotera Imaging Laboratory, Japan |
| Byung-Uk Lee | Ewha W. University, Korea |
| Ming Ronnier Luo | Zhejiang University / Leeds University, China |
| Lindsay Macdonald | University College London, UK |
| Yoshitsugu Manabe | Chiba University, Japan |
| Jan Morovic | HP Barcelona, Spain |
| Damien Muselet | Université Jean Monnet, France |
| Sergio Nascimento | University of Minho, Portugal |
| Ko Nishino | Kyoto University, Japan |
| Juan Luis Nieves | University of Granada, Spain |
| Jussi Parkkinen | University of Eastern Finland, Finland |
| Noël Richard | Université de Poitiers, France |

| Alessandro Rizzi | University of Milan, Italy |
| Yong Man Ro | Korea Advanced Institute of Science and Technology, Korea |
| Bogdan Smolka | Silesian University of Technology, Poland |
| Pei-Li Sun | National Taiwan University of Science and Technology, Taiwan |
| Jean-Baptiste Thomas | NTNU, Norway |
| Norimichi Tsumura | Japan |
| Maria Vanrell | Universitat Autònoma de Barcelona, Spain |
| Joost van de Weijer | Universitat Autònoma de Barcelona, Spain |
| Masahiro Yamaguchi | Tokyo Institute of Technology, Japan |

## Local Arrangements Committee

| Keita Hirai | Chiba University, Japan |

## Tutorials

| Shin'ya Nishida | NTT Communication Science Laboratories, Japan |
| Roland W. Fleming | University of Giessen, Germany |
| Ming Ronnier Luo | Zhejiang University, China/Leeds University, UK |
| Ko Nishino | Kyoto University, Japan |

## Invited Talks

| Takayuki Okatani | Tohoku University, Japan |
| Mathieu Hébert | University Jean Monnet of Saint-Etienne, France |
| Daisuke Iwai | Osaka University, Japan |
| Jon Y. Hardeberg | NTNU, Norway |

## Sponsoring Institutions

Chiba University, Institute for Global Prominent Research, Japan
Chiba University, Next Generation Research Incubator, Japan
"Creation of Imaging Science and Technology for Material Appearance"
University of Milano-Bicocca, Milan, Italy
Université Jean Monnet and Laboratoire Hubert Curien, Saint-Etienne, France
Groupe Français de l'Imagerie Numérique Couleur, France
Gruppo Italiano Ricercatori in Pattern Recognition, Italy
The Color Science Association of Japan
Association Française pour la Reconnaissance et l'Interprétation des Formes (AFRIF)
Special Interest Group on Foundations of Visual Information, CSAJ, Japan

# Contents

## Color Imaging for Material Appearance

# Invited Talks

# Improving Generalization Ability of Deep Neural Networks for Visual Recognition Tasks

Takayuki Okatani[1,2]([✉]), Xing Liu[1], and Masanori Suganuma[1,2]

[1] Graduate School of Information Sciences, Tohoku University, Sendai, Japan
okatani@vision.is.tohoku.ac.jp
[2] RIKEN Center for AIP, Tokyo, Japan
http://www.vision.is.tohoku.ac.jp

**Abstract.** This article discusses generalization ability of convolutional neural networks (CNNs) for visual recognition with special focus on robustness to image degradation. It has been long since CNNs were claimed to surpass human vision, for example, in an object recognition task. However, such claims simply report experimental results that CNNs perform better than humans on a closed set of testing inputs. In fact, CNNs can easily fail for images to which noises are added, when they have not learned the noisy images; this is the case even if humans are barely affected by the added noises. As a solution to this problem, we discuss an approach that first restores the clean image from an input distorted image and then uses it for the target recognition task, where a CNN trained only on clean images is used. For solutions to the first step, we show our recent studies of image restoration. There are multiple different types of image distortion, such as noise, defocus/motion blur, rain-streaks, raindrops, haze etc. We first introduce our recent study of architectural design of CNNs for image restoration targeting at a single, identified type of distortion. We then introduce another study, which proposes to use a single CNN to remove combination of multiple types of distortion with unknown mixture ratio. Although it achieves only lower accuracy than the first method in the case of a single, identified type of distortion, the method will be more useful in practical applications.

**Keywords:** Visual recognition · Convolutional neural networks · Generalization ability

## 1 Introduction

The emergence of convolutional neural networks has reshaped research in the field of computer vision in the past seven years. Their employment has brought about solutions to unsolved problems or contributed to (sometimes significant) improvements in performance (e.g., inference accuracy, computational speed etc.). It was claimed in the past years that CNNs can even surpass human vision in several visual recognition tasks, in particular, the task of object category classification [7].

© Springer Nature Switzerland AG 2019
S. Tominaga et al. (Eds.): CCIW 2019, LNCS 11418, pp. 3–13, 2019.
https://doi.org/10.1007/978-3-030-13940-7_1

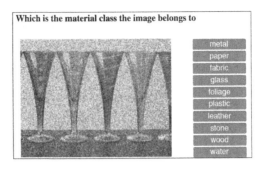

**Fig. 1.** Material classification from a noisy image. Humans and CNNs choose one of the ten material categories shown on the right.

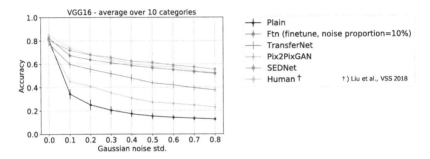

**Fig. 2.** Accuracy of material classification versus the strength of Gaussian noise added to the input images. Plain indicates a CNN trained only on clean images and Ftn is a CNN trained on both clean and noisy images.

However, we should be precise about the meaning (or underlying condition) of such claims. Each of them is made based on experiments that compare CNNs and humans on a recognition task using a *particular* dataset. The experimental results merely indicate that CNNs are better in terms of recognition accuracy than humans on a *closed* set of test inputs. In other words, CNNs may correctly classify inputs that are sampled from the same distribution as the training data they have learned, but will wrongly classify inputs sampled from a different distribution. The two distributions usually need to be very close; their difference is called *domain shift*, which is known as one of major causes that impede applications of CNNs to real-world problems.

One such example is shown in Fig. 1. The image shown on the left is a noisy version of a sample belonging to Flickr Material Databse (FMD) [18], which is a popular dataset for ten-class material classification task; the ten classes are shown on the right of the figure. We consider here the material classification task from noisy input images. The original images of FMDs are noise-free, and we add Gaussian random noises with a certain strength to them.

Figure 2 shows the results. It shows performance of various CNN models and humans for different strengths of additive Gaussian noises. An overall tendency is that humans and all the CNN models show similar accuracy in the noise-free case, and they all deteriorate as the noise strength increases. It is, however, seen that the performance decrease for humans is almost the smallest, while the CNN trained only on clean (i.e., noise-free) images performs the worst for noisy inputs. On the other hand, the CNN trained also on noisy images shows comparable performance to humans. This phenomenon demonstrates the aforementioned issue with neural networks; they work very well for trained data but can fail for inputs sampled from a slightly different distribution, even if the difference is mostly negligible for humans.

In this article, we consider how to cope with the issue with deep learning. We first discuss how to enable to perform visual recognition from degraded images such as noisy images considered above.

## 2 Image Restoration for Robust Visual Recognition

### 2.1 Visual Recognition Robust to Image Distortion

There are three approaches to visual recognition from distorted (or degraded) images, as shown in Fig. 3. The first approach, which is conceptually the simplest, is to train the CNN using not only clean images but noisy images. Then, the CNN will accurately recognize noisy inputs, as discussed above and shown in Fig. 2. However, this approach is often impossible to employ, since it requires to have training data of distorted images (i.e., noisy images in the aforementioned case), which need to be given labels (i.e., material or object categories), as well as to perform training on a larger dataset.

The second approach (Fig. 3(c)) is to make the CNN more robust to image distortion, so that it can correctly recognize distorted images even though it is trained only on clean images. This may be the most difficult one of the three approaches. In fact, there is only a few studies pursuing this approach. For example, Sun et al. [32] show that a type of activation functions mitigates decrease in recognition accuracy due to distortion of input images. However, the improvements are limited for real-world applications.

The third approach (Fig. 3(d)), which is the one we discussed in what follows, is to use another CNN model to restore quality of input images with distortions. We insert this CNN for image restoration before the CNN for classification (or other purposes); the first CNN estimate clean version of the input distorted image, which is fed to the second CNN for classification. We can use the CNN trained only on clean images for the second CNN. Instead, it is necessary to train the second CNN, which requires pairs of a distorted image and its clean version. On the other hand, it is not necessary to give the input distorted images labels for classification, which is advantageous. Moreover, the cost for creating the training data for image restoration (i.e., the second CNN) tends to be lower than the classification task.

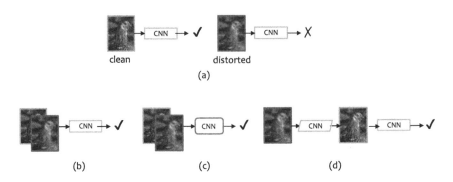

**Fig. 3.** Three ways to improve robustness of CNNs to image distortion. (a) A CNN trained only on clean images is vulnerable to distortion in input images. There are three methods to cope with this issue: (b) inclusion of distorted images in training data; (c) robustification of the CNN itself; and (d) cascading an image-restoration CNN to the CNN trained only on clean images.

Now, the problem is how to build a CNN that can perform image restoration with sufficient accuracy. We wish the first CNN to restore a clean image from an input distorted image and then the second CNN to correctly classify objects etc from the restored image. An example is the SEDNet shown in Fig. 2; it is a cascade of two CNNs (i.e., image restoration + classification) and it achieves slightly better performance than humans for inputs with large noises.

The problem of image restoration has been studied for a long time. In the past, researchers mainly tackle the problem by modeling natural images, where they consider their statistics based on edge statistics [4,16], sparse representation [1,25] etc. Recently, learning-based methods, particularly those using CNNs [8, 10] have shown better performance than those previous methods for the problems of denoising [21,24,28,29], deblurring [9,14,20], and super-resolution [2,11,30].

## 3   Image Restoration for Single Type of Distortions

We first consider the case where input images undergo a single type of distortion. This is a standard setting of image restoration, for which there have been a vast amount of studies conducted so far. Recent applications of CNNs have contributed to performance improvement. We have developed better architectural design of networks that can be shared across many tasks of image restoration. We briefly summarize the study here.

In the study, we pay attention to the effectiveness of paired operations on various image processing tasks. In [19], evolutionary computation is employed to search for optimal design of convolutional autoencoders for a few image restoration tasks; network structures repeatedly performing a pair of convolutions with a large- and small-size kernels perform well for image denoising. In [5], it is shown that a CNN iteratively performing a pair of up-sampling and down-sampling contributes to performance improvement for image-superresolution.

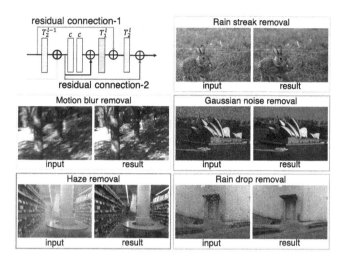

**Fig. 4.** Structure of the Dual Residual Block (DuRB) (upper left) and five popular image restoration tasks.

To accommodate such paired operation effectively, we propose a general architecture named Dual Residual Block (DuRN). A DuRN consists of an initial group of layers starting from the input layer, followed by an arbitrary number of blocks called Dual Residual Blocks (DuRBs), and the last group of layers ending at the output layer. Each DuRB has containers for the paired first and second operations. Normalization layers (such as batch normalization [6] or instance normalization [22]) and ReLU [15] layers can be incorporated when it is necessary.

In our experiments, we consider the five types of image distortions and restoration from them, as shown in Fig. 4. We design DuRBs for each of them; to be specific, we choose the two operations to be inserted into the containers $T_1^l$ and $T_2^l$ in the DuRBs. We have designed and used four different implementations, i.e., DuRB-P, DuRB-U, DuRB-S, and DuRB-US; DuRB-P are used for noise removal, rain-streak removal and raindrop removal, DuRB-U for motion blur removal, DuRB-S for raindrop removal, and DuRB-US for haze removal. For $[T_1^l, T_2^l]$, we specify [conv., conv.] for DuRB-P, [up-sampling + conv., down-sampling (by conv. with stride = 2)] for DuRP-U, [conv., channel-wise attention for DuRP-S, and [up-sampling + conv., channel-wise attention + down-sampling] for DuRB-US, respectively. We will show experimental results for noise removal, rain-streak removal, and motion-blur removal in what follows.

## 3.1 Noise Removal

We use DuRN-P for this task. Based on the findings in a study of neural architectural search [19], we choose convolution with large- and small-size receptive fields for $T_1$ and $T_2$, respectively. We also choose the kernel size and dilation rate for each DuRB so that the receptive field of convolution in each DuRB grows

**Fig. 5.** Some examples of the results by DuRN-P for additive Gaussian noise removal. Sharp images can be restored from heavy noises ($\sigma = 50$).

**Fig. 6.** Examples of motion blur removal on GoPro-test dataset.

its size with $l$. The entire network consisting of six DuRB-P's along with initial and final groups of layers is named DuRN-P. We train the network using $l_2$ loss (Fig. 5).

## 3.2   Motion Blur Removal

We use DuRN-U for this task. Following many previous works [9,23,27,31], we choose a symmetric encoder-decoder network for overall network structure. Then, following previous work [23] reporting the effectiveness of up- and down-sampling operations for this task, we employ the same operations for the paired operation. It achieves PSNR 29.9 dB and SSIM 0.91 on the GoPro-test dataset [14], while the state-of-the-art DeblurGAN (precisely, the "DeblurGAN-wild" introduced in the original paper [9]) achieved PSNR 27.2 dB and SSIM 0.95. Examples of deblurred images are shown in Fig. 6. It is seen that cracks on a stone-fence and numbers written on the car plate are restored well enough to be recognized.

*Object Detection from Deblurred Images.* We tested the two-step approach discussed earlier using the above CNN for motion blur removal. Given an image with motion blur, we first apply the above CNN, DuRN-U, to the input image and then use an object detector to the restored image. We follow the experimental procedure and dataset used in [9]. Note that DuRN-U is trained on the

GoPro-train dataset. For the object detector, we use YOLO v3 [17] trained on the Pascal VOC [3]. Table 1 shows quantitative results. The detection results for sharp images of the same YOLO v3 detector are used as the ground truths. It is seen that the proposed DuRN-U outperforms the state-of-the-art DeBlurGAN.

**Table 1.** Accuracy of object detection from deblurred images obtained by DeBlurGAN [9] and the proposed DuRN-U on Car Dataset.

|          | Blurred | DeBlurGAN[9] | DuRN-U (ours) |
|----------|---------|--------------|---------------|
| mAP (%)  | 16.54   | 26.17        | 31.15         |

## 4 Image Restoration for Combined Distortions

As explained above, there are many types of image distortion, such as various types of noises, defocus/motion blur, compression artifacts, haze, raindrops, etc. Thus, there are two cases for application of image restoration methods to real-world problems. One is the case where the user knows what image distortion need to be removed, e.g., a deblurring filter tool in a photo editing software. This is the case that we have considered above. The other is the case where the user wants to improve quality of an image but does *not* know what distortion(s) the image undergoes, e.g., applications to vision for autonomous cars or surveillance cameras.

We consider the second case here. Existing studies mostly consider the first case, which cannot be applied to the second case directly. However, real-world images usually suffer from a combination of different types of distortion, where we don't know mixture ratios and strengths of different distortion types in the input images. We need image restoration methods that work under such conditions.

There are only a few studies of this problem, such as Yu et al. [26]. The authors propose a method that adaptively selects and apply multiple light-weight CNNs; each CNN is trained for different image distortion. Their selection is done by an agent trained by reinforcemenet learning. However, the gain of accuracy obtained by their method is not so large, as compared with a dedicated method (CNN) for a single type of distortion.

We showed that a simple attention mechanism, named *operation-wise attention* layer, can better deals with the case of combined image distortions [13]. We propose a layer that performs many operations in parallel, such as convolution and pooling with different parameters. These operations are weighted by an attention mechanism built-in the layer, which is intended to work as a switcher of the operations. The attention weights are multiplied with the outputs of the operations, which are concatenated and transferred to the next layer. This layer can be stacked to form a multi-layer network that is fully differentiable. Thus, it can be trained in an end-to-end manner by gradient descent (Fig. 7).

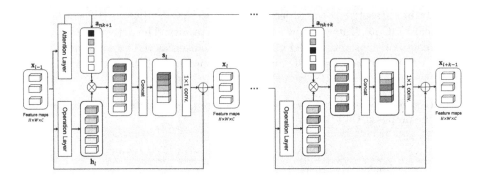

**Fig. 7.** Architecture of the operation-wise attention layer. It consists of an attention layer, an operation layer, a concatenation operation, and $1 \times 1$ convolution. Attention weights over operations of each layer are generated at the first layer in a group of consecutive $k$ layers. Note that different attention weights are generated for each layer.

We evaluated the proposed approach by using the DIV2K dataset, which was created in [26] to evaluate their proposed method, RL-Restore. The dataset consists of about 0.3 million image patches of $63 \times 63$ pixels. They have multiple types of distortion, i.e., a sequence of Gaussian blur, Gaussian noise and JPEG compression with random levels of distortion. The proposed method achieves improvements of 0.3–0.7 dB (PSNR) and 0.015–0.02 (SSIM) over RL-Restore.

As in the aforementioned experiments on single type distortion, we evaluate the performance of the proposed method on the task of object detection. That is, we first restore an input image having combined distortion and then apply an object detector (SSD300 [12]) to the restored image. Employing the images from the PASCAL VOC detection dataset, we synthesize combined distortion of Gaussian blur, Gaussian Noise, and JPEG compression with random levels of distortion. The proposed method improves detection accuracy by a large margin (around 30% mAP) compared to the case of applying the same detector to the distorted images. It outperforms RL-Restore for almost all categories of objects. Figure 8 shows a selected examples of detection results. It is observed that the proposed method eliminate the combined distortion effectively and contributes to more accurate object detection.

## 5    Summary

We have discussed how to improve generalization ability of CNNs for visual recognition tasks, particularly in the case where input images undergo various types of image distortion. We have first pointed out that CNNs trained only on clean images are vulnerable to distortion in input images. This may be regarded as co-variate shift, the issue with CNNs or any other machine learning methods. We have further discussed the three possible approaches to the issue, i.e., (i) training the CNN also on distorted images, (ii) building more robust CNNs that can deal with distorted images, even if they are trained on clean images

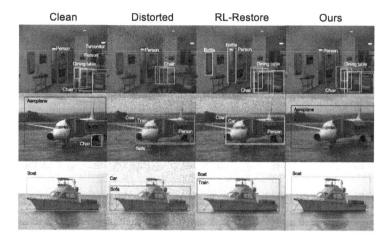

**Fig. 8.** Examples of results of object detection on PASCAL VOC. The box colors indicate class categories.

alone, and (iii) restoring a clean version from the input distorted image and then inputting it to a CNN trained only on clean images. We have then introduced two recent studies of ours that employ the third approach. The first study proposes an architectural design of CNNs for image restoration targeting at a single type of distortion. The second study proposes to use a single CNN that can restore clean image from an input image with combined types of distortion. The former provides better restoration performance but requires the type of distortion in input images to be identified beforehand. The latter is designed to be able to deal with unidentified type of image distortion, in particular, combined distortion of multiple types with unknown mixture ratios. We will be choosing between the two methods depending on conditions and requirements of applications. We believe that there will be room for further improvement in restoration accuracy, particularly for the second problem setting for unidentified distortion types. This will be studied in the future.

**Acknowledgments.** This work was partly supported by JSPS KAKENHI Grant Number JP15H05919, JST CREST Grant Number JPMJCR14D1, and the ImPACT Program "Tough Robotics Challenge" of the Council for Science, Technology, and Innovation (Cabinet Office, Government of Japan).

# References

1. Aharon, M., Elad, M., Bruckstein, A.: k-SVD: an algorithm for designing overcomplete dictionaries for sparse representation. IEEE Trans. Signal Process. **54**(11), 4311–4322 (2006)
2. Dong, C., Loy, C.C., He, K., Tang, X.: Learning a deep convolutional network for image super-resolution. In: Fleet, D., Pajdla, T., Schiele, B., Tuytelaars, T. (eds.) ECCV 2014, Part IV. LNCS, vol. 8692, pp. 184–199. Springer, Cham (2014). https://doi.org/10.1007/978-3-319-10593-2_13

3. Everingham, M., Eslami, S.M.A., Van Gool, L., Williams, C.K.I., Winn, J., Zisserman, A.: The pascal visual object classes challenge: a retrospective. Int. J. Comput. Vis. **111**, 98–136 (2015)
4. Fattal, R.: Image upsampling via imposed edge statistics. In: SIGGRAPH (2007)
5. Haris, M., Shakhnarovich, G., Ukita, N.: Deep back-projection networks for super-resolution. In: Proceedings of Conference on Computer Vision and Pattern Recognition (2018)
6. Ioffe, S., Szegedy, C.: Batch normalization: accelerating deep network training by reducing internal covariate shift. In: Proceedings of International Conference on Machine Learning (2015)
7. He, K., Zhang, X., Ren, S., Sun, J.: Delving deep into rectifiers: surpassing human-level performance on imagenet classification. In: Proceedings of International Conference on Computer Vision (2015)
8. Krizhevsky, A., Sutskever, I., Hinton, G.E.: Imagenet classification with deep convolutional neural networks. In: Proceedings of Neural Information Processing Systems (2012)
9. Kupyn, O., Budzan, V., Mykhailych, M., Mishkin, D., Matas, J.: DeblurGAN: blind motion deblurring using conditional adversarial networks. In: Proceedings of IEEE Conference on Computer Vision and Pattern Recognition (2018)
10. LeCun, Y., Bottou, L., Bengio, Y., Haffner, P.: Gradient-based learning applied to document recognition. Proc. IEEE **86**(11), 2278–2324 (1998)
11. Ledig, C., et al.: Photo-realistic single image super-resolution using a generative adversarial network. In: Proceedings of IEEE Conference on Computer Vision and Pattern Recognition (2017)
12. Liu, W., et al.: SSD: single shot multibox detector. In: Leibe, B., Matas, J., Sebe, N., Welling, M. (eds.) ECCV 2016, Part I. LNCS, vol. 9905, pp. 21–37. Springer, Cham (2016). https://doi.org/10.1007/978-3-319-46448-0_2
13. Suganuma, M., Lui, X., OKatani, T.: Attention-based adaptive selection of operations for image restoration in the presence of unknown combined distortions. CoRR abs/1812.00733 (2018)
14. Nah, S., Kim, T.H., Lee, K.M.: Deep multi-scale convolutional neural network for dynamic scene deblurring. In: Proceedings of IEEE Conference on Computer Vision and Pattern Recognition (2017)
15. Nair, V., Hinton, G.E.: Rectified linear units improve restricted boltzmann machines. In: Proceedings of International Conference on Machine Learning (2015)
16. Perrone, D., Favaro, P.: Total variation blind deconvolution: the devil is in the details. In: Proceedings of IEEE Conference on Computer Vision and Pattern Recognition (2014)
17. Redmon, J., Farhadi, A.: Yolov3: An incremental improvement. arXiv:1804.02767 (2018)
18. Sharan, L., Rosenholtz, R., Adelson, E.: Material perception: what can you see in a brief glance? J. Vis. **14**(9), 784 (2014)
19. Suganuma, M., Ozay, M., Okatani, T.: Exploiting the potential of standard convolutional autoencoders for image restoration by evolutionary search. In: Proceedings of International Conference on Machine Learning (2018)
20. Sun, J., Cao, W., Xu, Z., Ponce, J.: Learning a convolutional neural network for non-uniform motion blur removal. In: Proceedings of IEEE Conference on Computer Vision and Pattern Recognition (2015)
21. Tai, Y., Yang, J., Liu, X., Xu, C.: MemNet: A persistent memory network for image restoration. In: Proceedings of IEEE Conference on Computer Vision and Pattern Recognition (2017)

22. Ulyanov, D., Vedaldi, A., Lempitsky, V.S.: Instance normalization: the missing ingredient for fast stylization. arXiv:1607.08022 (2016)
23. Wieschollek, P., Hirsch, M., Schölkopf, B., Lensch, H.P.A.: Learning blind motion deblurring. In: Proceedings of International Conference on Computer Vision (2017)
24. Xie, J., Xu, L., Chen, E.: Image denoising and inpainting with deep neural networks. In: Proceedings of Neural Information Processing Systems (2012)
25. Yang, J., Wright, J., Huang, T.S., Ma, Y.: Image super-resolution via sparse representation. IEEE Trans. Image Process. 19(11), 2861–2873 (2010)
26. Yu, K., Dong, C., Lin, L., Change, L.C.: Crafting a toolchain for image restoration by deep reinforcement learning. In: Proceedings of IEEE Conference on Computer Vision and Pattern Recognition (2018)
27. Zhang, H., Patel, V.M.: Densely connected pyramid dehazing network. In: Proceedings of Conference on Computer Vision and Pattern Recognition (2018)
28. Zhang, K., Zuo, W., Chen, Y., Meng, D., Zhang, L.: Beyond a Gaussian denoiser: residual learning of deep CNN for image denoising. IEEE Trans. Image Process. 26(7), 3142–3155 (2017)
29. Zhang, K., Zuo, W., Zhang, L.: FFDNet: Toward a fast and flexible solution for cnn based image denoising. IEEE Trans. Image Process. 27(9), 4608–4622 (2018)
30. Zhang, Y., Li, K., Li, K., Wang, L., Zhong, B., Fu, Y.: Image super-resolution using very deep residual channel attention networks. In: Ferrari, V., Hebert, M., Sminchisescu, C., Weiss, Y. (eds.) ECCV 2018, Part VII. LNCS, vol. 11211, pp. 294–310. Springer, Cham (2018). https://doi.org/10.1007/978-3-030-01234-2_18
31. Zhu, J.Y., Park, T., Isola, P., Efros, A.A.: Unpaired image-to-image translation using cycle-consistent adversarial networks. In: Proceedings of International Conference on Computer Vision (2017)
32. Sun, Z., Ozay, M., Zhang, Y., Liu, X., Okatani, T.: Feature quantization for defending against distortion of images. In: Proceedings of Computer Vision and Pattern Recognition, pp. 7957–7966 (2018)

# Computational Imaging in Projection Mapping

Daisuke Iwai[✉] [iD]

Osaka University, Machikaneyama 1-3, Toyonaka, Osaka 560-8531, Japan
daisuke.iwai@sys.es.osaka-u.ac.jp
http://daisukeiwai.org/

**Abstract.** Projection mapping or spatial augmented reality (SAR) has been tremendously widespread over the world. The goal is to seamlessly merge physical and virtual worlds by superimposing computer generated graphics onto real surfaces. In projection mapping applications, target surfaces are generally not suitable for projection. They are textured and non-planar and conventional projectors are specifically designed to display high quality images onto uniformly white and flat surfaces only. Although researchers developed various algorithms to alleviate image quality degradations, the performances were limited by upper bounds resulting from the hardware. I briefly overview the recent advances in the projection mapping research field, particularly focuses on the computational imaging and display approach to overcome technical limitations of current projection hardware in terms of dynamic range, refresh rate, and depth-of-field. I also covers an emerging issue in the projection mapping research, which is dynamic projection mapping. This article is written by reorganizing a previously published state-of-the-art report paper by the same author [13] for an invited talk at the IAPR Computational Color Imaging Workshop (CCIW) 2019.

**Keywords:** Computational imaging · Computational display · Projection mapping · Spatial augmented reality (SAR) · Projector-camera system (procams)

## 1 Introduction

During the last decade, projection mapping or spatial augmented reality (SAR) has been tremendously widespread over the world. The goal is to seamlessly merge physical and virtual worlds by superimposing computer generated graphics onto real surfaces. One of the biggest differentiator compared to other augmentation techniques is the capability of projection mapping to let many users directly experience the augmentation without wearing glasses or any other devices. Constant improvements in size, pricing, and brightness of projectors have allowed many people to develop their own projection mapping projects. They used a large variety of surfaces as projection targets: large buildings, cars,

© Springer Nature Switzerland AG 2019
S. Tominaga et al. (Eds.): CCIW 2019, LNCS 11418, pp. 14–25, 2019.
https://doi.org/10.1007/978-3-030-13940-7_2

shoes, furniture, and even living creatures such as fish in an aquarium and human dancers. In the emerging application scenarios, there are strong demands for displaying desired appearances on non-planar, textured, and/or dynamically moving surfaces under environmental lightings.

Typically, projectors are designed and used to display images onto a planar, uniformly white, and static screen in a dark environment. Due to this fact, current projectors are not suitable for most projection mapping scenarios. Particularly, the dynamic range, frame-rate, latency, and depth-of-field (DOF) limit their applicability. These technical limitations of the projector hardware make it difficult to display desired appearances in the wanted visual quality even when the computational algorithms are applied. Researchers have applied the emerging "computational imaging and display" approach, which is a joint design of display hardware, optics and computational algorithms to overcome the limitations [26].

This invited talk summarizes the recent advances of projection mapping hardware solutions to display desired appearances onto non-optimized real surfaces in an enhanced visual quality. The following sections introduce computational display solutions to overcome the mentioned technical limitations and to achieve high dynamic range, high speed, and wide DOF projections. In addition, some works on an emerging technical issue in the projection mapping research, dynamic projection mapping, are introduced in the last part of the paper. Note that this article is written by reorganizing a previously published state-of-the-art report paper by the same author [13] for an invited talk at the IAPR Computational Color Imaging Worksop (CCIW) 2019. Therefore, some texts of this article are overlapped with the previous one.

## 2 High Dynamic Range Projection

The dynamic range or contrast of a projection display is defined as the ratio of the maximum to minimum luminance. The range of luminance values in the real world is extremely wide, from an outdoor scene in sunshine to an indoor scene under a candle light. Consequently, a high dynamic range (HDR) representation would be required to realistically render and display both natural and computer generated images. However, current projectors, except for laser-based devices, can support only a significantly limited dynamic range; i.e., a simultaneous in-scene contrast is typically limited to the range of between 1,000:1 and 6,000:1 [10]. Note that this section discusses the simultaneous dynamic range that is achieved without additional mechanical adjustments, such as auto-iris aperture control, which globally brightens or darkens all the pixels in a projection image and does not change the contrast within a single image. Theoretically, laser projectors are able to achieve extremely high dynamic range representations since they can be completely turn off the laser beam when displaying black pixels. Therefore, a laser projector would be one of the best choices in normal projector usage scenarios such as a theater. On the other hand, due to an eye safe issue, it is not practical in SAR or projection mapping applications where user's

Experimental setup          Under environment lighting      Under texture projection

**Fig. 1.** Experimental results of 3D HDR projection based on reflectance modulation using a full-color 3D printer [38].

eyes might be located between a projector and the augmented object. Several other solutions have been presented to overcome the contrast limitations. They can mainly be subdivided into methods trying to achieve that goal by reducing the black-level and hardware which locally amplifies the amount of photons. We will discuss them in the following paragraphs.

HDR projection has been achieved by applying the double modulation principle, by which the emission of a light source is spatially modulated twice at cascaded light blocking spatial light modulators (SLMs), e.g., a digital micromirror device (DMD) or a liquid crystal display (LCD), to reduce the luminance of dark pixels (or black level) while maintaining those of bright pixels. Researchers proposed several double modulation methods so far such as applying two LCD panels, and these successfully increased the dynamic range of a projected image by significantly lowering the black level luminance which is perceived when displaying zero intensity values (for more details, see a state-of-the-art report [8]). Recent works applied dual LCoS (Liquid crystal on silicon) designs [14,16].

Even when an ideal projector with infinite dynamic range is applied, environmental light and/or global illumination effects such as inter-reflection increases the reflected black level which consequently decreases the dynamic range of the projection. In particular, it is natural to assume that many projection mapping applications are run with a small amount of environment light contribution and non-flat, concave surfaces might be used as projection targets. Therefore, increasing the dynamic range of a projector is not sufficient, but the whole projection system including the surface must be optimized. To this end, researchers have proposed to spatially modulate the reflectance pattern of a projection surface to suppress the elevation of black level [7,18,19,38]. More specifically, the luminance of a projected light is theoretically computed as the multiplication of the reflectance of a surface and the incident light illuminance. Therefore, it is possible to avoid undesirable black level elevation by decreasing the reflectance at a place where dark image should be displayed.

Bimber and Iwai proposed to use printed media including an e-ink display for the reflectance modulation [7]. This was also extended to static 3D surfaces by applying a full-color 3D printer [38] (Fig. 1). Because these methods applied static or almost static reflection media, dynamic image contents such as movies are not suitable. Jones et al. proposed to optimize the surface reflectance pattern to display a short periodic movie sequence in HDR [19]. A dynamic modulation of the reflectance pattern was also investigated by Iwai et al. who proposed to cover the projection surface with a photochromic material such that the surface reflectance can be spatiotemporally controlled by applying UV illumination [18].

## 3  High Speed Projection

High speed projection systems enabling a much higher frame rate than a normal video rate (e.g., 60 Hz) are required in low latency scenarios. It has been achieved using DLP projectors that represent an 8-bit pixel intensity by controlling a MEMS mirror flip sequence, whether it reflects a light from a light source to the objective lens or not, at thousands of frames per second. Using the mechanism, researchers developed high speed projection systems.

Projection mapping applications generally require a precise alignment between a projected image and a physical surface. Even a small misalignment is salient, and thus, causes a significant degradation of the sense of immersion. This requirement becomes significantly more rigorous in dynamic projection mapping scenarios, in which a slight temporal delay of an even geometrically perfectly aligned projection causes a noticeable misalignment. For example, Ng et al. investigated the noticeable shortest latency for a touch panel interface [33]. They showed that participants perceived a misalignment when the latency between touch input and the display of this visual feedback on the touch position was greater than 6.04 ms. This maps to a minimum desired frame rate of approx. 165 Hz and challenging latency requirements.

Recently two solutions have been presented to overcome this latency issue. First, the direction of an image from a normal projector is rapidly controlled using a dual-axis scanning mirror galvanometer system to project images onto a moving surface without perceivable delays [34,40]. The latest work downsizes the system and realizes a portable high speed projector-camera system (procams) [27]. However, the frame rate of the projector is about 60 Hz and cannot interactively update the projected image content according to the movement of the surface without noticeable latency. Therefore, this method assumed that the perspective projection of the surface on the projector's image plane does not change while projecting, and consequently, the surface geometry is limited to simple shapes such as a sphere.

The second solution is to apply high-speed projectors that can display 8-bit images at several hundreds frames per second with low latencies. Watanabe et al. developed a projection device that has the ability to project 8-bit monochrome images at a frame rate of up to 1,000 Hz [42]. To achieve the 1,000 Hz projection, the DMD's mirror flip pattern as well as temporally adapting LED intensities are used. Combined with a high speed camera (1,000 FPS) this projector is able to achieve a dynamic projection mapping onto rigid and deformable surfaces without noticeable misalignments [31,32,41]. Kagami and Hashimoto achieved

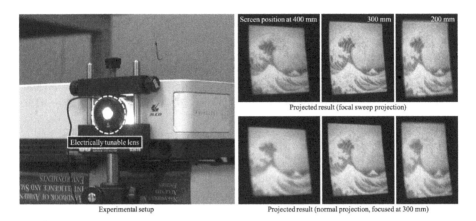

Fig. 2. Experimental results of focal sweep based extended DOF projection using an ETL [17].

to *stick* a projection image onto a moving planar surface using a customized high-speed procams [20,21]. Bermano et al. applied high speed procams to human face augmentation [5]. For the latter, a commercially available 480 Hz projector was used. When handheld or wearable projectors are used, the projectors rather than target surfaces move. Regan and Miller proposed a technique to reduce motion blur artifacts in such situations using a high speed projector [37]. Such systems have also been used in the fields of virtual and augmented reality other than projection mapping, where researchers have tried to minimize latency [24,45].

The latest work developed a projector that can embed spatially varying imperceptible binary codes (max. 64 bits) in a full color 24-bit image. The imperceptible codes can be used for optical communication to control various systems such as robots by projected lights while projecting meaningful images to human observers [15].

## 4    Increasing Focal Depth

Projectors are inherently designed with a large aperture to minimize the loss of light emitted from the light source. However, this optical design leads to a shallow depth of focus (DOF). Consequently, an image projected on a surface with large depth variance can become blurred quickly. Therefore, extending DOF of projectors is highly demanding issue especially in dynamic projection mapping applications where projection objects and/or projectors are moving in large spaces. Previous techniques fall into two categories: single-projector and multi-projector approaches.

Single-projector approaches digitally sharpen original images before projection so that an optically defocused projection closely approximates the original (i.e., unblurred) image. Defocus blur of a projected image is explained mathematically as the convolution of a PSF (point spread function) and the original image.

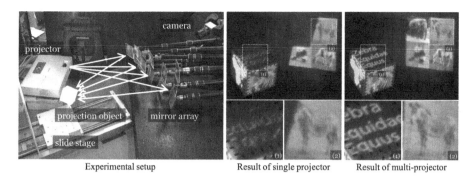

| Experimental setup | Result of single projector | Result of multi-projector |

**Fig. 3.** Experimental results of extended DOF projection using a mirror array based multi-projection system [29].

If the PSF of a projector on an object's surface is estimated correctly, a defocus-free image can be displayed by digitally correcting the original image using a deconvolution method, such as the Wiener filter [9]. Zhang and Nayar formulated image correction as a constrained optimization problem [44]. However, as summarized in a state-of-the-art report [8], such techniques suffer from the loss of high frequency components because PSFs of normal projectors are generally low pass filters. In the last 10 years, new optical designs have been introduced to enhance the performance of extending the DOF of a projector. For example, researchers apply coded apertures that have two-dimensional complex patterns instead of an ordinary circular aperture to make the PSFs more broadband [12,25]. Another strategy is to apply a focus tunable lens (FTL) (a.k.a. electrically tunable lens (ETL)) to sweep the focusing distance through the scene to make the PSF invariant to scene depths [17] (Fig. 2).

As a pioneering work of the multi-projector approach, Bimber and Emmerling realize multifocal projection using multiple projectors each with a focal plane at a unique distance [6]. For each point on a projection surface, they selected an optimal projector that could display the sharpest image at that spatial point location. Their multi-projector approach does not require deconvolution. However, when an object moves, it does require the projection of spatial pattern images on the surface to estimate PSFs from every projector. In addition, the black level rises with each superimposed projection. Nagase et al. proposed a model-based method that can select the optimal projector for each surface point even when the surface moves [29] (Fig. 3). This is achieved by estimating PSFs from geometric information, such as the shape of the surface and the relative pose of the surface to projectors. Multi-projector system with focal sweep technique realized a wide field-of-view and extended DOF projection [30]. A more general solution is to apply a multi-projector light transport matrix that models the influence of each projector pixel on a camera image that is regarded as an observed image [1,4,43]. Each projector image can be determined by computing the inverse light transport matrix (Fig. 4).

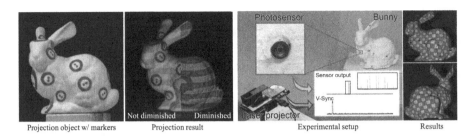

**Fig. 4.** Experimental results of dynamic projection mapping: (left) visual markers cancellation [2,3] and (right) scanning timing based online geometric registration for a laser projector [23].

## 5  Dynamic Projection Mapping

While projection mapping has been an active research field for a long time, most of the earlier research focused on the augmentation of static objects, or slowly and rigidly moving objects, since any dynamic projection system significantly adds up in system complexity and performance requirements. However, since the computational power of CPUs and GPUs evolved quickly according to Moore's law, and high-speed cameras and projectors are now becoming commercially available, more and more dynamic projection mapping systems have been published. These methods can be classified with respect to their degree of freedom when it comes to the dynamic components of the procam system. Most of the systems define *dynamic* in the sense that the scene rigidly transforms (or at least the non-rigid transformation is already known), or the projector or the camera is allowed to move. These approaches – although requiring significantly low latencies to generate convincing augmentations – can be supported by the application of known rigid geometry and potentially-available tracking information.

Methods for the augmentation of rigid dynamic objects do not require a full dense online surface reconstruction, but only a pose estimation of the projector with respect to the geometry to understand how the already known, geometrically rigid computer graphics needs to be rendered correctly by the devices. Applying a visual marker achieves a stable pose estimation. However, markers attached on a projection surface disturb projected results, as we can see the markers as a texture of the surface. This issue is resolved by combining a radiometric compensation technique to visually cancel the markers [2,3]. Other researchers replace the markers with tiny photosensors to measure the scanning timing of a projected beam from a laser projector [23]. Due to the raster-scanning mechanism, the pixel coordinate of the projected beam is uniquely identified from the measured time information. Once more than six photosensors measure the scanning timings and identify these pixel coordinates, the pose of the surface is estimated Leveraging a 1,000 Hz high speed procams (cf. Sect. 3), a visual marker-based method achieves a very low latency registration [41]. A stable marker position prediction is possible because the distance between the previous and current marker positions are short due to the small time difference (i.e., 1 ms).

A solution for dynamic projection mapping onto a deformable object is described by Punpongsanon et al. [36]: It is realized by painting invisible markers based on infrared ink onto the surface, which, being measured by an infrared camera, are used to estimate the surface's non-rigid deformation and to adapt the projection accordingly. A high-speed camera is used to robustly track dot cluster markers drawn by the same invisible inks [32]. Alternatively, retro-reflective markers are used to measure the surface deformation in the word of Fujimoto et al. [11]. However, a fully dynamic tracking is not achieved by this method. The dot cluster markers were extended to also allow the projection onto dynamic objects as shown by Narita et al. [31].

A system to dynamically augment human faces using projection was presented by Bermano et al. [5]. It applies markerless human face tracking, estimates blend shapes describing the current expression, deforms a base mesh and applies a texture which is dynamically adapted depending on estimated expression, time, desired lighting, as well as the spatial location of the face. To simplify the overall processing pipeline, projector and camera were optically aligned allowing the whole augmentation pipeline to work in 2D space. The overall latency of the presented prototype is less than 10 ms. Although this might sound sufficiently fast, an extended Kalman filter (EKF) needed to be incorporated for motion prediction to keep the inevitable delay of the projection onto the surface below the visual perception threshold. Recently, a similar system based on the usage of depth sensors was presented [39]. While they show how such an augmentation can be carried out with optically unaligned depth cameras and multiple projectors, the latency of the incorporated depth sensors makes it currently impractical for any fast and sudden motions. However, with more advanced and faster hardware, such limitations might be overcome.

The latest work realized real-time projections onto fully non-rigid, dynamic and unknown moving projection surfaces [28]. It applied a high speed photometric stereo in IR lights to estimate the normal directions of the projection target's surface and projected direction-dependent images onto the target.

## 6   Summary

This article described computational projection display technologies to overcome technical limitations stemming from projector hardware and improve projected image quality for arbitrary, imperfect surfaces beyond the capability of algorithmic solutions. It also covered the recent research trend, dynamic projection mapping. An interesting new research direction is to develop projection mapping technologies by taking into account the perceptual properties of human observers. There are several works already achieving illusory visual effects such as deforming real objects by projection mapping [22,35]. Another important direction is to integrate the techniques described in this article to develop an *ultimate* projection mapping system that can enhance the projected image quality regarding all the above mentioned technical issues. I believe the technologies introduced in this article will open up new application fields of the projection mapping and accelerate the development of useful products and services.

# References

1. Aliaga, D.G., Yeung, Y.H., Law, A., Sajadi, B., Majumder, A.: Fast high-resolution appearance editing using superimposed projections. ACM Trans. Graph. **31**(2), 13:1–13:13 (2012). https://doi.org/10.1145/2159516.2159518

2. Asayama, H., Iwai, D., Sato, K.: Fabricating diminishable visual markers for geometric registration in projection mapping. IEEE Trans. Vis. Comput. Graph. **24**(2), 1091–1102 (2018). https://doi.org/10.1109/TVCG.2017.2657634

3. Asayama, H., Iwai, D., Sato, K.: Diminishable visual markers on fabricated projection object for dynamic spatial augmented reality. In: SIGGRAPH Asia 2015 Emerging Technologies, SA 2015, pp. 7:1–7:2. ACM, New York, NY, USA (2015). https://doi.org/10.1145/2818466.2818477

4. Bermano, A., Brüschweiler, P., Grundhöfer, A., Iwai, D., Bickel, B., Gross, M.: Augmenting physical avatars using projector-based illumination. ACM Trans. Graph. **32**(6), 189:1–189:10 (2013). https://doi.org/10.1145/2508363.2508416

5. Bermano, A.H., Billeter, M., Iwai, D., Grundhöfer, A.: Makeup lamps: live augmentation of human faces via projection. Comput. Graph. Forum **36**(2), 311–323 (2017). https://doi.org/10.1111/cgf.13128

6. Bimber, O., Emmerling, A.: Multifocal projection: a multiprojector technique for increasing focal depth. IEEE Trans. Vis. Comput. Graph. **12**(4), 658–667 (2006). https://doi.org/10.1109/TVCG.2006.75

7. Bimber, O., Iwai, D.: Superimposing dynamic range. ACM Trans. Graph. **27**(5), 150:1–150:8 (2008). https://doi.org/10.1145/1409060.1409103

8. Bimber, O., Iwai, D., Wetzstein, G., Grundhöfer, A.: The visual computing of projector-camera systems. Comput. Graph. Forum **27**(8), 2219–2245 (2008). https://doi.org/10.1111/j.1467-8659.2008.01175.x

9. Brown, M.S., Song, P., Cham, T.J.: Image pre-conditioning for out-of-focus projector blur. In: 2006 IEEE Computer Society Conference on Computer Vision and Pattern Recognition (CVPR 2006). vol. 2, pp. 1956–1963 (2006). https://doi.org/10.1109/CVPR.2006.145

10. Damberg, G., Ballestad, A., Kozak, E., Minor, J., Kumaran, R., Gregson, J.: High brightness HDR projection using dynamic phase modulation. In: ACM SIGGRAPH 2015 Emerging Technologies, SIGGRAPH 2015, pp. 13:1–13:1. ACM, New York, NY, USA (2015). https://doi.org/10.1145/2782782.2792487

11. Fujimoto, Y., et al.: Geometrically-correct projection-based texture mapping onto a deformable object. IEEE Trans. Vis. Comput. Graph. **20**(4), 540–549 (2014). https://doi.org/10.1109/TVCG.2014.25

12. Grosse, M., Wetzstein, G., Grundhöfer, A., Bimber, O.: Coded aperture projection. ACM Trans. Graph. **29**(3), 22:1–22:12 (2010). https://doi.org/10.1145/1805964.1805966

13. Grundhöfer, A., Iwai, D.: Recent advances in projection mapping algorithms, hardware and applications. Comput. Graph. Forum **37**(2), 653–675. https://doi.org/10.1111/cgf.13387

14. Heide, F., Lanman, D., Reddy, D., Kautz, J., Pulli, K., Luebke, D.: Cascaded displays: spatiotemporal superresolution using offset pixel layers. ACM Trans. Graph. **33**(4), 60:1–60:11 (2014). https://doi.org/10.1145/2601097.2601120
15. Hiraki, T., Fukushima, S., Watase, H., Naemura, T.: Pixel-level visible light communication projector with interactive update of images and data. In: Proceedings of the International Display Workshops, pp. 1192–1195 (2018)
16. Hirsch, M., Wetzstein, G., Raskar, R.: A compressive light field projection system. ACM Trans. Graph. **33**(4), 58:1–58:12 (2014). https://doi.org/10.1145/2601097.2601144
17. Iwai, D., Mihara, S., Sato, K.: Extended depth-of-field projector by fast focal sweep projection. IEEE Trans. Vis. Comput. Graph. **21**(4), 462–470 (2015). https://doi.org/10.1109/TVCG.2015.2391861
18. Iwai, D., Takeda, S., Hino, N., Sato, K.: Projection screen reflectance control for high contrast display using photochromic compounds and UV leds. Opt. Express **22**(11), 13492–13506 (2014). https://doi.org/10.1364/OE.22.013492
19. Jones, B.R., Sodhi, R., Budhiraja, P., Karsch, K., Bailey, B., Forsyth, D.: Projectibles: optimizing surface color for projection. In: Proceedings of the 28th Annual ACM Symposium on User Interface Software & Technology, UIST 2015, pp. 137–146. ACM, New York, NY, USA (2015). https://doi.org/10.1145/2807442.2807486
20. Kagami, S., Hashimoto, K.: Sticky projection mapping: 450-fps tracking projection onto a moving planar surface. In: SIGGRAPH Asia 2015 Emerging Technologies, SA 2015, pp. 23:1–23:3. ACM, New York, NY, USA (2015). https://doi.org/10.1145/2818466.2818485
21. Kagami, S., Hashimoto, K.: A full-color single-chip-DLP projector with an embedded 2400-fps homography warping engine. In: ACM SIGGRAPH 2018 Emerging Technologies, SIGGRAPH 2018, pp. 1:1–1:2. ACM, New York, NY, USA (2018). https://doi.org/10.1145/3214907.3214927
22. Kawabe, T., Fukiage, T., Sawayama, M., Nishida, S.: Deformation lamps: a projection technique to make static objects perceptually dynamic. ACM Trans. Appl. Percept. **13**(2), 10:1–10:17 (2016). https://doi.org/10.1145/2874358
23. Kitajima, Y., Iwai, D., Sato, K.: Simultaneous projection and positioning of laser projector pixels. IEEE Trans. Vis. Comput. Graph. **23**(11), 2419–2429 (2017). https://doi.org/10.1109/TVCG.2017.2734478
24. Lincoln, P., et al.: From motion to photons in 80 microseconds: towards minimal latency for virtual and augmented reality. IEEE Trans. Vis. Comput. Graph. **22**(4), 1367–1376 (2016). https://doi.org/10.1109/TVCG.2016.2518038
25. Ma, C., Suo, J., Dai, Q., Raskar, R., Wetzstein, G.: High-rank coded aperture projection for extended depth of field. In: 2013 IEEE International Conference on Computational Photography (ICCP), pp. 1–9, April 2013. https://doi.org/10.1109/ICCPhot.2013.6528303
26. Masia, B., Wetzstein, G., Didyk, P., Gutierrez, D.: A survey on computational displays: pushing the boundaries of optics, computation, and perception. Comput. Graph. **37**(8), 1012–1038 (2013). https://doi.org/10.1016/j.cag.2013.10.003
27. Miyashita, L., Yamazaki, T., Uehara, K., Watanabe, Y., Ishikawa, M.: Portable lumipen: dynamic SAR in your hand. In: 2018 IEEE International Conference on Multimedia and Expo (ICME), pp. 1–6, July 2018. https://doi.org/10.1109/ICME.2018.8486514
28. Miyashita, L., Watanabe, Y., Ishikawa, M.: Midas projection: Markerless and modelless dynamic projection mapping for material representation. In: SIGGRAPH Asia 2018 Technical Papers, SIGGRAPH Asia 2018, pp. 196:1–196:12. ACM, New York, NY, USA (2018). https://doi.org/10.1145/3272127.3275045

29. Nagase, M., Iwai, D., Sato, K.: Dynamic defocus and occlusion compensation of projected imagery by model-based optimal projector selection in multi-projection environment. Virtual Real. **15**(2–3), 119–132 (2011). https://doi.org/10.1007/s10055-010-0168-4

30. Nakamura, T., Horisaki, R., Tanida, J.: Computational superposition projector for extended depth of field and field of view. Opt. Lett. **38**(9), 1560–1562 (2013). https://doi.org/10.1364/OL.38.001560

31. Narita, G., Watanabe, Y., Ishikawa, M.: Dynamic projection mapping onto deforming non-rigid surface using deformable dot cluster marker. IEEE Trans. Vis. Comput. Graph. **23**(3), 1235–1248 (2017). https://doi.org/10.1109/TVCG.2016.2592910

32. Narita, G., Watanabe, Y., Ishikawa, M.: Dynamic projection mapping onto a deformable object with occlusion based on high-speed tracking of dot marker array. In: Proceedings of the 21st ACM Symposium on Virtual Reality Software and Technology, VRST 2015, pp. 149–152. ACM, New York, NY, USA (2015). https://doi.org/10.1145/2821592.2821618

33. Ng, A., Lepinski, J., Wigdor, D., Sanders, S., Dietz, P.: Designing for low-latency direct-touch input. In: Proceedings of the 25th Annual ACM Symposium on User Interface Software and Technology, UIST 2012, pp. 453–464. ACM, New York, NY, USA (2012). https://doi.org/10.1145/2380116.2380174

34. Okumura, K., Oku, H., Ishikawa, M.: Lumipen: projection-based mixed reality for dynamic objects. In: 2012 IEEE International Conference on Multimedia and Expo (ICME), pp. 699–704, July 2012. https://doi.org/10.1109/ICME.2012.34

35. Okutani, N., Takezawa, T., Iwai, D., Sato, K.: Stereoscopic capture in projection mapping. IEEE Access **6**, 65894–65900 (2018). https://doi.org/10.1109/ACCESS.2018.2875905

36. Punpongsanon, P., Iwai, D., Sato, K.: Projection-based visualization of tangential deformation of nonrigid surface by deformation estimation using infrared texture. Virtual Real. **19**(1), 45–56 (2015). https://doi.org/10.1007/s10055-014-0256-y

37. Regan, M., Miller, G.S.P.: The problem of persistence with rotating displays. IEEE Trans. Vis. Comput. Graph. **23**(4), 1295–1301 (2017). https://doi.org/10.1109/TVCG.2017.2656979

38. Shimazu, S., Iwai, D., Sato, K.: 3D high dynamic range display system. In: 2011 10th IEEE International Symposium on Mixed and Augmented Reality (ISMAR), pp. 235–236, October 2011. https://doi.org/10.1109/ISMAR.2011.6092393

39. Siegl, C., Lange, V., Stamminger, M., Bauer, F., Thies, J.: FaceForge: markerless non-rigid face multi-projection mapping. IEEE Trans. Vis. Comput. Graph. **23**(11), 2440–2446 (2017). https://doi.org/10.1109/TVCG.2017.2734428

40. Sueishi, T., Oku, H., Ishikawa, M.: Robust high-speed tracking against illumination changes for dynamic projection mapping. In: 2015 IEEE Virtual Reality (VR), pp. 97–104, March 2015. https://doi.org/10.1109/VR.2015.7223330

41. Watanabe, Y., Kato, T., ishikawa, M.: Extended dot cluster marker for high-speed 3D tracking in dynamic projection mapping. In: 2017 IEEE International Symposium on Mixed and Augmented Reality (ISMAR), pp. 52–61, October 2017. https://doi.org/10.1109/ISMAR.2017.22

42. Watanabe, Y., Narita, G., Tatsuno, S., Yuasa, T., Sumino, K., Ishikawa, M.: High-speed 8-bit image projector at 1,000 fps with 3 ms delay. In: Proceedings of the International Display Workshops, pp. 1064–1065 (2015)

43. Wetzstein, G., Bimber, O.: Radiometric compensation through inverse light transport. In: 2007 15th Pacific Conference on Computer Graphics and Applications, PG 2007, pp. 391–399, October 2007. https://doi.org/10.1109/PG.2007.47

44. Zhang, L., Nayar, S.: Projection defocus analysis for scene capture and image display. ACM Trans. Graph. **25**(3), 907–915 (2006). https://doi.org/10.1145/1141911.1141974
45. Zheng, F., Whitted, T., Lastra, A., Lincoln, P., State, A., Maimone, A., Fuchs, H.: Minimizing latency for augmented reality displays: Frames considered harmful. In: 2014 IEEE International Symposium on Mixed and Augmented Reality (ISMAR), pp. 195–200, September 2014. https://doi.org/10.1109/ISMAR.2014.6948427

# On the Acquisition and Reproduction of Material Appearance

Aditya Sole, Davit Gigilashvili, Helene Midtfjord, Dar'ya Guarnera,
Giuseppe Claudio Guarnera, Jean-Baptiste Thomas,
and Jon Yngve Hardeberg[✉]

The Norwegian Colour and Visual Computing Laboratory,
NTNU – Norwegian University of Science and Technology, Gjøvik, Norway
jon.hardeberg@ntnu.no
http://www.colourlab.no

**Abstract.** Currently, new technologies (*e.g.* 2.5D and 3D printing processes) progress at a fast pace in their capacity to (re)produce an ever-broader range of visual aspects. At the same time, a huge research effort is needed to achieve a comprehensive scientific model for the visual sensations we experience in front of an object in its surrounding. Thanks to the projects *MUVApp: Measuring and Understanding Visual Appearance* funded by the Research Council of Norway, and *ApPEARS: Appearance Printing—European Advanced Research School* recently granted by the European Union, significant progress is being made on various topics related with acquisition and reproduction of material appearance, and also on the very understanding of appearance. This paper presents recent, ongoing, and planned research in this exciting field, with a specific emphasis on the *MUVApp* project.

**Keywords:** Colour · Gloss · Translucency · Texture · BRDF ·
Goniometry · Imaging · Soft metrology

## 1 Introduction

Humans are highly skilled in assessing the appearance of objects. By comparing the relative qualities of materials, such as whether they are flexible/rigid, soft/hard, smooth/rough, rotten/fresh, precious or cheap, we can for instance quickly tell if these are pleasing or may do us harm. Understanding the appearance of materials is also of great importance for commercial products. How these materials are used for different requirements and applications can be a key differentiator to the success or failure of a product. In computer vision, recognising materials is a key challenge, for instance for scene understanding.

The visual appearance of a material is generally classified into four appearance attributes (colour, gloss, translucency, and texture) that interact with each other [4]. This interaction is very complex and processed by the brain together with other information such as memory and viewing environment, to finally determine the perceived appearance of a surface or object. We can consider the study of appearance as an extension of colour science.

© Springer Nature Switzerland AG 2019
S. Tominaga et al. (Eds.): CCIW 2019, LNCS 11418, pp. 26–38, 2019.
https://doi.org/10.1007/978-3-030-13940-7_3

Visual appearance and material perception is drawing the attention of more and more vision scientists. Also within the field of imaging and printing there is an established interest in visual appearance, as evidenced for instance by the establishment of a conference series at the Electronic Imaging Symposium entitled Material Appearance.[1]

The reflectance properties of a material can be physically described by the spatially-varying Bidirectional Surface Scattering Reflectance Distribution Function (sv-BSSRDF) [32], which is an 8-dimensional function for each wavelength for non fluorescing materials. The simple BRDF model assumes that light entering a material exits at the same position. Simple measurements in fixed illumination and viewing geometries are commonly used to assess colour or gloss. Multi-angle instruments and BRDF measuring instruments have been developed to assess goniochromism, *i.e.* the dependency of perceived colour on the illumination and viewing geometry, which is especially important for special effect coatings, but also significant for other materials such as dyed papers [31]. A number of devices have been developed for specific applications, and the design of each of these devices is typically optimised for a specific parameter, while restricting other features. As a result, two instruments can give significantly different measurements.

Quantification of visual appearance requires modelling the relationship between physical stimuli (such as BRDF or a contrast-gloss physical measure) and psychophysical visual appearance attributes. The appearance of an object is however not determined solely by its sv-BSSRDF, as the viewing environment and the observer also significantly impacts on it. Some aspects of the problem are relatively well understood and can be solved with simpler measurement techniques, as for instance colour appearance modelling in the case of planar diffuse reflective surfaces under certain surround and illumination conditions, while for more complex object properties and illumination geometries research is needed. BRDF/BSSRDF models are also successfully used for photorealistic rendering of appearance in computer graphics, including translucency [20].

Material perception is a very complex process, and the appropriate dimensions, feature spaces and perception metrics are only beginning to be studied. It has been shown [30,45] that image statistics are promising for the problem of material recognition. However, for applications in training and design, the specification of material attributes are needed independently of a particular image, for example, a surgical training simulator must present different visualisations for various shapes and views, while an automotive design system must simulate the end product in different environments and weather conditions. The appearance of a material needs to be understood over the entire space of potentially relevant images – this is in part what makes material appearance modelling more challenging than understanding colour reproduction in the field of imaging. However, recent progress in soft metrology, computer graphics, virtual reality and neuroscience that allow us to explore a larger range of properties and imaging scenarios now allow us to tackle this more complex problem of material appearance.

---

[1] http://www.electronicimaging.org/.

## 2    Knowledge Challenges and Research Opportunities

Despite the importance of material perception, vision scientists have tended to simplify the research questions by using only simple flat and matte stimuli for their experiments to understand visual appearance, and disregarding the complexity of real world surfaces [2]. Recent progress in computer graphics have enabled vision scientists to simulate photo-realistic appearances of objects on the computer screen, but only a relatively small number of studies have used this approach to investigate the material perception of real objects [7]. On the contrary, the use of direct methods of measuring material properties of real objects have a long history in industrial applications [18,19], but were often specific to certain product types, and cannot be generalised to other materials or products. To know the exact relationships between human perception and physical properties, the measurement of physical properties should be precise and comprehensive, but such measurements are time consuming and expensive and inadequate, impossible, or e.g. limited to homogeneous materials without scattering for ellipsometry.

The measurement of the physical properties that, either singly or in combination, are related to psychophysical sensations is formally defined as soft metrology by the CIE [4]. Although aspects like colour appearance in fixed viewing geometries are reasonably well understood, key measurement challenges need to be overcome to measure and predict material appearance in a given environment. Taking into account optical properties such as gloss, colour, texture and translucency, image-based systems to estimate the BRDF [12,13] and sv-BSSRDF of 3D objects will offer fast measurements but also enable the building of visual appearance models with support of image statistics. Many studies on gloss have been performed on flat homogeneous surfaces without scattering (for ellipsometry) and assessing the perceived gloss of 3D objects raises a number of new problems related to the interaction of spatially varying visual attributes and viewing environment such as inter-reflection. The context or environment surrounding the object plays an important role in material perception [6]. While in many previous studies material surfaces are simulated by displaying rendered stimuli on a flat monitor, future work should explore the use of immersive Virtual Reality environments. In fact, even though the simulated physical and optical processes are elaborate, displaying a simulation just on a 2D monitor might not fully convey the appearance of a material, since a significant portion of the environment surrounding the observer is left outside the field of view. In order to overcome this drawback, it is important to generate samples that can be used as real physical objects to study material perception.

The *MUVApp: Measuring and Understanding Visual Appearance* project tries to address some of the above challenges to understand and study visual appearance. It is funded by the Research Council of Norway and supports 3 doctoral and 3 post-doctoral positions over a period of 5 years for research and networking activities. As illustrated in Fig. 1, it aims towards expanding key knowledge and understanding in the field of visual appearance reproduction and develop methodology to measure and understand visual appearance.

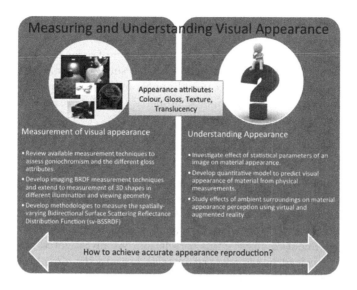

**Fig. 1.** MUVApp project research overview.

## 3   Optical Measurements and Functions of Appearance

Measuring physical properties of the material is important to understand visual appearance of the given material/object. These measurements help in material identification (whether it is food, textile, skin, metal, paper or plastic) by their correlation to the total appearance of an object as defined by CIE [4]. Next, we describe some of our different approaches towards appearance measurement.

### 3.1   Image Based Goniometric Measurements

For non-diffuse materials like metallic inks, measurements using the standard geometries as defined by CIE [3] are not sufficient to understand its visual appearance. Goniometric measurements are therefore performed to measure these materials at multiple illumination and viewing directions. Performing such a large set of measurements can be expensive and time consuming. Image based measurement setups are therefore proposed [17,28,39,43], which can be fast and cheap but less accurate compared to the reference goniospectrophotometers and commercially available multi-angle spectrophotometers. We propose such [28,43] an image based measurement setup to measure thin, flexible and homogeneous object material like printed paper material typically used in the packaging industry [37,39]. Such a setup can perform fast measurements and in line with production of these print and packaging materials. This can be an advantage over using the reference goniospectrophotometers and multi-angle spectrophotometers. The obtained measurements can be fitted to different surface reflection models to simulate and study the bidirectional reflectance properties of diffuse packaging material (wax-based inks printed on a packaging paper material) as demonstrated in [34, 38, 39]. The measurement setup has been evaluated against commercially available goniospectrophotometers and the accuracy of the image based setup is calculated by means of a propagation-of-error analysis [36]. Further, we have investigated the suitability of using such a measurement setup to measure materials with a complex visual appearance. These complex materials showed non-diffuse and gonio-chromatic properties which were difficult to model using well established reflection models [35].

### 3.2  Image Statistics and Contrast Measures

We have also investigated how contrast measures correlate with gloss perception in specific cases [42]. Indeed, contrast has been shown to play a role in gloss perception in the general case, *e.g.* [26, 27]. We made the observation that contrast metrics should correlate to contrast gloss in specific conditions, and we conducted an experiment to observe this correlation. We investigated how the state of the art of perceived image contrast metrics agreed with gloss perception for a specific viewing condition. Though preliminary, those results were promising. We are conducting further studies toward this direction to strengthen and limit those observations. Indeed, the results presented in [42] are strongly impacted by the effect of the background on the perceived image contrast computation, while we would prefer that the metrics only describe the near-to-specular area. Secondly, the samples were very simple in this experiment, and we probably described only a physical parameter of the generative model of BRDF used to generate the objects. This work is not expected to result in a model of contrast perception, neither a model of gloss perception. Instead, it will help defining the limits of the contribution of contrast in the perception of gloss, and to establish which contrast metrics is more suitable as a gloss indicator for some industries, *e.g.* the painting industries.

### 3.3  Colour and Spectral Image Acquisition

Acquisition of faithful colour data is indeed an important component of appearance measurements, often overlooked in the computer graphics and vision fields. Hence, we focused on the development of an effective technique for absolute colorimetric camera characterisation, suitable for use in a wide range of applications, including image-based reflectance measurements, spectral prefiltering and spectral upsampling for rendering and to improve color accuracy in HDR imaging. As demonstrated in [14], the characterised camera can be used as a 2D tele-colorimeter to obtain an estimate of the distribution of luminance and chromaticity in a scene, in physical units $(cd/m^2)$. Besides the aforementioned applications, such a characterised camera can be used for radiometric compensation, to project images on unoptimised surfaces [15] while compensating for the spatially varying background (see Fig. 2).

Beyond colour imaging, spectral and polarisation imaging may bring precious additional information to compute appearance attributes. The Spectral Filter Array technology [25] enables snapshot spectral imaging, which is valuable for

(a)                          (b)                          (c)

**Fig. 2.** In (a), textured surface used for projection. In (b), Uncompensated image projected on the textured surface. In (c), the compensated image, projected on the same surface. The estimation of the surface gamut partly relies on a camera characterised with our method [14].

computer vision. One advantage of this technology is that it is a very good candidate to perform multi-angle measurements and that the point of view of the imaging device is at a single location, differently from light-field cameras.

After defining the imaging pipeline for snapshot HDR spectral imaging [24], we handled the illumination [22,23] and the demosaicing [1,41]. We plan to extend this pipeline to the joint spectral and polarization imaging and to use this technology to capture data to measure appearance.

### 3.4   The Case of Textiles

The appearance of textiles is particularly interesting. In the context of the contract furniture business, woven cloth model acquisition must be rapid, since the volume of cloth swatches that need to be routinely processed is huge. Furthermore, results must be renderable in high quality even on a mobile device. To address such needs, a novel image-based technique was developed, for reverse engineering woven fabrics at a yarn level, which determines, from a single digital image, captured with a DSLR camera under controlled uniform lighting, the woven cloth structure and reflectance properties [16]. The developed technique finds applications also in other fields, and it is suitable for VR [16].

In the same direction, we also captured a database of hyperspectral images of textures, largely composed of textile. HyTexiLa [21] is available online and was, so far, used to study texture classification and to simulate imaging processes.

### 3.5   Appearance Translation Across Material Models

The production of 3D digital media content often requires collaboration among several departments, which exchange data and material models in order to simulate the visual appearance of objects and environments. A range of modelling and rendering tools is usually involved. Digital content could also be initially created with one material model, subsequently upgraded or changed over the lifespan. A lack of standards to exchange material parameters and data (between tools) requires the artists in digital 3D prototyping and design to manually match the appearance of materials to a reference image. To address the aforementioned issue, we developed a novel BRDF remapping technique, that automatically computes a mapping to match the appearance of a source material model [11]. Most notably, results obtained show that even when the characteristics of the models are substantially different, such as in the case of a phenomenological model and a physically-based one, the remapped renderings are indistinguishable from the original source model (Fig. 3).

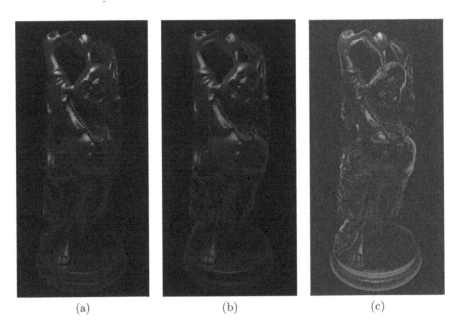

(a)                              (b)                              (c)

**Fig. 3.** Remapping from a phenomenological model, with no support for the Fresnel effect (a) to a physically based model (b). In (c) we report the error map. The appearance is correctly preserved, while the differences are mostly localised around the silhouette and due to the Fresnel effect, implemented in (b) but not in (a).

## 4    Visual Processes of Appearance Understanding

Eugène [5] defined appearance as "the visual sensation through which an object is perceived to have attributes as size, shape, colour, texture, gloss, transparency, opacity etc." However, he highlighted the lack of consensus on uniform description of appearance and mentioned that "this topic requires much more reflection and research". Next we describe briefly some of our attempts at achieving a better understanding of how we perceive and understand appearance.

## 4.1   Methods, Terminology, and Data

During our investigation of the state of the art, we have observed a dichotomy between the different research fields concerned with appearance. First, the terminology is not very clear, *e.g.* translucency refers clearly to the intrinsic optical property of scattering for the metrologist, while it may be considered as a perception feature for a psychologist. Second, there is quantity of quantitative research that describes very well a small part of the material appearance, but it is difficult to figure out a general hypothesis. Third, most of the work is conducted in virtual reality and it is not quantified how the findings relate to real optical properties of the material. To address these shortcomings we have realised a collection of real objects to generate research hypotheses through qualitative research and validate the state-of-the-art in real conditions; the *Plastique* collection [40].

## 4.2   Investigations

A behavioural investigation of the assessment of visual appearance was conducted [9]. Human observers were asked to describe the appearance of the physical objects from the *Plastique* collection, and perform appearance-based ranking tasks in uncontrolled similar to real-life conditions. The primary objective was to generate research hypotheses and outline future projects that eventually should lead to better insight into appearance perception. The study has revealed significant role of shape, colorant concentration and surface coarseness in translucency and gloss perception. One of the examples of shape outweighing the perceptual impact of intrinsic material properties is shown in Fig. 4. Further studies are currently being conducted to identify factors impacting translucency perception.

A study on the effect of blurring on translucency perception [8] revealed the interesting trend that identical objects are perceived less translucent when observed in blurred images. Images from the Flickr Material Database [33] were used (Fig. 5).

When describing appearance, it is interesting to understand if and why some attributes may appear more salient and prioritized by human observers. In another study [10] we analyzed how people cluster objects from the *Plastique* collection by their appearance, or how they order them in space "in a natural way". Apart from anticipated cross-individual similarities, very interesting cross-individual differences have been also observed (refer to Fig. 6) that opened a whole new direction for further study about the impact of individual subject background and experience on appearance assessment.

Related to the goal of developing a standard for ink opacity within ISO TC130, a psychophysical experiment was performed [29], where naïve observers rated the opacity of white ink, with different ink film thickness (IFT), printed on 3 different substrates. Five potential opacity metrics were tested. The proposed metrics showed good correlation with the visual assessments, and the metric of relative CIE lightness provided the most linear result.

**Fig. 4.** Considering its compact shape and high amount of colorant, the parallelepiped was almost unanimously ranked least translucent. However, decisions of the human subjects were inconsistent regarding a sphere and a female bust: although dye concentration in the sphere is obviously lowest, there was no statistically significant difference in perceived translucency between the sphere and the bust. One of the hypotheses we are currently examining further is that presence of the thin areas in the female bust compensates for the intrinsic material properties, and thus, shape can significantly impact translucency perception. Left: an example of the *sphere* being considered more translucent by an observer. Right: the *bust* being found more translucent.

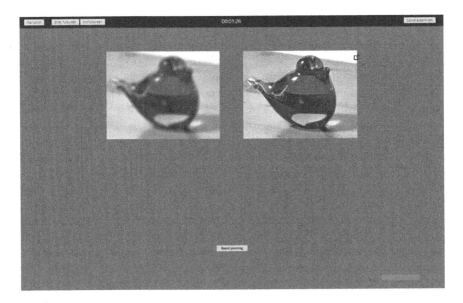

**Fig. 5.** A sample screen from a pair-comparison psychometric experiment carried out using the QuickEval web-based tool [44]. Human subjects were shown images of the glass objects with varying degree of Gaussian blur and asked to assess which object appeared more translucent. The study revealed that higher the image blur, less translucent is the object perceived.

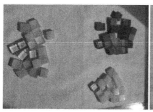

**Fig. 6.** Human observers were found to mostly use the colour attribute (either alone or in combination with translucency) to group those objects. In this group of objects, colour was prioritized for different reasons explained in the paper [10]. However, the number of groups for a given data set varied significantly. The left image illustrates grouping into 3 simple categories: "blue", "yellow", and "white"; The middle 4 categories: "blue", "yellow", "white", and "transparent"; while the right image is an example of clustering into 5 groups: "yellow", "orange", "dark blue", "pale blue", and "white". (Color figure online)

## 5  Conclusion and Perspectives

Visual appearance is still a very open research field, and, through our *MUVApp* projects we currently undertake an innovative transdisciplinary scientific approach involving fields like imaging science, vision science, and computer graphics. With support from this projects we aim to gain new knowledge of how human beings perceive the visual appearance of materials, objects and scenes, and to develop new methodologies for measuring and communicating visual appearance and appearance-related material and object properties.

In this paper we have summarised some of the recent and ongoing research activities and results within this project. For details, we would encourage the readers to refer to the cited articles. The understanding and hence control over the perception, measurement and eventually reproduction of visual appearance has potentially a very high societal impact. It is expected to be very potent in conjunction with the rapidly developing field of additive manufacturing (3D printing) for applications for instance in automotive industry, cultural heritage, and reconstructive surgery.

The capability to reproduce visual appearance using additive manufacturing techniques like 3D printing or 2.5D relief printing is still in its infancy. Additive manufacturing has more degrees of freedom than 2D printing for creating appearance effects beyond colour – such as gloss, translucency or goniochromatic effects – by mixing, for instance, transparent and opaque materials to control translucency, or by adding micro-facets on the object's surface to control directional reflectance. In many applications 3D printed objects must satisfy appearance as well as mechanical criteria, *e.g.* skin and dental prostheses. However, missing technology to match the desired appearance currently significantly limits the printer's applicability. The *ApPEARS* project funded by the European Union will address these limitations, exploring the complete material appearance reproduction workflow, from capturing optical material properties, communicating related appearance attributes, to modelling and controlling 2.5D/3D printing systems beyond colour.

*ApPEARS* focuses on the following key objectives: measurement and visual evaluation of material properties, reproduction of complex surface appearances, and predicting and minimizing reproduction errors. The exploitation of this complete reproduction workflow into high-impact application areas requires the development of end-use applications, combined with specialized training. With a start date in 2019 *ApPEARS* will train a group of 15 early stage researchers into highly-skilled researchers, who will form the next generation of scientists, engineers, designers and entrepreneurs in the field of visual appearance and printing. For more information refer to http://www.appears-itn.eu.

**Acknowledgment.** The work described in this paper has been partially funded by the Research Council of Norway, through the FRIPRO Toppforsk project *MUVApp – Measuring and Understanding Visual Appearance* (project number 250293). The contributions of other researchers affiliated with the project, within and beyond NTNU, are also acknowledged, as is the precious work of Osamu Masuda and Ludovic Coppel in the proposal phase.

# References

1. Amba, P., Thomas, J.B., Alleysson, D.: N-LMMSE demosaicing for spectral filter arrays. J. Imaging Sci. Technol. **61**(4), 40407-1–40407-11 (2017). https://doi.org/10.2352/J.ImagingSci.Technol.2017.61.4.040407
2. Brainard, D.H., Maloney, L.T.: Perception of color and material properties in complex scenes. J. Vis. **4**(9) (2004)
3. CIE15.2: Colorimetry. International Commission on Illumination (2004)
4. CIE175: A framework for the measurement of visual appearance. International Commission on Illumination (2006)
5. Eugène, C.: Measurement of "total visual appearance": a CIE challenge of soft metrology. In: 12th IMEKO TC1 and TC7 Joint Symposium on Man, Science and Measurement, Annecy, France, pp. 61–65, September 2008
6. Fleming, R.W.: Visual perception of materials and their properties. Vision Res. **94**, 62–75 (2014)
7. Giesel, M., Gegenfurtner, K.R.: Color appearance of real objects varying in material, hue, and shape. J. Vis. **10**(9), 10 (2010)
8. Gigilashvili, D., Pedersen, M., Hardeberg, J.Y.: Blurring impairs translucency perception. In: Color and Imaging Conference, pp. 377–382. Society for Imaging Science and Technology (2018)
9. Gigilashvili, D., Thomas, J.B., Hardeberg, J.Y., Pedersen, M.: Behavioral investigation of visual appearance assessment. In: Color and Imaging Conference, pp. 294–299. Society for Imaging Science and Technology (2018)
10. Gigilashvili, D., Thomas, J.B., Hardeberg, J.Y., Pedersen, M.: Material appearance: ordering and clustering. In: Electronic Imaging 2019 (2019)
11. Guarnera, D., et al.: Perceptually validated cross-renderer analytical BRDF parameter remapping. IEEE Trans. Visual. Comput. Graph. (2018). https://doi.org/10.1109/TVCG.2018.2886877

12. Guarnera, D., Guarnera, G., Ghosh, A., Denk, C., Glencross, M.: BRDF representation and acquisition. In: Computer Graphics Forum, vol. 35, no. 2, pp. 625–650 (2016). https://doi.org/10.1111/cgf.12867

13. Guarnera, D., Guarnera, G.C.: Virtual material acquisition and representation for computer graphics. In: Synthesis Lectures on Visual Computing, vol. 10. Morgan & Claypool Publishers (2018)

14. Guarnera, G.C., Bianco, S., Schettini, R.: Turning a digital camera into an absolute 2D tele-colorimeter. In: Computer Graphics Forum, pp. 1–12 (2018). https://doi.org/10.1111/cgf.13393

15. Guarnera, G.C., Bianco, S., Schettini, R.: DIY absolute tele-colorimeter using a camera-projector system. In: ACM SIGGRAPH 2018 Talks. SIGGRAPH 2018, pp. 23:1–23:2. ACM, New York (2018). https://doi.org/10.1145/3214745.3214777

16. Guarnera, G.C., Hall, P., Chesnais, A., Glencross, M.: Woven fabric model creation from a single image. ACM Trans. Graph. **36**(5), 165:1–165:13 (2017)

17. Guarnera, G.C., Peers, P., Debevec, P., Ghosh, A.: Estimating surface normals from spherical stokes reflectance fields. In: Fusiello, A., Murino, V., Cucchiara, R. (eds.) ECCV 2012. LNCS, vol. 7584, pp. 340–349. Springer, Heidelberg (2012). https://doi.org/10.1007/978-3-642-33868-7_34

18. Harrison, V., Poulter, S.: Gloss of papers. Nature **171**(4354), 651 (1953)

19. Ingersoll, L.: A means to measure the glare of paper. Electr. World **63**, 645–647 (1914)

20. Jakob, W., Arbree, A., Moon, J.T., Bala, K., Marschner, S.: A radiative transfer framework for rendering materials with anisotropic structure. ACM Trans. Graph. (TOG) **29**, 53 (2010)

21. Khan, H.A., Mihoubi, S., Mathon, B., Thomas, J.B., Hardeberg, J.Y.: HyTexiLa: high resolution visible and near infrared hyperspectral texture images. Sensors **18**(7), 2045 (2018). https://doi.org/10.3390/s18072045

22. Khan, H.A., Thomas, J.B., Hardeberg, J.Y., Laligant, O.: Illuminant estimation in multispectral imaging. J. Opt. Soc. Am. A **34**(7), 1085–1098 (2017). https://doi.org/10.1364/JOSAA.34.001085

23. Khan, H.A., Thomas, J.B., Hardeberg, J.Y., Laligant, O.: Spectral adaptation transform for multispectral constancy. J. Imaging Sci. Technol. **62**(2), 20504-1–20504-12 (2018). https://doi.org/10.2352/J.ImagingSci.Technol.2018.62.2.020504

24. Lapray, P.J., Thomas, J.B., Gouton, P.: High dynamic range spectral imaging pipeline for multispectral filter array cameras. Sensors **17**(6), 1281 (2017). https://doi.org/10.3390/s17061281

25. Lapray, P.J., Wang, X., Thomas, J.B., Gouton, P.: Multispectral filter arrays: recent advances and practical implementation. Sensors **14**(11), 21626 (2014). https://doi.org/10.3390/s141121626

26. Marlow, P.J., Anderson, B.L.: Generative constraints on image cues for perceived gloss. J. Vis. **13**(14), 2 (2013). https://doi.org/10.1167/13.14.2

27. Marlow, P.J., Kim, J., Anderson, B.L.: The perception and misperception of specular surface reflectance. Curr. Biol. **22**(20), 1909–1913 (2012). https://doi.org/10.1016/j.cub.2012.08.009

28. Marschner, S.R., Westin, S.H., Lafortune, E.P.F., Torrance, K.E., Greenberg, D.P.: Image-based BRDF measurement including human skin. In: Lischinski, D., Larson, G.W. (eds.) Rendering Techniques 1999. EUROGRAPH, pp. 139–152. Springer, Vienna (1999). https://doi.org/10.1007/978-3-7091-6809-7_13

29. Midtfjord, H., Green, P., Nussbaum, P.: A model of visual opacity for translucent colorants. Electron. Imaging **2018**(8), 1–6 (2018)

30. Motoyoshi, I., Nishida, S., Sharan, L., Adelson, E.H.: Image statistics and the perception of surface qualities. Nature **447**(7141), 206 (2007)
31. Neuman, M., Coppel, L.G., Edström, P.: Angle resolved color of bulk scattering media. Appl. Opt. **50**(36), 6555–6563 (2011)
32. Nicodemus, F.E., Richmond, J., Hsia, J.J., Ginsberg, I.W., Limperis, T.: Geometrical considerations and nomenclature for reflectance. National Bureau of Standards (1977)
33. Sharan, L., Rosenholtz, R., Adelson, E.H.: Accuracy and speed of material categorization in real-world images. J. Vis. **14**(9), 12 (2014)
34. Sole, A., Farup, I., Nussbaum, P.: Evaluating an image based multi-angle measurement setup using different reflection models. Electron. Imaging **2017**(8), 101–107 (2017). https://doi.org/10.2352/ISSN.2470-1173.2017.8.MAAP-280
35. Sole, A., Farup, I., Nussbaum, P., Tominaga, S.: Bidirectional reflectance measurement and reflection model fitting of complex materials using an image-based measurement setup. J. Imaging **4**(11), 136 (2018)
36. Sole, A., Farup, I., Nussbaum, P., Tominaga, S.: Evaluating an image-based bidirectional reflectance distribution function measurement setup. Appl. Opt. **57**(8), 1918–1928 (2018). https://doi.org/10.1364/AO.57.001918
37. Sole, A., Farup, I., Tominaga, S.: An image based multi-angle method for estimating reflection geometries of flexible objects. In: Color and Imaging Conference 2014, pp. 91–96, November 2014
38. Sole, A., Farup, I., Tominaga, S.: Image based reflectance measurement based on camera spectral sensitivities. Electron. Imaging **2016**(9), 1–8 (2016)
39. Sole, A.S., Farup, I., Tominaga, S.: An image-based multi-directional reflectance measurement setup for flexible objects. In: Segovia, M.V.O., Urban, P., Imai, F.H. (eds.) Measuring, Modeling and Reproducing Material Appearance 2015. SPIE Proceedings, vol. 9398, pp. 93980J–93980J-11 (2015). https://doi.org/10.1117/12.2076592
40. Thomas, J.B., Deniel, A., Hardeberg, J.Y.: The Plastique collection: a set of resin objects for material appearance research. In: Proceedings of the XIV Conferenza del Colore, pp. 1–12 (2018). http://jbthomas.org/Conferences/2018CDC.pdf
41. Thomas, J.B., Farup, I.: Demosaicing of periodic and random color filter arrays by linear anisotropic diffusion. J. Imaging Sci. Technol. **62**(5), 50401-1–50401-8 (2018). https://doi.org/10.2352/J.ImagingSci.Technol.2018.62.5.050401
42. Thomas, J.-B., Hardeberg, J.Y., Simone, G.: Image contrast measure as a gloss material descriptor. In: Bianco, S., Schettini, R., Trémeau, A., Tominaga, S. (eds.) CCIW 2017. LNCS, vol. 10213, pp. 233–245. Springer, Cham (2017). https://doi.org/10.1007/978-3-319-56010-6_20
43. Tominaga, S., Tanaka, N.: Estimating reflection parameters from a single color image. IEEE Comput. Graph. Appl. **20**(5), 58–66 (2000)
44. Van Ngo, K., Storvik, J.J., Dokkeberg, C.A., Farup, I., Pedersen, M.: QuickEval: a web application for psychometric scaling experiments. In: Image Quality and System Performance XII. SPIE Proceedings, vol. 9396 (2015)
45. Wiebel, C.B., Toscani, M., Gegenfurtner, K.R.: Statistical correlates of perceived gloss in natural images. Vis. Res. **115**, 175–187 (2015)

# Computational Color Imaging

# An Imaging System for Fourier Coefficients of Spectral Reflectance

Akira Kimachi[1]([✉]), Motonori Doi[2], and Shogo Nishi[1]

[1] Department of Engineering Informatics,
Faculty of Information and Communication Engineering,
Osaka Electro-Communication University, Neyagawa, Osaka 572-8530, Japan
kima@osakac.ac.jp
[2] Department of Telecommunication and Computer Networks,
Faculty of Information and Communication Engineering,
Osaka Electro-Communication University, Neyagawa, Osaka 572-8530, Japan

**Abstract.** This paper proposes a system for acquiring the images of complex Fourier coefficients of the spectral reflectance of an object up to the second order at an ordinary frame rate. This feature is realized by a correlation camera and a special illumination called sinusoidally-modulated phase-shift spectral illumination (SMPSSI). The correlation camera produces the temporal correlation between the intensity signal of incident light and external global reference signals pixel by pixel in every frame. The SMPSSI consists of a sum of spectral illuminations sinusoidally modulated at different frequencies with wavelength-linear phase shifts. The proposed system realizes high spectral resolution by performing spectral correlation with sinusoidal reference spectra in the wavelength domain, while maintaining the same temporal and spatial resolution as that of an ordinary video camera. An experimental system is developed with a digital correlation camera and a programmable spectral light source. Experimental results on color guide chips confirm that the proposed system extracted the Fourier coefficients up to the second order accurately.

**Keywords:** Spectral reflectance · Fourier coefficients ·
Correlation camera ·
Sinusoidally-modulated phase-shift spectral illumination

## 1    Introduction

Spectral reflectance or transmittance of objects tends to have unique features that originate from chemical composition or micro-structure of the surface, and thus serve strong clues to identifying the objects. In order to obtain spectral information as images, we need to acquire images for each wavelength of light sampled over the visible range. The resultant data are called spectral images, which are also regarded as a two-dimensional array of spectral data measured at

© Springer Nature Switzerland AG 2019
S. Tominaga et al. (Eds.): CCIW 2019, LNCS 11418, pp. 41–52, 2019.
https://doi.org/10.1007/978-3-030-13940-7_4

each pixel. The biggest problem in the acquisition of spectral images [1–4] is that it is inevitable to sacrifice either temporal or spatial resolution in exchange for increasing spectral resolution. A high-speed camera, although it can maintain both temporal and spatial resolution, suffers another problem of low signal-to-noise ratio because the light intensity, which is already weakened by narrow-band imaging, gets even weaker by shortened exposure time.

One of the solutions to this problem is the spectral matching imager [5–7], which performs spectral matching in a pixel-parallel manner by use of a correlation camera [8] to produce the correlation between the reference spectral reflectance of a target object and the spectral reflectance of the object in the scene. This system compresses multidimensional spectral information into just a few spectral correlation outputs on the focal plane. It realizes high spectral resolution by performing spectral correlation in the wavelength domain, while maintaining the same temporal and spatial resolution as that of an ordinary video camera, though it cannot measure the whole waveform of spectral reflectance of the object itself.

In this paper, as another solution to the problem with spectral imaging, we propose a system for acquiring the images of complex Fourier coefficients of the spectral reflectance of an object up to the second order at an ordinary frame rate. This remarkable feature is realized by two key components—a correlation camera and a special illumination called sinusoidally-modulated phase-shift spectral illumination (SMPSSI). The correlation camera, previously employed in the spectral matching imager [7] as mentioned above, is comprised of a time-domain correlation image sensor, which produces the temporal correlation between the intensity signal of incident light and external global reference signals pixel by pixel in every frame. The system proposed here is similar to the spectral matching imager to some extent, because it uses a correlation camera and the Fourier coefficients of spectral reflectance obtained from the correlation camera can be regarded as the correlations with sinusoidal reference spectra. The difference, however, lies in the spectral illumination used. The SMPSSI of the proposed system consists of a sum of spectral illuminations sinusoidally modulated at different frequencies with wavelength-linear phase shifts, while the spectral matching imager used a monochromatic illumination with a time-linear peak wavelength. The proposed system thus has an advantage of higher signal-to-noise ratio than that of the spectral matching imager because of much broader spectral power distribution of the SMPSSI and the temporal correlation with sinusoidal reference signals, for which the correlation camera achieves the highest accuracy. It can also be applied to spectral transmittance, of course, though the primary target of the current study is spectral reflectance.

Fourier representation of spectral reflectance has been mainly discussed in the context of color constancy models in human vision [9] and linear models for estimating spectral reflectance [10]. It has hardly been used, however, in most practical methods of spectral image processing. Meanwhile, Jia *et al.* recently proposed Fabry-Perot-type narrow-band filters with sinusoidal spectral transmittance [11], and developed a spectral imaging system with a mosaic array of the sinusoidal filters [12]. The use of filters with sinusoidal spectral transmittance can be regarded as a way of realizing Fourier transform during image acquisition. Their method, however, is inspired by Fourier transform spectroscopy and thus different from our system in three points. Firstly, they aim at the spectral power distribution of incident light itself coming directly from light sources or indirectly from reflective objects, not at the spectral reflectance of objects as in our method. Secondly, they do not use an active spectral illumination such as the SMPSSI used in our system. Thirdly, Fourier transform is not performed in the wavelength domain as in our method, but in the wavenumber domain.

The rest of this paper describes the principle of the proposed method, depicts the constructed imaging system, and shows experimental results obtained on the system.

## 2   Principle

### 2.1   Correlation Camera

The correlation camera has an input of external reference signals, which are supplied to all of the pixels. Let the frame time and its associated angular frame frequency denoted by $T$ and $\omega_0 = 2\pi/T$, respectively, and the intensity signal of incident light at a pixel $(x, y)$ and a time $t$ denoted by $f(x, y, t)$. In this study, we supply a pair of sinusoidal reference signals $\cos k\omega_0 t$ and $-\sin k\omega_0 t$ $(k = 1, 2, \ldots)$ to the correlation camera. The camera then produces the temporal correlation $g_k(x, y)$ between $f(x, y, t)$ and the complex sinusoidal reference signal $e^{-jk\omega_0 t} = \cos k\omega_0 t - j \sin k\omega_0 t$,

$$g_k(x, y) = \int_{-T/2}^{T/2} f(x, y, t)e^{-jk\omega_0 t}dt, \tag{1}$$

as well as the average intensity $g_0(x, y)$ (the same output as from an ordinary video camera),

$$g_0(x, y) = \int_{-T/2}^{T/2} f(x, y, t)dt, \tag{2}$$

at each pixel $(x, y)$, and outputs them as images in every frame $T$. Note that Eq. (1) treats the correlations with the pair of reference signals as a single complex number. In the following, we will omit the pixel coordinates $(x, y)$ because no spatial operations are involved in Eqs. (1) and (2).

### 2.2   Sinusoidally-Modulated Phase-Shift Spectral Illumination

The object is illuminated by sinusoidally-modulated phase-shift spectral illumination (SMPSSI). SMPSSI is defined with its spectral power distribution $E(\lambda, t)$ as

$$E(\lambda, t) = E_0(\lambda) \left[ C + \sum_{n=1}^{N} \cos(n\omega_0 t - \phi_n(\lambda)), \right] \tag{3}$$

where $\phi_n(\lambda)$ denotes the phase shift linear to wavelength $\lambda$

$$\phi_n(\lambda) = 2\pi n \frac{\lambda - \lambda_{\min}}{\lambda_{\max} - \lambda_{\min}}, \tag{4}$$

$[\lambda_{\min}, \lambda_{\max}]$ the effective wavelength range, $E_0(\lambda)$ the maximal spectral power distribution in the absence of modulation, and $C$ a constant satisfying

$$C \geq -\min_{t,\lambda} \sum_{n=1}^{N} \cos(n\omega_0 t - \phi_n(\lambda))$$

to guarantee the physical constraint $E(\lambda, t) \geq 0$. Equation (3) implies that each spectral component at wavelength $\lambda$ is modulated by a sum of sinusoidal carriers with integer multiples of the angular frame frequency $\omega_0$. Note that, in the limit of $N \to \infty$ in Eq. (3), we have

$$E(\lambda, t) \sim E_0(\lambda) \left[ C - \frac{1}{2} + \frac{T}{2} \sum_{m=-\infty}^{\infty} \delta\left( t - \frac{\lambda - \lambda_{\min}}{\lambda_{\max} - \lambda_{\min}} T - mT \right) \right], \tag{5}$$

where $\delta(t)$ denotes Dirac's $\delta$-function. Equation (5) implies that $E(\lambda, t)$ approaches to the monochromatic illumination used in the spectral matching imager [5,7], the peak wavelength of which is swept linearly to time $t$ from $\lambda_{\min}$ to $\lambda_{\max}$ in every frame.

## 2.3   Fourier Coefficient Imaging for Spectral Reflectance

Consider imaging an object with spectral reflectance $R(\lambda)$ under the SMPSSI in Eq. (3) by the correlation camera. We set the spectral power distribution $E_0(\lambda)$ inversely proportional to the spectral sensitivity of the correlation camera $S(\lambda)$, i.e. $E_0(\lambda) = K/S(\lambda)$ with a constant $K$. The intensity signal $f(t)$ of the incident light received by the correlation camera via $S(\lambda)$ is then expressed as

$$
\begin{aligned}
f(t) &= \int_{\lambda_{\min}}^{\lambda_{\max}} E(\lambda, t) R(\lambda) S(\lambda) d\lambda \\
&= K \int_{\lambda_{\min}}^{\lambda_{\max}} d\lambda R(\lambda) \left[ C + \sum_{n=1}^{N} \cos(n\omega_0 t - \phi_n(\lambda)) \right].
\end{aligned} \tag{6}
$$

Note that the spectral sensitivity $S(\lambda)$ is canceled out by $E_0(\lambda)$. For $f(t)$, each pixel of the correlation camera produces the temporal correlation $g_k$ with a complex sinusoidal reference signal $e^{-jk\omega_0 t}$ ($k = 1, 2, \ldots$) as well as the average intensity $g_0$ over a frame time $T$ as

$$g_0 = \int_{-T/2}^{T/2} f(t)dt$$

$$= \int_{-T/2}^{T/2} dt \cdot K \int_{\lambda_{\min}}^{\lambda_{\max}} d\lambda R(\lambda) \left[ C + \sum_{n=1}^{N} \cos\left(n\omega_0 t - \phi_n(\lambda)\right) \right]$$

$$= KCT \int_{\lambda_{\min}}^{\lambda_{\max}} d\lambda R(\lambda)$$

$$\equiv KCT(\lambda_{\max} - \lambda_{\min})\mathcal{R}_0, \tag{7}$$

$$g_k = \int_{-T/2}^{T/2} f(t)e^{-jk\omega_0 t}dt$$

$$= \int_{-T/2}^{T/2} dt e^{-jk\omega_0 t} \cdot K \int_{\lambda_{\min}}^{\lambda_{\max}} d\lambda R(\lambda) \left[ C + \sum_{n=1}^{N} \cos\left(n\omega_0 t - \phi_n(\lambda)\right) \right]$$

$$= \frac{KT}{2} \int_{\lambda_{\min}}^{\lambda_{\max}} d\lambda R(\lambda) \sum_{n=1}^{N} (e^{-j\phi_n(\lambda)}\delta_{kn} + e^{j\phi_n(\lambda)}\delta_{k,-n})$$

$$= \frac{KT}{2} \int_{\lambda_{\min}}^{\lambda_{\max}} d\lambda R(\lambda) \exp\left[ -j2\pi k \frac{\lambda - \lambda_{\min}}{\lambda_{\max} - \lambda_{\min}} \right]$$

$$\equiv \frac{KT}{2}(\lambda_{\max} - \lambda_{\min})\mathcal{R}_k, \tag{8}$$

where $\mathcal{R}_k$ $(k = 0, 1, 2, \ldots, N)$ denotes the Fourier coefficients of $R(\lambda)$ over $\lambda_{\min} \leq \lambda \leq \lambda_{\max}$,

$$\mathcal{R}_k = \frac{1}{\lambda_{\max} - \lambda_{\min}} \int_{\lambda_{\min}}^{\lambda_{\max}} R(\lambda) \exp\left[ -j2\pi k \frac{\lambda - \lambda_{\min}}{\lambda_{\max} - \lambda_{\min}} \right] d\lambda. \tag{9}$$

Equations (7) and (8) imply that $g_0$ and $g_k$ are respectively equivalent to the 0-th and $k$-th Fourier coefficients of the spectral reflectance of the object, and are output from each individual pixel in every frame.

Note that it is also possible to obtain Fourier coefficients of a spectral reflectance $\rho(\kappa) = R(\lambda)\frac{d\lambda}{d\kappa}$ represented as a function of wavenumber $\kappa = 2\pi/\lambda$ by shifting the modulation phase, instead of $\phi_n(\lambda)$ in Eq. (3), by $\psi_n(\kappa) = 2\pi(\kappa - \kappa_{\min})/(\kappa_{\max} - \kappa_{\min})$, where $\kappa_{\max} = 2\pi/\lambda_{\min}$, $\kappa_{\min} = 2\pi/\lambda_{\max}$. The spectrum of the SMPSSI under the wavenumber-linear phase shift $\psi_n(\kappa)$, however, is less easy to understand than that under the wavelength-linear phase shift $\phi_n(\lambda)$. Spectra in the visible range are usually measured as functions of wavelength $\lambda$, instead of wavenumber $\kappa$, by a spectrometer. The spectrum of the SMPSSI $E(\lambda, t)$ in Eq. (3) is observed as a sum of traveling sinusoidal waves with the same velocity toward longer wavelengths with an envelope $E_0(\lambda)$. The observed $E(\lambda, t)$ is not sinusoidal under the wavenumber-linear phase shift $\psi_n(\kappa)$. Moreover, it is difficult to relate Fourier coefficients defined for a wavenumber-domain spectrum $\rho(\kappa)$ to its wavelength-domain waveform $R(\lambda)$.

# 3  System Construction

## 3.1  Digital Correlation Camera

We constructed an imaging system for Fourier coefficients of spectral reflectance as shown in Fig. 1. We used a correlation camera of the digital accumulation type (DCI1 by Reglus Co., Ltd.), the specifications of which are listed in Table 1. DCI1 first captures a consecutive sequence of 32 image frames at 1,000 fps with the embedded image sensor, then produces the average intensity image $g_0(x, y)$ by simply accumulating them, and the temporal correlation image $g_k(x, y)$ by accumulating them with weights of the complex sinusoidal reference signals $\cos k\omega_0 t$ and $\sin k\omega_0 t$ for the real and imaginary parts, respectively, and finally outputs $g_0(x, y)$ and $g_k(x, y)$ at the frame rate of 31.25 fps. DCI1 can distribute reference signals of one to four different frequencies to every $2 \times 2$ pixels as a unit. This implies that, for example, we can acquire four complex correlation images $g_k(x, y)$

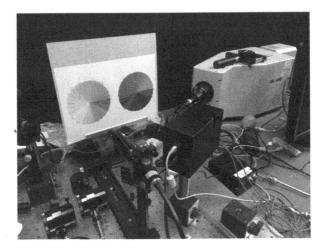

**Fig. 1.** A constructed system for imaging Fourier coefficients of spectral reflectance.

**Table 1.** Specifications of the digital correlation camera.

| Image sensor | Brookman BT130AM03 (monochrome) |
|---|---|
| No. of pixels | $1280 \times 1024$ |
| Pixel dimension | 5.6 μm × 5.6 μm |
| Output bits | 12 (average)/10 (correlation) |
| Exposure | Global shutter |
| Frame rate | |
|     Image sensor | 1,000 fps |
|     Camera | 31.25 fps (accumulating 32 frames) |
| Reference signals | 1 to 4 frequencies |

**Table 2.** Specifications of the programmable spectral light source.

| | |
|---|---|
| Wavelength range | 450–700 nm (max. 380–780 nm) |
| Wavelength resolution | 5 nm (min.) |
| Intensity level | 0–768 |
| Spectrum switching rate | 7,830 times/s (max. 12,500 times/s) |
| Lamp | Xe 500 W |
| Output power | 200 mW (max.) |

($k = 1, 2, 3, 4$) to the maximum, but suffer the lowest resolution (half of the full resolution). In Sect. 4, as a compromise, we acquire up to the second-order complex correlation images $g_1(x, y)$, $g_2(x, y)$ in a checkerboard manner with $1/\sqrt{2}$ of the full resolution. Each low-resolution correlation image is interpolated by discrete Fourier transform. The camera also provides the frame synchronization signal as a trigger for the SMPSSI.

### 3.2 Programmable Spectral Light Source for SMPSSI

We implemented the SMPSSI on a programmable spectral light source (Optronic Laboratories Inc. OL490) [13], which we employed in the spectral matching imager [7]. In OL490, the light from a Xe lamp is diffracted onto the DMD (digital micromirror device), which consists of a two-dimensional array of micromirror pixels to switch the direction of reflected light in a binary manner, and the reflected light is collected and output through optics. We can change the spectral power distribution of the output light at a high speed by writing a sequence of binary images of "wavelength" and "intensity" dimensions on the DMD. The output light illuminates the object in a $5 \times 5$ cm$^2$ area with almost uniform spectral irradiance.

Table 2 shows the specifications of OL490. We limited the wavelength range to 450–700 nm from the original 380–780 nm, because the output light intensity is very low in shorter and longer wavelength regions and the sensitivity of the correlation camera is also low at shorter wavelengths. The switching rate for spectral power distribution amounts to 250 times for every trigger input from the correlation camera ($31.25$ fps $\times 250 = 7812.5 \approx 7830$ fps). The number of modulation frequencies was chosen to $N = 2$. These settings delay the modulation phase by $2\pi/250$ at $\omega_0$ and by $4\pi/250$ at $2\omega_0$ for each 1-nm increment of wavelength, making the spectral power distribution appear to travel toward longer wavelengths in every frame.

The maximal spectral power distribution in the absence of modulation, $E_0(\lambda)$, must be adjusted to satisfy $E_0(\lambda) = K/S(\lambda)$. To realize this, we acquired a sequence of images of a white reflectance standard with a flat spectral reflectance under monochromatic illumination from OL490 while its peak wavelength was swept. We attained the condition $E_0(\lambda) = K/S(\lambda)$ after adjusting three times the intensity of the monochromatic illumination to equalize the image intensity of the reflectance standard, which is proportional to $E_0(\lambda)S(\lambda)$, for all peak wavelengths.

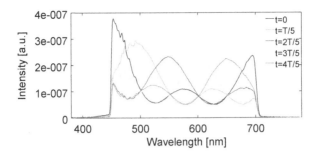

**Fig. 2.** Measured spectral power distribution of the SMPSSI.

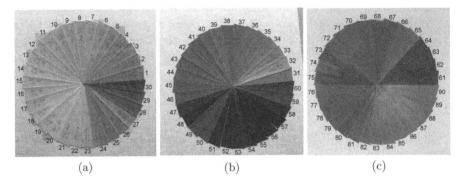

**Fig. 3.** Experimental objects consisting of DIC color guide chips.

The spectral power distribution of the SMPSSI after adjusting $E_0(\lambda)$ is plotted in Fig. 2. It is confirmed that the spectral waveform travels toward longer wavelengths over time. It is also observed that the spectral envelope monotonically decreases toward longer wavelength, which is the direct result of adjusting $E_0(\lambda)$.

## 4 Experimental Results

### 4.1 Image Acquisition

We conducted experiments for the objects shown in Fig. 3. They are three discs in each of which 30 wedge-shaped color chips, selected out of DIC Color Guide Part 1 [14] with high Munsell chroma, are circularly placed side by side with their hue varying gradually. Figure 4 shows the images of the objects illuminated in the central $5 \times 5$ cm$^2$ region by the SMPSSI and captured from an oblique direction by the correlation camera. Figure 4(a), (b) and (c) respectively correspond to the average intensity image $g_0(x, y)$, and the temporal correlation images $g_1(x, y)$ and $g_2(x, y)$ with complex sinusoidal reference signals $e^{-j\omega_0 t}$ and $e^{-j2\omega_0 t}$. $g_1(x, y)$

and $g_2(x, y)$, which are complex-valued, have their magnitude represented in brightness, and their argument in hue according to the chart in Fig. 4(d). The horizontal order of the images in Fig. 4(a)–(c) coincides with that in Fig. 3(a)–(c).

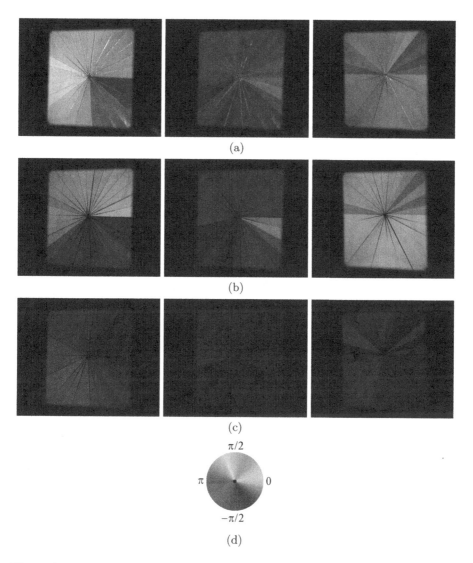

**Fig. 4.** Captured images of the objects in Fig. 3. (a) Average intensity $g_0(x, y)$. (b) Temporal correlation $g_1(x, y)$ with $e^{-j\omega_0 t}$. (c) Temporal correlation $g_2(x, y)$ with $e^{-j2\omega_0 t}$. (d) Hue representation of argument.

## 4.2 Error Analysis

Figure 5(a) and (b) respectively plot the magnitude and argument of $g_1(x, y)$ and $g_2(x, y)$ averaged within each color chip region of the objects, along with the Fourier coefficients $\mathcal{R}_1$ and $\mathcal{R}_2$ computed from the spectral reflectances of the color chips. Figure 5(c) and (d) respectively plot the errors of the averaged magnitude and argument of $g_1(x, y)$ and $g_2(x, y)$ from those of $\mathcal{R}_1$ and $\mathcal{R}_2$. The abscissas represent the index of the color chips. The magnitudes $|g_1(x, y)|$ and $|g_2(x, y)|$ are scaled to the Fourier coefficients by a factor $\mathcal{R}_0/g_0(x, y)$. The Fourier coefficients $\mathcal{R}_0$, $\mathcal{R}_1$ and $\mathcal{R}_2$ are computed in the same range of 450–700 nm as that of the SMPSSI.

From Fig. 5(b) and (d), we observe that $\angle g_1(x, y)$ agrees well to $\angle \mathcal{R}_1$, while the errors of $\angle g_2(x, y)$ from $\angle \mathcal{R}_2$ are larger than those of $\angle g_1(x, y)$ from $\angle \mathcal{R}_1$, especially for the color chips with very small magnitude $|g_2(x, y)|$. In this case, the argument $\angle g_2(x, y)$ is not well-defined and thus vulnerable to noise. We also find that $\angle g_1(x, y)$ and $\angle \mathcal{R}_1$ monotonically increase in Fig. 5(b). This agrees well to the gradual change in hue of the color chips as well as to the peak shift in the spectral reflectance of the color chips toward shorter wavelengths.

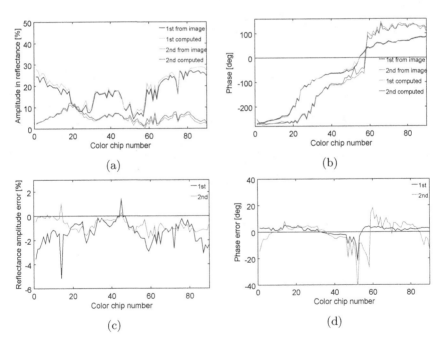

**Fig. 5.** (a) Magnitude and (b) argument of $g_1(x, y)$ and $g_2(x, y)$ averaged within each color chip region, along with the Fourier coefficients $\mathcal{R}_1$ and $\mathcal{R}_2$ computed from the spectral reflectances of the color chips. (c) Magnitude error and (d) argument error of the averages of $g_1(x, y)$ and $g_2(x, y)$ from $\mathcal{R}_1$ and $\mathcal{R}_2$. (Color figure online)

## 4.3    Reconstruction of Spectral Reflectance

Figure 6 plots the spectral reflectances of color chips #14, 31, 39, 52, 59 and 90, which all have large errors in either magnitude or argument of $g_1(x,y)$ and $g_2(x,y)$ in Fig. 5(c), (d). The black, red, blue, green and magenta curves respectively represent the spectrum that was measured, reconstructed from $g_1(x,y)$ only, reconstructed from $g_1(x,y)$ and $g_2(x,y)$, approximated from $\mathcal{R}_0$ and $\mathcal{R}_1$, or approximated from $\mathcal{R}_0$, $\mathcal{R}_1$ and $\mathcal{R}_2$. The reconstruction and approximation were done in the same range of 450–700 nm as that of the SMPSSI. In all of the plots, we see that the reconstructed spectra agree well to the approximates, and that the whole waveform of the reconstructed spectra gets closer to that of the measured spectra when both $g_1(x,y)$ and $g_2(x,y)$ were incorporated than when only $g_1(x,y)$ was used.

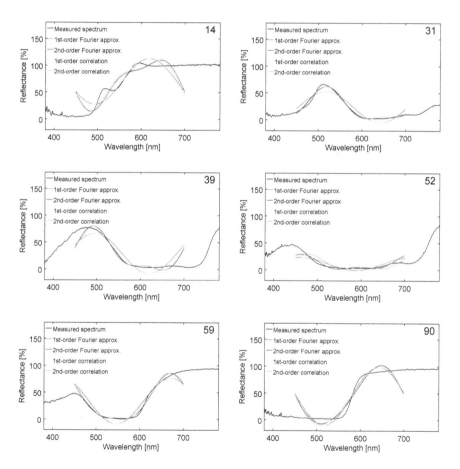

**Fig. 6.** Spectral reflectances of color chips #14, 31, 39, 52, 59 and 90, measured (black), reconstructed from $g_1(x,y)$ only (red), reconstructed from $g_1(x,y)$ and $g_2(x,y)$ (blue), approximated from $\mathcal{R}_0$ and $\mathcal{R}_1$ (green), and approximated from $\mathcal{R}_0$, $\mathcal{R}_1$ and $\mathcal{R}_2$ (magenta). (Color figure online)

## 5   Conclusion

We proposed a system for acquiring the images of complex Fourier coefficients of the spectral reflectance of an object up to the second order at an ordinary frame rate. We developed an experimental system with a digital correlation camera and a programmable spectral light source to realize the sinusoidally-modulated phase-shift spectral illumination. Experimental results on color guide chips confirm that the proposed system extracted the Fourier coefficients up to the second order accurately, and that the spectra reconstructed from the output images approximated well the measured spectra of the color chips.

## References

1. Tominaga, S.: Multichannel vision system for estimating surface and illuminant functions. J. Opt. Soc. Am. A **13**(11), 2163–2173 (1996)
2. Tominaga, S.: Spectral imaging by a multi-channel camera. J. Electron. Imaging **8**(4), 332–341 (1999)
3. Haneishi, H., Hasegawa, T., Hosoi, A., Yokoyama, Y., Tsumura, N., Miyake, Y.: System design for accurately estimating the spectral reflectance of art paintings. Appl. Opt. **39**(35), 6621–6632 (2000)
4. Hardeberg, J.Y., Schmitt, F., Brettel, H.: Multispectral color image capture using a liquid crystal tunable filter. Opt. Eng. **41**(10), 2532–2548 (2002)
5. Kimachi, A., Imaizumi, T., Kato, A., Ando, S.: Spectral matching imager using correlation image sensor. Trans. IEE Jpn. **122–E**(4), 200–206 (2002)
6. Kimachi, A., Ikuta, H., Fujiwara, Y., Masumoto, M., Matsuyama, H.: Spectral matching imager using amplitude-modulation-coded multispectral light-emitting diode illumination. Opt. Eng. **43**(4), 975–985 (2004)
7. Kimachi, A., Ando, S., Doi, M., Nishi, S.: Three-phase quadrature spectral matching imager using correlation image sensor and wavelength-swept monochromatic illumination. Opt. Eng. **50**(12), 127208-1–127208-8 (2011)
8. Ando, S., Kimachi, A.: Correlation image sensor: two-dimensional matched detection of amplitude-modulated light. IEEE Trans. Electron Devices **50**(10), 2059–2066 (2003)
9. D'Zmura, M., Lennie, P.: Mechanisms of color constancy. J. Opt. Soc. Am. A **3**(10), 1662–1672 (1986)
10. Wandell, B.A.: The synthesis and analysis of color images. IEEE Trans. Pattern Anal. Mach. Intell. **PAMI–9**(1), 2–13 (1987)
11. Jia, J., Ni, C., Sarangan, A., Hirakawa, K.: Fourier multispectral imaging. Opt. Express **23**(17), 22649–22657 (2015)
12. Jia, J., Barnard, K.J., Hirakawa, K.: Fourier spectral filter array for optimal multispectral imaging. IEEE Trans. Image Process. **25**(4), 1530–1543 (2016)
13. Fong, A., Bronson, B., Wachman, E.: Advanced photonic tools for hyperspectral imaging in the life sciences. SPIE Newsroom, April 2008
14. http://www.dic-graphics.co.jp/products/cguide/dic_color_guide.html

# Finding a Colour Filter to Make
# a Camera Colorimetric by Optimisation

Graham D. Finlayson$^{(\boxtimes)}$ and Yuteng Zhu$^{(\boxtimes)}$

University of East Anglia, Norwich NR4 7TJ, UK
{g.finlayson,yuteng.zhu}@uea.ac.uk

**Abstract.** The Luther condition states that a camera is colorimetric if its spectral sensitivities are a linear transform from the XYZ colour matching functions. Recently, a method has been proposed for finding the optimal coloured filter that when placed in front of a camera, results in effective sensitivities that satisfy the Luther condition. The advantage of this method is that it finds the best filter for all possible physical capture conditions. The disadvantage is that the statistical information of typical scenes are not taken into account.

In this paper we set forth a method for finding the optimal filter given a set of typical surfaces and lights. The problem is formulated as a bilinear least-squares estimation problem (linear both in the filter and the colour correction). This is solved using Alternating Least-Squares (ALS) technique. For a range of cameras we show that it is possible to find an optimal colour correction filter with respect to which the cameras are *almost* colorimetric.

**Keywords:** Digital camera · Filter design · Colorimetry

## 1  Introduction

Mapping the raw RGBs measured by a camera to either display coordinates (such as sRGB) or the XYZ tristimuli - a human vision system referenced colour space - is called colour correction. Colour correction is an essential procedure in the camera pipeline since cameras do not "see" the world as humans do. Fundamentally, this is because the relationship between the spectral sensitivities of a camera and human visual matching functions is not a linear mapping. Explicitly, the Luther condition is not satisfied [1].

Many different algorithms have been developed for solving the colour correction problem. The most common method is to apply a linear correction transform mapping RGBs to XYZs (or display RGBs). While linear correction generally works well, it can still fail in a large number of cases, especially for saturated colours. In order to address this issue, polynomial regression methods [2–5],

G. D. Finlayson and Y. Zhu—Co-first authors.
Granted by EPSRC and Apple Inc.

S. Tominaga et al. (Eds.): CCIW 2019, LNCS 11418, pp. 53–62, 2019.
https://doi.org/10.1007/978-3-030-13940-7_5

look-up-table methods [6] and artificial neural networks have been proposed [7]. However, most non-linear methods are not invariant to exposure change. In Finlayson *et al.* [8] a root-polynomial method is developed that is exposure invariant. Indeed, given two input RGBs $\underline{p}$ and $k\underline{p}$, the outputs of colour correction are $\underline{q}$ and $k\underline{q}$ if it is exposure invariant.

Another way of achieving better colour fidelity is to make more than three measurements [9]. However, when more sensors are used, the acquisition is generally more complex and suffers from problems such as reduced resolution (when sensor filter mosaic is used) or registration problem (when multiple pictures are captured). Multispectral camera systems are much more expensive than conventional cameras and are not widely deployed.

An alternate approach to increase the dimensionality of a camera system is to take two pictures of every scene with and without a coloured filter [10]. Of course this approach requires the two images to be registered (a far from easy problem to solve). Finlayson *et al.* [11] also proposed a prefiltering solution but the aim here was not to increase the dimensionality of capture. Rather a filter was found such that the device sensitivities multiplied by the filter and then linearly transformed by a $3 \times 3$ matrix were as close as possible to the XYZ colour matching functions. We call this method **spectral-based colorimetric filter design**. Surprisingly, for some cameras there exists a filter that makes them *almost* colorimetric. In [11] a filter is sought that will allow a camera to capture colorimetric data for all possible spectra. Yet, we know that the spectra we measure in the world are not arbitrary. In particular, surface reflectances are smooth and can be well approximated by lower dimensions [12].

In this paper we wish to find the filter that makes a camera as colorimetric as possible for a given set of measured lights and surfaces. Figure 1 illustrates our approach. Here we see a standard D65 illuminant lighting a colour target with known reflectances. Given these spectra and the spectral sensitivities of the camera and XYZ colour maching functions, we can calculate the camera RGB responses and XYZ triplets respectively. In our optimisation we seek to find a colour filter (red ellipse in the Figure) in combination with a $3 \times 3$ colour correction transform.

Mathematically, we will show that the simultaneous calculation of the colour filter and colour correction matrix is a bilinear optimisation problem. We show that this can be solved using Alternating Least-Squares (ALS). We regulate the optimisation to allow us to control the shape of the filter (e.g. its transmittance property).

Experiments validate our approach. For a large corpus of data we solve for the best filter for a large range of cameras. We show a filter can always be found, with which the camera system becomes much more colorimetric.

The paper is organized as follows. In Sect. 2, we present the background on image formation and linear colour correction. Section 3 discusses the formulation and calculation of a filter and a transform matrix. The colorimetric performance is evaluated in comparing with two other methods in Sect. 4. The paper concludes in Sect. 5.

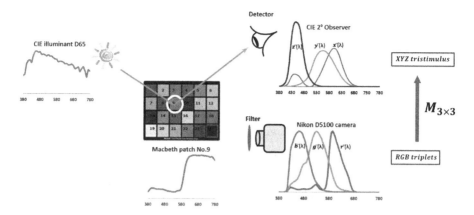

**Fig. 1.** Schematic diagram of colour measurement for an object viewed under a given illuminant. We try to determine a filter (placed in front) for a corresponding camera such that the RGB outputs after a linear mapping become the same as perceptual XYZ tristimulus results. Note that the human eye and camera system should be placed at the same viewing geometry in practice. (Color figure online)

## 2    Background

Suppose a light $E(\lambda)$ strikes a surface $S(\lambda)$ then, under the Lambertian model of image formation, the reflected light $C(\lambda)$ is proportional to $E(\lambda)S(\lambda)$. Given a set of three spectral sensitivity functions, $\underline{Q}(\lambda)$, then the sensor response is defined as:

$$\underline{\rho} = \int_{\omega} C(\lambda)\underline{Q}(\lambda)d\lambda \qquad (1)$$

where the integral is taken over the visible spectrum $\omega$. Similarly, the colour response of human visual system can be defined as

$$\underline{x} = \int_{\omega} C(\lambda)\underline{\chi}(\lambda)d\lambda \qquad (2)$$

where $\chi(\lambda)$ represents the observer colour matching functions (including long-, medium- and short- wavelengths).

In practice, the spectral data is measured through sampling across the visible spectrum, i.e. typically from 400 nm to 700 nm at a 10 nm interval. Given a discrete representation of our data, the integrals shown above can be replaced by vector-matrix multiplication.

$$\underline{\rho} = Q^{t}\underline{c} \qquad (3)$$

$$\underline{x} = \chi^{t}\underline{c} \qquad (4)$$

$\underline{c}$ denotes one colour signal spectrum as a $31 \times 1$ vector. $Q$ and $\chi$ are $31 \times 3$ matrices. The 3-vector camera response $\underline{\rho}$ and visual system response $\underline{x}$ are $3 \times 1$ vectors.

Given a $31 \times N$ matrix $C$ of colour signal spectra (one spectrum per column) then, respectively, the camera responses and XYZ tristimuli are $N \times 3$ matrices written as

$$P = C^t Q \tag{5}$$

$$X = C^t \chi \tag{6}$$

In linear colour correction we solve for the best $3 \times 3$ matrix $M$ that best maps camera RGBs to XYZ tristimuli. Therefore, we minimize:

$$\min_{M} \| PM - X \| \tag{7}$$

The matrix $M$ can be solved for in closed form (using the Moore-Penrose inverse)

$$M = P^+ X = [P^t P]^{-1} P^t X \tag{8}$$

where the superscript $^+$ and $^t$ denote the pseudo-inverse and transpose operation respectively.

Finally, in the next section, we are interested in designing a filter that makes a camera more colorimetric. How then can we model the effect of a filter given the linear algebra formulation of color formation we have been developing in this section? Suppose $f(\lambda)$ denotes a transmissive filter and $C(\lambda)$ a colour signal spectrum. Physically, the light passing though a filter is equal to the product of the spectra $f(\lambda)C(\lambda)$. In the discrete domain our spectral functions are now represented by the 31-vectors $\underline{f}$ and $\underline{c}$. Unfortunately, component-wise multiplication of vectors do not exist in linear algebra. Rather we must re-express $\underline{f}$ as a diagonal matrix:

$$D(\underline{f}) = diag(\underline{f}) \begin{cases} D(\underline{f})_{ij} = 0 & \text{if } i \neq j \\ D(\underline{f})_{ij} = f_i & \text{otherwise} \end{cases} \tag{9}$$

Now, $D(\underline{f})\underline{c}$ equals the component-wise multiplication of $\underline{f}$ and $\underline{c}$.

## 3   Optimisation-Based Filter Design

Let us return to Fig. 1. For a given set of measured colour signal spectra and camera sensitivities, we can calculate the camera RGBs and the corresponding tristimuli. Now we wish to find a transmissive filter - that we can place in front of the camera - that will allow the RGBs to be corrected more accurately. That is, when we carry out a least-squares regression of the filtered RGBs we are closer to the ground-truth XYZs.

A high-level mathematical formulation of the optimisation - for finding the optimal filter supporting colour correction - can be addressed as:

$$\min_{\underline{f},M} \| C^t diag(\underline{f}) QM - C^t \chi \| \tag{10}$$

As before $C$ denotes a set of $N$ combinations of colour signal spectra. Respectively, $Q$ and $\chi$ are the $31 \times 3$ matrices encoding the spectral sensitivities of the camera and XYZ colour matching functions. The colour filter is denoted by the $31 \times 1$ vector $\underline{f}$. Remember the function $diag()$ turns a vector into a diagonal matrix where the filter components are mapped to the diagonal of the matrix (see the end of Background Section) for a description. Finally, $M$ denotes a colour correction matrix.

The form of Eq. 10 is *bilinear*. That is to say we are solving for $\underline{f}$ and $M$, and if one (or the other) is held fixed the problem becomes a simple linear optimisation. We exploit this insight to solve for the overall optimisation problem. See Algorithm 1 below for the details.

---

**Algorithm 1.** Alternative Least-squares Regression Algorithm for filter and linear matrix calculation

---
1: $i = 0, M^0_{3\times3} = I, R^0 = C^t Q$
2: **repeat**
3:    $i = i + 1$
4:    $\min\limits_{\underline{f}^i} \| C^t diag(\underline{f}^i)QM^{i-1} - C^t\chi \|$ , subject to $0 \le \underline{f}^i \le 1$
5:    $\min\limits_{M^i} \| C^t diag(\underline{f}^i)QM^i - C^t\chi \|$
6:    $R^i = C^t diag(\underline{f}^i)QM^i$
7: **until** $\| R^i - R^{i-1} \| < \epsilon$
8: **return** $\underline{f} = \underline{f}^i$   and   $M = M^i$

---

Most of the optimisation shown in Algorithm 1 is straightforward. Particularly in Step 5, we are solving a normal linear regression (and can use the Moore-Penrose inverse). However, solving for the filter $\underline{f}$ is more complex. It is still linear, ultimately, and can be solved using the Moore-Penrose inverse but there is some 'book-keeping' (equation rearranging) to be done.

First, let us rewrite $diag(\underline{f})$ in the following way

$$
diag(\underline{f}) = f_1 \begin{pmatrix} 1 & & \\ & 0 & \\ & & \ddots \\ & & & 0 \end{pmatrix} + f_2 \begin{pmatrix} 0 & & \\ & 1 & \\ & & \ddots \\ & & & 0 \end{pmatrix} + \dots + f_{31} \begin{pmatrix} 0 & & \\ & 0 & \\ & & \ddots \\ & & & 1 \end{pmatrix} \tag{11}
$$

$$
= f_1 D_1 + f_2 D_2 + \dots + f_3 D_{31}
$$

where matrix $D_i$ is a sparse matrix having one non-zero value in the $i^{th}$ diagonal. Based on this property, the calculation of $C^t diag(\underline{f})QM$ can be expressed as follows

$$
C^t diag(\underline{f})QM = f_1 C^t D_1 QM + f_2 C^t D_2 QM + \dots + f_{31} C^t D_{31} QM \tag{12}
$$

Let us define a vector $\underline{V}_i = vec(C^t D_i Q M)$ where the $vec()$ function strips out a matrix into a vector. A new matrix $V = [V_1, V_2, ..., V_{31}]$ can now be constructed accordingly (the vector $V_1$ is placed in the first column followed by the second $V_2$ and the third $V_3$ etc.). Similarly, we vectorise on the human response and define $X = vec(C^t \chi)$. Step 4 of our algorithm can now be reformulated as:

$$\min_{\underline{f}} \| V\underline{f} - X \| \tag{13}$$

The same vectorisation is operated on the matrix $X$. Apparently, the filter can now be easily solved by least-squares regression as $f = V^+ X$.

Using this newly calculated filter $\underline{f}$, next we can solve the mapping matrix $M$ as

$$M = (C^t diag(\underline{f})Q)^+ (C^t \chi) \tag{14}$$

Because solving for the filter or the colour correction matrix is to solve a least-squares problem, then the error reduces at each stage in the optimisation process. Further it is well known that Alternating Least-Squares problems (of which Algorithm 1 is a particular case) also converge [13].

It is important to note that from a physical perspective, the transmittance of the filter must be within the range [0, 100%]. Therefore Eq. 13 is solved subject to $0 \leq f \leq 1$. This linear constraint condition can be achieved using Quadratic programming (least-squares problem as in Eq. 13 can be easily converted into quadratic problem) where we apply the upper and lower constraints upon the parameters [14].

## 4      Experimental Results

In this work, we find the best colour pre-filter for a set of 28 digital cameras [15]. The colour signal tested here is a combination of the CIE standard illuminant D65 [16] with SFU-1995 reflectance data set [17]. The filter optimization is based on the best mapping between RGBs (after filtering and linear correction) and reference XYZs as formulated in Eq. 10.

### 4.1      Spectral Transmission of Filter

The filter and the corresponding transform matrix for each camera device with given testing colour signal inputs are calculated through Algorithm 1. Note that in order to simulate a physically reliable filter, we constrain its parameters in the range of [0, 100%] and for the current method, the experimental results presented here (in Table 1) are based on this constraint. For Canon D50 we show the filter found by bilinear least-squares at the top of Fig. 2a representing the transmittance within [0, 100%]. Actually, by using the Quadratic programming technique, the boundaries for filter parameters can be easily adjusted. In Fig. 2b we also show a variant where the filter transmittance is higher constrained to be between 50% and 100% (it can be regarded as a high-transparent filter which can result in less noise issues).

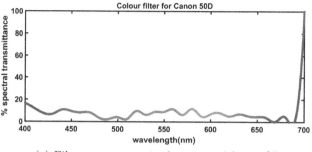

(a) Filter parameters in the range of (0, 100%)

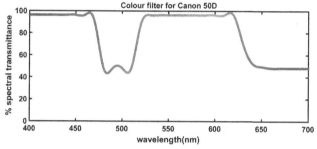

(b) Filter parameters in the range of (50%, 100%)

**Fig. 2.** Filters results for Canon D50 under different constraints

## 4.2   Colour Evaluation

We evaluate our method compared to simple least-squares and the previous "spectral-based" colorimetric filter design method as in [11]. Our results are summarized for all 28 cameras in Table 1.

In the first three columns of the table, we record the mean, median and 95 percentile of colour difference errors in terms of CIELAB $\Delta E^*_{ab}$ for the SFU-1995 reflectance data set viewed under a CIE D65 illuminant. In the second set of three columns we record the performance of the prior filter design method (that tries to find a filter so a camera best matches the Luther Condition). Finally, in the last three columns we record the colour correction performance by our new method. The overall colour correction performance is drawn in Fig. 3 listing the results by these three methods (from left to right).

The current filtering method can achieve as small error as $0.98 \pm 0.28 \Delta E^*_{ab}$ by averaging the whole camera set. The overall medium error is even smaller, reaching $0.59 \pm 0.17 \Delta E^*_{ab}$. Clearly, our new method finds filters which support a step change in our ability to correct camera colour responses. Compared to the linear colour correction and according to the mean, median and 95% percentile error measures, the recorded error by current method is much less. Previously, we

**Table 1.** Comparison of colour correction results between different methods

| Camera name | Linear correction | | | Spectral-based method | | | Current method | | |
|---|---|---|---|---|---|---|---|---|---|
| | Mean | Median | 95 pct | Mean | Median | 95 pct | Mean | Median | 95 pct |
| Canon50D | 1.03 | 0.64 | 2.82 | 0.47 | 0.29 | 1.47 | 0.68 | 0.42 | 2.20 |
| Canon60D | 1.08 | 0.65 | 3.09 | 0.51 | 0.32 | 1.55 | 0.88 | 0.55 | 2.74 |
| Canon500D | 1.09 | 0.65 | 3.14 | 0.48 | 0.29 | 1.44 | 0.91 | 0.58 | 2.80 |
| NikonD40 | 1.11 | 0.75 | 3.30 | 1.61 | 1.08 | 4.97 | 0.81 | 0.51 | 2.50 |
| Sony_Nex5N | 1.12 | 0.64 | 3.55 | 1.49 | 1.00 | 4.63 | 0.47 | 0.31 | 1.39 |
| Canon600D | 1.28 | 0.78 | 3.69 | 0.49 | 0.31 | 1.50 | 0.51 | 0.32 | 1.54 |
| Canon300D | 1.30 | 0.69 | 4.13 | 1.02 | 0.60 | 3.29 | 0.81 | 0.51 | 2.50 |
| Canon1D Mark III | 1.33 | 0.72 | 4.33 | 0.48 | 0.24 | 1.61 | 0.64 | 0.41 | 1.93 |
| PentaxQ | 1.36 | 0.90 | 4.06 | 0.85 | 0.45 | 3.03 | 0.61 | 0.39 | 1.82 |
| PentaxK5 | 1.39 | 0.83 | 4.35 | 1.56 | 1.06 | 4.81 | 1.68 | 1.13 | 5.14 |
| NikonD700 | 1.40 | 0.80 | 4.59 | 1.62 | 1.07 | 4.98 | 1.05 | 0.61 | 3.42 |
| NokiaN900 | 1.41 | 1.01 | 3.86 | 0.60 | 0.35 | 1.90 | 1.01 | 0.58 | 3.30 |
| NikonD50 | 1.43 | 0.97 | 4.45 | 1.73 | 1.14 | 5.35 | 0.99 | 0.58 | 3.16 |
| NikonD3 | 1.45 | 0.84 | 4.63 | 1.60 | 1.06 | 4.92 | 1.09 | 0.65 | 3.51 |
| Nikon3dx | 1.46 | 0.83 | 4.76 | 1.65 | 1.11 | 5.06 | 0.95 | 0.56 | 3.07 |
| NikonD200 | 1.50 | 0.91 | 4.82 | 1.66 | 1.10 | 5.12 | 1.03 | 0.59 | 3.25 |
| NikonD90 | 1.54 | 0.87 | 5.05 | 1.66 | 1.11 | 5.11 | 1.06 | 0.63 | 3.41 |
| NikonD5100 | 1.61 | 0.91 | 5.12 | 1.59 | 1.06 | 4.89 | 0.99 | 0.58 | 3.15 |
| Canon40D | 1.65 | 1.03 | 4.92 | 0.46 | 0.25 | 1.47 | 1.03 | 0.59 | 3.45 |
| Canon5D Mark II | 1.65 | 1.03 | 4.92 | 0.46 | 0.25 | 1.47 | 1.05 | 0.62 | 3.31 |
| NikonD300s | 1.70 | 0.94 | 5.48 | 1.59 | 1.06 | 4.86 | 1.15 | 0.72 | 3.59 |
| Olympus_EPL2 | 1.77 | 1.15 | 5.56 | 1.33 | 0.85 | 4.15 | 1.22 | 0.70 | 3.83 |
| NikonD80 | 1.91 | 1.14 | 6.19 | 1.62 | 1.07 | 4.91 | 1.03 | 0.60 | 3.31 |
| Phase_One | 1.95 | 1.18 | 6.24 | 0.74 | 0.43 | 2.37 | 1.00 | 0.55 | 3.32 |
| Canon20D | 2.01 | 1.13 | 6.60 | 0.68 | 0.43 | 2.15 | 0.85 | 0.51 | 2.76 |
| PointGreyG | 2.45 | 1.74 | 7.28 | 1.43 | 0.98 | 4.38 | 1.44 | 0.87 | 4.52 |
| Hasselblad | 2.65 | 1.65 | 8.45 | 0.89 | 0.57 | 2.78 | 1.61 | 0.94 | 5.13 |
| PointGreyG2 | 3.03 | 2.07 | 9.38 | 1.60 | 1.08 | 4.90 | 0.98 | 0.57 | 3.06 |
| Mean | 1.60 | 0.98 | 4.96 | 1.14 | 0.74 | 3.54 | 0.98 | 0.59 | 3.11 |

proposed the filter design for colorimetric purpose based on Luther condition [11]. Comparing to the former spectral-based colorimetric filter design, the current method outperforms overall, especially for the Nikon cameras which illustrate a significant improvement. Among the camera set, Sony Nex5N provides the best results which are all under Just Noticeable Difference [18].

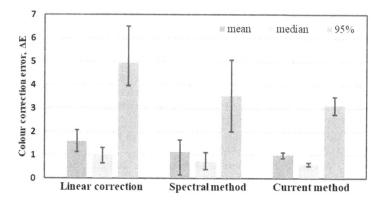

**Fig. 3.** Overall colour correction performance in terms of mean, median, 95 percentile colour differences with error bars.

## 5  Conclusion

In this article, we develop a method to find the optimal filter (to be placed in front of a camera) to make a device most colorimetric via optimisation. Experiments show that this method provides dramatic improvement over direct linear correction operating on raw unfiltered RGBs. Compared to normal linear correction the errors (calculated as mean, median or 95% $\Delta E_{ab}^*$) are reduced by 20% to 70% on average.

**Acknowledgments.** We would like to express special thanks to our colleagues Dr. Javier Vazquez and Miss Ellie Bowler for their helpful discussions and proofreading.

## References

1. Luther, R.: Aus dem Gebiet der Farbreizmetrik. Zeitschrift fur Technische Physik **8**, 540–558 (1927)
2. Hong, G., Luo, M.R., Rhodes, P.A.: A study of digital camera colorimetric characterization based on polynomial modeling. Color Res. Appl. **26**(1), 76–84 (2001)
3. Finlayson, G.D., Mohammadzadeh, D.M., Mackiewicz, M.: The alternating least squares technique for non-uniform intensity color correction. Color Res. Appl. **40**(3), 232–242 (2015)
4. Finlayson, G.D., Drew, M.S.: Constrained least-squares regression in color spaces. J. Electron. Image **6**(4), 484–493 (1997)
5. Vazquez-Corral, J., Connah, D., Bertalmio, M.: Perceptual color characterization of cameras. Sensors **14**(12), 23205–23229 (2014)
6. Hung, P.-C.: Colorimetric calibration in electronic imaging devices using a look-up-table model and interpolations. J. Electron. Image **2**(1), 53–61 (1993)
7. Li, X.: A new color correction model for based on BP neural network. Adv. Inf. Sci. Serv. Sci. **3**(5), 72–78 (2011)
8. Finlayson, G.D., Mackiewicz, M., Hurlbert, A.: Color correction using root-polynomial regression. Trans. Image Process. **24**(5), 1460–1470 (2015)

9. Liang, H.: Advances in multispectral and hyperspectral imaging for archaeology and art conservation. Appl. Phys. A **106**(2), 309–323 (2012)
10. Farrell, J., Wandell, B.: U.S. Patent No. 5479524, U.S. Patent and Trademark Office, Washington, DC (1995)
11. Finlayson, G.D., Zhu, Y., Gong, H.: Using a simple colour pre-filter to make cameras more colorimetric. In: 26th Color Imaging Conference (2018)
12. Marimont, D.H., Wandell, B.A.: Linear models of surface and illuminant spectra. J. Opt. Soc. Am. A **9**(11), 1905–1913 (1992)
13. Zhang, T., Golub, G.H.: Rank-one approximation to high order tensors. SIAM J. Matrix Anal. Appl. **23**(2), 534–550 (2001)
14. Nocedal, J., Wright, S.J.: Numerical Optimization, 2nd edn. Springer, New York (2006). https://doi.org/10.1007/978-0-387-40065-5
15. Jiang, J., Liu, D., Gu, J., Süsstrunk, S.: What is the space of spectral sensitivity functions for digital color cameras? In: IEEE Workshop on Applications of Computer Vision, pp. 168–179 (2013)
16. Ohta, N., Robertson, A.: Colorimetry: Fundamentals and Applications. Wiley, New York (2005)
17. Barnard, K., Martin, L., Funt, B., Coath, A.: A data set for color research. Color Res. Appl. **27**(3), 147–151 (2002)
18. Wyszecki, G., Stiles, W.S.: Color Science: Concepts and Methods, Quantitative Data and Formulae, 2nd edn. Wiley, New York (1982)

# Conditional Color Gamut for Color Management of Multiview Printed Images

Nicolas Dalloz[1,2(✉)] and Mathieu Hébert[1]

[1] Univ Lyon, UJM-Saint-Etienne, CNRS, Institut d Optique Graduate School,
Laboratoire Hubert Curien, UMR 5516, Saint-Etienne, France
[2] HID Global CID SAS, Suresnes, France
nicolas.dalloz@hidglobal.com

**Abstract.** A number of printing or surface coloration technologies have recently emerged, able to print color images on various kinds of supports with various benefits in terms of color rendering. Some of them are even able to produce image with variable colors, where each point in the print can display two or more colors according to the illumination or observation conditions (modes). For most printing systems presenting these variable color properties, the colors displayable in one mode depend on the colors that we want to display in the other modes. Because of this interdependence of the colors displayable in the different modes, the color gamut concept as defined for traditional printing is not sufficient anymore to perform efficient color management. We propose to extend it by taking into account the constraints induced by the selection of colors in some modes, and introduce the concept of conditional color gamut, illustrated through the case of recto-verso halftone prints viewed in reflection or transmission modes, where gamuts can be easily predicted thanks to prediction models.

**Keywords:** Color reproduction · Computational printing ·
Recto-verso printing · Multiview printed image

## 1  Introduction

The color reproduction domain, associated with computational printing, evolves rapidly towards new usages and observation scenarios for which the color management methods developed for standard 2D printing are not directly adapted. Methods relying on ICC profiles often fail with these new printing technologies, mainly because of the number of measurements which would be required. This is especially true in the case of multi-ink printing, more and more used for a spectral reproduction instead of simply color reproduction [1–4], or in the case of 2.5 and 3D printings which intend to reproduce not only color but also other visual attributes such as gloss, texture and translucency [5–7]. This is also true in the case of the multi-view printing technologies which emerge thanks to the progress of computational printing [8–11] or plasmonic color effects [12–16]. Multi-view prints are surfaces (or multilayer supports) able to display different colors, and even different images, according to the way they are illuminated and/or observed. Their characterization is not necessarily a big challenge, except in the case of the plasmonic surfaces which are often very specular and need a

© Springer Nature Switzerland AG 2019
S. Tominaga et al. (Eds.): CCIW 2019, LNCS 11418, pp. 63–76, 2019.
https://doi.org/10.1007/978-3-030-13940-7_6

high measurement precision offered only by specific optical instrumentation [17], and probably also extended perception models for their structural colors. But for the technologies based on more conventional printing, for example paper with special inks [8–10], standard inks on special supports [11], or recto-verso prints viewed in reflection or transmission [18, 19], usual spectrophotometers often suffice. The main difficulty lies on the fact that the colors achievable in one viewing mode may depend on the color targeted in the other modes [20]. This is obvious with structural colors, where the micro- or nano-structure determines the colors displayed under every angle and polarization of the incident light. In ink-based printing, the presence of a certain amount of inks on the support gives a certain tint to the print in all viewing modes, or at least discards certain colors in some modes. The color management methods which seem to have been used so far to obtain the multi-view color images in the contributions mentioned above rely either on manual color selections, or on look-up tables listing expansively the sets of displayable colors in the different viewing modes according to the printing command parameters, i.e. on time-consuming methods which need to be repeated each time one parameter is modified in the printing setup.

In order to cope with the issue of interdependence of the colors displayable in different viewing modes, we propose to refine the color gamut concept while including these interdependence constraints, by introducing the concept of conditional color gamut. This concept could be illustrated through any multi-view printing technology. We selected the recto-verso halftone printing on paper for observation in reflection and transmission, whose color gamuts can be easily generated thanks to the accurate spectral reflectance and transmittance models available today, and whose advantage is also to be familiar to anybody as it is close to conventional ink printing.

The paper is structured as follows: first, in Sect. 2, we present the characteristics of recto-verso halftone prints and review the models allowing the prediction of their spectral reflectance and transmittance, thereby their color in reflection and transmission modes. We show the color gamuts associated with these modes for office paper printed on both sides with an electrophotography printer. In Sect. 3, we introduce the concept of conditional color gamut after having explained the constraints on the reproduction of certain colors in the transmission mode once the colors in the reflection mode have been selected. The interest of the conditional color gamut concept is revealed in Sect. 4 when we want to display different images in reflection and transmission modes, which requires to match the colors of different areas of the print based on different recto-verso halftones. We show that the intersection of conditional color gamuts is a convenient way to verify that color matching is possible, or to select colors in the two modes such that we are certain that color matching is possible. In Sect. 5, we address the question of the contrast which can be obtained in the images displayed in the reflectance and transmittance modes, knowing that in recto-verso printing, a good contrast in one of the two mode is to the detriment of the contrast in the other mode [20]. Section 6 finally draws the conclusions.

## 2   Recto-Verso Print in Different Illumination Conditions

A recto-verso color print is a support, preferably strongly scattering but not opaque, printed on both sides with different halftone colors, each halftone being characterized by the surface coverages of the different inks. As the examples presented hereinafter will be based on CMY color printing, we will denote as $c, m, y$ the surface coverage of the three inks cyan, magenta and yellow on the recto side, and $c', m', y'$ their surface coverage on the verso side. Four flux transfer factors characterize the macroscopic optical properties of the print: its reflectance $R(\lambda)$ and transmittance $T(\lambda)$ for an illumination of the recto side, and its reflectance $R'(\lambda)$ and transmittance $T'(\lambda)$ for an illumination of the verso side (Fig. 1).

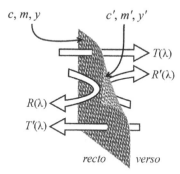

**Fig. 1.** Flux transfers in a recto-verso print. (Color figure online)

We usually consider that the observer looks at the recto side of the print, whose color appearance vary according to the illumination of the two sides. In the most general case, the irradiances on the recto and verso sides can be different, with different spectral power distributions (SPDs) and different magnitudes. We will consider in this study that the two irradiances have similar SPDs, denoted as $E_i(\lambda)$, and only their magnitude can differ. In the case where only the recto side is lit, we are in the *reflectance mode*. The observer received the spectral radiance:

$$L_R(\lambda) = \frac{1}{\pi} R(\lambda) E_i(\lambda) \tag{1}$$

In the opposite case where the print is backlit without illumination of the recto side, we are in the *transmittance mode*, and the observed radiance is:

$$L_T(\lambda) = \frac{1}{\pi} T'(\lambda) E_i(\lambda) \tag{2}$$

In the case where light comes from both sides, with an irradiance $(1 - \alpha)E_i(\lambda)$ on the recto side and an irradiance $\alpha E_i(\lambda)$ on the verso side, we are in an $\alpha$-*transmittance mode*, and the observed radiance is:

$$L_{\alpha T}(\lambda) = \frac{1}{\pi}[(1 - \alpha)R(\lambda)E_i(\lambda) + \alpha T'(\lambda)E_i(\lambda)] \tag{3}$$

The pure reflectance and transmittance modes correspond respectively to $\alpha = 0$, and $\alpha = 1$. The reflectance mode is usual: each time we read a document, a newspaper or a book, we are in this configuration since we generally avoid backlighting. The pure transmittance mode is rarer because it needs to prevent ambient light susceptible to illuminate the recto side, therefore to be in the dark. The $\alpha$-T transmittance mode corresponds to the lighting configuration where we have ambient light and a light source (e.g. a window) behind the document that we are reading. We estimated that when a document is viewed in front of the window of a white room, $\alpha$ is around 0.9 [20].

Various models are now available to predict the spectral reflectance and transmittance of recto-verso prints, therefore their color in the different illumination scenarios mentioned above. The first model proposed by Hébert and Hersch [21, 22] extends the Clapper-Yule [23] and Williams-Clapper models [24] thanks to a generalized two-flux approach. The reflectance model is calibrated from reflectance measurements on a limited number of halftone patches printed on the recto side, permitting to assess the intrinsic optical parameters of the support and the inks as well as the ink dot spreading on the support [25]. The transmittance model is calibrated from transmittance measurement on the same set of halftone color patches as the one used for calibrating the reflectance model. Recent improvements of this two-flux approach have been proposed by Mazauric *et al.* by using flux transfer matrices, leading to the Duplex printing reflectance-transmittance (DPRT) model [19], and the Double-layer reflectance transmittance (DLRT) model [18]. Another family of models extend the Yule-Nielsen modified spectral Neugebauer model which has become classical for the reflectance prediction of halftone prints: a first version for the transmittance of recto-verso prints has been proposed by Hebert and Hersch [26], again refined by Mazauric *et al.* by using flux transfer matrices and avoiding the empirical determination of the Yule-Nielsen $n$ parameter [27]. These different approaches provide good prediction accuracy for conventional printing on common or high quality papers, or white polymer supports.

Throughout the present paper, we will consider a printing setup based on a common 80 g/m$^2$ office paper, printed on both sides with the Xerox Phaser 6500DN PS electrophotography printer, by using only the cyan, magenta and yellow inks (no black ink) deposited according to a rotated clustered dot halftoning technique at 120 lpi. The paper is similar on both sides, and the same printer, inks and halftoning technique are used on both sides. The DLRT model [18], specially calibrated for this printing setup, has shown good prediction accuracy, with an average $\Delta E94$ value of 0.89 unit between predicted and measured spectra over a large set recto-verso halftone colors used for verification of the model. The good color prediction accuracy is also confirmed by the color matching between different recto-verso halftone colors that we could obtain on real prints with ink surface coverages computed by using the DLRT model in an inversed approach, as shown later in Figs. 4 and 6.

We thus predicted thanks to the DLRT model the spectral reflectances and transmittances of $11^6$ recto-verso halftone colors where each of the surface coverages $c$, $m$, $y$, $c'$, $m'$, $y'$ varies from 0 to 1 in steps of 0.1. The predicted spectral reflectances and transmittances were converted into spectral radiances perceived in reflection mode, resp. transmission mode, according to Eq. (1), resp. Eq. (2), by considering an irradiance $E_i(\lambda)$ whose SPD corresponds to the one of the D65 illuminant. The spectral radiances were then converted into CIE1931 XYZ tristimulus values, then into

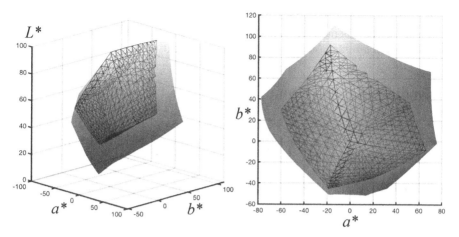

**Fig. 2** Color gamuts obtained in reflection mode (volumes featured by the black meshed surface) and transmission mode (featured by the volumes in color) for common office paper printed on both sides with an electrophotography printer. (Color figure online)

CIE1976 L*a*b* color coordinates by using the XYZ tristimulus values of the unprinted paper as "white stimulus" for the chromatic adaptation [28].

The obtained color gamuts in reflection and transmission modes are shown in Fig. 2. In reflection mode, the colors are due only to the inks printed on the recto side, whereas in transmission mode, they are determined by the inks printed on both sides. The gamut in transmission mode looks larger than the one in reflection mode. This is a consequence of the white color selected for the conversion of the XYZ tristimulus values into L*a*b* color coordinates, corresponding to the tristimulus values of the unprinted paper in each mode. Notice that the radiance of the unprinted white depends on the observation mode, as it can be seen in Fig. 4, but it has the highest luminance in each mode. It is therefore suitable to use it as the "white stimulus" in the calculation of the CIE1976 L*a*b* color coordinates, in observation scenarios where nothing around the print is brighter than the unpinted paper. This is not obvious in the transmission mode where the light source behind the print can be observed simultaneously with the print. We assume here that the light source is not visible, but this has no consequence on the concepts developed in the next sections.

Notice that an $\alpha$-transmission mode, with $0 < \alpha < 1$, would yield a gamut different from the ones displayed in Fig. 2.

The color gamut concept is central in color reproduction to ensure optimal reliability of the printed colors in comparison to the original image that we want to print. For example, gamut mapping techniques, known to provide optimal color rendering for images reproduced with a given printing system, rely on this color gamut concept [29]. However, gamut mapping is possible only in one illumination-observation mode, based on the gamut associated with this mode. When the print is intended to be observed in more than one mode, we must take into account the fact that the color wanted in one mode can constrain the colors reproducible in the other modes. As far as we know, no "multi-gamut mapping" technique has ever been proposed which could take these constraints into consideration. One first step towards this direction relies on the concept of conditional color gamut that we introduce in the next section.

## 3  Conditional Color Gamut

When the print is intended to be viewed in more than one illumination mode, in our case in the reflection and transmission modes, the set of colors reproducible in one mode may depend upon the colors that we want to display in the other modes. For example, if we want a yellow color in reflection mode, we must print on the recto side of the support a halftone color containing mainly yellow ink; consequently, whatever is the halftone color printed on the verso side, the color viewed in transmission mode will necessarily look yellowish. The set of colors actually displayable in the transmission mode is reduced in comparison to the global color gamut in this mode, and we will call this reduced set "conditional color gamut in transmission mode associated with this yellow color wanted in reflection mode".

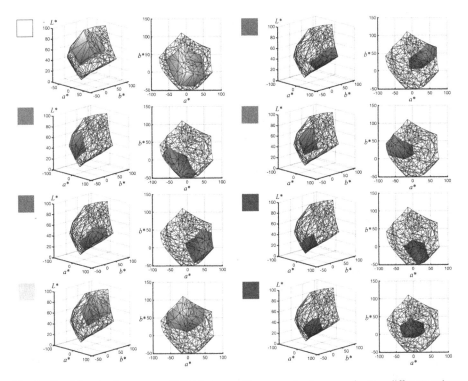

**Fig. 3**  Conditional color gamuts $G_t(C_r)$ in transmittance mode shown under two different points view in the CLE1976 L*a*b* color space, associated with eight different colors $C_r$ wanted in reflectance mode featured by the colored squares on the left of the gamuts. The volumes featured by a meshed surface correspond to the global color gamut in transmittance mode, already displayed in color in Fig. 2. (Color figure online)

More generally, we will denote as $G_t(C_r)$ the conditional color gamut in transmission mode associated with a color $C_r$ in reflection mode. Figure 3 shows eight examples of conditional color gamuts associated with eight different colors selected for the reflection mode corresponding to the eight Neugebauer primaries that we have in CMY printing: white ($c = m = y = 0$), cyan ($c = 1, m = y = 0$), magenta ($c = y = 0, m = 1$), yellow ($c = m = 0, y = 1$), red ($c = 0, m = y = 1$), green ($c = y = 1, m = 0$), blue ($c = m = 1, y = 0$), and black ($c = m = y = 1$). For each color $C_r$, we considered the $11^3$ halftone colors on the verso side where $c', m', y'$ are varied from 0 to 1 in steps of 0.1, we predicted the spectral transmittances of these recto-verso halftone patches, and converted them into CIE1976 L\*a\*b\* color coordinates. The obtained conditional gamut is displayed under the form of a color volume and compared to the global gamut associated with the transmission mode, already shown as a color volume in Fig. 2 and represented here by the black meshed surfaces.

If we focus on the case of the yellow color in the reflection mode, displayed at the bottom left of the figure, we clearly see that the corresponding conditional color gamut is a small subset of the global conditional gamut associated with the transmission mode, and covers only the most yellowish colors.

## 4 Color Matching and Intersection of Conditional Color Gamuts

The interest of prints displaying different colors in different illumination modes is the possibility to display with one printed support different images or graphical contents in the different modes. Figure 4 shows a simple example of paper printed with the same printing setup as the one described in Sect. 4, displaying two different images in reflection and transmission modes, one containing four colors, the other one containing two gray colors. The printed area is a square subdivided into four squares with same area, surrounded by the unprinted paper whose color, different in the two modes, is considered as the white reference for the calculation of the CIE1976 L\*a\*b\* color coordinates in each mode. In the reflection mode, the four squares have four different colors, labelled $C_{r1}$, $C_{r2}$, $Cr_3$ and $C_{r4}$. In transmission mode, the two squares on the top

**Fig. 4** Recto-verso print produced with the printing setup described in Sect. 4, viewed in (a) reflectance mode, and (b) transmittance mode (uncalibrated color pictures). (Color figure online)

have the same gray color $C_{r1}$ and the two square on the bottom have the same gray color $C_{r2}$, thus forming the image composed of two gray rectangles. Notice that the color pictures have been taken with an uncalibrated camera.

The possibility to display four colors in reflection mode and only two colors in transmission mode relies on a color matching operation: the four halftone colors printed on the recto side have been selected in order to obtain identical colors in transmission mode for the two squares on the top, and for the two squares on the bottom. The frontier between the squares is not visible anymore inside the rectangles.

Obtaining one color $C_{t1}$ in transmission mode knowing that two colors $C_{r1}$ and $C_{r2}$ are displayed in reflection mode means that $C_{t1}$ belong to both conditional gamuts $G_t(C_{r1})$ and $G_t(C_{r2})$, therefore to the intersection of the two conditional gamuts, $G_t(C_{r1}) \bigcap G_t(C_{r2})$. The color matching between the two areas is possible when the intersection is non-empty, and any other color belonging to the intersection could have been selected to fulfill the rectangle.

Figure 5 shows a pair of conditional color gamuts in transmittance mode (featured by the black meshed surfaces) associated with a pair of gray colors wanted in reflection mode, as well as their intersection represented by the volume in red whose size is assessed by a volume quantity $V$ expressed in arbitrary unit. This volume of intersection is computed as follows [30]: since each conditional gamut is originally represented by a set of points in the CIE1976 L*a*b* color space computed from a set of predicted spectral transmittances, an alpha-shape is computed from this set of points in order to draw its envelope, thanks to the function *alphaShape* in Matlab©. The alpha value was set to 30, which gives a satisfying accuracy of the 3D shape. Once the

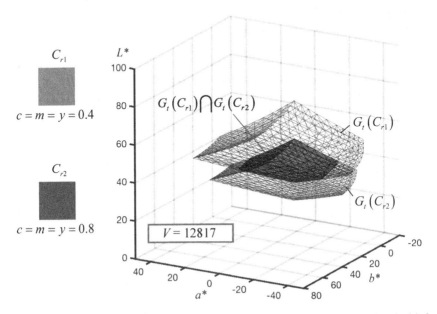

**Fig. 5** Conditional color gamuts $G_t(C_{r1})$ and $G_t(C_{r2})$ in transmission mode associated with four different pairs of gray colors $C_{r1}$ and $C_{r2}$ wanted in the reflection mode (meshed surfaces), and their intersection (volume in red). (Color figure online)

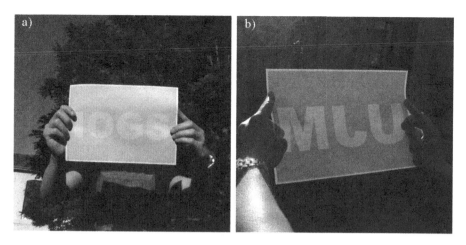

**Fig. 6** Recto-verso print printed in inkjet showing two different binary color images in (a) reflectance mode, and (b) transmittance mode (uncalibrated color pictures). (Color figure online)

envelopes of the two conditional gamuts $G_t(C_{r1})$ and $G_t(C_{r2})$ are obtained, the points of $G_t(C_{r1})$ contained into the alpha-shape enveloping $G_t(C_{r2})$ and the points of $G_t(C_{r1})$ contained into the alpha-shape enveloping $G_t(C_{r2})$ are gathered into a new set of points, from which is computed a third alpha-shape enveloping the intersection of the two conditional color gamuts. Then, the volume of this alpha-shape is computed by summing the volume of all tetrahedral contained into the alpha-shape, which can be done automatically thanks to the function *volume* in Matlab©.

Figure 6 shows another sample printed in inkjet, where two different binary color images are displayed in reflectance and 0.9-transmittance modes whose colored areas do not coincide with each other. The recto-verso print has been decomposed into four areas. In reflectance mode, areas A and B are filled with the blue color $C_{r1}$, and the two other areas C and D with the yellow color $C_{r2}$. In transmittance mode, areas A and C display the yellowish color $C_{t1}$, and areas B and D display the pinkish color $C_{t2}$. Obviously, only two halftone colors have been printed on the recto side of the paper to display the wanted colors $C_{r1}$ and $C_{r2}$, whereas four different halftone colors have been printed on the verso side to display the colors $C_{t1}$ and $C_{t2}$. The color matchings between areas A and C on the one hand, and between areas B and D on the other hand, were possible because both $C_{t1}$ and $C_{t2}$ belong to the intersection of the condition colors gamuts in transmission attached to the colors $C_{r1}$ and $C_{r2}$ wanted in reflection, i.e. $G_t(C_{r1}) \cap G_t(C_{r2})$. This latter was sufficiently large to select two colors $C_{t1}$ and $C_{t2}$ well distinct from each other, and therefore obtain enough contrast between the letters and the background in the image viewed in transmission mode.

Guaranteeing a good contrast in the images displayed in both reflection and transmission modes is not obvious, as illustrated by Fig. 7 through the intersection of conditional gamuts in transmission mode associated with four pairs of gray colors wanted in reflection mode (one gray color in the pair being the same in the four cases). The conditional color gamuts are represented in the same way as in Fig. 5. This figure illustrates the fact that when colors $C_{r1}$ and $C_{r2}$ in the reflection mode are more distant from each other, which is preferred to have a good contrast in the image displayed in reflection mode, they generate conditional color gamuts in the transmission mode whose intersection is smaller, and it is more difficult to find in this intersection two well distinct colors $C_{t1}$ and $C_{t2}$.

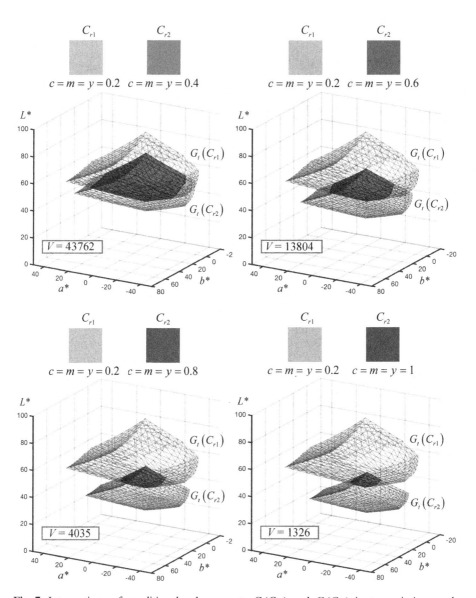

**Fig. 7** Intersections of conditional color gamuts $G_t(C_{r1})$ and $G_t(C_{r2})$ in transmission mode associated with four different pairs of gray colors $C_{r1}$ and $C_{r2}$ wanted in reflection mode, represented in the same way as in Fig. 5. (Color figure online)

## 5 Contrasts in Multiple Binary Images

Let us study more deeply the influence of the color distance between the colors wanted in the reflection mode on the volume of intersection of the conditional color gamuts they generate in the transmission mode.

The volume of the intersection between two conditional color gamuts in the transmittance mode associated with two different colors selected for the reflection mode seems to be a good indicator of the possibility to find in the transmission mode two well distinct colors. We can also consider that $C_{r1}$ has already been selected and observe how the intersection volume varies when $C_{r2}$ is varied, as illustrated in the previous section by Fig. 7. In this case, it looks convenient to compute the ratio of the volume of $G_t(C_{r1}) \cap G_t(C_{r2})$ to the volume of $G_t(C_{r1})$, which defines a *relative intersection volume* induced by $C_{r2}$ in respect to $C_{r1}$, denoted as $V_t(C_{r2}|C_{r1})$. The relative intersection volume tends to 1 when $C_{r2}$ tends to $C_{r1}$, and it is 0 when the conditional color gamuts associated with $C_{r1}$ and $C_{r2}$ are disjoint. The blue curves plotted in Fig. 8 show how the relative intersection volume $V_t(C_{r2}|C_{r1})$ varies for various gray colors $C_{r1}$ when $C_{r2}$ is also a gray color varying from white (gray value = $c = m = y = 0$) to black (gray value 1). On the same graph is plotted in red the color distance between $C_{r1}$ and $C_{r2}$, assessed by the $\Delta E_{94}$ metric. This confirms that when the two colors in the reflection mode are close from each other (small $\Delta E_{94}$ value between $C_{r1}$ and $C_{r2}$) the relative intersection volume is high, and reciprocally.

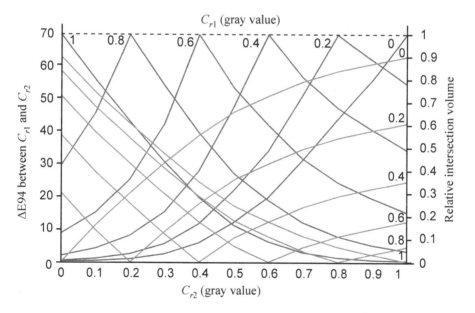

**Fig. 8** Relative intersection volume $V_t(C_{r2}|C_{r1})$ of the conditional color gamuts $G_t(C_{r1})$ and $G_t(C_{r2})$ in the transmission mode associated with gray colors $C_{r1}$ and $C_{r2}$ wanted in reflection mode, and color distance $\Delta E94$ between these gray colors $C_{r1}$ and $C_{r2}$, plotted as functions $C_{r2}$ from 0 (black) to 1 (white), for various gray colors $C_{r1}$. (Color figure online)

In order to assess more accurately the color contrast in the images, even though this concept is not clearly defined, we can consider the maximal color distance that we can find in the intersection of the conditional gamuts, in $\Delta E_{94}$ units. Alternatively to the $\Delta E_{94}$ metric, since according to Fairchild [31] humans would be more sensible to contrasts in lightness than in hue and chroma, the maximal $\Delta L^*$ value could also be considered.

The graph of Fig. 9 shows, again with gray colors, how the maximal $\Delta E_{94}$ color distance that we can obtain in the image in transmittance mode (colors $C_{t1}$ and $C_{t2}$) depends on the $\Delta E_{94}$ color distance between the two colors $C_{r1}$ and $C_{r2}$ selected for the image in reflection mode. Once again we see that if the colors in reflectance mode are very different, the two colors in transmittance mode must be close from each other. This graph enable determining the best gray colors to select in reflection mode and transmission mode giving the best contrast in the images displayed in each one.

For example, if $C_{r1}$ is a gray value of 0.3 (i.e. $c = m = y = 0.3$) and we want a contrast of 30 $\Delta E_{94}$ units between $C_{r1}$ and $C_{r2}$, it is preferable to select a gray value for $C_{r2}$ of 0 (no ink) or close to 1 (full coverage by the three inks), but the maximal contrast that we can obtain in transmission mode is around 35 $\Delta E_{94}$ units in the first case and only 15 $\Delta E_{94}$ units in the second case. It is therefore preferable to choose the lightest gray value for $C_{r2}$ in reflection mode to have a better contrast in transmission mode.

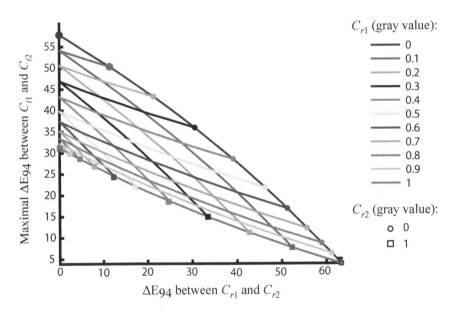

**Fig. 9** Maximal $\Delta E_{94}$ value that can be obtained between the two colors in the image viewed in transmission mode, as a function of the $\Delta E_{94}$ value between the colors in the image viewed in reflection mode, for various colors $C_{r1}$ and a variation of color $C_{r2}$. (Color figure online).

# 6   Conclusions

The present paper intended to take into account color reproduction constraints in multi-view printing for technologies able to produce supports which display different color images under different illumination or observation conditions (modes). It introduces the concept of conditional color gamut, which denotes the set of colors that can be displayed in an area of the print in one mode knowing the colors wanted for the same area in the other modes. The color matching between areas necessary to reproduce the different images in the different modes, which is not always possible, can be checked by verifying that the expected colors belong to the intersection of the conditional color gamuts of the colors wanted in the other modes. These concepts have been illustrated through the example of the recto-verso CMY printing on paper observed in two modes (reflection and transmission), which has the particularity to guarantee a good color contrast in the reflection mode in detriment to the color contrast in the transmission mode, and reciprocally. The intersection of conditional color gamuts helps to identify an optimal contrast in both modes. These concepts can be useful to help color management for multi-view printing obtained with many other technologies.

**Acknowledgement.** This work was supported by the French National Research Agency (ANR) within the program "Investissements d'Avenir" (ANR-11-IDEX-0007), in the framework of the LABEX MANUTECH-SISE (ANR-10-LABX-0075) of Université de Lyon.

# References

1. Tzeng, D.-Y., Berns, R.S.: Spectral-based six-color separation minimizing metamerism. In: Proceedings of the IS&T/SID Color Imaging Conference, pp. 342–347 (2000)
2. Gerhardt, J., Hardeberg, J.Y.: Characterization of an eight colorant inkjet system for spectral color reproduction. In: Proceedings of the CGIV, pp. 263–267 (2004)
3. Le Moan, S., Blahová, J., Urban, P., Norberg, O.: Five dimensions for spectral color management. J. Imaging Sci. Technol. **60**(6), 60501-1–60501-9 (2016)
4. Urban, P., Berns, R.S.: Paramer mismatch-based spectral gamut mapping. IEEE Trans. Image Process. **20**, 1599–1610 (2011)
5. Baar, T., Samadzadegan, S., Ortiz-Segovia, M.V., Urban, P., Brettel, H.: Printing gloss effects in a 2.5D system. In: Proceedings of the SPIE, vol. 9018, Paper 90180 M (2014)
6. Arikan, C.A., Brunton, A., Tanksale, T.M., Urban, P.: Color-managed 3D printing with highly translucent printing materials. In: Proceedings of the SPIE, vol. 9398, Paper 93980S (2015)
7. Brunton, A., Arikan, C.A., Tanksale, T.M., Urban, P.: 3D printing spatially varying color and translucency. ACM Trans. Graph. (TOG) **37**, 157 (2018)
8. Hersch, R.D., Collaud, F., Emmel, P.: Reproducing color images with embedded metallic patterns. ACM Trans. Graph. **22**, 427–436 (2003). Proceedings of the SIGGRAPH 2003
9. Babaei, V., Hersch, R.D.: Color reproduction of metallic-ink images. J. Imaging Sci. Technol. **60,** Paper 030503 (2016)
10. Rossier, R.. Hersch, R.D.: Hiding patterns with daylight fluorescent inks. In: Proceedings of the IS&T 19th Color and Imaging Conference, pp. 223–228 (2011)
11. Pjanic, P., Hersch, R.D.: Color changing effects with anisotropic halftone prints on metal. ACM Trans. Graph. **34**, Article 167 (2015). Proceedings of the SIGGRAPH 2015

12. Destouches, N., et al.: Permanent dichroic coloring of surfaces by laser-induced formation of chain-like self-organized silver nanoparticles within crystalline titania films. In: Conference on Synthesis and Photonics of Nanoscale Materials X, Proceedngs of SPIE, vol. 8609–860905 (2013)

13. Kumar, K., et al.: Printing colour at the optical diffraction limit. Nature nanotechnology Nat. Nanotechnol. **7**, 557–561 (2012)

14. Miyata, M., et al.: Full-color subwavelength printing with gap-plasmonic optical antennas. Nano Lett. **16**(5), 3166–3172 (2016)

15. Sun, S., et al.: All-dielectric full-color printing with $TiO_2$ metasurfaces. ACS Nano **11**, 4445–4452 (2017)

16. Nam, H., et al.: Inkjet printing based mono-layered photonic crystal patterning for anti-counterfeiting structural colors. Sci. Rep. **6**, 30885 (2016)

17. Hébert, M., et al.: Characterization by hyperspectral imaging and hypercolor gamut estimation for structural color prints. In: Bianco, S., Schettini, R., Trémeau, A., Tominaga, S. (eds.) CCIW 2017. LNCS, vol. 10213, pp. 211–222. Springer, Cham (2017). https://doi.org/10.1007/978-3-319-56010-6_18

18. Mazauric, S., Fournel, T., Hébert, M.: Fast-calibration reflectance-transmittance model to compute multiview recto-verso prints. In: Bianco, S., Schettini, R., Trémeau, A., Tominaga, S. (eds.) CCIW 2017. LNCS, vol. 10213, pp. 223–232. Springer, Cham (2017). https://doi.org/10.1007/978-3-319-56010-6_19

19. Mazauric, S., Hebert, M., Simonot, L., Fournel, T.: Two-flux transfer matrix model for predicting the reflectance and transmittance of duplex halftone prints. J. Opt. Soc. Am. A **31**, 2775–2788 (2014)

20. Dalloz, N., Mazauric, S., Fournel, T., Hébert, M.: How to design a recto-verso print displaying different images in various everyday-life lighting conditions. In: IS&T Electronic Imaging Symposium, Materials appearance, Burlingame, USA, 30 January–2 February 2017 (2017)

21. Hébert, M., Hersch, R.D.: Reflectance and transmittance model for recto-verso halftone prints: spectral predictions with multi-ink halftones. J. Opt. Soc. Am. A **26**, 356–364 (2009)

22. Hébert, M., Hersch, R.D.: Reflectance and transmittance model for recto-verso halftone prints. J. Opt. Soc. Am. A **23**, 2415–2432 (2006)

23. Clapper, F.R., Yule, J.A.C.: The effect of multiple internal reflections on the densities of halftone prints on paper. J. Opt. Soc. Am. **43**, 600–603 (1953)

24. Williams, F.C., Clapper, F.R.: Multiple internal reflections in photographic color prints. J. Opt. Soc. Am. **43**, 595–597 (1953)

25. Hébert, M., Hersch, R.D.: Review of spectral reflectance prediction models for halftone prints: calibration, prediction and performance. Color Res. Appl. Paper 21907 (2014)

26. Hébert, M., Hersch, R.D.: Yule-Nielsen based recto-verso color halftone transmittance prediction model. Appl. Opt. **50**, 519–525 (2011)

27. Mazauric, S., Hébert, M., Fournel, T.: Revisited Yule-Nielsen model without fitting of the n parameter. J. Opt. Soc. Am. A **35**, 244–255 (2018)

28. Wyszecki, G., Stiles, W.S.: Color Science: Concepts and Methods, Quantitative Data and Formulae, 2nd edn. Wiley, Hoboken (1982)

29. Morovič, J.: Color Gamut Mapping. Wiley, Hoboken (2008)

30. Cholewo, T.J., Love, S.: Gamut boundary determination using alpha-shapes. In: Color and Imaging Conference, 7th Color and Imaging Conference Final Program and Proceedings, pp. 200–204, 5 (1999)

31. Fairchild, M.D.: Color Appearance Models, 3rd edn. Wiley, Hoboken (2013)

# Multispectral Imaging

# Acquisition of 3D Data and Spectral Color by Using RGBD Camera and Programmable Light Source

Motonori Doi$^{(\boxtimes)}$, Norifumi Nishida, Akira Kimachi, and Shogo Nishi

Osaka Electro-Communication University,
18-8 Hatsu-cho, Neyagawa, Osaka 572-8530, Japan
doi@osakac.ac.jp

**Abstract.** Measurement of shape and color of three-dimensional (3D) object surface is important in many fields including display, digital archives, computer graphics, and computer vision. For instance, the reproduction of object color appearance under various illuminations requires spectral color information of the object surface, and the shape information of the object surface is important for the shading. This paper proposes a method for acquisition of 3D data and spectral color of the object surface by a system consisted of RGBD camera and a programmable light source that can emit narrow band lights. We use Kinect v2 as the RGBD camera. The Kinect has auto white balance and auto contrast, and user cannot control these color compensation functions. Therefore, we estimated the reflection from object in each narrow band image by using achromatic color patches as references. In experiments, we confirmed the estimation accuracy by using achromatic color patches. The results showed that average root mean square error (RMSE) for the spectral color estimation of six color patches was 0.035 in the range in which perfect reflection is defined as 1. We also generated spectral images from 12 band images and reproduced color images under several lighting conditions from the spectral images. Then, we combined the 3D data and the reproduced color image in PLY format. We showed that it is possible to measure 3D data and spectral color of the object by the system consisted of the RGBD camera and the programmable light source.

**Keywords:** Spectral reflectance · Three-dimensional data · RGBD camera · Programmable light source

## 1 Introduction

Measurement of shape and color of three-dimensional (3D) object surface is important in many fields including display, digital archives, computer graphics, and computer vision. For instance, the reproduction of object color appearance under various illuminations requires spectral color information of the object surface, and the shape information of the object surface is important for the shading. Conventional imaging systems cannot meet the recording of such high-order information.

There are several methods to take spectral color information and shape information simultaneously. Manabe et al. proposed a method to measure both of shape and

S. Tominaga et al. (Eds.): CCIW 2019, LNCS 11418, pp. 79–88, 2019.
https://doi.org/10.1007/978-3-030-13940-7_7

spectrum based on color coded patterns projection [1], and the authors proposed stereo matching based on multiband imaging [2]. These methods were available for some applications. However, the 3D shape estimations in these methods are not accurate in comparison with recent 3D measurement methods, such as time of flight (ToF) [3].

In this paper, we propose the acquisition of 3D data and spectral color of the object surface by a system consisted of recent RGBD camera and a programmable light source that can emit narrow band light. We use Microsoft Kinect v2 [4] (referred to as Kinect) as the RGBD camera. The Kinect is a popular low-cost RGBD camera that can obtain RGB image with depth information (RGBD) data by using ToF method. The depth is related to the distance from the camera and obtained for each pixel in the image as the depth image. The 3D information of the scene is reconstructed from the depth image.

Therefore, we attempt to use Kinect for acquisition of 3D data and spectral color. The Kinect has auto white balance and auto contrast. However, we can't find how to fix the white balance and contrast of the camera by the user. There are works for spectral color recovery from RGB images [5–7]. In our case, the camera parameters are unknown and changed for different scenes. Therefore, it is difficult to estimate the spectral color by the conventional methods. The available information for the estimation is the observed colors of the objects of those reflectances are known. Therefore we estimate the spectral color on the objects in each narrow band image by using the gray values of achromatic color patches in the image as references.

## 2  Measurement System

The measurement system consisted of a RGBD camera, a programmable light source and PCs for control of them. Figure 1 shows the system setting. Narrow band light is emitted from the light guide of the programmable light source. The light is diffused by a diffuser and illuminate target objects. The distribution of the light is compensated by the image of a large white board taken in advance at the position of the target object.

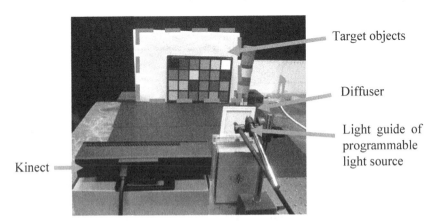

**Fig. 1.** Measurement system

## 2.1   RGBD Camera

RGBD camera is the camera that can capture RGB image and depth image simultaneously. As the RGBD camera, we use Kinect that launched in 2014. The Kinect is a game controller by using gesture recognition. The system is low cost and the software development kit (SDK) is provided. Therefore, the Kinect is used in various research areas. The resolution of RGB image is 1920 × 1080, and that of depth image is 512 × 424. The Kinect obtains the depth data by ToF.

## 2.2   Programmable Light Source

It is difficult to control the spectral power distribution of illumination by using conventional light source. We use a programmable light source (Gooch&Housego, Inc. OL490) to control the illumination spectra. Figure 2 shows the programmable light source. The light source can emit light with arbitrary spectral-power distribution. The programmable light source is composed of a xenon lamp source, a grating, a digital micro mirror device (DMD) chip, and a liquid light guide. The light beam of xenon is separated by the grating into its constituent wavelength. The intensity of the light on each wavelength is controlled by the DMD chip.

# 3   Spectral Reflectance Estimation Using Achromatic Color Patches

The simple model for the surface reflection defines the gray value observed by a camera as the following equation,

$$g = \int E(\lambda)R(\lambda)S(\lambda)d\lambda \tag{1}$$

where $E(\lambda)$ is the spectral power distribution of the illumination, $R(\lambda)$ is the spectral reflectance of the object surface, and $S(\lambda)$ is the spectral sensitivity of the camera. At a wavelength $\lambda_\alpha$, the observed gray value $g(\lambda_\alpha)$ on the object surface is simply defined as the following equation,

**Fig. 2.** Programmable light source

$$g(\lambda_\alpha) = E(\lambda_\alpha)R(\lambda_\alpha)S(\lambda_\alpha) \tag{2}$$

When the reflectance of the standard white is supposed as 1, the observed gray value of the standard white is defined as the following equation,

$$w(\lambda_\alpha) = E(\lambda_\alpha)S(\lambda_\alpha) \tag{3}$$

Therefore, $R(\lambda_\alpha)$, the reflectance at a wavelength $\lambda_\alpha$, is calculated from the gray value of the object surface $g(\lambda_\alpha)$ and standard white $w(\lambda_\alpha)$ under illumination with wavelength $\lambda_\alpha$ by simple division as the following equation,

$$R(\lambda_\alpha) = g(\lambda_\alpha)/w(\lambda_\alpha) \tag{4}$$

This conventional estimation is based on the linearity of the camera response. The precision of the estimation depends on the value of $w(\lambda_\alpha)$.

In our case, the white balance and contrast of our camera was uncontrollable, and we think the camera response is nonlinear. To solve this problem, we used achromatic color patches as the reference. The spectral reflectance data of the achromatic patches are measured in advance. The estimation of spectral reflectance on object surface is done by the following steps;

1. Acquisition of RGB images of object with achromatic color patches under narrow band illuminations.
2. Detection of gray values of the achromatic patches in each band image.
3. Estimation of reflectance at each pixel on objects by the piecewise linear interpolation of reflectances of achromatic patches those have brighter and darker gray values for the gray value of the pixel in the narrow band image.

The piecewise linear interpolation is done by the following equation,

$$R(\lambda_\alpha) = \frac{g(\lambda_\alpha) - gd(\lambda_\alpha)}{gb(\lambda_\alpha) - gd(\lambda_\alpha)}(Rb(\lambda_\alpha) - Rd(\lambda_\alpha)) + Rd(\lambda_\alpha) \tag{5}$$

where $g(\lambda_\alpha)$ is the gray values at the pixel, $gb(\lambda_\alpha)$ is the gray value of brighter achromatic patch, $gd(\lambda_\alpha)$ is the gray value of darker achromatic patch, $Rb(\lambda_\alpha)$ is the reflectance of brighter achromatic patch, and $Rd(\lambda_\alpha)$ is the reflectance of darker achromatic patch. The difference between $gb(\lambda_\alpha)$ and $gd(\lambda_\alpha)$ is related to the estimation precision.

## 4  Experiments

### 4.1  Spectral Reflectance Estimation by Using Achromatic Color Patches

The camera response for narrow band illumination was low. Therefore, we set the bandwidth to 20 nm and captured images were integrated over some shots. We took 12-band images at 20 nm intervals in the wavelength range of 420–640 nm. The target object is a color chart (X-rite Color Checker CLASSIC) at 675 mm distance from the RGBD camera. The illumination distributions in taken images were compensated by the image of white board taken in advance.

The spectral reflectance estimation was done for 6 primary colors of blue (B), green (G), red (R), yellow (Y), magenta (M) and cyan (C) in the color chart (Fig. 3). The gray value of each color patch was defined as the averaged value of 40 × 40 pixels areas in each patch. The achromatic color patches used for the estimation are white (W), n8, n6.5, n5, n3.5, and black (Bl) as shown in Fig. 3. In our investigation, the reflectances of these patches were close to 0.87, 0.58, 0.36, 0.19, 0.09, and 0.03 in all wavelength, respectively. In this experiment, the reflection of the color patches was regarded as the Lambertian reflection.

Figure 4 shows the result of spectral reflectance estimation by the proposed method using achromatic color patches. In Fig. 4, solid lines indicate estimated values and dotted lines indicate measured values by spectrophotometer (Konica Minolta, CM-2600d). For the comparison, we also estimated spectral reflectance of these color patches by using only the white patch as shown in Fig. 5. Table 1 shows the root mean square error (RMSE) in the estimation by using achromatic patches and the estimation by using only white patch. These results show that the estimation by using achromatic patches is better than the conventional estimation by using only white reference.

## 4.2   Spectral Images

We obtained images of a color objects with the color chart under 12 narrow band illuminations. The scene of objects is shown in Fig. 6 and the 12 narrow band images are shown in Fig. 7. Spectral reflectance at each pixel in the center area of the image is estimated by the proposed method. Then, images of spectral color are generated as shown in Fig. 8. Each pixel of the image of a wavelength has the reflection at the wavelength as 8bit value. The images in short wavelength range include noise because the camera response in the range is low.

Figure 9 shows the images reproduced from the spectral images as the image under illumination of D65 and LEDs of warm white, cool white, and daylight. In the reproduction, the spectral data at each pixel are converted to the XYZ tristimulus values and then to the sRGB color values. The influence of noise in short wavelength range is negligible in the results.

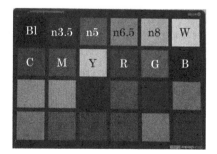

**Fig. 3.** Measured color chart (Color figure online)

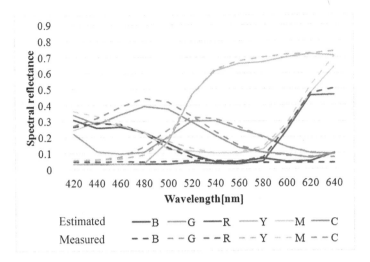

**Fig. 4.** Spectral reflectance estimation by using achromatic references (Color figure online)

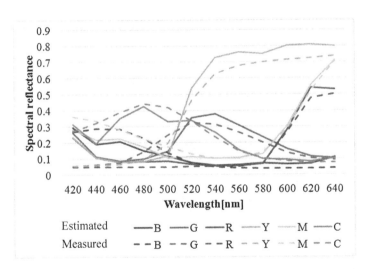

**Fig. 5.** Spectral reflectance estimation by using only white reference. (Color figure online)

**Table 1.** Estimation error (RMSE)

| Color | Blue | Green | Red | Yellow | Magenta | Cyan | Average |
|---|---|---|---|---|---|---|---|
| White reference | 0.050 | 0.074 | 0.062 | 0.084 | 0.052 | 0.049 | 0.062 |
| Achromatic references | 0.027 | 0.053 | 0.020 | 0.026 | 0.046 | 0.036 | 0.035 |

**Fig. 6.** Target objects (Color figure online)

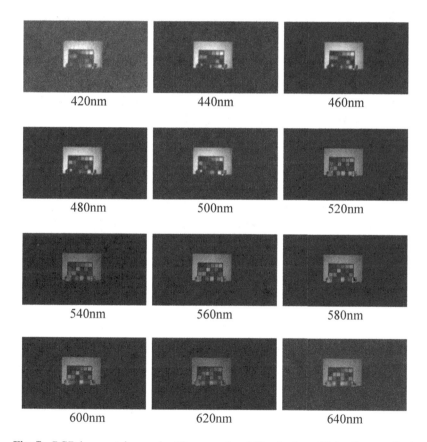

**Fig. 7.** RGB images taken under 12 narrow band illuminations (Color figure online)

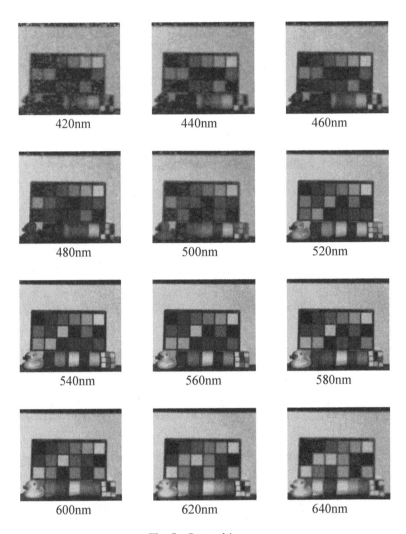

420nm     440nm     460nm

480nm     500nm     520nm

540nm     560nm     580nm

600nm     620nm     640nm

**Fig. 8.** Spectral images

### 4.3 Reproduction of Color Images with Depth Data

We also obtained 3D data of objects in PLY (Polygon File) format by the Kinect. Figure 10 shows the obtained depth data visualized by MeshLab [8]. In the PLY format, it is possible to describe each vertex data of polygons by 3D (x, y, and, z) position and RGB data. In our investigation, the resolution of the data in the image plane (x-y plane) was 1.77 mm and the resolution in depth (z-axis) was 1.1 mm at the target position. We replaced the RGB data to that of the reproduced color images in 4.2. A visualization of one of the results is shown in Fig. 11. The reproduced colors from spectral images are shown on 3D object surface.

In this experiment, we obtained high-resolution color image and low-resolution depth data. Then, we fitted the reproduced color image to low-resolution depth data by taking reference points from each data manually. Therefore, the fitting was not so strict, and the side of duck toy includes the color of the background color patch in Fig. 11. The precise fitting is one of future works.

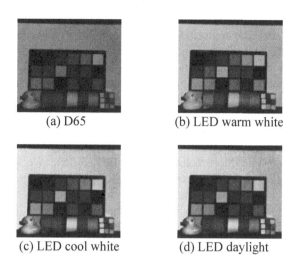

(a) D65                (b) LED warm white

(c) LED cool white        (d) LED daylight

**Fig. 9.** Reproduced color images under various illumination color (Color figure online)

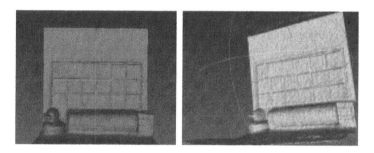

**Fig. 10.** 3D data of objects

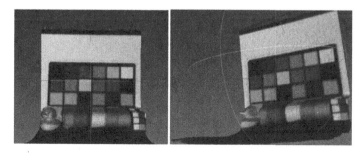

**Fig. 11.** 3D visualization of objects with the reproduced color image under illumination of LED warm white (Color figure online)

## 5  Conclusions

This paper proposed a method for acquisition of 3D data and spectral color of the object surface by a system consisted of RGBD camera and a programmable light source that can emit narrow band light. We use Kinect as the RGBD camera. The Kinect has auto white balance and auto contrast. However, we can't fix the white balance and the contrast by using the SDK. Therefore, we estimated the reflectance on object in each narrow band image by using achromatic color patches as references. In experiments, we estimated spectral colors from 12-band images at 20 nm intervals in the wavelength range of 420–640 nm by using the reflectances of the achromatic color patches. The results showed that RMSE for the spectral color estimation of six color patches was 0.035. We also generated spectral images from 12 band images and reproduced color images under several lighting conditions from the spectral images. Then, we combined the 3D data and the reproduced color image in PLY format. We showed that it is possible to measure 3D data and spectral color of the object by the system consisted of the RGBD camera and the programmable light source.

## References

1. Manabe, Y., Parkkinen, J., Jääskeläinen, T., Chihara, K.: Three dimensional measurement using color structured patterns and imaging spectrograph. In: Proceedings of the ICPR2002, pp. 202–205 (2002)
2. Doi, M., Minami, A., Tominaga, S.: Accurate stereo matching based on multiband imaging. In: Proceedings of the SPIE/IS&T EI2011, vol. 6499 (2011)
3. Gokturk, S.B., Yalcin, H., Bamji, C.: A time-of-flight depth sensor - system description, issues and solutions. In: Proceedings of the CVPRW 2004, p. 35 (2004)
4. Kinect for Windows. https://developer.microsoft.com/en-us/windows/kinect
5. Park, J., Lee, M., Grossberg, M.D., Nayar, S.K.: Multispectral imaging using multiplexed illumination. In: Proceedings of the ICCV 2007, pp. 1–8 (2007)
6. Jiang, J., Gu, J.: Recovering spectral reflectance under commonly available lighting conditions. In: Proceedings of the CVPRW 2012, pp. 1–8 (2012)
7. Haneishi, H., Hasegawa, T., Hosoi, A., Yokoyama, Y., Tsumura, N., Miyake, Y.: System design for accurately estimating the spectral reflectance of art paintings. Appl. Opt. **39**(5), 6621–6632 (2000)
8. MeshLab. http://www.meshlab.net/

# HDR Spectral Video Measurement System

Takayuki Tsuruta[✉], Yoshitsugu Manabe, and Noriko Yata

Chiba University, Chiba, Japan
tsuruta@chiba-u.jp

**Abstract.** This paper describes a method for measurement of HDR spectral video. In recent years, it is necessary to record images with more accurate color information in various fields such as digital archive, electronic museum, telemedicine, and so on. HDR images and spectral images are one of solutions to the problem. However, in order to acquire these images, it is generally necessary to lengthen the exposure time or replace the filter. Due to these problems, it took time and effort to acquire HDR images and spectral images. So, we propose a system that combines HDR image and spectral image by using four filters and RGB camera. In this paper, after introducing the technology of the previous research, we explain about the proposed method and finally evaluate the result.

**Keywords:** HDR image · Spectral image · High dynamic range · CMY-ND filter

## 1 Introduction

In recent years, we can obtain information on remote place more easily by the development of digital society. In addition, various fields such as digital archiving [1], online shopping, telemedicine are developing. Since users know things and information through images, the reliability of the color is very important. For example, if the color of the product image differs from the real product in the online shopping, the user will purchase undesirable items. Also, in the case of telemedicine, the doctor needs to judge the accurate position and state of the affected part based on the image information. So, the color information of the image is very important. However, there are some difficulties with typical RGB cameras. The first problem is that capturing natural scenes with high dynamic range content using conventional RGB cameras generally results in saturated and underexposed image. It is occurred because of the narrow dynamic range of common 8-bit (256 gradations) images. A method to solve the problem is an HDR image. The second problem is that the color that a typical RGB image can represent is less than the color that human beings can be perceived. To solve the problem, a spectral image having high dimensional spectral information for each pixel is effectively.

In previous studies, large equipment was required for HDR image measurement, and color reproduction was often insufficient. Therefore, we propose a system to measure HDR image and spectral image comprehensively.

S. Tominaga et al. (Eds.): CCIW 2019, LNCS 11418, pp. 89–101, 2019.
https://doi.org/10.1007/978-3-030-13940-7_8

## 2    Related Work

In this section, we explain what kind of images are HDR image and spectral image. In addition, we introduce the previous research and clarify the problem to overcome in the research.

### 2.1    HDR Image

A typical RGB image has luminance values represented by 8 bits (256 gradations) of red, green and blue. Capturing natural scenes with high dynamic range content using conventional RGB cameras generally results in saturated and underexposed image shown as Fig. 1. The phenomenon occurs because the dynamic range that conventional RGB images can express is narrow.

**Fig. 1.**   Saturated and underexposed image. The left image is too bright, and floor is white. On the other hand, the right image is too dark. (Color figure online)

There is a high dynamic range (HDR) image that can be generated by synthesizing images with different brightness in order to solve the problem. The HDR image has luminance information of 8bits or more, so it is possible to prevent the lack of information at bright and dark area.

Debevec et al. proposed a method of generating HDR images by acquiring multiple images with different exposure times [2]. Haneishi et al. proposed a system to measure HDR spectral images using a multiband camera [3]. In this method, two pairs of R, G and B band (6 bands) images obtained by changing the exposure time are used. However, color reproduction was not sufficient when they tried to express a wide range using only two kinds of brightness. There was also a problem that the camera system was large.

### 2.2    Spectral Image

The spectral image has information on spectral reflectance which is the physical characteristic of the object for each pixel. Since spectral image has higher dimensional information than the typical RGB image, it can reproduce more colors and has paid attention in many fields in recent years. For example, there is research to identify objects with different spectral reflectance by using spectral information [4]. However, we need an expensive equipment and capturing becomes complicated to measure spectral information.

### 2.3    Problems of Previous Research

The conventional HDR method has a problem that it is difficult to shoot dynamic object. In addition, there were few researches to combine HDR images and spectral images. Therefore, we propose an HDR spectral video measurement system which does not require filter exchange by using complementary color filters, neutral density filter, and RGB camera.

## 3    Method

In this section, we propose HDR spectral video measurement system using complementary color filters, neural density filter, and RGB camera. In HDR processing we show two algorithms.

### 3.1    Image Acquisition

In this research, we use the camera system shown as Fig. 2. The system has four filters and a beam splitter that divides incident light into four. Therefore, it can capture four images with different colors at once. Mechanism of optical element of the camera system is shown in Fig. 3. The system has cyan (C), magenta (M), yellow (Y) and neutral density (ND) filters. The image with ND filter is used in HDR processing, and the image with complementary color filters are used in spectral estimation. The spectral transmission characteristics of the CMY-ND filters are shown in Fig. 4.

**Fig. 2.** HDR spectral video measurement system. The image on the left shows the camera with the optical element. The optical element has the beam splitter and the filter cartridge shown on the right figure. The cartridge has four filters.

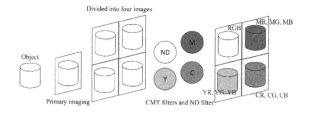

**Fig. 3.** The mechanism of optical element. (Color figure online)

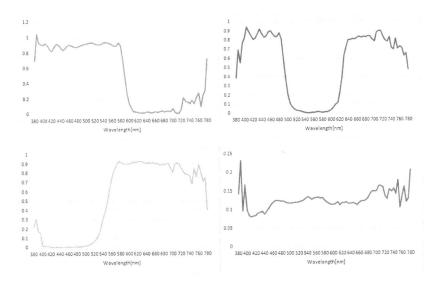

**Fig. 4.** The spectral transmission characteristics of the CMY-ND filter

## 3.2   Image Alignment

The introduced camera system can capture images connected with four color images as shown in Fig. 5. The captured image is divided into four, but the pixel positions of four images are slightly shifted from each other. For the reason, we align the positions of the four filtered images using homography transformation. Homography transformation is a method of projecting the coordination of a certain plane onto another plane. In our method, we use the image with ND as the reference image and adjust other three images to it. The transformation requires a homography matrix and we calculate the matrix using a 17 × 20 checker board shown in Fig. 7.

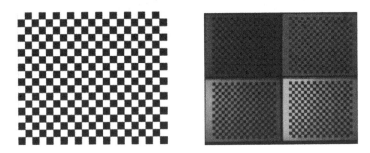

**Fig. 5.** The **17 × 20** checkerboard. The right image is an obtained image by capturing a checkerboard with the camera system.

By capturing the checkerboard with the camera system, 340 feature points can be extracted for each filtered image. The homography matrix can be calculated by the Eq. (1) using the coordination of these feature points and the pseudo inverse matrix.

$$\mathbf{X}' = \mathbf{HX},$$
$$\mathbf{H} = \mathbf{X}'\mathbf{X}^{\mathrm{T}}(\mathbf{XX}^{\mathrm{T}})^{-1}, \tag{1}$$

where $\mathbf{H}$ is the homography matrix, $\mathbf{X}'$ is the coordination of feature points in ND image, and $\mathbf{X}$ is the coordination in the CMY images to be aligned. By multiplying the CMY images by the homography matrix, it is possible to match the position of all the images to the ND image.

### 3.3  Estimate of Spectral Information

In this research, spectral information is estimated using RGB values captured through CMY-ND filters. Here, the relationship between the nine values and the spectral information is represented by Eq. (2).

$$\mathbf{r} = \mathbf{Xg},$$
$$\mathbf{X} = \mathbf{rg}^{\mathrm{T}}(\mathbf{gg}^{\mathrm{T}})^{-1}. \tag{2}$$

To calculate the transformation matrix $\mathbf{X}$, we use the x-rite color-checker shown in Fig. 6. The color-checker has 24 color patches, and we measure the spectral distribution and the value of 9 bands for each color. $\mathbf{r}$ represents spectrum, and $\mathbf{g}$ represents nine values. We measure the spectral distribution data of the color-checker for 5 nm interval in the range of 380 nm–780 nm using a spectroradiometer.

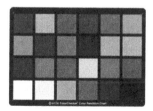

**Fig. 6.** x-rite color-checker. (Color figure online)

### 3.4  HDR Processing

We propose two kinds of HDR processing. In both cases, HDR images are generated using the value of the ND image at the same position as the pixel value saturated in the CMY images. However, these methods are different algorithms and will be explained one by one.

## HDR Processing Using Luminance Ratio of Filtered Images

The first is a method using the ratio of the luminance values of each CMY image with respect to the ND image [5]. The ratios are obtained beforehand by shooting a white object using the camera system and dividing the luminance values of each CMY images by the value of the ND image as shown in the Fig. 7.

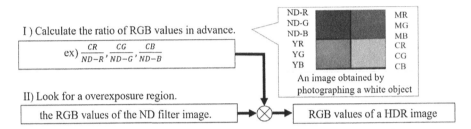

Fig. 7. The procedure of the HDR process.

When HDR processing is performed, an HDR image is generated by multiplying the value of the ND image by this ratio.

## HDR Processing Using Spectral Transmission Characteristics of Filters

We propose HDR processing method using the spectral transmission characteristics of filters. The flow of HDR processing is shown in Fig. 8. In this method, we calculate the ratios of the spectral transmission characteristic of the CMY color filter to the ND filter and perform the HDR processing using the ratio.

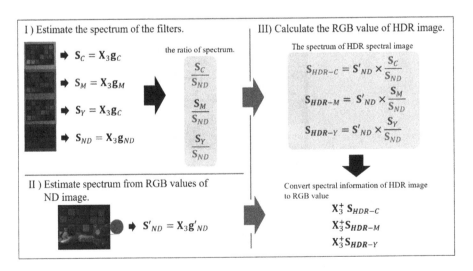

Fig. 8. The flow of HDR processing.

The spectral ratio is the transmission characteristic of the CMY color filters divided by the ND filter for each sampled wavelength. Although the camera system can acquire four images at once, the brightness of these images differs depending on the position before division. In an image captured without filters shown in Fig. 9, the top left of the image is dark, and the bottom right is bright. We estimate the spectrum of filters using the RGB values obtained through the filters to consider such an optical problem of the equipment.

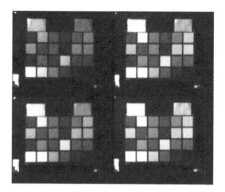

**Fig. 9.**  Captured image without filters.

The spectrum of each CMY-ND image can be estimated as shown in Eq. (3). We calculate for 24 patches of color checker.

$$
\begin{aligned}
\mathbf{S}_C &= \mathbf{X}_{3band}\mathbf{g}_C, \\
\mathbf{S}_M &= \mathbf{X}_{3band}\mathbf{g}_M, \\
\mathbf{S}_Y &= \mathbf{X}_{3band}\mathbf{g}_Y, \\
\mathbf{S}_{ND} &= \mathbf{X}_{3band}\mathbf{g}_{ND}.
\end{aligned}
\tag{3}
$$

$\mathbf{X}_{3band}$ is a matrix for estimating spectral from values of 3 bands. $\mathbf{g}_C, \mathbf{g}_M, \mathbf{g}_Y$ and $\mathbf{g}_{ND}$ are captured values with camera system and $\mathbf{S}_C, \mathbf{S}_M, \mathbf{S}_Y$ and $\mathbf{S}_{ND}$ are spectrum estimated from them. The ratio of filter can be calculated by dividing the spectrum of the CMY color filter by the spectrum of ND filter and calculating the average of 24 colors (Eq. (4)).

$$
\begin{aligned}
\mathbf{r}_{C/ND} &= \frac{1}{24}\sum_{i=1}^{24}(\mathbf{S}_{Ci}/\mathbf{S}_{NDi}), \\
\mathbf{r}_{M/ND} &= \frac{1}{24}\sum_{i=1}^{24}(\mathbf{S}_{Mi}/\mathbf{S}_{NDi}), \\
\mathbf{r}_{Y/ND} &= \frac{1}{24}\sum_{i=1}^{24}(\mathbf{S}_{Yi}/\mathbf{S}_{NDi}).
\end{aligned}
\tag{4}
$$

When a saturated pixel is found in the CMY images, we extract the value of the ND image with the same coordinates. $\mathbf{g}_{LDR-ND}$ is the value of the ND image, and its spectrum $\mathbf{S}_{LDR-ND}$ can be calculated by the Eq. (5) using transformation matrix $\mathbf{X}_{3band}$.

$$\mathbf{S}_{LDR-ND} = \mathbf{X}_{3band}\mathbf{g}_{LDR-ND}. \tag{5}$$

The accurate spectral information of the saturated pixel is estimated by multiplying this $\mathbf{S}_{LDR-ND}$ by the ratio of the Eq. (5). The calculation is shown as Eq. (6).

$$
\begin{aligned}
\mathbf{S}_{HDR-C} &= \mathbf{S}_{LDR-ND} \times \mathbf{r}_{C/ND}, \\
\mathbf{S}_{HDR-M} &= \mathbf{S}_{LDR-ND} \times \mathbf{r}_{M/ND}, \\
\mathbf{S}_{HDR-Y} &= \mathbf{S}_{LDR-ND} \times \mathbf{r}_{Y/ND},
\end{aligned}
\tag{6}
$$

where $\mathbf{S}_{HDR-C}, \mathbf{S}_{HDR-M}$ and $\mathbf{S}_{HDR-Y}$ represent the spectrum of the HDR spectral image. Finally, these spectra are inversely converted to RGB value (Eq. (7)).

$$
\begin{aligned}
\mathbf{g}_{HDR-C} &= \mathbf{X}_{3band}^{+}\mathbf{S}_{HDR-C}, \\
\mathbf{g}_{HDR-M} &= \mathbf{X}_{3band}^{+}\mathbf{S}_{HDR-M}, \\
\mathbf{g}_{HDR-Y} &= \mathbf{X}_{3band}^{+}\mathbf{S}_{HDR-Y}.
\end{aligned}
\tag{7}
$$

## 4    Experiment

We experimented in the darkroom to block external light. Table 1 shows the specification of the camera system.

**Table 1.** The specification of camera system.

| Used camera | Grasshopper GS3-U3-51S5C-C |
|---|---|
| Library | Point Grey FlyCap2 |
| Resolution | $2448 \times 2048$ |
| Frame rate | 15 [fps] |

### 4.1    Output of HDR Spectral Image

We captured the image shown in Fig. 10 with the camera system and generated HDR spectral images by the propose two HDR methods.

First, an output image without HDR processing is shown in Fig. 11 and the tone mapping image of HDR spectral images by two methods are shown in Fig. 12. There are places where noticeable differences occur in these images. Figure 13 shows images which enlarged a part of the Figs. 11 and 12. In the image without HDR processing, the pink pattern disappears due to saturation, but the pattern is preserved in the HDR image using second HDR method. Moreover, it can be seen that the false contour occurring in

**Fig. 10.** Captured image with the filters.

the output image using the first HDR method is disappeared in the image using the second method. From this result, it can be said that the second HDR method is superior in color reproduction.

**Fig. 11.** Output image without HDR processing.

**Fig. 12. HDR images.** The left image is output in the first method, and the right image is in the second method.

**Fig. 13.** Enlarged views of Figs. 11 and 12. These are shown enlarging the lower right of the output images in Figs. 11 and 12. The left image is output image without HDR processing, the middle is the first method, and the right is the second method.

## 4.2 Spectral Evaluation After HDR Processing

To evaluate the proposed method quantitatively, we check how accurately the output image can reproduce the spectral information.

First, we capture the x-rite color-checker in a bright environment. We generate HDR spectral images from captured images by the two HDR processing method, and evaluate the spectral information estimated for each patch against the correct value. The correct data was obtained by measurement the patches of 24 colors with a spectrora-diometer. The mean squared error between the estimated spectrum and correct data are used for the evaluation. We define the patch number as shown in Fig. 14. The evaluation results are shown in Fig. 15. In this graph, the vertical axis represents the mean squared error and the horizontal axis represent the patch number. Also, the green bars are result of the first HDR processing method and orange bars are the second.

We experiment in a bright environment, but not all patches were saturated. The saturated patches are represented by red numbers in the Fig. 15. As a result of the experiment, the second HDR method has better color reproducibility with many colors.

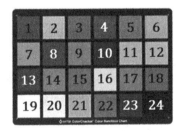

**Fig. 14.** The patch number of x-rite color checker (Color figure online)

## 4.3 Evaluation of Luminance Linearity by HDR Processing

Since cameras receive light on the sensor while opening the shutter, the shutter speed and brightness of image are proportional. Therefore, we check whether the luminance of the HDR spectral image has linearity with respect to the shutter speed. First, we

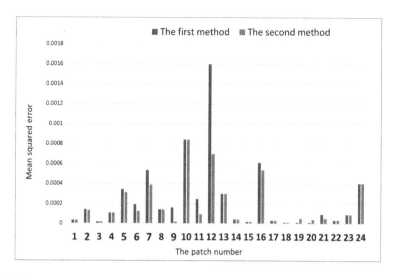

**Fig. 15.** The mean squared error of spectra after HDR processing. (Color figure online)

capture a white object at various shutter speeds. HDR spectral images are outputted from these images, and luminance $L$ are calculated by the Eq. (8).

$$L = 0.2126 \times R + 0.7152 \times G + 0.07722 \times B. \tag{8}$$

The relationship between the luminance $L$ and the shutter speed shown in Fig. 16. In this graph, the solid lines of red blue, and gray indicate luminance of the output image when the first method, the second method and without the HDR processing, respectively. Also, the yellow line represents the ideal proportional relationship. The correlation between the luminance of the three methods and ideal are shown in Table 2.

**Table 2.** the correlation between the luminance of the three methods and ideal.

| The first method | The second method | non HDR |
|---|---|---|
| 0.9824 | 0.9927 | 0.7701 |

## 5   Discussion

In this research, we proposed HDR spectral video measurement system using filter and RGB camera. We performed HDR processing using the RGB value of the ND image when the CMY images were saturated. As a result, the reproducibility of many colors improved in the spectral evaluation experiment at Sect. 4.2. However, in the case of achromatic color, our method can't improve the colors. It is considered that the conventional method is an algorithm specialized for achromatic color. In Sect. 4.3, we evaluated the linearity of luminance by HDR processing. As a result, it was found that

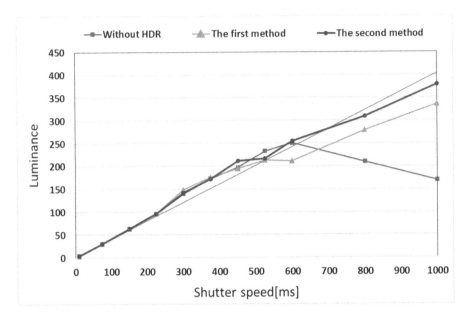

**Fig. 16.** The relationship between the luminance and the shutter speed. (Color figure online)

the saturated pixel values can be interpolated by the HDR processing, and linearity is established between the luminance of the out put image and the exposure time.

We will further improve the color reproduction of the HDR processing by preparing more patches and applying machine learnings. We also want to improve the estimation accuracy of spectral information by considering the optical error of the camera system.

## 6 Conclusions

In this research, we proposed an HDR spectral video measurement system to improve the color reproduction of images. The previous research required a large scale equipment to generate HDR images, but the proposed method solved the problem by using complementary color filters, neutral density filter, and RGB camera. In addition, we proposed two HDR processes and experiments. As a result, the color reproduction of the HDR spectral image can be improved by performing these HDR processes. Particularly, the HDR method using spectral information reduces color shift in HDR processing and solve the problem of false contours. Although, the proposed system can't generate video in real time, it can measure HDR spectral video from previously captured video. Spectral information and HDR processing technology are very important. We want to improve the accuracy of color reproduction and expand the range of use.

# References

1. Miyake, Y., Yokoyama, Y.: Obtaining and reproduction of accurate color images based on human perception. In: Proceedings of the SPIE Color Imaging, vol. 3300, pp. 190–197 (1998)
2. Debevec, P.E., Malik, J.: Recovering high dynamic range radiance maps from photographs. In: Proceedings of the SIGGRAPH, pp. 369–378 (1997)
3. Haneishi, H., Miyahara, S., Yoshida, A.: Image acquisition technique for high dynamic range scenes using a multiband camera. Color Res. Appl. **31**(4), 294–302 (2006)
4. Manabe, Y., Sato, K., Inokuchi, S.: Material Classification from Spectral Images for Object Recognition. The transactions of the Institute of Electronics, Information and Communication Engineers. D-II (1996)
5. Onishi, Y., Manabe, Y., Yata, N.: HDR spectral video measurement system using complementary color filter and neutral density filter. In: Proceedings of the 13th AIC Congress 2017, PS03-77, October 2017

# Spectral Estimation of Chromatically Adapted Corresponding Colors

Tanzima Habib$^{(\boxtimes)}$ and Phil Green

Norwegian University of Science and Technology, 2815 Gjovik, Norway
syedath@stud.ntnu.no

**Abstract.** This paper reviews the estimation of spectral reflectance for corresponding colors in XYZ color space, including both corresponding color data sets and chromatically adapted colorimetry. For use in color management workflows, the performance of an inverse transform of the chromatically adapted data was evaluated using spectral estimation. These estimated spectra were then evaluated against the estimated spectral reflectances of reference corresponding color data to analyze the similarity. The results show that established methods using PCA can be used to obtain good spectral estimates, and the methods described in this paper can be implemented in a color managed workflow where spectral processing and output are desired.

**Keywords:** Spectral estimation · Principal component analysis · Corresponding color data · Chromatic adaptation transform

## 1 Introduction

Increasing use is now being made of spectral data in color reproduction workflows. Spectral source data is available through measurement or from multispectral and hyperspectral cameras, and there is also an increasing need for output that is spectral (reflectance, emission or even bi-spectral, in the case of fluorescence). Such data may be required for the final output, or may be used in an intermediate processing step prior to calculation of final output values. With the introduction of ICCMAX in color management it is now possible to connect spectral data, using a spectral Profile Connection Space or transforming to or from colorimetric representations [1]. Spectral data is also closely related to material property. ICCMAX can be used to exploit this relationship and adjust for material properties.

Another application of spectral output is data hiding using spectral reflectance. Bala et al. have encoded watermark by using metameric matches that can be detected using narrow band illumination but goes visually undetected under wide band illumination [2].

Spectral data is extensively used in color science and the color reproduction industries. In a color reproduction workflow, it is common to perform a chromatic adaptation step to ensure the appearance is correct in the intended viewing condition, or in the PCS. Chromatic adaptation transforms are defined for colorimetric data, via a transform in a 3-dimensional cone space, but when this is done there is no spectral representation of the adapted colorimetry.

© Springer Nature Switzerland AG 2019
S. Tominaga et al. (Eds.): CCIW 2019, LNCS 11418, pp. 102–117, 2019.
https://doi.org/10.1007/978-3-030-13940-7_9

Another sensor adjustment transform is based on material equivalency. Derhak developed a normalization method that transforms sensor excitation to material equivalent representation described by the Wpt (Waypoint) color space. Such Wpt based material adjustment transform reduces the difference introduced by observer and illuminant [3]. In this paper, we review the use of spectral estimation using PCA for various corresponding color datasets and evaluate its performance.

## 1.1    Spectral Estimation

The colorimetric value of an object defined as three co-ordinate representation is easily available. But this colorimetric value is not a signature attribute of the object but rather depends on the viewing conditions such as illuminant and observer function. Tristimulus colorimetry is computed from the spectral reflectance of the object, with the illuminant and colorimetric observer as input [4]. For cases where the spectral reflectance is not known, a number of methods have been described for the estimation or reconstruction of spectral reflectance from colorimetry. We will further discuss the reconstruction of spectral reflectance from tristimulus values in the next section.

## 1.2    Training Datasets

For spectral estimation one of the most important steps is to decide and create a database of spectral reflectances. This database is used to provide spectral reflectance information and nature with respect to its colorimetric response and to obtain a transformation matrix for estimation.

The training data should be selected based on the test data properties and it is important to have a large number of measured spectral reflectances that is spread over a range of colors distinguishable under various lighting conditions and preferably under the test conditions. We will establish this importance of training data selection with respect to test data later in the results section. We are using the following spectral reflectances for training (Table 1).

**Table 1.** Description of training datasets used.

| Dataset | No. of samples | Specification |
| --- | --- | --- |
| FOGRA51 [5] | 1617 | 380 nm–730 nm at 10 nm |
| CC240 | 240 | 380 nm–1080 nm at 2 nm |
| Munsell Glossy Corrected [6] | 1600 | 380 nm–780 nm at 5 nm |
| Munsell Matt [7] | 1269 | 380 nm–780 nm at 1 nm |
| ISO 17321 [8] | 24 | 380 nm–830 nm at 5 nm |

The FOGRA51 spectral reflectance dataset represents characterization data for printing by offset litho on premium coated paper [5]. It was extrapolated to 780 nm by repeating the spectral reflectance value at 730 nm over the range 735–780 nm. The CC240 dataset are measurements of 240 Macbeth Colour Checker samples obtained using a hyperspectral camera. The above datasets are divided into two sets of training spectral reflectances, the first training dataset comprises 1563 spectral reflectances of FOGRA51 and the remainder of the 54 spectral reflectances are reserved as the ground truth for the testing phase. The second training set comprises of the CC240, Munsell Glossy corrected, Munsell Matt and ISO17321 spectral reflectances for a total of 3135 spectral reflectances. All the spectral reflectances are converted to 380–780 nm range in steps of 10 nm for spectral estimation.

## 2   Spectral Estimation Methods

In this section, we discuss the methods used for spectral estimation of corresponding color data i.e. reconstruction of spectral reflectance from tristimulus values. Tristimulus values are defined as the product of surface spectral reflectance, spectral distribution of illuminant and observer color matching functions. One of the simplest methods is the pseudo inverse method that uses minimization of least square errors to obtain the estimated spectral reflectance [9]. This method uses a set of training spectral reflectances multiplied to the Moore-Penrose pseudo inverse of their tristimulus values under a given viewing condition to generate the transformation matrix [10]. This matrix can then reconstruct spectral reflectance given a tristimulus value. Another widely used method is principal component analysis (PCA), described by Fairman and Brill [11]. "The K eigenvectors having the highest associated eigenvalues will be the first K principal components of the spectral reflectances.", as stated by Fairman and Brill suggest to choose a number of eigenvectors as principal components that store the highest variance of mean centered training spectral reflectances. To find the suitable number of principal components, the percentage of variance can be calculated. In our case, the percentage of variance for three principal components for the 3135 spectral reflectance i.e. the second training dataset in the range of 380 nm-780 nm at an interval of 10 nm is 96.74% and for six principal components it is 99.44%. While for 1563 spectral reflectances of the FOGRA51 dataset in the same wavelength range a 99.53% of variance information is obtained with just three principal components. Therefore, if the training dataset is large and comprises spectral reflectance of varied type of measured samples then it is recommended to increase the number of components to allow more variance information. The percentage of variance obtained by Fairman and Brill using 3534 spectral reflectances in the wavelength range of 400 nm to 700 nm at 10 nm interval for the first three principal components is 98.9% and for the first six principal components is 99.8%. This suggest that apart from the amount of training spectral reflectances, the range of wavelength also affects the percentage of variance stored in the principal components. From a mathematical point of view, we know that the principal components of a certain data set let us obtain the least number of dimensions by which to effectively describe the data and its internal variability. Therefore, it would indeed be prudent to perform more analysis and experiment on this type of data where variance information is lower than expected within the first three principal components. We are discussing the number of principal components in multiples of three because the PCA method described by Fairman and Brill can be used with only in multiples of three as discussed later. In this paper we will consider PCA based methods. We refer to the simple PCA method proposed by Fairman and Brill as classical PCA, and a variant of this method proposed by Agahian et al. known as weighted PCA. They are described below.

## 2.1  Spectral Estimation Using Classical PCA

Let E be a 41 × 3 matrix that contains the first three principal components column-wise of the training spectral reflectance set Q (41 × n) where n is the number of spectral reflectances in the training set. For the second training dataset n is 3135. Eo is a 41 × 1 matrix that contains the mean spectral reflectance of matrix Q given by:

$$Eo = \left( \sum_r Q \right) / n$$

where $\sum_r$ is row-wise summation applied on matrix Q.

For a spectral reflectance R with dimensions 41 × 1, the co-ordinates C (3 × 1) of the principal components will have the following desired relationship according to Fairman and Brill:

$$EC = R - Eo. \tag{1}$$

$$or \ R = Eo + EC \tag{2}$$

Let, A (41 × 3) be the weight set for tristimulus integration, R is the spectrum which is being integrated. Therefore, the relationship between the tristimulus value T (3 × 1) and spectral reflectance R (41 × 1) is:

$$T = A^T R \tag{3}$$

Matrix A is of the form $A_{i\lambda}$ where i changes from 1 to 3 and $\lambda$ changes from 380 nm to 780 nm at an interval of 10 nm and it is given by:

$$A_{1\lambda} = k \left( \sum S_\lambda \bar{x}_\lambda \right), A_{2\lambda} = k \left( \sum S_\lambda \bar{y}_\lambda \right) \text{ and } A_{3\lambda} = k \left( \sum S_\lambda \bar{z}_\lambda \right)$$

Where S is the spectral power distribution of the illuminant and $\bar{x}$, $\bar{y}$ and $\bar{z}$ are the colour matching functions stored column-wise in the same wavelength range 380 nm to 780 nm at an interval of 10 nm. Scalar k is used for normalization and is given by:

$$k = 1 / \left( \sum S_\lambda \bar{y}_\lambda \right)$$

Using Eqs. (2) and (3) a relationship between the co-ordinates and the tristimulus values can be drawn as below:

$$T = A^T Eo + (A)^T EC$$

$$or \ C = \left( A^T E \right)^{-1} \left( T - A^T Eo \right) \tag{4}$$

Equation 4 is now a relationship between the principal components co-ordinates and the tristimulus values, hence, they are called the tristimulus-constrained principal component co-ordinates. These co-ordinates can be used with the PCA method to estimate spectral reflectance as in Eq. 2. Therefore, we can rewrite the Eq. 2 using the tristimulus constrained principal component co-ordinates as below:

$$R = Eo + E\left((A^T E)^{-1}(T - A^T Eo)\right) \tag{5}$$

As can be seen the term $A^T Eo$ is the tristimulus value of the mean spectral reflectance of the training data. This equation can be modified to use more principal components in multiples of three and for each increase in the set of principal components, we will also need to include a new illuminant with observer function and a corresponding tristimulus value computed under the new illuminant, more information can be found in [11]. This limitation arises because the principal component co-ordinates are constrained by the tristimulus values which are three dimensional. Moreover, to obtain the corresponding tristimulus values with the new illuminant we have to use a regression method. Therefore, for simplicity, we will use this method with three components considering the trade-off in variance percentage is reasonable. By improving the selection of the training spectral reflectances, the variance percentage for three principal components can be increased.

### 2.2    Spectral Estimation Using Weighted PCA

Agahian et al. proposed a weighted PCA where the training spectral reflectances are assigned weights computed as the inverse of colorimetric difference $d$ between the tristimulus values computed using the training spectral reflectances and the test tristimulus value. The smaller the difference, higher will be the weight. These weights form an nxn diagonal matrix which are multiplied by the training spectral reflectance matrix Q, and then PCA is applied as above. To avoid division by zero, Agahian et al. adds a small value $s = 0.01$ to the colorimetric difference d. This method allows the mean reflectance to have a shape according to the test tristimulus value's closeness to the training spectral reflectance when tristimulus is computed from them using the test illuminant and observer function. Therefore, the reconstructed spectral reflectance should be closer to the original spectral reflectance compared to the reconstructed spectra obtained by classical PCA [12].

We used both classical PCA and weighted PCA to estimate spectral reflectance and compare the results.

## 3    Uses of Spectral Estimation on Corresponding Colors

A corresponding color transform allows an observer adapted to an illuminant to change a stimulus under it to match visually to the original stimulus viewed under a reference illuminant. This change in the stimulus is usually applied to the colorimetric data, but the implication is that there is no corresponding spectral reflectance. Here we show how spectral estimation can be used to estimate a spectral reflectance from a corresponding color. The two spectral estimation methods discussed above are applied on various datasets and scenarios.

## 3.1   Testing the Method on Known Spectral Reflectances

First, we apply the methods to tristimulus values for which we know the measured spectral reflectances in order to test their accuracy. We used spectral reflectances from a characterization data set provided by Fogra [5]. It should be noted that this data was obtained not from single measurements, but from many measurements of a test chart printed according to a specific printing condition. After averaging, further manipulation was performed to ensure the data set had certain desired properties including smoothness and consistency in single-channel tone steps. Such steps are believed to improve the model accuracy in color management [13] (Table 2).

**Table 2.** Description of corresponding color datasets used.

| Dataset | No. of samples | Reference illuminant | Test illuminant | Method |
|---------|----------------|----------------------|-----------------|--------|
| Helson | 59 | C | A | Memory |
| Lam & Rigg | 58 | D65 | A | Memory |
| Kuo & Luo (A) | 40 | D65 | A | Magnitude |
| Lutchi (A) | 43 | D65 | A | Magnitude |
| Lutchi (D50) | 44 | D65 | D50 | Magnitude |

## 3.2   Spectral Estimation of Corresponding Color Datasets

Both classical PCA and weighted PCA were applied on the reference tristimulus values and visually matched corresponding tristimulus values of each corresponding color dataset using training set 2. The standard two-degree observer color matching function was used for all the cases while the illuminant for spectral estimation is the illuminant under which the XYZ value is calculated. The estimated spectral reflectances would help in analyzing how well PCA based spectral estimation can convert tristimulus values to their respective spectral reflectance. They would also help in finding the similarity between the estimated spectra of the reference XYZ and its corresponding XYZ and if these spectra can be used for chromatic adaptation in the spectral domain. Since we don't have the measured spectral reflectances for the corresponding datasets we can only make approximations based on reasonable assumptions.

## 3.3   Spectral Estimation of Chromatically Adapted Data

A CAT is optimized to predict corresponding color data [14]. By estimating spectra of chromatically adapted tristimulus values it is possible to observe the changes in the stimulus in the spectral domain. To calculate chromatically adapted tristimulus values from the reference corresponding color in XYZ color space, we used three CATs, namely, Bradford, CAT02 and CAT16.

The reference XYZ values of a corresponding color dataset are taken and different CATs are applied to obtain the chromatically adapted XYZ values under the test illuminant of that corresponding color dataset. CAT02 and CAT16 have been implemented using the two-step transform with equi-energy illuminant transform as an intermediate step proposed by Li et al. [15]. We then apply classical PCA and weighted PCA on these various chromatically adapted XYZ values using second training dataset. Second training dataset has been used because it consists of a large number of spectral reflectances for a variety of natural and synthetic objects to predict a match for corresponding datasets. The characteristics of the estimated spectra for these adapted tristimulus values are discussed in the results section.

### 3.4    Spectral Estimation of Inverse of Chromatically Adapted Data

In color management it is important to be able to invert a transform, for example in order to obtain a preview of a color on a different medium from the intended target. To understand how well this inverse can be accomplished, the inverse transform was implemented on the chromatically adapted tristimulus values and spectral reflectance was estimated for these back transformed tristimulus values. When the inverse CAT is applied, we only obtain the original reference color value if a linear CAT such as linear Bradford is used. For the inverse CAT estimation, we have used Bradford CAT and CAT16. The spectral estimation of these inverse CAT tristimulus values for each corresponding color dataset were performed using the two PCA methods.

## 4    Results and Discussion of Spectral Estimation

In order to visualize the performance of the spectral estimation on the data set, we select the spectra which correspond to the 5th, 50th and 95th percentile RMS errors. The results are discussed in the following sections.

### 4.1    Spectral Estimation of FOGRA51 Data

Spectral estimation of fifty-four FOGRA51 samples whose XYZ values were computed using D65 illuminant and D50 illuminant respectively were performed using two sets of training data. The first training set comprises of 1563 FOGRA51 spectral reflectances and the second training set comprises of 3135 spectral reflectances. The results using the first and the second training sets with classical PCA method applied on tristimulus values of FOGRA51 dataset are shown in Figs. 1 and 2 respectively.

In Fig. 1, the estimated spectra are very similar to their respective measured spectra while the estimated spectra in Fig. 2 are not as accurate. This demonstrates the degree to which the training set used influences the outcome. The same effect can be seen in Figs. 3 and 4 where the FOGRA 51 samples were estimated using weighted PCA for the two training sets 1563 FOGRA51and 3135 spectral reflectances respectively. To improve accuracy, we need to choose training data whose surface properties are as similar to the test data as possible.

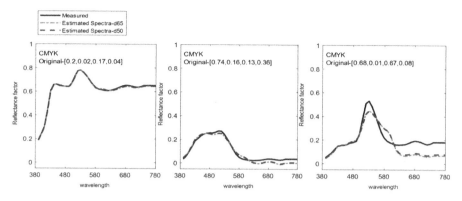

**Fig. 1.** Estimated reflectances of FOGRA51 using classical PCA and FOGRA51 training set: 5<sup>th</sup>, 50<sup>th</sup> and 95<sup>th</sup> percentile RMS errors.

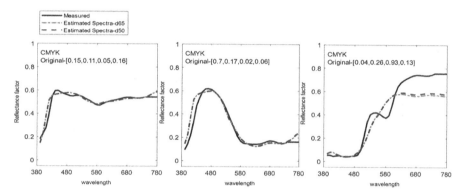

**Fig. 2.** Estimated reflectances of FOGRA51 using classical PCA and 3135 training set: 5<sup>th</sup>, 50<sup>th</sup> and 95<sup>th</sup> percentile RMS errors

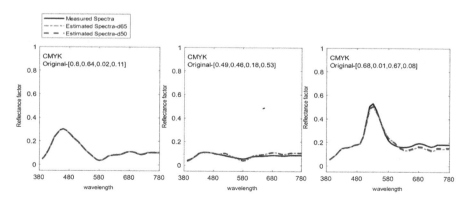

**Fig. 3.** Estimated reflectances of FOGRA51 using weighted PCA and 1563 FOGRA51 training set: 5<sup>th</sup>, 50<sup>th</sup> and 95<sup>th</sup> percentile RMS errors.

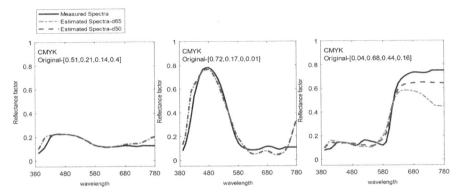

**Fig. 4.** Estimated reflectances of FOGRA51 using weighted PCA and 3135 training set: 5th, 50th and 95th percentile RMS errors.

If we compare Figs. 1 and 3 where the training set is the same but the spectral estimation method differs, we see that weighted PCA results are closest to the measured spectra. In this, the mean RMSE between measured spectra and estimated spectra of D65 XYZ values is 0.0153 and the mean RMSE between measured spectra and estimated spectra of D50 XYZ values is 0.0104, which are the lowest. Now, if we compare the two estimated spectra obtained from D65 XYZ and D50 XYZ values, an opposite behaviour can be seen where the two estimated spectra using classical PCA are similar while the dissimilarity between them increases when weighted PCA is used. This is because in classical PCA every training spectral reflectance equally influences the test tristimulus value and the Vo matrix is global, while in weighted PCA the influence of every spectral reflectance increases as its colorimetric similarity under an illuminant increases with the test tristimulus value, and in this case the Vo matrix is locally calculated. Although small the mean RMSE is higher for weighted PCA than classical PCA.

The metamerism index suggests that the spectra estimated are acceptable for D50, C and A illuminant according to mean $\Delta E_{00}$ difference. However, for cases using D65 as source illuminant with PCA, the color difference is high for some spectra with test illuminant A.

It can be seen from the result above that if we wish to estimate spectra that are closer to the original spectra then weighted PCA with carefully chosen training data will perform best. But if we require the estimated spectra of XYZ values measured under different illuminants to be closer to each other while being a good approximation of the original spectra then classical PCA will perform better. When XYZ is recalculated using the estimated spectral reflectance, the CIELAB difference is close to zero, differing only at the fourteenth decimal place when calculated against the actual XYZ. As our aim in this paper is to estimate the spectral reflectance of corresponding color datasets which are measured under different illuminants and compare them with other CAT estimates, getting estimated spectral reflectances of reference XYZ values that are similar to the estimated spectral reflectances of corresponding color XYZ values will be more useful. Therefore, in the rest of the paper we will only discuss results obtained with classical PCA.

## 4.2  Spectral Estimation of Corresponding Color Dataset

For the Helson, Lam & Rigg, Kuo & Luo (A), Lutchi (A) and Lutchi (D50) corresponding color datasets, spectral reflectances were estimated using classical PCA for both reference and test XYZ values using the second training dataset with 3135 spectral reflectances. The results of three samples chosen with $5^{th}$, $50^{th}$ and $95^{th}$ RMS difference for Lutchi (A) and Lutchi (D50) are shown in Figs. 5 and 6. We need to note here that in the corresponding color datasets the reference and test white points do not exactly match the white points of standard illuminants, but as we need to use the illuminant spectral power distribution in calculating the matrix [S.O], we use the standard illuminant for this purpose which introduces a small error. For this reason, estimated spectral reflectances will not be as accurate an estimate of the original spectral reflectance as in the case of calculated XYZ values of FOGRA51 dataset. Moreover, as the corresponding color XYZ data are chromatically adapted data, they differ slightly from the calculated corresponding XYZ values under respective illuminants. Hence, we can see that the difference between the two estimated spectra are higher than in the case of FOGRA 51 data under the two illuminants. Nonetheless, the estimated spectral reflectances have similar shape. The mean RMS difference is given in Table 3.

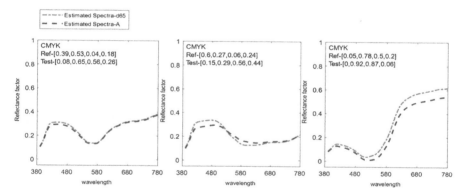

**Fig. 5.** Estimated reflectances of Lutchi (A) using classical PCA:$5^{th}$, $50^{th}$ and $95^{th}$ percentile RMS difference.

Due to this the obtained estimated spectral reflectances will not be as accurate an interpretation of the original spectral reflectance as in the case of calculated colorimetric values of FOGRA51 dataset. Hence, we can see that the difference between the two estimated spectra are higher than in the case of FOGRA51 data under the two illuminants. But nonetheless, the estimated spectral reflectances have similar shape. The mean RMS difference is given in Table 3. The Lutchi D50 data has the smallest mean RMS difference and max RMS difference (Table 4).

The above Table 5 shows the metamerism index for the estimated spectra. Illuminant D65 has been considered as reference light and illuminant D50, A and C as the test lights. The mean $\Delta E_{00}$ difference was below 1.0 for every dataset under different test illuminants and only the Lutchi D50 with test illuminant A has a mean $\Delta E_{00}$ difference greater

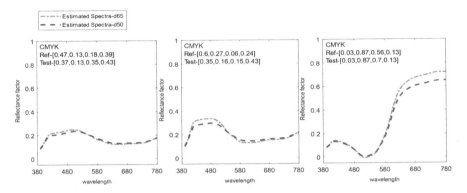

**Fig. 6.** Estimated reflectances of Lutchi (D50) using classical PCA: 5th, 50th and 95th percentile RMS difference

**Table 3.** Metamerism Iindex for estimated reference and test spectra using classical PCA and weighted PCA methods with reference illuminant D65 and three test illuminants D50, A and C.

|  | Mean $\Delta E_{00}$ difference | | | Max $\Delta E_{00}$ difference | | |
|---|---|---|---|---|---|---|
|  | D65/D50 | D65/C | D65/A | D65/D50 | D65/C | D65/A |
| C-PCA D65 | 0.5504 | 0.1867 | 1.9604 | 4.4409 | 1.9676 | 12.5713 |
| C-PCA D50 | 0.5804 | 0.1731 | 0.9053 | 5.9405 | 2.5142 | 4.5225 |
| W-PCA D65 | 0.2619 | 0.0993 | 0.9460 | 4.6212 | 1.5358 | 13.8484 |
| W-PCA D50 | 0.1839 | 0.0659 | 0.3586 | 0.8470 | 0.3354 | 1.4914 |

**Table 4.** Weighted mean RMS difference and weighted max RMS difference between the estimated reference reflectance and estimated test reflectance.

|  | Weighted mean RMSD | Weighted max RMSD |
|---|---|---|
| CCD | 0.0028 | 0.0079 |

than 0.5. For all datasets test illuminant, A has the highest mean $\Delta E_{00}$ difference. This is expected because the difference between D65 which is bluish light and illuminant A which is reddish light is high. Also, when the reference spectra are estimated using D65 or C it adds an error i.e. biased towards bluish light, similarly, for the test spectra the test illuminant adds an error.

As expected, when making a corresponding color match under a test illuminant that is less blue than the reference illuminant, both the corresponding color colorimetry and estimated spectral reflectance are also less blue.

### 4.3    Spectral Estimation of Chromatically Adapted Data

Below are the plots for estimated spectral reflectance for each of the reference XYZ values of the corresponding color dataset and estimated spectral reflectance of its

**Table 5.** Color accuracy for the estimated reference and test spectra using reference illuminant D65 and three test illuminants D50, A and C

|  | Weighted mean $\Delta E_{00}$ difference | | | Weighted max $\Delta E_{00}$ difference | | |
|---|---|---|---|---|---|---|
|  | D65/D50 | D65/A | D65/C | D65/D50 | D65/A | D65/C |
| CCD | 0.0617 | 0.5410 | 0.0593 | 0.8243 | 0.1713 | 0.7750 |

respective chromatically adapted XYZ values using the four transforms namely Bradford CAT, CAT02 and CAT16. From the visual plots we can see that the estimated spectral reflectances of the chromatically adapted XYZ values are quite similar in shape to the estimated spectral reflectance of the reference XYZ values. The CAT02 (blue) and CAT16 (green) estimated spectral reflectance have similar characteristics. Bradford CAT spectra had the lowest mean RMS difference for every dataset except Lutchi D50 where CAT02 slightly performs better. CAT16 spectra have the highest mean RMS difference for every dataset. The larger RMS differences indicate a larger change in colorimetry (and therefore in the spectral reflectance estimated) in the transform (Fig. 7).

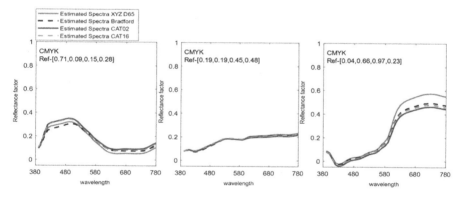

**Fig. 7.** Estimated reflectances of reference Lutchi(A) and reference data chromatically adapted to ill. A using Bradford CAT, CAT02 and CAT16 respectively: 5th, 50th and 95th percentile RMS difference. (Color figure online)

Spectra estimation was also done for Wpt MAT adapted XYZ values and were closest to the spectral estimation of reference corresponding color XYZ values. As Wpt MAT has been developed to maintain sameness of material property and since spectral reflectance is an intrinsic property of a material, therefore, we should recover a very similar spectral reflectance. This topic will be further investigated in the future (Fig. 8 and Table 6).

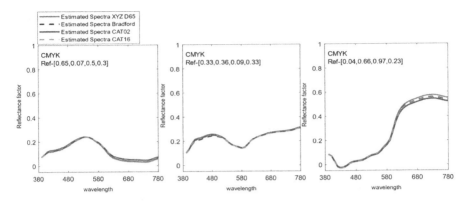

**Fig. 8.** Estimated reflectances of reference Lutchi (D50) and reference data chromatically adapted to ill. D50 using Bradford CAT, CAT02 and CAT16 respectively: 5$^{th}$, 50$^{th}$ and 95$^{th}$ percentile RMS difference.

**Table 6.** Weighted mean RMS difference and weighted max RMS difference between the estimated reflectance of reference corresponding color data vs estimated reflectance of chromatically adapted data.

|  | Weighted mean RMSD | | | Weighted max RMSD | | |
|---|---|---|---|---|---|---|
|  | Bradford | CAT16 | CAT02 | Bradford | CAT16 | CAT02 |
| CCD | 0.0225 | 0.0428 | 0.0278 | 0.0746 | 0.1455 | 0.0802 |

Additionally, we have also calculated the weighted mean of CIELAB difference for 11 corresponding color datasets and their respective chromatically adapted data using Bradford, CAT02 and CAT16 as shown in Table 7. This is to check the CAT performance with respect to other known experimental data.

**Table 7.** Weighted mean of CIELAB difference of each of the corresponding color datasets to its chromatically adapted data.

| Datasets | No. of samples | Bradford | CAT16 | CAT02 |
|---|---|---|---|---|
| Weighted mean | 560 | 6.51 | 6.94 | 6.48 |

### 4.4 Spectral Estimation of Inverse of Chromatically Adapted Data

Selected results of spectral estimates for the inverse of chromatically adapted reference XYZ of every corresponding color dataset are plotted against its respective estimated spectral reflectance of reference XYZ values. The inverse transform has been performed only for Bradford CAT and CAT16. Again, spectra obtained for the back transformed XYZ values are very similar in shape to the spectral reflectance obtained for the reference XYZ values (Table 8). The mean RMS difference and mean $\Delta E_{00}$ are low overall and lowest for the Bradford CAT. This demonstrates that the inverse transform can successfully be used in a color management workflow (Figs. 9 and 10).

**Table 8.** Weighted mean RMS difference and weighted max RMS difference of estimated spectra inverse of chromatically adapted XYZ and its respective reference XYZ reflectance.

|  | Weighted mean RMSD | | Weighted max RMSD | | Weighted mean $\Delta E_{00}$ | |
|---|---|---|---|---|---|---|
|  | Bradford | CAT16 | Bradford | CAT16 | Bradford | CAT16 |
| CCD | 0.0050 | 0.0107 | 0.0196 | 0.0382 | 0.1661 | 0.2804 |

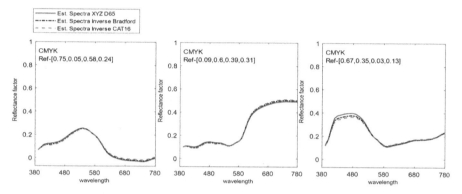

**Fig. 9.** Estimated reflectances of reference Lutchi (A) and inverse of chromatically adapted reference XYZ to ill. A using Bradford CAT, CAT02 and CAT16 respectively: 5th, 50th and 95th percentile RMS difference.

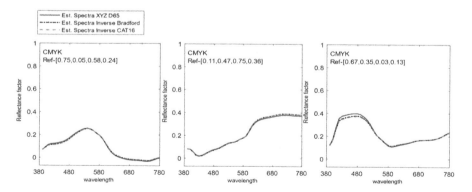

**Fig. 10.** Estimated reflectances of reference Lutchi (D50), inverse of chromatically adapted reference XYZ to ill. D50 using Bradford CAT, CAT02 and CAT16 respectively: 5th, 50th and 95th percentile RMS difference.

## 5   Conclusion

Spectral estimation of corresponding color data has been performed to find the intrinsic relationship between original stimuli and chromatically adapted colorimetric data. We showed that for a recovery to be performed well we have to select training data which has similar characteristics to the test data.

Classical PCA has successfully estimated spectra for the reference XYZ and corresponding XYZ of corresponding color datasets and have shown to have a similar spectral shape. The estimated spectral reflectances of the chromatically adapted XYZ values show that spectra estimated from Bradford CAT adapted XYZ values are closest to the reference XYZ values of corresponding color dataset. This can also be seen in the inverse transform, where the Bradford CAT had a lower mean RMS difference compared to CAT16. If the source white point in the forward transform is same as the destination white point in the inverse transform, then the inverse transform will be complete and we should recover same spectra as the spectra obtained from the reference XYZ values. The low values of RMS difference suggest that the classical PCA on the respective chromatically adapted XYZ values has been consistent in estimating spectral reflectance.

The results demonstrate that, by using appropriate methods such as classical PCA, it is possible to obtain good spectral estimates of corresponding colors, and therefore that spectral estimation can be used in conjunction with chromatic adaptation in a color managed workflow.

Spectral estimation of corresponding colors can readily be implemented within the ICCMAX color management architecture, where the transform can be encoded either in matrix form (preferably), or as a multidimensional look-up table with PCS XYZ input and adapted spectral reflectances as output.

## References

1. International Color Consortium. "iccMAX". http://www.color.org/iccmax.xalter. Accessed 9 May 2018
2. Bala, R., Braun, K.M., Loce, R.P.: Watermark encoding and detection using narrowband illumination. In: Color and Imaging Conference, pp. 139–142. Society for Imaging Science and Technology (2009)
3. Derhak, M.W., Berns, R.S.: Introducing Wpt (Waypoint): a color equivalency representation for defining a material adjustment transform. Color Res. Appl. **40**, 535–549 (2015)
4. Fairchild, M.D.: Color Appearance Models. Wiley, New York (2013)
5. Fogra FOGRA51. http://www.color.org/chardata/fogra51.Xalter. Accessed 10 May 2018
6. University of Eastern Finland, Munsell colors glossy (Spectrophotometer measured). http://www.uef.fi/web/spectral/munsell-colors-glossy-spectrofotometer-measured,last.    Accessed 10 May 2018
7. University of Eastern Finland, Munsell colors matte (Spectrophotometer measured). http://www.uef.fi/web/spectral/munsell-colors-matt-aotf-measured. Accessed 10 May 2018
8. ISO 17321-1. Graphic technology and photography – Colour characterisation of digital still cameras (DSCs) – Part 1: Stimuli, metrology and test procedures (2012)

9. Zhao, Y., Taplin, L., Nezamabadi, M.: Using the matrix R method for spectral image archives. In: 10th Congress of the International Colour Association, pp. 469–472 (2005)
10. Babaei, V., Amirshahi, S.H., Agahian, F.: Using weighted pseudo-inverse method for reconstruction of reflectance spectra and analyzing the dataset in terms of normality. Color Res. Appl. **36**, 295–305 (2011)
11. Fairman, H.S., Brill, M.H.: The principal components of reflectances. Color Res. Appl. **29**, 104–110 (2004)
12. Agahian, F., Amirshahi, S.A., Amirshahi, S.H.: Reconstruction of reflectance spectra using weighted principal component analysis. Color Res. Appl. **33**, 360–371 (2008)
13. Green, P.: Accuracy of colour transforms. In: Color Imaging XI: Processing, Hardcopy, and Applications. SPIE (2006)
14. Luo, M.R., Rhodes, P.A.: Corresponding-colour datasets. Color Res. Appl. **24**, 295–296 (1999)
15. Li, C., et al.: Comprehensive color solutions: CAM16, CAT16, and CAM16-UCS. Color Res. Appl. **42**, 703–718 (2017)

# Perceptual Model and Application

# Using the Monge-Kantorovitch Transform in Chromagenic Color Constancy for Pathophysiology

Ghalia Hemrit[1(✉)], Futa Matsushita[2], Mihiro Uchida[2], Javier Vazquez-Corral[1], Han Gong[1], Norimichi Tsumura[2], and Graham D. Finlayson[1]

[1] University of East Anglia, Norwich NR4 7TJ, UK
ghalia.hemrit@gmail.com
https://www.uea.ac.uk/computing/colour-and-imaging
[2] Chiba University, Chiba 263-8522, Japan
http://www.mi.tj.chiba-u.jp/

**Abstract.** The Chromagenic color constancy algorithm estimates the light color given two images of the same scene, one filtered and one unfiltered. The key insight underpinning the chromagenic method is that the filtered and unfiltered images are linearly related and that this linear relationship correlates strongly with the illuminant color. In the original method the best linear relationship was found based on the assumption that the filtered and unfiltered images were registered. Generally, this is not the case and implies an expensive image registration step.

This paper makes three contributions. First, we use the Monge-Kantorovich (MK) method to find the best linear transform without the need for image registration. Second, we apply this method on chromagenic pairs of facial images (used for Kampo pathophysiology diagnosis). Lastly, we show that the MK method supports better color correction compared with solving for a $3 \times 3$ correction matrix using the least squares linear regression method when the images are not registered.

**Keywords:** Color constancy · Chromagenic computer vision

## 1 Introduction

Color constancy is the vision property that allows humans to identify the color of an object independently of the color of the light source. For example, we are able to perceive a banana as yellow both in a room illuminated with a tungsten bulb – i.e. under reddish light – and outside in a cloudy day i.e. under bluish light. This property means that solving for color constancy – in other words, removing the color of the light – is a fundamental step in digital color image processing.

GH, JVC, HG and GF have received funding from the British Government's EPSRC programme under grant agreement EP/M001768/1, and funding from Apple Inc. GH, FM, MU and NT have received funding from Chiba University.

ⓒ Springer Nature Switzerland AG 2019
S. Tominaga et al. (Eds.): CCIW 2019, LNCS 11418, pp. 121–133, 2019.
https://doi.org/10.1007/978-3-030-13940-7_10

The chromagenic method for color constancy [3,4] solves for the illuminant color given 2 images of the same scene, one captured with a color filter and another without. This method can be decomposed in two different steps. In the first step, a set of linear transform matrices are calculated using a set of pairs of filtered and unfiltered images. In particular, each of these matrices relates a particular unfiltered image to its filtered counterpart. In the second step, given a pair of new chromagenic images, the method estimates the light color (the illuminant estimation step) by finding the best transform among the ones calculated in the pre-processing step.

The chromagenic color constancy approach can deliver good estimates of the illuminant [5]. However, the filtered and the unfiltered images need to be registered [7]. This is a limitation for some real-life applications as image registration is usually time-consuming and computationally expensive. In fact, image registration is still an important field of research on its own [6] and cannot always be solved reliably.

In this paper, we present an approach that aims at avoiding the need for image registration in the first step of the chromagenic color constancy algorithm. In particular, we propose to use the Monge-Kantorovitch (MK) transform for obtaining the linear relations between the filtered and unfiltered images.

To show the effectiveness of our new method, we introduce a new *pilot* database of 63 scenes of chromagenic facial images (to be used in Kampo diagnosis). Using this dataset we demonstrate that our new method supports better color correction compared with assuming registered images (when registration cannot be carried out or is insufficiently accurate).

While the focus of this paper is color correction – of a normal capture and a second image taken though a colored filter – without registration we have investigated using the discovered color corrections for illuminant estimation using the full chromagenic algorithm. However, we found that the dataset is too small to conclude much about estimation performance. Indeed, for this small dataset, we found the modified chromagenic algorithm can work almost perfectly (and conversely chromagenic working with unregistered images can fail). But, in order to study algorithm performance in depth we will need to capture a much large corpus of images. We plan to compile a large set of chromagenic face images in the near future.

This paper is organized as follows. We start by recalling the background of our research: color constancy, the chromagenic color constancy, and an overview of what is the image-based Kampo diagnosis system. Then, we introduce our new dataset of facial images. Section 4 presents our approach. This is followed by the experiments and results. Finally, the paper is summed up in the conclusions.

## 2    Research Background

### 2.1    Color Constancy

Color constancy is the ability of a visual system to see objects with same colors regardless of the lighting conditions. In Fig. 1, we can see that the gray ball color varies with the color of the light, this happens when color constancy is not performed, here in the case of a digital camera.

While the human visual system is designed to achieve color constancy, machines – in particular modern digital cameras – need algorithms to accomplish this function (also known as white-balancing in digital photography). In computer vision, color constancy is achieved by first determining the color of the light under which the image scene was captured. Once the light color is estimated, it can be "divided out". Illuminant estimation is a core component of modern digital cameras reproduction pipelines.

**Fig. 1.** The rendering of a gray ball under various lights. The image is from the SFU gray-ball dataset [8], appeared in [9].

Illuminant estimation algorithms can be split into two broad classes: algorithms that estimate the illuminant via a 'bag of pixels' statistical approach [14–17], and learning-based methods [18,19] (including deep learning [20,21]). There are also less commonly used methods that look for physical insights to drive the light estimation. For example, in the specular highlight method [22], highlights are sought in the scene. It is then assumed that the highlight color is the same as the illuminant color (true for dielectic materials). Another example is the blackbody-model-based algorithm [30,31] that uses the sensors responses to form an illuminant invariant color space and estimate the power spectrum of the illuminant. Another physics based method is the eponymous chromagenic algorithm [3,4,7], see Sect. 2.2, below.

Color constancy – the ability to estimate and then remove the color bias due to illumination – is important in several applications including, object tracking [12], facial recognition [11] and scene understanding [13]. In this paper we focus on a medical application requiring color constancy. Matsushita et al. [2] developed a pathophysiology system to reproduce a Kampo medical diagnosis for number of diseases based on facial images. The method only works when face color in an image is directly related to the physical reflectance properties of a face. This condition is only accomplished when the light illuminating the scene is equienergetic (i.e. achromatic), meaning that color constancy should be applied.

### 2.2  Chromagenic Color Constancy

In the chromagenic color constancy approach two images are taken of each scene. The first image is a normal capture and the second is an image taken through a specially chosen chromagenic filter. Given reasonable assumptions about the dimensionality of lights and surfaces it was shown in [7] that the filtered and unfiltered responses are related by a linear transform and that this relationship varies with (is intrinsic to) the illuminant color. Put another way, the relationship between filtered and unfiltered RGBs indexes – and so identifies – the illumination.

Mathematically, by adopting the Lambertian model of image formation, if we denote as $\rho$ the normal captured image, and $\underline{\rho}_F$, the image captured by placing a color filter in front of the camera, we can write:

$$\begin{aligned} \rho_k &= \int_\omega E(\lambda)S(\lambda)Q_k(\lambda)d\lambda \\ \underline{\rho}_{F,k} &= \int_\omega E(\lambda)S(\lambda)F(\lambda)Q_k(\lambda)d\lambda \end{aligned} \tag{1}$$

where $\lambda$ denotes a particular wavelength, $\omega$ the visual spectrum (normally from 380 to 740 nm), $E$ is the illuminant, $S$ is the set of scene objects reflectances, $k$ corresponds to R, G or B, the color channels of the digital camera, $Q$ is the camera sensitivity function, and $F$ is the spectral response of the selected filter.

As stated above, it was shown in [7] that under reasonable assumptions about the dimensionality of lights and surfaces, the unfiltered and filtered responses should be related by a $3 \times 3$ linear transform:

$$\underline{\rho}_F \approx T_E^F \underline{\rho} \tag{2}$$

The chromagenic algorithm works in two steps. First, in pre-processing, we calculate a range of illuminant transform matrices $T_i$ (for $i = 1, .., N$ illuminants) using a least squares approach. In a second step, given a chromagenic pair of images $\underline{I}(x, y)$ and $\underline{I}_F(x, y)$, we determine the illuminant color by minimizing:

$$argmin_i(\Sigma_x \Sigma_y || T_i \underline{I}(x, y) - \underline{I}_F(x, y)||) \tag{3}$$

where $(x, y)$ represents a particular pixel of the image.

A limitation of chromagenic color constancy is that images need to be registered. Image registration is required both in the least squares minimization of the first step and also in the selection of $T_i$ in the second step. In this work, we present a method to avoid the need for registration in the first step.

## 2.3 Kampo Medical Diagnosis

Kampo medicine is the traditional Japanese medicine used in Japan and, in alternate forms, across Asia. A Kampo medical diagnosis [25] requires a visual observation, an olfactory examination, an inquiry and a palpation. A face-only diagnosis is, however, possible for various diseases: blood stagnation (due to a poor blood circulation), blood deficiency (resulting from the lack of blood, in other terms when the blood is not regenerated in normal proportions) and yin deficiency (which is a sign of a lack of water at the face level).

Matsushita et al. [2] developed an image-based system for facial Kampo diagnosis. The system emits a diagnosis in the form of a score (from 1 to 5) where 1 indicates a non-disease state and 5 indicates a severe disease state. The Kampo system works as follows. First, given an image of an ill patient, the system generates a hemoglobin density image and a gloss image. The hemoglobin image is the result of a pigmentation component separation by independent component analysis (ICA) [23] and the gloss image is obtained by using a polarizer (the face is captured with and without a polarizing plate) [24]. Five regions of interest are extracted for each of the two images: one region from the forehead area in the image, 2 regions under the eyes and 2 other regions at the cheeks level. A final region is the sum of all these 5 regions. Five features values are calculated from the RGBs values of these 5 regions. In total 60 features are extracted from the images. The system emits a diagnosis by support vector regression (an optimization problem).

In [2], the system was evaluated and tested on a dataset of images generated from images of healthy patients (taken in a lab under a white light) by the modulations of gloss and hemoglobin. The results were compared to Kampo medical doctor diagnostic. In this paper, we also present a new dataset of images we collected for Kampo diagnosis, in order to allow the testing of the system under different lights. However, here we capture every scene with and without a colored filter.

# 3  A Chromagenic Face Image Dataset for Pathophysiology

We introduce in this section a new dataset of facial images for Kampo pathophysiology diagnosis. The dataset has 63 initial scenes (a set of three facial images of a healthy subject taken under a determined light). Every scene was captured 3 times: one time without a filter and 2 other times with a red and a yellow filter (respectively a Tiffen 85 and a Tiffen 81EF). The images were taken in Chiba University in Japan during the Summer 2018. Nine participants took part in the data collection. All images were taken with a Nikon D5200 camera in a lighting room equipped with 2 Thouslite LED cubes (which allowed us to simulate a range of illuminant color temperatures).

**Fig. 2.** Two images of the same scene from the dataset showing the ColorChecker chart, the left image is a normal capture and the right image was captured through a red filter, note that these 2 images are the camera pipeline outputs.

The left of Fig. 2 shows one normal image from our dataset, the right shows the same capture but through the red filter. The right image is, of course, redder in appearance. The images are not registered but the experiment conditions were very well controlled, for this reason the difference in the images alignment is not easily noticeable in this case. Notice that there is a ColorChecker in the scene and this is true for all our images. Placing a ColorChecker in every scene is useful for two reasons.

First, we can use it to measure the white point (the RGB of the color of the light). In line with [10] this is defined to be the RGB taken from the brightest unsaturated gray patch of the ColorChecker. In Fig. 4 we show the ground-truth chromaticities for the illuminants in the 63 scenes of the dataset. It is clear that our dataset has a range of illuminant colors.

Second, given a chromagenic pair of images, with the Macbeth ColorChecker in each image, we can solve for the best possible $3 \times 3$ matrix relating the colors of the two color charts (without requiring the pixel-wise registration of the images in this case). We will consider this ColorChecker-based $3 \times 3$ matrix transform as our reference when solving for the linear transform in the case of non-registered images (see Sect. 5). Of course, usually there is no ColorChecker in the scene and solving for the best possible transform is not possible.

While Fig. 2 shows the capture environment, in the Kampo diagnosis we need only the face image. In Fig. 3 we show two sets of 3 images for two of our subjects. From left to right we show the original image. Then there is the same person imaged through a yellow and a red filter.

In the future, we will generate new images with various diseases states from this dataset. These images will be obtained by modulations of gloss and hemoglobin [2].

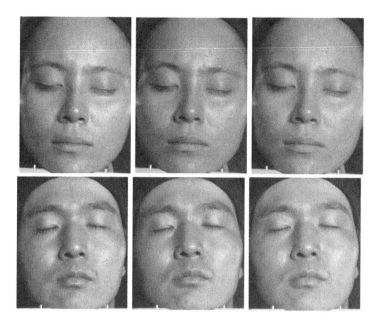

**Fig. 3.** Two sets of filtered and unfiltered images from the dataset. The 2 sets represent 2 scenes (2 subjects), from left to right: normal capture, image with yellow filter and image with red filter. (Color figure online)

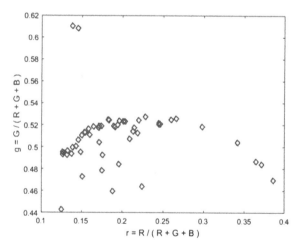

**Fig. 4.** Ground-truth chromaticities of the Kampo images dataset.

# 4    Color Correction Without Registration: The Monge-Kantorovitch Linear Transform

The chromagenic color constancy algorithm works in two steps. In the pre-processing step we solve for the best $3 \times 3$ matrices relating unfiltered to filtered RGBs for a large range of scenes and illuminants. Each transform by construction is associated with a light color. Then in the second step, when we have a chromagenic image pair for an unknown illuminant, we test each of the pre-computed transforms in turn to see which when applied to the unfiltered RGBs best predicts the filtered counterparts. The color of the light is then defined to be the associated light color.

Both the pre-processing step and the application part of the chromagenic algorithm (estimating the illuminant using a pair of chromagenic images) requires registered pairs of images. Unfortunately, even after decades of investigation, image registration remains a hard problem and even when it works it delivers imperfect results [6]. Further, even images that are only slightly out of registration can result in significantly different transforms ($3 \times 3$ matrices) that best relate the unfiltered to filtered RGBs. This is the case for our dataset where the differences in the alignment of the unfiltered and filtered images of the same scene is not significantly visible but this difference still impacts on the transforms (see results in Sect. 5).

In what follows, we only focus on the pre-processing step of the chromagenic method. In particular, we propose using the Monge-Kantorovitch (MK) linear transform to replace the $3 \times 3$ matrix relating the images in the chromagenic pair without registration. Note that the MK transform is a 3-D similarity transform. MK has its roots in the Earth Movers Distance (EMD) [26] (or Wasserstein Metric [28]) which has proven to be a useful tool in image recognition [27]. Imagine we have a few piles of earth. Equal to the volume of all the earth we have several holes to deposit the earth. Clearly if we wish to move the earth into the holes to minimize the energy expelled, we wish to move each shovel full of earth as little as possible. The minimum distance we have to move all the earth is exactly the earth movers distance. It can be efficiently solved using linear programming [29].

Rather usefully, there is a simple and closed form linear restriction to EMD. Given $M \times N$ data matrices $A$ and $B$ (where $N > M$) the classic linear least squares minimization solves:

$$\min_{T} ||TA - B|| \tag{4}$$

Of course to solve the above then we exploit the fact the columns of $A$ and $B$ are in correspondence (not the case for non-registered images). In the linear restriction EMD, we seek to find a transform $T$ such that the correlation structure of $AT$ and $B$ matches and that $TA$ is as close to $A$ as possible (that is the colors in $A$ move as little as possible). Specifically, we minimize

$$\min_{T} ||TA - A|| \; s.t. \; TAA^tT^t = BB^t \tag{5}$$

Pitié et al. [1] have shown that MK (or linear restriction to EMD) can be used in color grading (to map the colors of an input image to match the look and feel of a target image).

Here we use Eq. 5 to find the transform relating an RGB image to its filtered counterpart. In Eq. 5, $A$ would contain the pixels from the unfiltered image and $B$ pixels for the same scene captured through a colored filter. The pixels in $A$ and $B$ may not be in correspondence. Indeed, there is no constraint that the number of pixels in the filtered and unfiltered images need to be the same.

## 5    Experiments and Results

In order to evaluate the effectiveness of our approach, we compare the results given by our method (Eq. 5; $MK$) to those obtained by the usual least squares procedure (Eq. 4; $LST$) on our Kampo dataset.

As a reference point, we use the fact that a Macbeth ColorChecker chart is included in our images. This allows us to compute the best possible linear transform between the two images ($T_{CC}$) by computing the least squares regression only considering those colors of the color charts. Thanks to this, we can now evaluate the difference between the best linear transform and the two other solutions as

$$\epsilon_m = ||T_{CC}A - f_m(A)||$$

where A is the unfiltered image and $f_m$ states the method being computed where $m = \{LS, MK\}$.

Figure 5 plots the individual errors for all images: the upper graph is the result for the red filter and the lower graph is the result for the yellow filter. These results are summarized in Table 1, where we present the mean and RMS errors for the dataset. Our method improves the usual procedure by at least 75%. Note all image values are in the interval [0,1] so a mean error of 0.01 corresponds to a 1% error.

Visual examples of our results are presented in Fig. 6 where we show from left to right: an unfiltered image, the image corrected by using the ColorChecker (i.e., the best possible result or reference), the image corrected using MK (the approach proposed in this paper), and the image corrected with the LST approach. The upper example was generated with the red filter and the lower with the yellow filter. The images were linearly converted from RAW format and demosaiced. We can clearly see that our approach generates colors that are very close to the best possible solution.

**Table 1.** Mean and RMS error for MK vs LST approaches with red and yellow filters

| Filter | Mean | | RMS | |
|--------|------|------|------|------|
| | MK | LST | MK | LST |
| Red | **0.0024** | 0.0140 | **0.0033** | 0.0236 |
| Yellow | **0.0025** | 0.0123 | **0.0031** | 0.0207 |

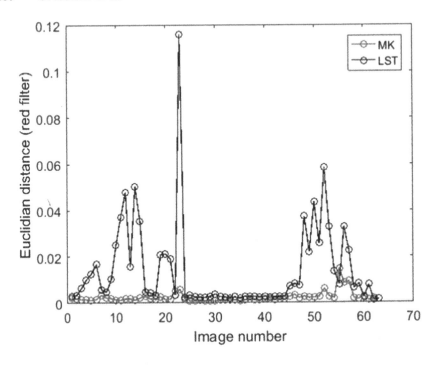

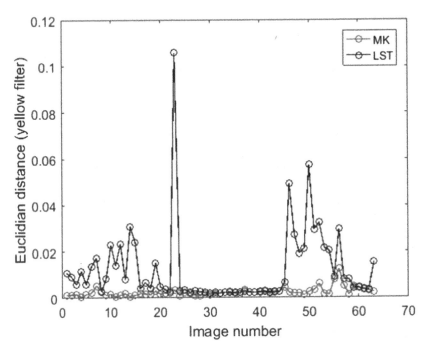

**Fig. 5.** Chromagenic distance when using MK vs the least squares transform LST. Top: red filter. Bottom: yellow filter. (Color figure online)

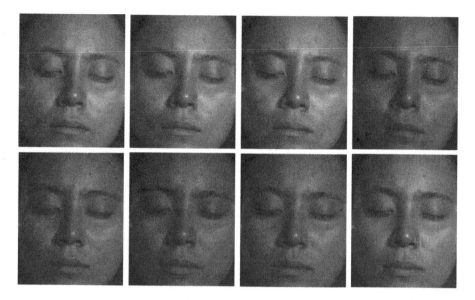

**Fig. 6.** Two scenes from the dataset (upper with red filter and lower with yellow filter), from left to right: the original unfiltered image, the color corrected image with CCT (the ColorChecker-based transform), the color corrected image with MK and the color corrected image with LST. (Color figure online)

## 6    Conclusion

This paper introduces a new image dataset comprising 63 scenes of facial images taken under a variety of lights and, novelly, with and without a color filter. Given a pair of filtered and unfiltered images it will be possible to use the chromagenic approach to illuminant estimation. The chromagenic algorithm has two parts: first we need to relate the unfiltered to filtered image using a linear transform. Second, we need to identify the illuminant by searching for the best transform. This paper focuses on the first question only.

We show, using the Monge-Kantorovitch (MK) transform, how we can solve for the linear map without the need to register the images. This is of significant practical importance. Not only is registration a hard problem it cannot always be solved in a pixel-wise manner. Here we remove the need for registration altogether. Moreover, we show that the MK method outperforms direct least squares (where we assume good registration when this not the case) by a factor of about 4:1.

Looking to the future our plan is to capture a larger set of facial images so we can test the second part of the chromagenic algorithm. That is, we will investigate whether MK suffices to allow the chromagenic algorithm to estimate the illuminant for face images.

# References

1. Pitie, F., Kokaram, A.: The linear Monge-Kantorovitch linear colour mapping for example-based colour transfer. In: IET 4th European Conference on Visual Media Production, pp. 23–23 (2007)
2. Matsushita, F., Kiyomitsu, K., Ogawa, K., Tsumura, N.: System for evaluating pathophysiology using facial image. In: Color and Imaging Conference, pp. 274–279 (2017)
3. Finlayson, G.D., Fredembach, C., Drew, M.S.: Detecting illumination in images. In: IEEE 11th International Conference on Computer Vision (2007)
4. Finlayson, G.D., Hordley, S.D., Morovic, P.: Colour constancy using the chromagenic constraint. In: IEEE Conference on Computer Vision and Pattern Recognition, pp. 1079–1086 (2005)
5. Fredembach, C., Finlayson, G.D.: The bright-chromagenic algorithm for illuminant estimation. J. Imaging Sci. Technol. **52**, 137–142 (2008)
6. Zitova, B., Flusser, J.: Image registration methods: a survey. Image Vis. Comput. **21**, 977–1000 (2003)
7. Finlayson, G.D., Hordley, S., Morovic, P.: Chromagenic filter design. In: 10th Annual Congress of the International Colour Association, pp. 1023–1026 (2005)
8. Ciurea, F., Funt, B.V.: A large image database for color constancy research. In: Color and Imaging Conference, pp. 160–164 (2003)
9. Gijsenij, A., Gevers, T., Van De Weijer, J.: Computational color constancy: survey and experiments. IEEE Trans. Image Process. **20**, 2475–2489 (2011)
10. Hemrit, G., et al.: Rehabilitating the ColorChecker dataset for illuminant estimation. In: Color and Imaging Conference, pp. 350–353 (2018)
11. Samal, A., Iyengar, P.A.: Automatic recognition and analysis of human faces and facial expressions: a survey. Patt. Recognit. **25**, 65–77 (1992)
12. Yilmaz, A., Javed, O., Shah, M.: Object tracking: a survey. ACM Comput. Surv. **38**, 1–45 (2006)
13. Li, L.J., Socher, R., Fei-Fei, L.: Towards total scene understanding: classification, annotation and segmentation in an automatic framework. In: IEEE Conference on Computer Vision and Pattern Recognition, pp. 2036–2043 (2009)
14. Buchsbaum, G.: A Spatial processor model for object colour perception. J. Franklin Inst. **310**, 1–26 (1980)
15. Land, E.H., McCann, J.J.: Lightness and retinex theory. J. Opt. Soc. Am. **61**, 1–11 (1971)
16. Finlayson, G.D., Trezzi, E.: Shades of gray and colour constancy. In: Color and Imaging Conference, pp. 37–41 (2004)
17. Vazquez-Corral, J., Vanrell, M., Baldrich, R., Tous, F.: Color constancy by category correlation. IEEE Trans. Image Process. **21**, 1997–2007 (2012)
18. Gehler, P.V., Rother, C., Blake, A., Minka, T., Sharp, T.: Bayesian color constancy revisited. In: IEEE Conference on Computer Vision and Pattern Recognition, pp. 1–8 (2008)
19. Gijsenij, A., Gevers, T.: Color constancy using natural image statistics. In: IEEE Conference on Computer Vision and Pattern Recognition, pp. 1–8 (2007)
20. Bianco, S., Cusano, C., Schettini, R.: Color constancy using CNNs. In: IEEE Conference on Computer Vision and Pattern Recognition, pp. 81–89 (2015)
21. Barron, J.T., Tsai, Y.-T.: Fast fourier color constancy. In: IEEE Conference on Computer Vision and Pattern Recognition (2017)

22. Tan, R.T., Nishino, K., Ikeuchi, K.: Color constancy through inverse-intensity chromaticity space. J. Opt. Soc. Am. A. **21**, 321–334 (2004)
23. Tsumura, N., et al.: Image-based skin color and texture analysis/synthesis by extracting hemoglobin and melanin information in the skin. ACM Trans. Graph. **22**, 770–779 (2003)
24. Ojima, N., Minami, T., Kawai, M.: Transmittance measurement of cosmetic layer applied on skin by using processing. In: 3rd Scientific Conference of the Asian Societies of Cosmetic Scientists, p. 114 (1997)
25. Sato, Y., Hanawa, T., Arai, M., Cyong, J.C., Fukuzawa, M., M.K.: Introduction to Kampo: Japanese traditional medicine. Japan Soc. Orient. Med. (2005)
26. Rubner, Y., Tomasi, C.: The Earth mover's distance. Percept, Metrics Image Database Navig (2001)
27. Rubner, Y., Tomasi, C., Guibas, L.J.: Earth mover's distance as a metric for image retrieval. Int. J. Comput. Vis. **40**, 99–121 (2000)
28. Vasershtein, L.N.: Probl. Pered. Inform. **5**, 64 (1969)
29. Dantzig, G.B., Orden, A., Wolfe, P.: Generalized simplex method for minimizing a linear form under linear inequality restraints. Pac. J. Math. **5**, 183–195 (1955)
30. Ratnasingam, S., Hernández-Andrés, J.: Illuminant spectrum estimation at a pixel. J. Opt. Soc. Am. A. **28**, 696–703 (2011)
31. Ratnasingam, S., Collins, S., Hernández-Andrés, J.: Optimum sensors for color constancy in scenes illuminated by daylight. J. Opt. Soc. Am. A. Opt. Image Sci. Vis. **27**, 2198–2207 (2010)

# Chromatic Adaptation in Colour Management

Phil Green$^{(\boxtimes)}$ and Tanzima Habib

Norwegian University of Science and Technology, 2815 Gjovik, Norway
philip.green@ntnu.no

**Abstract.** Chromatic adaptation transforms are used to predict corresponding colours viewed under a different adapting illuminant. In colour management it is often necessary to apply such a transform in order to achieve a corresponding-colour match on a reproduction medium. A linear version of the Bradford CAT has been standardized for this purpose, due to its advantages of computational simplicity and invertibility. Despite being in use in colour management since 2001 the performance of this linear Bradford transform has had limited evaluation. In this paper it is tested for the first time on a comprehensive corresponding-colour data set, and it is shown that the performance is not significantly different from the original Bradford transform, and is a little better than the more recent CAT16 transform. Other issues related to the use of chromatic adaptation in colour management workflows are also discussed.

**Keywords:** Chromatic adaptation · Colour management · ICC

## 1 Introduction

Colour management is the set of procedures that are used to achieve a colour reproduction goal on an output system or encoding, given a data source from a different system or encoding – or, as described by the International Color Consortium (ICC), to "make colour seamless between device and documents" [1].

In colour management, rather than create a transform to connect every pair of data encodings, the resulting potential combinatorial explosion is avoided by connecting each encoding to a reference intermediate colour space based on the appearance of the colour under specified observing conditions. In the widely used ICC v2 [2] and v4 [3] specifications for colour profiles (collectively known as ICC.1), this is known as the Profile Connection Space (PCS). The PCS is defined as CIE colorimetry based on a D50 illuminant and the CIE 1931 Standard Colorimetric Observer, and can be considered primarily as an exchange space rather than a source or destination colour space.

Since the source and destination encoding are usually different, the match made between source and destination is not exact colorimetry but corresponding colour [4]. The set of procedures required to give acceptable results will include adjustments for the actual viewing conditions and the colour gamuts of the source and destination encoding. Of interest in the present paper is the procedures adopted when source and destination encodings have different white points for either or both of the media and adopted white point. Having a fixed PCS requires that the connection to or from the PCS includes chromatic adaptation into the fixed observing conditions of the PCS.

© Springer Nature Switzerland AG 2019
S. Tominaga et al. (Eds.): CCIW 2019, LNCS 11418, pp. 134–144, 2019.
https://doi.org/10.1007/978-3-030-13940-7_11

Experience has also shown that acceptable matches require that the media white of the source be matched to the media white of the destination by default, while the somewhat rarer case that D50 colorimetry is matched regardless of any differences in the media white points (resulting in either dark or clipped white points in the reproduction) is also supported. In ICC colour management, this is the case for the Media-Relative Colorimetric and ICC-Absolute Colorimetric rendering intents respectively. (The Perceptual intents are also based on media-relative colorimetry but some additional procedures are required to map PCS colours into a reference gamut).

In order to consistently achieve a good corresponding-colour match when source and destination illuminants are different, a number of requirements are imposed on the chromatic adaptation transform in use in colour management. First, it should give a good prediction of the corresponding colour as seen by an observer with normal colour vision. Second, it should give the same results when transforming in two stages via the PCS as when transforming directly from source to destination illuminant. Finally, it should be readily invertible so that a round trip transform from source to PCS and back to source results in the same values within the usual limits of precision. The purpose of this paper is to evaluate the current solutions in the light of these criteria.

## 2    Chromatic Adaptation

A chromatic adaptation transform predicts corresponding colours by transforming XYZ colorimetry into cone space, performing the adaptation by applying ratios of cone excitations for the source and destination illuminant, and converting back to XYZ. Many of the elements in this process are linear matrix operations which can be concatenated. Below we outline the particular forms of chromatic adaptation transform considered in this paper.

### 2.1    The Linear Bradford CAT

The ICC v4 specification [3] recommends a particular CAT, which is based on the Bradford CAT [5] but where the non-linear exponent has been eliminated. A linear CAT has a number of major advantages: for a given combination of source and destination illuminant it can be applied directly to XYZ PCS data as a $3 \times 3$ matrix, making it computationally efficient. The matrix is also analytically invertible, which permits data to be converted in both forward and inverse transforms without accumulating errors. These are both important considerations in colour management.

The linear Bradford transform is described in Annex E of the v4 ICC specification, with a recommendation to use it in almost all cases, using alternatives "only to address specific known issues, recognizing that the resulting profile will most likely produce different results than profiles from other sources" [3]. Where alternative CATs are used, there may be a loss of interoperability with profiles that use the linear Bradford transform.

The linear Bradford transform was introduced in a proposal approved by ballot of ICC members [6] in 2000. The proposal was included in the v4 ICC profile specification from 2001 onwards. In this workflow, all colorimetry is chromatically adapted to the D50 PCS, and the $3 \times 3$ matrix used to perform the adaptation is stored in the profile as a 'chad' tag. Five cases can be then considered in a colour managed workflow:

1. No transform. The colorimetry in a profile is already D50, in which case the 'chad' matrix is identity and no conversion is required.
2. A non-D50 illuminant in source or destination. A corresponding-colour match to or from the ICC PCS is required and is provided by the CAT. By inverting the 'chad' matrix in the profile, the tristimulus values of the non-D50 white point and the untransformed data can be obtained if required.
3. A non-D50 illuminant in both source and destination. The source and destination colorimetry are the same, but different from D50. In this case the inverse CAT (PCS to destination) transform is the inverse of the forward CAT (source to PCS), and the step of converting to intermediate PCS colorimetry has no effect on the final output.
4. Different non-D50 illuminants in source and destination. Both source and destination colorimetry are different from each other and from the ICC PCS. This case is similar to the two-step method of converting via a daylight reference illuminant recommended by Li et al. [8]. The linear conversion to and from an intermediate illuminant cancel each other out when the degree of adaptation set to 1, so that the two-step method implied in an ICC workflow gives identical results to converting directly from source to destination using the linear Bradford transform.
5. Undefined. The colorimetry in a profile is not D50 and no 'chad' tag is present. In this case the meaning of the data in the PCS is unknown. This situation is permitted in v2 profiles, but in a v4 profile would render the profile invalid. The removal of this ambiguity is a primary reason for recommending the v4 profile format.

The linear Bradford transform was reviewed by Finlayson and Süsstrunk [7], who evaluated it on a limited data set, but some questions remain unanswered:

– How well does linear Bradford perform in predicting corresponding colours across a broader range of test data?
– Should linear Bradford be replaced by a more recent transform such as CAT16?
– How significant is the difference between the predictions of linear Bradford and those of other CATs?

Some other issues relating to the appropriate use of chromatic adaptation in a colour management workflow are also discussed in this paper.

## 2.2   CAT16

The CAT16 transform was proposed by Li et al. [8], partly to avoid the widely-acknowledged computational problems with the CAT02 transform used in CIE-CAM02. CAT16 was derived by replacing, the matrices $M_{02}$ and $M_{HPE}$ by a single matrix $M_{16}$, derived by optimization on a combined corresponding-colour data set, as shown in Eqs. 1–3.

$$M_{16} = \begin{matrix} 0.401288 & 0.650173 & -0.051461 \\ -0.250268 & 1.204414 & 0.045854 \\ -0.002079 & 0.048952 & 0.953127 \end{matrix} \qquad (1)$$

The CAT16 transform is then represented by:

$$\Phi_{r,t} = M_{16}^{-1} \Lambda_{r,t} M_{16} \qquad (2)$$

where $\Lambda_{r,t}$ is the diagonal adaptation matrix, and when the luminance of the test and reference illuminants match is given by:

$$\Lambda_{r,t} = \begin{pmatrix} D\frac{R_{wr}}{R_w}+1-D & 0 & 0 \\ 0 & D\frac{G_{wr}}{G_w}+1-D & 0 \\ 0 & 0 & D\frac{B_{wr}}{B_w}+1-D \end{pmatrix} \qquad (3)$$

where $[R_w, G_w, B_w]$ and $[R_{wr}, G_{wr}, B_{wr}]$ are the results of applying $M_{16}$ to the XYZ values of the test (source) and reference (destination) illuminant respectively, and $D$ is the degree of adaptation. $D$ is computed as in CAT02 and CIECAM02, and when adaptation is not complete ($D < 1$) the transform is not transitive and it is recommended that a two-step transform is applied – first to a reference, daylight illuminant, and secondly to a final destination illuminant using the inverse of Eq. 2 [8].

The simplified structure of CAT16 (when compared with other CATs such as Bradford or CAT02) has the effect that for a given test and reference illuminant $\Phi_{r,t}$ is a $3 \times 3$ matrix and its implementation within an ICC profile would have the same form as linear Bradford. Conversion from source to destination via the ICC PCS is a two-step transform with D50 as the reference illuminant, thus satisfying the above recommendation.

CAT16 has been shown to perform well in predicting corresponding-colour data [8], and a summary of its performance in comparison with the Bradford transform is included in Table 1 below.

**Table 1.** Performance of Bradford, linear Bradford and CAT16 chromatic adaptation transforms in estimating corresponding-colour data on 584 sample pairs

| | Bradford | | Linear bradford | | CAT16 | |
|---|---|---|---|---|---|---|
| | $\Delta E^*_{ab}$ | $\Delta E_{2000}$ | $\Delta E^*_{ab}$ | $\Delta E_{2000}$ | $\Delta E^*_{ab}$ | $\Delta E_{2000}$ |
| Median | 5.52 | 3.42 | 5.55 | 3.49 | 6.04 | 3.78 |
| Max | 34.55 | 17.13 | 35.03 | 17.17 | 44.78 | 18.82 |

## 2.3  Degree of Adaptation

The degree of observer adaptation to an adapting illuminant has been widely studied, e.g. [9, 10]. Full adaptation only takes place when the adapting illuminant is close to daylight and/or the Plankian locus for the black body radiator [11], and in a real viewing environment is likely that there are multiple potential sources of adaptation. Many colour appearance models and CAT transforms include a factor for the degree of adaptation to the test illuminant. It has also been found that for printed surface colours there is a degree of adaptation to the colorimetry of the substrate [12–15].

Matching colours using an assumption of partial adaptation can give good results [13, 14], but are outside the scope of this paper. One difficulty in implementing a partial adaptation is that an estimated partially-adapted white point may be outside the gamut of the reproduction medium.

In the linear Bradford transform there is no parameter for the degree of adaptation and hence full adaptation to the destination illuminant is assumed. In the ICC v4 it is in effect assumed that the observer is fully adapted to the display white for emissive colours, and to the perfect diffuse reflector for surface colours.

## 2.4    Media-Relative Colorimetry

Scaling to media-relative colorimetry has been used for many years in ICC colour management with considerable success, since it meets the most common user requirement of matching media white points. In ICC-Absolute colorimetry, the PCS white point is a perfect diffuse reflector viewed under a D50 illuminant, with CIELAB values of [100,0,0]. In media-relative colorimetry, the PCS white point is also [100,0,0], but to match this the $X$, $Y$ and $Z$ components are scaled by Eq. 4 [3].

$$X_r = \frac{X_{D50}}{X_{MW}} X_a$$
$$Y_r = \frac{Y_{D50}}{Y_{MW}} Y_a \qquad (4)$$
$$Z_r = \frac{Z_{D50}}{Z_{MW}} Z_a$$

where $X_r$, $Y_r$, $Z_r$ are the media-relative XYZ values, $X_{D50}$, $Y_{D50}$ and $Z_{D50}$ are the colorimetry of the D50 illuminant, $X_{MW}$, $Y_{MW}$ and $Z_{MW}$ are the measured XYZ values of the media white point (chromatically adapted to D50) and $X_a$, $Y_a$ and $Z_a$ are the measured XYZ values of the stimulus after chromatic adaptation to D50.

Because Eq. 4 has the same form as what is known as a 'wrong von Kries' transform, it is sometimes assumed that media-relative scaling is a kind of chromatic adaptation. It is important to understand that media-relative scaling is applied solely to data that is already chromatically adapted to D50, and that the operation is simply a linear scaling to ensure that it is possible to connect source and destination white points. Because the ratio of $X$, $Y$ and $Z$ components may be altered by media-relative scaling, there can be a change in chromaticity which can become evident if the source and destination media white points are significantly different.

The XYZ values of the media white point, chromatically adapted to D50, are stored in the profile in the mediaWhitePointTag [3]. This allows the CMM to compute ICC-absolute colorimetric values from media-relative values when required by undoing the scaling in Eq. 4.

In the ICC v2 specification the PCS is D50 but requirement to chromatically adapt all data to the PCS is less clearly expressed. If the data is not chromatically adapted, the media-relative scaling is then also performing a 'wrong von Kries' adaptation with potential for inconsistent results, especially when the media white point tag stored in the profile is not adapted to D50.

# 3  Evaluating Chromatic Adaptation Transforms

Three criteria for chromatic adaptation transforms used in colour management workflows were outlined in Sect. 1 above. As shown in Sect. 2, the criteria of invertibility and of equivalence between a one-step transform and a transform via the PCS are satisfied by the use of a single $3 \times 3$ matrix to convert to and from the PCS. The remaining criterion, of good prediction of corresponding colour, is reviewed below.

Since a chromatic adaptation transform predicts the change in appearance of a given stimulus when the adapting illuminant changes, there is no corresponding measurement and the transform can only be evaluated by comparing its predictions with data obtained through psychophysical experiments. It is acknowledged that such visual data will always be intrinsically noisy, and so deriving a good CAT requires attention to the principles and objectives of a corresponding colour transform rather than solely fitting to minimize the errors in a data set.

Finlayson and Süsstrunk [7] compared the performance of linear Bradford in predicting the corresponding-colour data set of Lam and Rigg [5] used in deriving the Bradford transform, with that of the original Bradford transform and a 'sharp' version, derived by optimizing the transform matrix to minimize the RMS error in XYZ between the corresponding-colour sample pairs for D65 and Illuminant A. It was found that the original Bradford performed better than either the sharp transform or linear Bradford, but the differences were not statistically significant.

The Lam and Rigg data comprises 58 sample pairs. A more comprehensive data set, based on 21 corresponding-colour experimental data sets with a total of 584 sample pairs (and including the Lam and Rigg data), was accumulated by Li et al. [8] to evaluate the new CAT16 transform. We used this data set to compare the performance of Bradford, linear Bradford and CAT16, and the results are shown in Table 1. Where a degree of adaptation factor, $D$, is present in the transform, it was set to 1, assuming complete adaptation. (This gave slightly better results for CAT16 than calculating $D$ according to [8] with parameters for 'average' viewing condition). The median error provides the best estimate of central tendency for data that is not normally distributed, and the maximum is included since in colour management workflows this can sometimes be of greater importance than the central tendency.

It can be seen from Table 3 that the linear Bradford transform performs only slightly less well than the original Bradford, which suggests there is no advantage in using the greater complexity of the original Bradford transform to predict corresponding colours in a colour management workflow. CAT16 performs a little worse than both linear Bradford and the original Bradford transform.

Of the different data sets included in the test, only one (Lutchi D65 to D50) is directly relevant to the use case of converting to or from the ICC PCS, and it is interesting to note that in this case linear Bradford actually performs best. However, this single data set is too small (44 sample pairs) to draw conclusions from.

To determine the statistical significance of the differences between the predictions of the different CATs, a two-tailed Student's t-test was performed on paired samples in $X$, $Y$ and $Z$, between the predictions of the different CATs and between the CATs and the perceptual data accumulated by Li et al. [8]. Table 2 shows the resulting $p$ values indicating the probability that the data are significantly different, where $p < 0.05$ indicates a significant difference at the 95% level.

**Table 2.** Results of the Student's t-test comparing the significance of differences between predictions of the CATs for 584 sample pairs in the corresponding-colour data set (CCD) [8]

|  | $X$ | $Y$ | $Z$ |
|---|---|---|---|
| Bradford-linear bradford | 0.29152 | 0.23225 | 0 |
| Linear bradford – CAT16 | 0 | 0 | 0 |
| Bradford – CAT16 | 0 | 0 | 0 |
| CCD-Bradford | 0.00022 | 0.62246 | 0 |
| CCD-linear bradford | 0.00027 | 0.61030 | 0 |
| CCD-CAT16 | 0 | 0.00002 | 0 |

The results show that the corresponding colours predicted by all the CATs differ significantly from each other and from the perceptual data, with the following exceptions: Bradford and Linear Bradford only differ in the prediction of $Z$, and both Bradford transforms predict $Y$ values that do not differ significantly from the perceptual data.

## 4  Material Equivalence

In this section we review the role of material equivalence transforms in colour management and summarise previous results comparing such transforms with chromatic adaptation transforms.

In a corresponding-colour transform, a source stimulus viewed under one adapting condition is transformed to a different stimulus which visually matches the original source stimulus when the observer is adapted to a different viewing condition. In colour management, a chromatic adaptation transform is always required when the colorimetry of source or destination is not D50.

However, in certain cases the source colour is a reflectance whose colorimetry has simply been computed using a different illuminant from the PCS illuminant, and there is no source viewing condition to consider. In this case the intended viewing condition is represented by the destination illuminant, not by the illuminant actually used to calculate the colorimetry, and the correct procedure would be compute the colorimetry from the reflectance using the destination illuminant (if using an ICC profile the destination illuminant will be D50). In the absence of the 'correct' colorimetry or the spectral reflectance from which to compute it, it is appropriate to make the best estimate which is equivalent to the original reflectance computed using the D50 illuminant. Material equivalence has been discussed in a number of papers including [16–18].

Derhak proposed an intermediate color equivalency representation, Waypoint that is an estimate of the material color is used. Waypoint Wpt coordinates are obtained using normalization matrices $(T)$, where matrix $T_1$ transforms tristimulus values $(C_{src})$ under the source observer function and source illuminant to its equivalent Wpt representation and similarly, matrix $T_2$ is a Wpt normalization matrix to the destination conditions.

Similarly to a CAT, the Wpt based MAT is then used to transform $C_{src}$ to destination tristimulus values $(C_{dest})$ and is then given by:

$$C_{dest} = T_2^{-1}TC_{src} \tag{4}$$

Derhak et al. [18] compared the performance of four different transforms in predicting the colorimetry under one illuminant given the colorimetry under a different illuminant. D65, D50, F11 and A were used as the reference and test illuminants, with all pairs of these as reference and test evaluated. The results showed that the Waypoint material adjustment transform (Wpt MAT), originally trained on Munsell reflectances [15], gave the best overall performance in predicting the colorimetry of both the Munsell data and the in-situ natural reflectances provided in ISO 17321, while for certain illuminant pairs linear Bradford gave a slightly better performance in predicting the colorimetry of the ISO 17321 data. The overall results of Derhak et al. [18] for linear Bradford, Waypoint MAT and CAT16 are summarized in Table 3.

**Table 3.** Performance of linear Bradford, Waypoint MAT and CAT16 in predicting material equivalence for combinations of D65, D50, F11 and A as reference and test illuminants

| Data set | Transform | Mean error |
|---|---|---|
| Munsell reflectances | CAT16 | 3.86 |
| | Linear bradford | 3.02 |
| | Wpt MAT | 1.58 |
| ISO 17321 in-situ reflectances | CAT16 | 5.78 |
| | Linear bradford | 5.25 |
| | Wpt MAT | 5.00 |

It is interesting to note that linear Bradford has a similar performance to Waypoint MAT in predicting a test data set different from the training set. Although a material adjustment transform is not intended to produce the same results as a chromatic adaptation transform, the results in Derhak et al. suggest that linear Bradford could reasonably be used for both purposes.

A MAT transform would fall into the category of a 'reason to use a different CAT' [3] and its output could validly be encoded in a v4 profile in place of linear Bradford for situations where a material equivalent representation is desired. Alternatively, a

MAT transform can be encoded in an ICC.2 (iccMAX) profile [19] and used to convert source data to either the D50 PCS or to a custom PCS as required. We suggest that a MAT could be determined that was optimal for a wider set of training data, and also that a custom MAT could be computed that was optimal for a particular class of colour data (such as specific printing conditions or display types).

# 5  iccMAX

ICC has adopted a next-generation colour management architecture, known as icc-MAX, which has been standardized as ICC.2 [19] and ISO 20677 [20]. A goal of iccMAX is to permit "greater flexibility for defining colour transforms and profile connection spaces" by allowing "PCS transform results to be relative to arbitrary illuminants and observers" [19], while also continuing to achieve unambiguous transform results. This is achieved by removing the requirement to use D50 for all PCS data; instead, the spectralViewingConditionsTag can used to encode the colorimetric observer and the illuminant which constitute the PCS of the profile. A customToS-tandardPCS transform ('c2sp') (and its inverse, standardToCustomPCS or 's2cp') is required to be present when the PCS of the profile is not D50, in order to support cases where the PCS of the profile does not match the PCS of the profile to be connected to.

iccMAX also supports spectral source and destination data and a spectral PCS. Thus it is possible, for example, to have a spectral source data encoding (reflectance, transmittance or bi-directional reflectance) and transform it to a colorimetric PCS using any colorimetric observer and/illuminant [18]. The greater flexibility of transform encodings in iccMAX make it possible to implement a chromatic adaptation transform or even a full colour appearance model within the profile if required. The choice of spectralViewingConditionsTag can also be deferred to run-time, so that the user can select the colorimetric PCS required for a particular workflow without having a pro-liferation of profiles.

Thus in ICC.2 it is possible to achieve the same results as in a profile created according to the v4 specification, but additionally non-D50 illuminants, spectral data, custom observers, alternative CATs, MATs and colour appearance models can all be supported. To ensure that transforms using profiles built according to the new archi-tecture are unambiguous, ICC recommends that Interoperability Conformance Speci-fications are defined for ICC.2 workflows [19].

# 6  Conclusions

Current solutions for chromatic adaptation in colour management have been evaluated using a comprehensive corresponding-colour data set. The linear Bradford transform used in ICC colour management performs reasonably well, and also has a number of advantages that make it suitable for use in ICC v4 colour management: notably its computational simplicity, its analytic invertibility and its ability to transform colours into and out of the ICC PCS with no loss in accuracy.

Two main cases have been identified in the present paper where an alternative to linear Bradford may be preferred. The first is where a state-of-the art CAT with best performance on corresponding colour data sets is required. Although CAT16 avoids the computational problems of CAT02, it does not perform better than linear Bradford, and there is no compelling reason to use it in preference. The second case is where a material equivalence transform is needed in order to predict the colorimetry under a different illuminant, rather than corresponding colour appearance. In this case Waypoint MAT may give a better performance, although it is possible that it could be optimized further for particular types of reflectance or emission. However, linear Bradford can continue to be used with confidence for most colour management applications, and it is not proposed here that it should be superseded for ICC v4.

For cross-media colour reproduction workflows with more advanced requirements that go beyond the D50 colorimetric PCS, the ICC.2 architecture provides a range of potential solution. These include the use of different CATs as well as MATs and colour appearance transforms.

**Acknowledgements.** The authors thank Ronnier Luo, Eric Walowit and the ICC members who provided helpful discussion and suggestions.

# References

1. International Color Consortium. http://www.color.org/
2. ICC.1:2001-04 File Format for Color Profiles
3. ISO 15076-1:2010 Image technology colour management - Architecture, profile format, and data structure
4. Hunt, R.: Objectives in colour reproduction. J. Photographic Sci. **18**, 205–215 (1970)
5. Lam, K.L.: Metamerism and Colour Constancy. Ph.D. thesis, University of Bradford (1985)
6. Swen, S., Wallis, L.: Chromatic Adaptation Tag Proposal, ICC Votable Proposal Submission, No. 8.2 (2000)
7. Finlayson, G.D., Süsstrunk, S.: Spectral sharpening and the bradford transform. In: Proceedings of Color Imaging Symposium, University of Derby, pp. 236–243 (2000)
8. Li, C., et al.: Comprehensive color solutions: CAM16, CAT16, and CAM16-UCS. Color Res. Appl. **42**, 703–718 (2017)
9. Katoh, N.: Appearance match between soft copy and hard copy under mixed chromatic adaptation. In: 3rd IS&T/SID Color Imaging Conference, pp. 22–25 (1995)
10. Henley, S.A., Fairchild, M.D.: Quantifying mixed adaptation in crossmedia color reproduction. In: 8th IS&T/SID Color Imaging Conference, pp. 305–310 (2000)
11. Zhai, Q., Luo, M.R.: A study of neutral white and degree of chromatic adaptation. In: 25th IS&T Color Imaging Conference, pp. 93–97 (2017)
12. Green, P.J., Otahalova, L.: Determining visually achromatic colors on substrates with varying chromaticity. In: Proceedings of Color Imaging VIII: Processing, Hardcopy, and Applications, SPIE 2003, pp. 356–364 (2003)
13. Green, P.J., Oicherman, B.: Reproduction of colored images on substrates with varying chromaticity. In: Color Imaging IX: Processing, Hardcopy, and Applications. SPIE, pp. 91–100 (2003)

14. Baah, K., Green, P., Pointer, M.: Perceived acceptability of colour matching for changing substrate white point. In: Color Imaging XVIII: Displaying, Processing, Hardcopy, and Applications, 86520Q (2013)
15. High, G., Green, P., Nussbaum, P.: Content-dependent adaptation in a soft proof matching experiment, In: Color Imaging XXII: Displaying, Processing, Hardcopy, and Applications, pp. 67–75 (2017)
16. Derhak, M.W., Berns, R.S.: Introducing Wpt (Waypoint): A color equivalency representation for defining a material adjustment transform. Color Res. Appl. **40**, 535–549 (2015)
17. Liu, Q., Wan, X., Liang, J., Liu, Z., Xie, D., Li, C.: Neural network approach to a colorimetric value transform based on a large-scale spectral dataset. Color. Technol. **133**, 73–80 (2017)
18. Derhak, M., Green, P., Conni, M.: Color appearance processing using iccMAX. In: Color Imaging XXIII: Displaying, Processing, Hardcopy, and Applications, pp. 323-1–323-6, no. 6 (2018)
19. ICC.2:2018 Image technology colour management - Extensions to architecture, profile format, and data structure
20. ISO 20677:2019 Image technology colour management - Extensions to architecture, profile format, and data structure

# Web Browsers Colorimetric Characterization

Philippe Colantoni[1]([✉]) and Alain Trémeau[2]

[1] Université de Lyon, Université Jean Monnet, Centre Interdisciplinaire d'Études
et de Recherches sur l'Expression Contemporaine, EA 3068, Saint-Etienne, France
`philippe.colantoni@univ-st-etienne.fr`
[2] Université de Lyon, Université Jean Monnet,
Laboratoire Hubert Curien, UMR 5516, Saint-Etienne, France
`alain.tremeau@univ-st-etienne.fr`

**Abstract.** The great heterogeneity of mobile display devices currently available on the market makes the implementation of universal color management difficult. To address this problem, we have targeted a common feature of these devices: their ability to run web browsers. In this article we describe a colorimetric characterization tool, uncorrelated to the hardware and operating system used, which is an essential element in the implementation of an universal color management process in web browsers. This tool consists of a software that controls a calorimeter running on a computer located in the same local network as the mobile device running the web browser. It uses colorimetric parameters that allow us to obtain, for the metrics we want to optimize, accurate color transformation models (with maximum errors in $\Delta E_{1994}$ and $\Delta E_{2000}$ up to 2 times lower than the state of the art).

**Keywords:** Color management · Colorimetric characterization · Colorimetric calibration · Web browser color calibration

## 1 Introduction

The great heterogeneity of mobile display devices (smartphones and tablets) currently available on the market makes the implementation of an universal color management process difficult. To address this problem we have targeted a common feature of these devices: their ability to run web browsers. Smartphones and tablets are mobile devices that capture (with one or more cameras) and reproduce (through their displays) RGB images. In both cases the RGB images manipulated are dependent on the input and output devices that are used. The result is a color inconsistency that can be a problem. To face this issue a color management workflow must be used to compensate for any colorimetric differences between input and output images, and to ensure that a color scene is accurately acquired and displayed on a display.

© Springer Nature Switzerland AG 2019
S. Tominaga et al. (Eds.): CCIW 2019, LNCS 11418, pp. 145–161, 2019.
https://doi.org/10.1007/978-3-030-13940-7_12

The implementation of a color management system is therefore necessary. In this paper, we want to complete and improve the work we published in previous papers [12,13] toward an optimal colorimetric characterization that works for any display technology, with the aim to transpose it to mobile devices displays. In particular, we will focus on setting up the two main elements (the colorimetric characterization and calibration) necessary to create a color management module that can be fully executed within a web browser on a mobile device.

The colorimetric characterization and the colorimetric calibration of a mobile device are not trivial for end-users as it exists in the state of the art several solutions for which the efficiency varies from one device to another one, or from one product to another one of the same device model. In [4] the authors reported that the most efficient colorimetric characterization models tested in their study perform well for all tested iPhone displays, but that these models were ranked differently on two iPhones of the same model (iPhone 4), which suggests that the intra-model consistency may be an issue for the colorimetric characterization of smartphone (or tablet) displays. Furthermore, available solutions and free software are in general not user-friendly and not simple to use, as several parameters may impact the accuracy of these tasks. In this paper, we propose an alternative solution to conventional approaches based on a web application. To the best of our knowledge, only [4] addressed this problem in the literature. However, their solution contains less functionalities than the one we propose.

In this article we propose to address the issue of color characterization and calibration in a web browser with a dedicated tool (see Sect. 4). To allow the characterization of a very large number of display system types (desktop, mobile and VR headset displays), we will see in Sect. 5 that our solution includes some optimizations that improve the accuracy of our calibration models. Before that in Sects. 2 and 3 we will introduce the concept of color management and color characterization adapted for this case of study. Although also suitable for the characterization of VR headsets, we will focus, in this article, on mobile devices. However, we will briefly describe the method we use for virtual reality devices in Sect. 6.

## 2   Color Management

Color management consists in a controlled transformation between the color representations of different devices. Forward color transform consists to convert device dependent color image data, e.g. RGB values, into device independent color data, e.g. $XYZ$ or $L^*a^*b^*$ values. Device independent color spaces such as $CIEXYZ$ or $CIELAB$ space represent colors in an absolute manner independent from any capturing or display device using the concept of standard observer. The development of a forward color transform (a forward model) requires knowledge of the image acquisition device (or a display device which can also be considered as an input device). This transform can be inverted by an inverse device transform (a backward model) adapted to the display device used that produces display device dependent color data, e.g. again RGB values, that ensures the accurate reproduction of the color defined by the device independent color data.

Device characterization and calibration are closely linked. They are the two key components of a color management system, they enable color images to be communicated and exchanged in a device independent color space. The aim of the device characterization is to model in the most accurate way how input values are processed by a device, it also provides several complementary information about this device such as the gamut of its primaries or the color channels correlation. Characterization is based on measurements of input values (e.g. RGB input values of a display) and output values (e.g. XYZ values measured on the display by a colorimeter or spectrometer). Color characterization enables to estimate, with a strong reliability, the color output of a display device while knowing the input color, and vice versa for an input device. The reliability of the characterization depends of the number of measures used to do this characterization, and of the set of colors (color patches) which are measured. It also allows to define the color gamut of the device.

While the characterization process defines the relationship that links the device dependent color space to the device independent color space, the calibration defines the setting up of this device, i.e. it defines how to match color values provided by this device to another one. The calibration step comes after the characterization step. The aim of the calibration step is to adjust the accuracy of output values produced by a device by comparison with a standard. Color calibration consists in set up a model from the set of color values used for the characterization and from the model resulting from this characterization, to ensure correct color reproduction of these color values.

The color management process is implemented through a Color Management Module (CMM). This CMM have to deal with the fact that the color gamut of different devices vary in range which makes an accurate reproduction impossible. For this reason, it has to implement a gamut mapping algorithm [3]. The gamut clipping is one of the simplest forms of gamut mapping that can be used.

# 3    Colorimetric Characterization

The colorimetric characterization of a device consists to model accurately how color values are transformed by this device. This can be done only by using a device independent color space such as the $CIEXYZ$ or the $CIELAB$ color space, as device dependent color spaces (such as the RGB color space) produce color values which differ from device to device.

Three main categories of colorimetric characterization methods can be found in the literature [1]. The first one aims to physically model the behavior of a color device. Generally, physical models are based on a number of simplifying conditions such are channel independence, chromaticity constancy, angle view independence [2]. The main disadvantage of physically models is the need to draw, test and validate assumptions which is time consuming and not simple for a wide range of end-users.

The second category corresponds to methods based on numerical models. Several numerical methods exist in the state of the art, such as polynomial regression methods, Radial Basis Functions (RBFs), neural networks [2]. These methods are based on a training set which is used to estimate the optimal parameters for the numerical functions used. In comparison with the physical methods, numerical methods are able to accurately model devices without assumption of channel independence. However, when precision is needed these methods are expensive in terms of measurement and computation time.

The third category corresponds to methods that are using 3D Look Up Tables (3D LUT). In general 3D LUT are built on a regular lattice of the RGB cube. Nevertheless, more accurate LUT can be built on a regular lattice of the CIELAB color space [5]. The accuracy of this kind of methods depends on the number of measurements done to create the table and on the efficiency of the interpolation method used to estimate the color data that are between measurement points. 3D LUT are also used for the computation of ICC profiles. The main advantage of 3D LUT methods is that they do not need to make any assumption regarding the device used. On the other hand, their main disadvantage is the need of a huge number of measurements.

To the best of our knowledge very few studies have been focused on colorimetric characterization of mobile displays. According to [2] only Piecewise Linear Model Assuming Constant Chromaticity (PLCC), Piecewise Linear Model Assuming Variation in Chromaticity (PLVC), and masking models have been applied on mobile device displays. In their paper [2] the authors proposed a model based on Radial Basis Functions (RBF) and polyharmonic splines which outperforms the other methods. They also tested Artificial Neural Networks (ANN) but the main problem with ANN models is that the accuracy of results depends strongly of the number of neurons in the hidden layer(s). An increase of neurons in the layer(s) in general improves accuracy. However according [2], sometime when the number of neurons in the hidden layer(s) reaches a threshold there is no further improvement.

The main advantage of the PLVC model is that it needs only a small number of measured samples. Moreover, it is very simple in terms of implementation. On the other hand, this model does not take into account channel interdependence. PLVC model is able to model channel interdependence for all three primaries but only if we use a polynomial regression of 3rd degree with 19 variables that raises estimation problems especially on gamut boundary. The main difficulty with the RBF model is to choose optimal parameters and an adequate basis function to obtain a good accuracy which is not simple. The best results obtained by [2] were for polyharmonic spline kernel of 4th order.

The investigation done by [2] showed the importance of the size of a training set, their study leads to conclusion that the optimum size for ANN and RBF is around 150 samples, while for Polynomial regression models is around 100 samples. Good average accuracy could be obtained with smaller training sets, but the maximum color difference is then not acceptable. The distribution of color samples in the training set has also an impact on the overall accuracy. The quality of a colorimetric characterization is generally evaluated in terms of colorimetric accuracy but other factors must be analyzed, such as the smoothness of the 3D LUT - based color transform used [8].

In Sect. 3.4 we will develop a new color characterization technique based on the solution proposed in [13]. Our intent is to extend the field of use of this technique in order to improve the accuracy of our calibration models when they are evaluated with perceptually accurate metrics such as the $\Delta E_{1994}$ and $\Delta E_{2000}$. For this purpose, we will introduce in the following sub sections 2 related concepts: the forward and backward transformation models (see Sect. 3.2) and the target color space (TCS) (see Sect. 3.3). But before that, we will discuss the opportunity to use ICC profiles for mobile devices.

### 3.1   Can We Use ICC Profiles?

The International Color Consortium (ICC) provides a solution by defining standards to store calibration data in ICC profiles. ICC profiles describe the color attributes of an input or an output device by defining a mapping model between these devices and a Profile Connection Space (PCS). This PCS can be either the CIEXYZ or the CIELAB ($L^*a^*b^*$). Mappings may be specified using Look Up Tables (LUT), to which interpolation is applied, or through a series of parameters for transformations. ICC profiles can be used by many software enabling color management. Considering that some browsers do not support ICC profiles, one option is to use the default ICC profile of the mobile display used; another option consists to compute the profile of the mobile device using the settings defined by the user.

Associated with the sRGB color space which is the standard color space used by browsers that support color profiles [6], ICC profiles can be a good solution but it will not cover all possible scenarios (operating systems and web browsers).

### 3.2   The Forward and Backward Transformation Models

The forward and backward forward transformation models correspond to the following parts of a color workflow:

- $RGB_{src} \rightarrow XYZ_{src} \rightarrow L^*a^*b^* \rightarrow TCS$
- $TCS \rightarrow L^*a^*b^* \rightarrow XYZ_{dst} \rightarrow RGB_{dest}$

As described in [13]: the forward transformation used is based on polyharmonic splines (a subset of the Radial Basis Functions that can be used for interpolating or approximating arbitrarily distributed data); the backward transformation used (or inverse transformation) is based on a tetrahedral interpolation.

### 3.3   Target Color Space

The **Target Color Space** (TCS) is different from the Profile Connection Space used with ICC profiles. The TCS used in our method is based on CIELAB but we adapted it to any color metrics (i.e. any $\Delta E_m$) that a user would like to optimize. In [5] we proposed a sampling method of the CIELAB color space based on non-Euclidean color differences. Here, we propose to use this sampling method to improve the accuracy of any color metric (with the aim to minimize the maximum error). Different sampling strategies can be used depending of the color metric used (e.g. $\Delta E_{1976}$, $\Delta E_{1994}$, $\Delta E_{CMC}$, $\Delta E_{BFD}$ or $\Delta E_{2000}$) and of the sampling distance considered. This sampling does no impact the accuracy of the forward and backward transforms. The only additional errors that may result from this sampling are related to numerical errors resulting from the geometrical model and from the interpolation method used. On the other hand, this uniform sampling, based on a 3D close packed hexagonal grid, has a strong impact on the geometrical shape of the resulting gamut (see Fig. 1). Not only the shape near the borders of the gamut and the volume of the gamut are concerned but also its centroid.

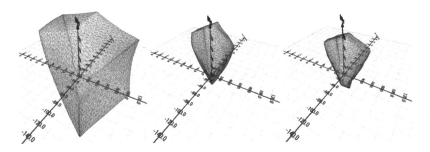

**Fig. 1.** Gamut of a Google Nexus 9 with 3 TCS based on $\Delta E_{1976}$, $\Delta E_{1994}$ and $\Delta E_{2000}$

In this new paper we will focus on 3 TCS based on $\Delta_{1976}$, $\Delta_{1994}$ and $\Delta_{2000}$ corresponding to a tabulated version of $CIELAB$, which can be found at the following url address [10] (see [5] and Fig. 2).

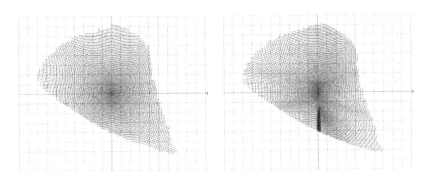

**Fig. 2.** $CIELAB$ Sampling corresponding to $\Delta_{1994}$ and $\Delta_{2000}$

## 3.4   Characterization Process

Considering that we want to characterize a display with N colors, the characterization method that we propose is based on the following steps:

1. Create a dataset of $27 + 24 = 51$ samples, built on a $3 \times 3 \times 3$ lattice of the RGB cube (i.e. 27 samples) complemented by 4 samples for each face (i.e. 24 samples) of the RGB cube (inter points of the $3 \times 3$ RGB values), as learning set (which will be used for the initialization of the interpolation process).
2. Measure the initial dataset and compute (as [13]) the forward and backward models (with predefined non optimal parameters).
3. Create a second dataset of N-51 samples from a uniform sampling of the target color space based on a 3D close packed hexagonal grid (see Fig. 3). The color values defined depend of the color metric used and of the color gamut of the display (see Sect. 3.3). This dataset will be used as optimization dataset.
4. The N-51 color values of the new dataset are ordered by decreasing Lightness (L*) value (as in [13]). This order defines the order of color values that will be measured during the characterization process. In order to be displayed on the screen, next measured, the N-51 L*a*b* color values are sequentially converted (and refined) in RGB values using the backward transform.
5. We refine the accuracy of the estimation model by adding to the current learning dataset the 1st color value on the top of the current optimization dataset. The model and the optimization dataset are recomputed (the forward and backward models) and refined at each iteration of the process value (as [13]), i.e. each time a new color value is taken into account (i.e. added to the learning set and consequently removed from the optimization set).
6. Create a test dataset of 64 samples, built on a $4 \times 4 \times 4$ lattice of the RGB cube, as validation set. The color values of this dataset are by definition (due to the over sampling) different from those of the 1st learning set and of the 1st optimization set. Analyze the accuracy of the estimation model from this dataset.

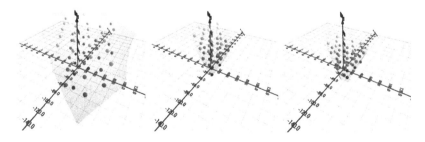

**Fig. 3.** 49 color samples for a Google Nexus 9 with 3 TCS ($\Delta E_{1976}$, $\Delta E_{1994}$ and $\Delta E_{2000}$) from a uniform sampling based on a 3D close packed hexagonal grid.

This characterization method is similar as the one which was proposed in [13], nevertheless now the choice of the target color space significantly changes the color distribution. This enables us to decrease the maximum errors. A more precise description of the implementation of this method is available in Sect. 4.1.

# 4   A New Tool for Web Browser Color Characterization

We introduced a first color management pipeline in [12] devoted to display calibration that included a screen characterization tool. This tool can only work on operating systems able to drive a colorimeter, i.e. Windows, MacOS and Linux. The main novelty of the new tool that we propose is to remove this limitation and thus to extend the area of use to Android and iOS operating systems. To reach this objective, we developed a web application that is able to drive, on a smartphone (or on a tablet, a VR headset), the display of colors from a computer connected on the same local network.

Most of web browsers support Color Management System (CMS) and ICC color profiles. With some smartphones users can customize the color profile of their display thanks to its Operating System (OS) color management. With other smartphones, the web browser does not have this option due to the operating system used. In this case, users are dependent of the default color management settings set by the manufacturer of this device. To face this issue we propose a characterization method that is placed above the existing CMS already present (or not) in the web browser.

The web application is provided by our software which includes a web server (the web application module). The mobile application module is used to display input color values sent by the web application module (through generated web pages). The colorimeter module is used to measure output color values displayed on the screen of the mobile phone (or the tablet, the VR headset) and to send these values to the color calibration module. The computer drives the colorimeter. The web application module has three main functionalities: (i) colorimetric characterization, (ii) colorimetric calibration and (iii) colorimetric correction.

The second novelty of this new color characterization module is that the new sampling method used for the TCS gives more accurate results than the previous one [13].

## 4.1   Tool Description

Performing colorimetric characterization of mobile devices can be an issue for end-user because the number of measurements to be done to perform this process is very tedious and time consuming if performed by hand. According [4], in the case of conventional displays connected to a PC with a Windows/Linux operating system this task can be easily automated by means of a simple cross-platform application which instructs a spectroradiometer to take measurements and displays a series of color patches on the display in a synchronized manner. However, there is no common programming environments for all mobile devices. For mobile devices there are various programming environments, e.g. Objective-C for iOS application on iPhone, Java or C/C++ for Android application, Windows Mobile 8, Firefox OS and Tizen. In [4] the authors proposed a solution that makes use of the WebSocket API in the HTML5 standard which allows bi-directional, full-duplex communications between a web browser and a server. The measurement setup consists of a smartphone which runs a web browser and a PC which runs a web server and the control software of the spectroradiometer. As long as the smartphone's web browser supports Web-Sockets, the framework can run without any problem.

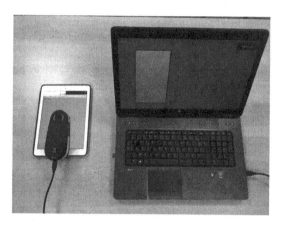

**Fig. 4.** Our software characterizing an iPad 2

The application that we propose (see Fig. 4), as the solution proposed by [4] aims to overcome this problem, i.e. to avoid of developing different control applications for all platforms separately. Written in C++ available on MacOS on Windows, we describe below how this tool works:

1. Launch the application on the server computer, enter the following parameter values: N the number of color values that will have to be measured (where N = 51 samples of the 1st learning set + Nb of samples of the optimization set); $\Delta E_m$ is the $CIELAB$ color metric which defines the TCS that will be used by the calibration model (e.g. $\Delta E_{76}$, $\Delta E_{94}$, $\Delta E_{CMC}$, $\Delta E_{BFD}$ or $\Delta E_{00}$); and lastly the type of device to characterize (e.g. a mobile display).
2. The application displays the URL to be used by the client on his web browser. The user has to enter this URL in the web browser to start the characterization process. The web page generated by the server is set to follow the instructions sent by the server.
3. The server sends a request to the user: "Start the characterization process". If the user is not familiar with the application, an help explains how to use the spectrocolorimeter in order to measure colors displayed on a screen. The spectrocolorimeter must be set in front of the center of the web browser window. The color of the background of this window is set to red and a message "Wait" is displayed in this window.

4. The characterization tool process the 51 colors of the learning set by sending them, one by one, from the server to the mobile device. For each color, the mobile device receives an instruction from the server to refresh the window in order to set the color of the background with the current color. The client web browser informs the server that it is ready for a new measure. Then, the spectrocolorimeter receives an instruction from the server to proceed the color measurement which send the measured values to the server. Next, the server proceeds to the next color or ends the process.

5. A first estimation model is computed by the server computer from these 51 pairs of input and output values.

6. A first optimization dataset of N colors is computed by the server computer.

7. Next, the N-51 colors ($CIELAB$ based on $\Delta_m$ values sequentially backward transformed in $RGB$ values) of the optimization set are sent, one by one, by the server to the client web browser of the mobile device. For each color, the client receives an instruction from the server to refresh the window in order to set the color of the background with the targeted color. The client informs the server that it is ready for a new measure. Then, the spectrocolorimeter receives an instruction from the server to proceed color measurement and send the measured values to the server. Next, the server proceeds to the next color or ends the process.

8. The learning dataset is updated by the server computer according the iterative process defined in Sect. 3.4.

9. A refined estimation model (the forward and backward transformations) is computed by the server computer from the new learning dataset created. From one iteration to the next one, the learning set is enriched by a new color with a lower lightness than the previous one added before, as a consequence the optimization dataset must be improved also.

10. The current optimization dataset is updated by the server computer according to the new learning dataset computed, next step 7 is re-iterated until all the N-51 colors are measured.

11. During the validation process the 64 colors of the validation set (see Sect. 3.4) are sent, one by one, by the server to the client web browser of the mobile device. For each color, the client web browser receives an instruction from the server to refresh the window in order to set the color of the background with the current color. The client informs the server that it is ready for a new measure. Then, the spectrocolorimeter receives an instruction from the server to proceed color measurement and send the measured values to the server. Next, the server proceeds to the next color or ends the process.

12. Optimization of the model parameters (color space used for the transformation $CIELab$ or $CIEYXZ$, polyharmonic kernels and smoothing factor) by the server computer using a brute-force process, as in [13].

13. Saving of the resulting file and of the corresponding ICC profile (in a data format corresponding to a 3D LUT).

## 4.2   Calibration Files

The file format that we propose to encode our calibration data is not compatible with ICC 4.2 specifications but can be easily converted in this format. We have opted for a calibration file format from which the set of colors used (for forward and backward transforms) are directly readable by a text editor. It is based on pairs of values:

- the RGB device-dependent color values that the output device can reproduce. This set of color values will be addressed by our color management system to ensure correct color reproduction on the output device.
- the corresponding xyY device-independent color values that the output device can reproduce. This set of color values corresponds to the set of color values measured during the characterization step which will be processed in the Target Color Space used.

The files also contains the additional set of 64 pairs of values to ensure the accuracy of the color management solution. This additional set of color values will be first used as a test set to check the accuracy of the calibration test, next will be integrated in the learning base to refine the accuracy of the forward and backward models. Additional data containing the parameters of the calibration model are also included in our files (these parameters can be found in [13]). They allow, when reading the files, to generate an optimal calibration.

# 5   Results

We chose to test our characterization process with 4 devices: 1 smartphone with an OLED display (an OnePlus 5 from OnePlus) and 3 tablets with LCD screens (an Apple iPad 2, a Google Pixel C and a Google Nexus 9). For all these devices we used Mozilla Firefox as web browser.

To test the accuracy of our characterizations, we have chosen to avoid any external lighting source and to use absolute colorimetry. For this purpose, all our CIEXYZ to CIELAB conversions use as white reference the XYZ value corresponding to the RGB triplet $(1, 1, 1)$ (each channels of RGB values vary between 0 and 1). This allows us to avoid any chromatic adaptation.

Table 1 shows the results we obtained for the 4 devices tested with 100 color samples. For each of these devices we carried out 3 characterizations corresponding to the following 3 TCS: $CIELAB$ based on $\Delta_{1976}$, $CIELAB$ $\Delta_{1994}$ and $CIELAB$ $\Delta_{2000}$. Each of these characterizations took 5 minutes with a X-Rite i1 Pro 2 Spectrocolorimeter. Table 2 shows the results we obtained for 2 of these devices tested with 2 TCS ($CIELAB$ $\Delta_{1976}$ and $CIELAB$ $\Delta_{2000}$) with 100, 150 and 200 samples, respectively. For these 2 tables, each line, which corresponds to a complete characterization, displays 3 accuracy indexes (the average error, the maximum error and the 95 percentile value) of the forward model's accuracy. The model accuracy was calculated from the N samples when compared to the 64 colors of the test base.

**Table 1.** Forward transform $\Delta E$ accuracy - Results for the 4 devices tested with 100 samples

| Devices | Samples | TCS | Average $\Delta E_{1976}$ | $\Delta E_{1994}$ | $\Delta E_{2000}$ | Max TCS | $\Delta E_{1976}$ | $\Delta E_{1994}$ | $\Delta E_{2000}$ | 95 TCS | $\Delta E_{1976}$ | $\Delta E_{1994}$ | $\Delta E_{2000}$ |
|---|---|---|---|---|---|---|---|---|---|---|---|---|---|
| iPad 2 | 100 | 1976 | 0.686 | 0.369 | 0.354 | 1976 | 3.448 | 3.343 | 3.969 | 1976 | 1.603 | 0.668 | 0.642 |
| iPad 2 | 100 | 1994 | 0.632 | 0.320 | 0.301 | 1994 | 2.215 | 1.330 | 1.019 | 1994 | 1.388 | 0.618 | 0.695 |
| iPad 2 | 100 | 2000 | 0.874 | 0.448 | 0.417 | 2000 | 4.565 | 1.448 | 1.361 | 2000 | 1.824 | 1.194 | 1.125 |
| Nexus 9 | 100 | 1976 | 1.482 | 0.675 | 0.628 | 1976 | 4.364 | 2.404 | 2.120 | 1976 | 3.049 | 1.407 | 1.343 |
| Nexus 9 | 100 | 1994 | 1.475 | 0.639 | 0.597 | 1994 | 4.754 | 1.383 | 1.402 | 1994 | 2.829 | 1.253 | 1.176 |
| Nexus 9 | 100 | 2000 | 1.780 | 0.765 | 0.708 | 2000 | 7.484 | 2.279 | 1.996 | 2000 | 3.905 | 1.750 | 1.507 |
| Pixel C | 100 | 1976 | 0.986 | 0.558 | 0.546 | 1976 | 2.392 | 1.933 | 2.568 | 1976 | 1.995 | 1.263 | 1.208 |
| Pixel C | 100 | 1994 | 0.894 | 0.522 | 0.486 | 1994 | 2.199 | 1.637 | 1.324 | 1994 | 1.912 | 1.142 | 1.056 |
| Pixel C | 100 | 2000 | 1.058 | 0.610 | 0.556 | 2000 | 3.166 | 1.760 | 1.562 | 2000 | 2.193 | 1.424 | 1.352 |
| OnePlus 5 | 100 | 1976 | 1.155 | 0.597 | 0.565 | 1976 | 4.860 | 3.073 | 2.510 | 1976 | 2.388 | 1.217 | 1.327 |
| OnePlus 5 | 100 | 1994 | 1.271 | 0.602 | 0.583 | 1994 | 3.163 | 1.633 | 1.611 | 1994 | 2.580 | 1.264 | 1.345 |
| OnePlus 5 | 100 | 2000 | 1.521 | 0.674 | 0.650 | 2000 | 3.737 | 2.254 | 1.857 | 2000 | 3.474 | 1.265 | 1.450 |

**Table 2.** Forward transform $\Delta E$ accuracy - Results for 2 devices tested (Google Pixel C and Google Nexus 9) with 100, 150 and 200 samples

| Devices | Samples | TCS | Average $\Delta E_{1976}$ | $\Delta E_{1994}$ | $\Delta E_{2000}$ | Max TCS | $\Delta E_{1976}$ | $\Delta E_{1994}$ | $\Delta E_{2000}$ | 95 TCS | $\Delta E_{1976}$ | $\Delta E_{1994}$ | 2000 |
|---|---|---|---|---|---|---|---|---|---|---|---|---|---|
| Pixel C | 100 | 1976 | 0.986 | 0.558 | 0.546 | 1976 | 2.392 | 1.933 | 2.568 | 1976 | 1.995 | 1.263 | 1.208 |
| Pixel C | 150 | 1976 | 0.894 | 0.520 | 0.480 | 1976 | 2.847 | 1.587 | 1.347 | 1976 | 2.172 | 1.130 | 0.995 |
| Pixel C | 200 | 1976 | 0.739 | 0.406 | 0.383 | 1976 | 1.930 | 1.266 | 1.252 | 1976 | 1.454 | 0.977 | 0.995 |
| Nexus 9 | 100 | 2000 | 1.780 | 0.765 | 0.708 | 2000 | 7.484 | 2.279 | 1.996 | 2000 | 3.905 | 1.750 | 1.507 |
| Nexus 9 | 150 | 2000 | 1.327 | 0.606 | 0.574 | 2000 | 4.789 | 1.741 | 1.676 | 2000 | 2.848 | 1.268 | 1.101 |
| Nexus 9 | 200 | 2000 | 1.115 | 0.561 | 0.529 | 2000 | 4.027 | 1.691 | 2.182 | 2000 | 2.338 | 1.289 | 1.199 |

**Table 3.** Backward transform $RGB$ accuracy - Results for the 4 devices tested with 100 samples

| Devices | Samples | TCS | Average | Max | 95 |
|---------|---------|-----|---------|-----|-----|
| iPad 2 | 100 | $\Delta E_{1976}$ | 0.0062 | 0.0163 | 0.0116 |
| iPad 2 | 100 | $\Delta E_{1994}$ | 0.0064 | 0.0222 | 0.0140 |
| iPad 2 | 100 | $\Delta E_{2000}$ | 0.0086 | 0.0240 | 0.0202 |
| Nexus 9 | 100 | $\Delta E_{1976}$ | 0.0291 | 0.1616 | 0.0885 |
| Nexus 9 | 100 | $\Delta E_{1994}$ | 0.0282 | 0.1766 | 0.0845 |
| Nexus 9 | 100 | $\Delta E_{2000}$ | 0.0319 | 0.1331 | 0.0924 |
| Pixel C | 100 | $\Delta E_{1976}$ | 0.0095 | 0.0233 | 0.0203 |
| Pixel C | 100 | $\Delta E_{1994}$ | 0.0103 | 0.0264 | 0.0201 |
| Pixel C | 100 | $\Delta E_{2000}$ | 0.0105 | 0.0290 | 0.0208 |
| OnePlus 5 | 100 | $\Delta E_{1976}$ | 0.0094 | 0.0328 | 0.0189 |
| OnePlus 5 | 100 | $\Delta E_{1994}$ | 0.0113 | 0.0348 | 0.0243 |
| OnePlus 5 | 100 | $\Delta E_{2000}$ | 0.0121 | 0.0280 | 0.0262 |

Tables 3 and 4 show the results for the backward model with the same 3 accuracy indexes (the average error, the maximum error and the 95 percentile value).

**Table 4.** Backward transform $RGB$ accuracy - Results for 2 devices tested (Google Pixel C and Google Nexus 9) with 100, 150 and 200 samples

| Devices | Samples | TCS | Average | Max | 95 |
|---------|---------|-----|---------|-----|-----|
| Pixel C | 100 | $\Delta E_{1976}$ | 0.0095 | 0.0233 | 0.0203 |
| Pixel C | 150 | $\Delta E_{1976}$ | 0.0082 | 0.0205 | 0.0175 |
| Pixel C | 200 | $\Delta E_{1976}$ | 0.0067 | 0.0202 | 0.0147 |
| Nexus 9 | 100 | $\Delta E_{2000}$ | 0.0319 | 0.1331 | 0.0924 |
| Nexus 9 | 150 | $\Delta E_{2000}$ | 0.0242 | 0.1426 | 0.0867 |
| Nexus 9 | 200 | $\Delta E_{2000}$ | 0.0158 | 0.1276 | 0.0579 |

As we can see in Tables 1 and 2, the results are in line with our assumptions done in Sect. 3.3. The use of a given TCS allows to obtain much lower maximum error and 95 percentile values when these accuracy indexes are calculated with the corresponding metric. The results are particularly good with the TCS based on $\Delta E_{1994}$ regardless of the device characterized. The TCS based on $\Delta E_{2000}$ is lagging because of the lower quality of its sampling (see Fig. 2 and Ref. [5]).

Unfortunately, as one can see in Tables 3 and 4, the improvement of the forward model does not benefit from its inverse model for TCS based on $\Delta E_{1994}$ and $\Delta E_{200}$. On the contrary, we even notice a loss of precision due to 2 concomitant factors: for these 2 TCS the gamuts undergo significant distortions which degrade the tetrahedral interpolation used in the calculations of this model; the inverse model being based on a sampling obtained with the classical model it undergoes an accumulation of numerical errors (due to the resampling of the CIELAB space among others).

Tables 2 and 4 show us that in any case the increase in the number of colors improves the accuracy of the forward and reverse models. However, the increase in the number of colors mechanically increases the time required for characterization (5 min for 100 colors, 8 min for 200 colors). However, the accuracy of the models is limited by the stability of the display device (its ability to reproduce the same color identically) and the quality of the spectrophotometer used to perform the measurements.

## 6  Usage and Perspectives

The first possible usage of this tool is to create, from the characterization files we have produced, standard ICC profiles in order to use them in classic color workflows based on Microsoft, Adobe or Apple Color Management Modules or possibly open source CMMs like lcms2. We have chosen to offer a higher level of integration by implementing a color workflow based on a CMM entirely executed by web browsers (a WebCMM) with a simple javascript interface.

In the Sect. 3.2 we presented the two transformations which define our calibration model, our Color Management Module (CMM). Written in C++, theses transformations are not linked to any external software module. The entire calibration process is therefore performed by our code independently of any function of the system on which it is performed. It is for this reason that we were able to generate a particular version of our library entirely compiled in WebAssembly. WebAssembly, or wasm, is a low-level binary programming language for developing applications in web browsers. This is a standard of the "World Wide Web" consortium that has been designed to complement JavaScript with superior performance. Since WebAssembly only specifies a low-level language, bytecode is usually produced by compiling a higher-level language. Supported languages include C and C++, compiled with Emscripten. The transformation of our code into wasm allowed us to define interface functions in Javascript. These functions now allow us to run our color management system within web browsers using standard html pages. We therefore have a color management module dedicated to the Web (a WebCMM).

The second possible usage of this tool is for characterizing Virtual Reality headsets. To do this, we have developed a specific procedure for generating web pages in our characterization tool. The generated pages use *a-frame* [9] a Javascript library that allows to produce and manipulate 3D objects in a virtual environment displayed in a virtual reality headset. The pages we produce generate a virtual environment with a uniform color that is displayed on the screens integrated into the headset using the *WebVR* standard. To make colorimetric measurements we use a simple fixing system that allows us to hold the sensor of our spectrocolorimeter on the surface of one of the helmet lenses. We thus have a tool capable of characterizing all the display devices that modern web browsers can manage.

Now that we have a complete color management system dedicated to browsers (and VR headset driven by *WebVR*) we can start porting other tools to the Web. Our objective in the coming months will be to offer the first web framework to natively manage multi and hyperspectral images in a web browser. This framework will have a complete management of all calculations (performed in real time using WebGL shaders) that will allow the following transformations: reflectance to color (using a color reconstruction and an illuminant) then color to RGB using our WebCMM.

## 7   Conclusion

In this paper we have presented an innovative software tool dedicated to color characterization of web browsers. This tool, is able of driving any Web browser running on the same computer or located on the same local network. This tool was developed to characterize many types of display devices: smartphones, tablets, monitors, virtual reality headsets. It integrates an algorithm that allows it to dynamically select color patches according to several criteria. These criteria, which depend of the number of sample colors and of the TCS, define the precision of the models (forward and backward) that will be produced.

The quality of the generated models depends largely on the stability of the display device that is characterized. It cannot be possible to produce a good predictive model if the color measurements are not stable. However, we shown in this study that the increase in the number of colors significantly improves the accuracy of the models produced. If a characterization must be performed to produce a quality forward model, we advise to use a number of sample colors greater than 200 associated with a TCS based on the $\Delta E_{1994}$, meanwhile for the reverse model we advise to also use a number of sample colors greater than 200 but associated this time with a TCS based on the $\Delta E_{1976}$.

## References

1. Thomas, J.-B., Hardeberg, J.Y., Foucherot, I., Gouton, P.: The PLVC display color characterization model revisited. Color Res. Appl. **33**(6), 449–460 (2008). https://doi.org/10.1002/col.20447
2. Poljicak, A., Dolic, J., Pibernik, J.: An optimized Radial Basis Function model for color characterization of a mobile device display. Displays **41**, 61–68 (2016)
3. Morovic, J.: Color Gamut Mapping. Wiley, Chichester (2008). ISBN: 978-0-470-03032-5
4. Byshko, R., Li, S.: Characterization of iPhone displays: a comparative study. In: Workshop Farbbildverarbeitung, Darmstadt (2012)

5. Colantoni, P., Thomas, J.B., Trémeau, A.: Sampling CIELAB color space with perceptual metrics. Int. J. Imaging Robot. **16**(3), 1–22 (2016)
6. Javorsek, D., Mocnik, J., Staresinic, M.: Analysis of colour appearances on different display devices. Tekstilec **58**(2), 100–107 (2015)
7. Velea, R., Gordon, N.: Evaluating gamut coverage metrics for ICC color profiles. Int. J. Chaotic Comput. (IJCC) **4**(2), 113–117 (2016)
8. Aristova, A.: Smoothness of color transformations. Master i Teknologi - Medieteknikk, Hogskolen, Gjovik (2010)
9. https://aframe.io/. Accessed 26 Sept 2018
10. https://data.couleur.org/deltaE/. Accessed 26 Sept 2018
11. https://viva-arts.univ-st-etienne.fr/spectralviewer.html. Accessed 26 Sept 2018
12. Colantoni, P., Thomas, J.-B.: A color management process for real time color reconstruction of multispectral images. In: Salberg, A.-B., Hardeberg, J.Y., Jenssen, R. (eds.) SCIA 2009. LNCS, vol. 5575, pp. 128–137. Springer, Heidelberg (2009). https://doi.org/10.1007/978-3-642-02230-2_14
13. Colantoni, P., Thomas, J.B., Hardeberg, J.Y.: High-end colorimetric display characterization using an adaptive training set. J. Soc. Inf. Disp. **19**, 520–530 (2011)

# Color Image Evaluation

# Evaluation of Automatic Image Color Theme Extraction Methods

Gianluigi Ciocca[ID], Paolo Napoletano[(✉)][ID], and Raimondo Schettini[ID]

Department of Informatics, Systems and Communication,
University of Milano-Bicocca, Milan, Italy
{ciocca,napoletano,schettini}@disco.unimib.it
http://www.ivl.disco.unimib.it/

**Abstract.** Color themes are quite important in several fields from visual and graphic art design to image analysis and manipulation. Color themes can be extracted from an image manually by humans or automatically by a software. Plenty of automatic color theme extraction methods, either supervised or unsupervised, have been presented in the state of the art in the last years. Evaluation of a color theme goodness with respect to a reference one is based on visual and subjective comparisons, that may be affected by cultural and social aspects, they are time consuming and not costless. In this paper we experiment several supervised and unsupervised state-of-the-art methods for color theme extraction. To overcome the burden of a subjective evaluation, we experiment the use of a computational metric based on the Earth Mover's distance for goodness evaluation instead of a subjective one. Results show the best color theme is extracted by using a supervised method based on a regression model trained on user-defined color themes and that the computational metric adopted is comparable to a subjective one.

**Keywords:** Color theme extraction · Color palette evaluation · Earth Mover's Distance

## 1 Introduction

In the field of visual and graphic art design the choice of an attractive set of colors (also called color theme or color palette) can be a very complex process [21]. The perceived quality of a color decision can be affected by subjective-culture, trending fashions, and individual preference [23,30,32]. Artists and designers often choose colors by taking inspiration from other premade color themes [1, 11,12] or themes extracted from images [23]. A color theme of an image is a finite set of color (usually from 3 to 7) that best represents an image [21].

Color themes are useful in many tasks such as image recoloring, color blending, photo segmentation and editing, image enhancement and manipulation [31]. Color theme can be also adopted as signatures (or feature vectors) for the indexing of images in a content-based image retrieval system [19,25,33,35]. A user

© Springer Nature Switzerland AG 2019
S. Tominaga et al. (Eds.): CCIW 2019, LNCS 11418, pp. 165–179, 2019.
https://doi.org/10.1007/978-3-030-13940-7_13

can query the system by choosing a color, or a set of colors, and then retrieve a set of images that are relevant to that query, or in another way a set of images for which the colors of the query are representative [4,35].

Whatever is the application domain, being able to automatically extract a color theme from an image can facilitate color-related applications such as color picking interfaces, color mood transfer from one image to another, or color harmonization [18,23,26,33]. Human beings are able to recognize millions of colors and more important they are able to describe an image by selecting just a few of them [15,20]. While human beings perform this task quite effortlessly, algorithms does not perform this task easily especially from the computational-cost point of view.

A plenty of automatic color theme extraction methods have been presented in the last years. There are methods based on clustering [8,15,27], that are unsupervised, while other methods are supervised, such as the one by Lin et al. [21]. They presented a regression model trained on user-defined color themes. Very recently a deep-learning based solution has been presented for a discrete-continuous color gamut representation that extends the color gradient analogy to three dimensions and allows interactive control of the color blending behavior [31]. Mellado et al. presented a graph-based palette representation to find a theme as a minimization problem [24].

The evaluation of color theme goodness, that is how much a set of colors is representative of a given image, involves human beings and therefore is highly subjective. Such evaluations are time consuming and not costless. To overcome the limits of subjective evaluations, computational metrics can be adopted. In this paper we experiment several supervised and unsupervised state-of-the-art methods for color theme extraction from images and we exploit a computational metric based on the Earth Mover's distance (EMD) for the automatic evaluation of the goodness of a color theme extracted with respect to a human-based reference theme. Results show that the best method is the one based on a regression model trained on user-defined themes [21] and that the EMD is a quite robust measure of color theme goodness and thus comparable to a subjective one.

## 2    Methods for Color Theme Extraction

In this section we review the methods for automatic color theme extraction experimented in this paper. Concerning the size of the color theme, previous studies found that the most common value is five [27], therefore the following methods, where possible, will take into account this value as input constraint.

### 2.1    Color Histogram

This is the simplest algorithm for theme extraction [17]. It is based on the concept of 3D color histogram of an image, that is defined as a distribution over each possible triplet of colors $\mathbf{c_i} = (c_1, c_2, c_3)_i$ of within the color space considered. The distribution is calculated as percentage of the image pixel that assumes a given color value $c_i$. Since the number of all possible triplets is enormous, the 3D histogram is usually quantized in small number of volume partitions. We consider a uniform quantization of each color channel of size 3 thus we have $3 \times 3 \times 3 = 27$ partitions $v$. The color theme is obtained by selecting the $K$ partitions with the highest number of pixels inside and then selecting the $K$ colors $\mathbf{c_v} = (\mu_1, \mu_2, \mu_3)_v$ representing each partition: $\mu_1$ is the mean of the colors belonging to the partition $v$. Figures 1 and 2 show some color-histogram-based themes obtained with $K = 5$. This method is very simple and at low computational cost. Besides its simplicity, this method may fail because the quantization can aggregate colors that in practice need to be divided, and more important the color representing the volume $v$ may be a color not present in the original image because is obtained as average of all the colors of the partition $v$. These drawbacks are mostly due to the fact that the quantization is performed uniformly. This method, apart from the choice of the number of volume partitions $K$, is unsupervised.

## 2.2   Median Cut

This algorithm is based on the concept of 3D color histogram [17]. In this case, the color space is divide not uniformly by taking into account the distribution of pixels within the three color channels. The algorithm takes as input a maximum number of groups $K$ and works as follows. At the beginning, all the image pixels belong to the same group or partition. The color channel with the highest range of values is chosen as reference $c_R$. The median value $m_{c_R}$ of the selected color channel is computed and two subgroups are formed by selecting pixels that are higher or lower than the median value $m_{c_R}$. If the number of subgroups is equal to $K$ then the algorithm stops, otherwise it starts again from the selection of the subgroup with the highest color range. The algorithm stops when the number of subgroups equals $K$.

   The final color theme is obtained, as for the color histogram, by selecting the $K$ volumes with the highest number of pixels inside and then selecting then colors representing each volume. This method is considered unsupervised. Figures 1 and 2 show some examples obtained with $K = 5$.

   The color space is partitioned in a smarter way than the color histogram, but in those cases where a huge partition is composed of similar colors, the algorithm splits this partition in two or more partitions (see the greenish colors in Fig. 1 column 3) penalizing those colors that are not so present in the image but are semantically important (look at the bluish color that is reported in the r2 of third column of Fig. 1.

## 2.3   K-Means and C-Means

Unsupervised clustering methods are largely adopted in machine-learning-based applications. One of the most famous and adopted clustering method is the k-means [22,34]. Given $m$ points $\{x_1, \ldots, x_m\}$ belonging to a $n-$dimensional space $R^n$, and a given number of clusters $K$, the k-means algorithm search for the centroids of the clusters $\{c_1, \ldots, c_K\}$ belonging to $R^n$ such that the sum of the distances between each point $x_i$ belonging to a cluster $l$ and its centroid $c_l$ is minimized:

$$\min_{\{c_1, \ldots, c_K\}} = \sum_{i=1}^{m} \min_{l=1 \ldots K} \|x_i - c_l\|$$

K-means is influenced by the initialization step. In this paper we consider two variations of k-means. The first variant (k-means1) is the one adopted by Lin et al. [21] where the initial seeds are stratified randomly sampled within the CIELab color representation of the image. The second (k-means2) is the original k-means with a special initialization where the initial seeds are chosen uniformly over a set of colors ordered from the brightest to darkest.

One of the drawbacks of the k-means is that it does not take into account spatial arrangement of the colors in the image, and can thus wash out important image regions [21].

Fuzzy c-means clustering is quite similar to k-means, except on how the pixels are assigned to the clusters. Here the assignment is soft instead of hard [10]. This makes the algorithm less subject to the outliers problem and so more robust to catch colors related to small (but important) details of the image. For both k-means and c-means the number $K$ is set to 5. Figures 1 and 2 show some examples of color themes obtained with k-means1, k-means2 and c-means.

## 2.4   ISODATA

ISODATA clustering [16] is an unsupervised classification method alternative to k-means. Unlike the latter, it is not necessary to set in advance the number of final clusters because, during execution, the algorithm checks whether to merge or divide the clusters in order to better fit the distribution of input data. The execution in fact continues until the preset thresholds of variance and distance between the clusters are not below the parameters established by the user. The best set of parameters are not easy to be found and it requires a "trial and error" stage. Even though we need not to set the number K, the disadvantage of the algorithm is that the output color theme may include a higher number of colors than k-means. Figures 1 and 2 show some examples of color themes obtained with ISODATA. This algorithm is considered unsupervised.

## 2.5   Mean Shift

Mean shift is a clustering algorithm based on the concept of kernel density estimation. The algorithm considers the color space as a empirical probability density function $f(x)$ and the image pixels are considered as sampled from the underlying probability density function. Dense regions (or clusters) in the color space correspond to the mode (or local maxima) of the probability density function. The aim of the algorithm is to find those local maxima [9]. Given the pixels

$x_i$ of the input image, the algorithm applies a kernel $K(x_i - x)$ to each pixel around an initial pixel $x$. For each pixel, the algorithm defines a window around it and computes the weighted mean $m(x)$ of the pixel as:

$$m(x) = \frac{\sum_{x_i \in N(x)} K(x_i - x)x_i}{\sum_{x_i \in N(x)} K(x_i - x)}$$

where $N(x)$ is the set of neighbours of $x$ for which $K(x_i) \neq 0$. Now the algorithm shifts the center of the window to the mean $(x \leftarrow m(x))$ and repeats the estimation until $m(x)$ converges. The difference $m(x) - x$ is called mean shift. Given a kernel $K$, bandwidth parameter $h$, we chose a Gaussian kernel: $K(x_i - x) = e^{-\frac{\|x_i - x\|^2}{h}}$. The parameter $h$ influences the width of the kernel and then the granularity of the cluster and implicitly the number of clusters.

As in the case of ISODATA, the number of clusters can be determined automatically. As drawbacks, the choice of the right value for $h$ is a "trial and error" process, and the number of clusters is usually higher than 5. Figures 1 and 2 show some examples of color themes obtained with Mean shift. This algorithm is considered unsupervised.

## 2.6 Diffused Expectation Maximization

Diffused expectation maximisation (DEM) is an algorithm for image segmentation. The method models an image as a finite mixture, where each mixture component corresponds to a region class and uses a maximum likelihood approach to estimate the parameters of each class, via the expectation maximisation algorithm, coupled with anisotropic diffusion on classes, in order to account for the spatial dependencies among pixels [5,6]. Each image is conceived as drawn from a mixture of Gaussian density function, so that for any pixel we have:

$$p(x_i|\theta) = \sum_{k=1}^{K} p(x_i|k, \theta)P(k)$$

and the likelihood of the image data is

$$\mathcal{L} = p(x|\theta) = \prod_{i=1}^{N} p(x_i|\theta)$$

Image segmentation can be achieved by finding the set of labels that maximise the likelihood $\mathcal{L}$. The final set of labels are used to select the Gaussians. The mean values of the Gaussians are the colors of the final color theme. The algorithm takes the number of Gaussians $K$ as input and uses k-means for the initialization of the Guassian' parameters. One of the problem of this method is that due to the anisotropic diffusion spatial dependencies between pixels are taken into account. It causes the lost of those pixels that are associated to very small (but important) regions. Figures 1 and 2 show some examples of color themes obtained with DEM. This algorithm, apart from the choice of $K = 5$ is considered unsupervised.

## 2.7   Regression

This method has been presented by Lin et al. [21]. It is based on a regression model trained on 1,600 color themes extracted from a set of 40 images by 160 different human subjects recruited through the Amazon Mechanical Turk platform. They were asked to pick 5 different colors that would "best represent the image and order them in a way that would capture the image well." Part of these color themes (1,000) have been used to fit a linear model of the training set through the LASSO regression and the remaining for testing. Before training, target scores for each theme on how close it is to human-extracted themes has been computed. 79 features have been extracted from each color theme by considering six types of features to describe each theme: saliency, coverage error both for pixels and for segments, color diversity, color impurity, color nameability, and cluster statistics. To score the goodness of a color theme with respect to the human-based ones during the training process, the authors defined the following distance:

$$score(p) = 1 - \frac{1}{|H|} \sum_{h \in H} \frac{dist(p,h)}{maxDist}$$

where $p$ is the given theme, $H$ is the set of human-extracted themes, $dist$ is the Euclidean error between the two themes in the CIELab color space, and $maxDist$ is some maximum possible distance between two themes. The theme scores are then scaled between 0 and 1 for each image, so that each image gets equal weight in training. Themes with scores closer to 1 are more perceptually similar to human themes on average than themes with scores closer to 0. Given the distance metric and the human-extracted themes for each image, an optimal oracle color theme, that is closest on average to all the human-extracted themes is calculated. Due to the fact that this method requires a training process, it is considered a supervised approach. Figures 1 and 2 show some examples of color themes obtained with the regression method.

## 2.8   Clarifai

Clarifai (https://clarifai.com/) is an online service for visual recognition. Given an image is possible, through a set of API, to get tags related to the contents of the image, and the color theme. The number of colors of the theme can not be set, thus the output is variable in lengths. Figures 1 and 2 show some examples of color themes obtained with the Clarifai API.

## 2.9   Random Color Theme

To evaluate the goodness of the color theme methods discussed above, as a baseline, we consider also a random color theme approach. It extracts $K = 5$ colors from a 3D histogram representation of the input image. To reduce the number of possible themes we consider 27 volumes of the 3D histogram by performing a $3 \times 3 \times 3$ channels quantization. The random algorithm is executed 10 times and the themes showed in Figs. 1 and 2 is the best in terms of similarity with respect to the ground truth.

## 3   Evaluation Metrics

The qualitative analysis of the color themes extracted using the methods described in the previous section is of limited utility, because it is based on visual and subjective comparisons (see Figs. 1 and 2). To score the goodness of the methods analyzed and quantitatively calculate the similarity between the palettes it is necessary to define a suitable metric.

Lin et al. [21] adopted a subjective metric by asking human subjects to evaluate a set of color themes and rate "how well they represent the color theme of the image". Subjective evaluations strictly depends on the number of subjects and may be affected by cultural and social aspects related to the profiles of the human subjects involved. More important, they are not costless and are time consuming.

To overcome these problems, and so to ease the evaluation step, we introduce an objective metric based on the Earth Mover's Distance (EMD) [28,29]. EMD considers each color theme as a probability distribution, so given two distributions, it performs a quantitative measure of their dissimilarity. EMD measures the minimal cost that must be paid to transform one distribution into the other. As we have seen in the previous section, each theme extraction method outputs a variable number of colors, usually from 3 to 7, so most of the time distributions to be compared are of different length. The EMD by definition can operate on variable-length representations of the distributions and thus is more suitable than traditional histogram matching metrics, like euclidean distance. Moreover, to make the EMD metric capable of approximating perceptual dissimilarity as well as possible, we perform evaluations in the CIE-Lab color space that is more perceptually linear than other color spaces [36]. Within the CIE-Lab color space, a change of the same amount in a color value should produce a change of about the same visual importance.

The EMD definition is based on the notion of distance between the basic features that are aggregated into the distributions, in our case the single colors of the theme. This distance is called ground distance and measures dissimilarity between individual colors in the CIE-Lab space: $\mathbf{c} = \{c_L, c_a, c_b\}$. Given two colors $\mathbf{c_i}$ and $\mathbf{c_j}$, the ground distance $d_{ij}$ is the euclidean distance between the two colors,

$$d_{ij} = \sqrt{(c_L^i - c_L^j)^2 + (c_a^i - c_a^j)^2 + (c_b^i - c_b^j)^2}.$$

The concept of EMD is based on the concept of signature that coincides with the concept of color theme itself. Each signature is made of $m$ clusters and then each color of the theme is the centroid of each of the $m$ clusters. Let us consider two signatures $P = \{(\mathbf{p_1}, w_{\mathbf{p_1}}), \ldots, (\mathbf{p_m}, w_{\mathbf{p_m}})\}$ and $Q = \{(\mathbf{q_1}, w_{\mathbf{q_1}}), \ldots, (w_{\mathbf{q_n}})\}$ of size $m$ and $n$ respectively, where $\mathbf{p_i}$ and $\mathbf{q_j}$ are two different colors or centroids of the clusters, $w_{\mathbf{p_i}}$ and $w_{\mathbf{q_j}}$ are the weights associated to each cluster.

The computation of the EMD between two signatures is obtained as linear programming optmization. The aim of the linear programming solver is, given two signatures made of different sets of clusters and related cluster weights, to fill in the cluster weights of the second signature with the cluster weights of the first signature in a way that the work needed to move these weights from a signature to another is minimum. Intuitively, the solution of this linear programming optimization is the amount of work needed to transform a signature into another.

More formally, the aim is to find a flow $\mathbf{F} = [f_{ij}]$, with $f_{ij}$ the flow between $\mathbf{p}_i$ and $\mathbf{p}_j$, that minimizes the overall cost

$$WORK(P, Q, \mathbf{F}) = \sum_{i=1}^{m} \sum_{j=1}^{n} d_{ij} f_{ij},$$

subject to the following constraints:

$$f_{ij} \geq 0, 1 \leq i \leq m, 1 \leq j \leq n \tag{1}$$

$$\sum_{i=1}^{m} f_{ij} \leq w_{\mathbf{p}_i}, 1 \leq i \leq m \tag{2}$$

$$\sum_{j=1}^{n} f_{ij} \leq w_{\mathbf{q}_j}, 1 \leq j \leq n \tag{3}$$

$$\sum_{i=1}^{m} \sum_{j=1}^{n} f_{ij} = min \left( \sum_{i=1}^{m} w_{\mathbf{p}_i} \sum_{j=1}^{n} w_{\mathbf{q}_j} \right) \tag{4}$$

The first constraint allows to move weights only from $P$ to $Q$ but not the opposite. The second two constraints limit the weights that can be moved from a cluster of $P$ and $Q$ respectively. The last constraint forces to move the maximum amount of weights from $P$ to $Q$.

Once the optimal flow $\mathbf{F}$ is found, the EMD is defined as follows:

$$EMD(P, Q) = \frac{\sum_{i=1}^{m} \sum_{j=1}^{n} d_{ij} f_{ij}}{\sum_{i=1}^{m} \sum_{j=1}^{n} f_{ij}}$$

The denominator of the EMD formula is a normalization factor that is the total weight of the smaller signature. The ground distance $d_{ij}$ can be any distance, but if it is a metric and the total weights of two signatures are equal, the EMD is a true metric [29].

## 4    Experiments

In this Section we present the results of our experiments. In Subsect. 4.1 we discuss the data employed for the evaluation of the methods and all the parameters adopted for the themes extraction process. In Subsect. 4.2 we present the color themes extracted using each of the considered methods and we present the results of the evaluation metric adopted.

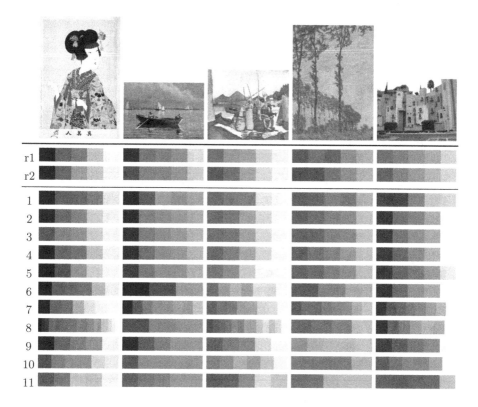

**Fig. 1.** 1-Regression, 2-c-means, 3-k-means1, 4-k-means2, 5-Median Cut, 6-Clarifai, 7-ISODATA, 8-Mean Shift, 9-Color Histogram, 10-DEM, 11-Random. Color themes extracted by each method from the first 5 images of the test set. From the top, color theme are listed from the best to the worst. The first two rows represent the color themes achieved throughthe Mechanical Turk (r1) or provided by the artists (r2). (Color figure online)

## 4.1  Data and Experimental Setup

For the evaluation we employ the test part of the dataset presented by Lin et al. [21]. The dataset has been collected by asking 160 different human subjects recruited through the Amazon Mechanical Turk platform, to extract themes from a set of 40 images. These images consisted of 20 paintings and 20 photographs. The paintings were chosen from five artists with different artistic styles (Impressionist, Expressionist, Pointillist, Realist, and Ukiyoe prints). The photographs were Flickr Creative Commons images chosen from the categories Landscape, Architecture, Interior, Closeup, and Portrait.

The authors required participants to choose exactly 5 colors from candidate color swatches generated by running k-means clustering on the image. As we have discussed above, color theme of size 5 are considered the most common size on online theme sharing sites. Each participant extracted themes from either

**Fig. 2.** 1-Regression, 2-c-means, 3-k-means1, 4-k-means2, 5-Median Cut, 6-Clarifai, 7-ISODATA, 8-Mean Shift, 9-Color Histogram, 10-DEM, 11-Random. Color themes extracted by each method from the last 5 images of the test set. From the top, color theme are listed from the best to the worst. The first two rows represent the color themes achieved through the Mechanical Turk (r1) or provided by the artists (r2). (Color figure online)

10 paintings or 10 photographs. The authors asked the participants to pick 5 different colors that would "best represent the image and order them in a way that would capture the image well." The total number of themes collected was 1,600 (40 themes for each image).

For comparison purposes, the authors choose a subset of 10 images (5 paintings and 5 photographs) and asked 11 art students to extract themes from those images. This set of 10 images is the test set adopted by Lin et al. [21] and also adopted in this paper. Using the distance $score(p)$ defined in Sect. 2.7 and the human-extracted themes for each image, an optimal oracle color theme can be found, that is the closest on average to all the human-extracted themes. Thus, for the test set we have two oracles: the Amazon-Mechanical-Turk (r1) one and the Artists one (r2). See the first two rows of the Figs. 1 and 2.

We extract from the 10 test images all the color themes using the 11 methods discussed in Sect. 2: 1-Regression, 2-c-means, 3-k-means1, 4-k-means2, 5-

Median Cut, 6-Clarifai, 7-ISODATA, 8-Mean Shift, 9-Color Histogram, 10-DEM, 11-Random. For all the methods that require an input number of cluster we consider $K = 5$. The regression, the c-means and k-means1 methods are obtained from the author resources that are available at https://github.com/sharondl/color-themes.

**Table 1.** EMD measured between each color theme obtained using the evaluated methods and the color theme achieved through Amazon Mechanical Turk or provided by the Artists. The last column shows the sum of the average over the two references and the standard deviation. The methods are sorted by the minimum distance.

| Method | Mech. Turk | | Artist | | |
|---|---|---|---|---|---|
| | avg (max) | ±std | avg (max) | ±std | avg + std |
| Regression | **14.29** (24.14) | 5.25 | **17.63** (24.93) | 5.11 | **21.14** |
| c-means | 18.81 (27.79) | 4.89 | 18.85 (29.07) | 6.43 | 24.49 |
| k-means1 | 19.39 (28.75) | 5.39 | 20.14 (28.81) | 5.59 | 25.26 |
| k-means2 | 20.32 (29.43) | 5.17 | 20.91 (30.42) | 6.42 | 26.41 |
| Median Cut | 21.93 (28.12) | 4.34 | 21.91 (28.93) | 5.26 | 26.72 |
| Clarifai | 20.48 (29.14) | 4.91 | 22.37 (37.27) | 7.13 | 27.44 |
| ISODATA | 21.98 (32.79) | 4.83 | 22.52 (34.63) | 6.04 | 27.68 |
| Mean Shift | 24.87 (30.83) | **4.02** | 23.57 (32.47) | **4.78** | 28.62 |
| Color Histogram | 26.05 (39.17) | 7.44 | 25.24 (39.81) | 7.08 | 32.90 |
| DEM | 25.97 (40.44) | 6.70 | 26.44 (41.21) | 7.46 | 33.29 |
| Random | 32.76 (40.23) | 6.43 | 31.50 (43.64) | 6.43 | 38.56 |

To check how many colors the extracted color themes have in common with the ground truth we adopt the color names mapping defined by the ISCC–NBS system proposed in the 1955 by the Inter-Society Color Council and the National Bureau of Standards (NBS, now NIST) [2]. The system was designed to describe colours in non-technical, everyday terms that anybody could understand. The backbone of the system is based on the following 13 names: Pink, Red, Orange, Brown, Yellow, Olive, Yellow green, Green, Blue, Purple, White, Gray, Black. From these names, other subcategories have been derived and the final number of colors is 267 [7]. This color mapping allows to represent each color theme (also the ground truth) with a set of a limited number of color. In this way it is more likely that two color themes can share the same colors.

## 4.2  Results

Qualitative results are showed in Figs. 1 and 2. The first row of each figure are the test images, the following two rows are the oracle themes r1 (Mechanical Turk) and r2 (Artists) respectively. The remaining 11 rows are the color themes

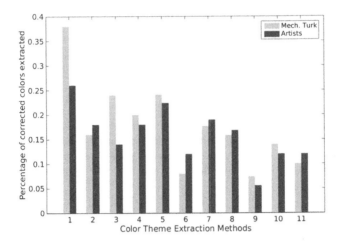

**Fig. 3.** 1-Regression, 2-c-means, 3-k-means1, 4-k-means2, 5-Median Cut, 6-Clarifai, 7-ISODATA, 8-Mean Shift, 9-Color Histogram, 10-DEM, 11-Random. Average percentage of colors in common between the given method and Mechanical Turk or Artists ground truth (light and dark grey respectively). The percentage is the number of colors in common divided by the number of colors extracted by the given method.

extracted using the corresponding methods. The method are sorted in terms of goodness measured through the EMD. It is quite evident also from a visual analysis that the regression method in most of the cases outputs a color theme that is closer to the reference ones than other methods. Clarifai, ISODATA and mean shift found in most of the cases higher colors than 5.

Table 1 shows the quantitative results expressed in terms of EMD between each method and the two reference color palette. For each method it is showed the average over the 10 test images, the maximum distance and the standard deviation. The last column is the sum between the average and the standard deviation of all the distance computed with the two references. The list of the methods are sorted by the minimum distance, that is by similarity to the reference themes. The results show that the regression method is the best performing in terms of similarity with respect to the ground truth. In particular, the regression method is able to produce palette more similar to the Mechanical Turk ground truth than the Artist ground truth. C-means, k-means1 and k-means2 are quite similar both in terms of visual output and similarity with respect to the ground truth. Color histogram, DEM and random themes are the worst with a EMD value much higher than the value achieved by the regression method. Mean shift achieves the standard deviation lower than other methods. It depends mostly on the fact that the size of the generated palette is, on average, larger than the others. They more likely contains more colors of the reference themes than the other methods, that means that the distance between the mean shift themes and the reference themes are quite similar between each other.

The sorting obtained by the EMD metric is similar to the sorting obtained by Lin et al. [21] using a subjective metric. In this paper, the authors asked humans to evaluate how well a set of themes represented the color themes of the test set. The themes compared included the themes extracted by the regression method, ground truth and k-means1. This further demonstrates the goodness of the EMD as metric for color theme goodness evaluation.

Figure 3 shows the percentage of colors that are in common between the 11 methods and the two reference themes. The percentage is computed by dividing the number of colors in common between the two color themes and the length of the color theme computed with the given state-of-the-art method. Bars represent the average behavior across all the test images. This figure confirms that the regression method is the best performing also in terms of number of colors in common with both ground truth. Following this evaluation the worst ones are Clarifai and color histogram. Bad evaluation of Clarifai color themes is influenced by the fact that the size of the themes is often slightly higher than 5. This also happens to the mean shift and ISODATA methods that output more colors than Clarifai and so they have higher probability to match the ground-truth colors.

## 5    Conclusion

In this paper we compared several state-of-the-art methods for color theme extraction from images: supervised, unsupervised and a commercial service. The methods have been evaluated by adopting an objective metric that measures the similarity between user-defined themes and color themes achieved by the methods. The metric is based on the Earth Mover's distance (EMD) that allows to handle the variable size of the color palettes obtained by the methods. The EMD is based on the definition of the ground distance that is the distance between two colors belonging to two different themes. We have adopted the Euclidean distance as ground distance measured in the CIE-Lab color space that models the perceptual dissimilarity between colors better than other color spaces. Results on a test set of 10 images demonstrated that a supervised method based on a regression model trained on a set of user-defined color theme performs better than the other methods although unsupervised clustering methods are also quite good in terms of performance. A comparison between the EMD metric and subjective one adopted in [21] shows that the two metrics are quite similar for color theme goodness evaluation. As a future work, we plan to perform a more extensive evaluation with a larger set of images. More specifically, a direct comparison between the objective metric and a human-based/subjective metric will be carried out. It would be interesting in the future to explore the use of deep learning for color theme extraction [3] and other alternative machine learning approaches [14]. Another aspect that would deserve to be taken into account is how image complexity influences color theme extraction [13].

**Acknowlegment.** The authors wish to thank Marco Verna because part of this work has been developed during his thesis. Published in the context of the projects: FooDesArt - Food Design Arte - L'Arte del Benessere, CUP (Codice Unico Progetto): E48I16000350009 - Call "Smart Fashion and Design", cofunded by POR FESR 2014–2020 (Programma Operativo Regionale, Fondo Europeo di Sviluppo Regionale); E4S: ENERGY FOR SAFETY Sistema integrato per la sicurezza della persona ed il risparmio energetico nelle applicazioni di Home & Building Automation, CUP: E48B17000310009 - Call "Smart Living".

# References

1. Adobe Color CC: Adobe 2017 (2017). https://color.adobe.com
2. Agoston, G.A.: Color Theory and Its Application in Art and Design, vol. 19. Springer, Heidelberg (2013). https://doi.org/10.1007/978-3-540-34734-7
3. Bianco, S., Cadene, R., Celona, L., Napoletano, P.: Benchmark analysis of representative deep neural network architectures. IEEE Access **6**, 64270–64277 (2018)
4. Bianco, S., Ciocca, G.: User preferences modeling and learning for pleasing photo collage generation. ACM Trans. Multimedia Comput. Commun. Appl. (TOMM) **12**(1), 6 (2015)
5. Boccignone, G., Ferraro, M., Napoletano, P.: Diffused expectation maximisation for image segmentation. Electron. Lett. **40**(18), 1 (2004)
6. Boccignone, G., Napoletano, P., Caggiano, V., Ferraro, M.: A multiresolution diffused expectation-maximization algorithm for medical image segmentation. Comput. Biol. Med. **37**(1), 83–96 (2007)
7. Centore, P.: sRGB centroids for the ISCC-NBS colour system. Munsell Colour Sci. Painters (2016)
8. Chang, H., Fried, O., Liu, Y., DiVerdi, S., Finkelstein, A.: Palette-based photo recoloring. ACM Trans. Graph. (TOG) **34**(4), 139 (2015)
9. Cheng, Y.: Mean shift, mode seeking, and clustering. IEEE Trans. Pattern Anal. Mach. Intell. **17**(8), 790–799 (1995)
10. Chuang, J., Stone, M., Hanrahan, P.: A probabilistic model of the categorical association between colors. In: Color and Imaging Conference. vol. 2008, pp. 6–11. Society for Imaging Science and Technology (2008)
11. Colormind: Colormind.io (2018). http://colormind.io/
12. COLOURlovers: Colourlovers (2017). http://www.colourlovers.com
13. Corchs, S., Ciocca, G., Bricolo, E., Gasparini, F.: Predicting complexity perception of real world images. PLoS ONE **11**(6), e0157986 (2016)
14. Cusano, C., Napoletano, P., Schettini, R.: Remote sensing image classification exploiting multiple kernel learning. IEEE Geosci. Remote Sens. Lett. **12**(11), 2331–2335 (2015)
15. Delon, J., Desolneux, A., Lisani, J.L., Petro, A.B.: Automatic color palette. In: IEEE International Conference on 2005 Image Processing, ICIP 2005, vol. 2, pp. II-706. IEEE (2005)
16. Dunn, J.C.: A fuzzy relative of the ISODATA process and its use in detecting compact well-separated clusters. J. Cybern. **3**, 32–57 (1973)
17. Gonzalez, R.C., Woods, R.E., et al.: Digital Image Processing. Prentice Hall, Upper Saddle River (2017)
18. Greenfield, G.R., House, D.H.: Image recoloring induced by palette color associations. J. WSCG **11**, 189–196 (2003)

19. Gudivada, V.N., Raghavan, V.V.: Content based image retrieval systems. Computer **28**(9), 18–22 (1995)
20. Hubel, D.H.: Eye, Brain, and Vision. Scientific American Library/Scientific American Books, New York (1995)
21. Lin, S., Hanrahan, P.: Modeling how people extract color themes from images. In: Proceedings of the SIGCHI Conference on Human Factors in Computing Systems, pp. 3101–3110. ACM (2013)
22. MacQueen, J., et al.: Some methods for classification and analysis of multivariate observations. In: Proceedings of the Fifth Berkeley Symposium on Mathematical Statistics and Probability, Oakland, CA, USA, vol. 1, pp. 281–297 (1967)
23. Meier, B.J., Spalter, A.M., Karelitz, D.B.: Interactive color palette tools. IEEE Comput. Graph. Appl. **3**, 64–72 (2004)
24. Mellado, N., Vanderhaeghe, D., Hoarau, C., Christophe, S., Brédif, M., Barthe, L.: Constrained palette-space exploration. ACM Trans. Graph. (TOG) **36**(4), 60 (2017)
25. Napoletano, P.: Hand-crafted vs learned descriptors for color texture classification. In: Bianco, S., Schettini, R., Trémeau, A., Tominaga, S. (eds.) CCIW 2017. LNCS, vol. 10213, pp. 259–271. Springer, Cham (2017). https://doi.org/10.1007/978-3-319-56010-6_22
26. Obrador, P.: Automatic color scheme picker for document templates based on image analysis and dual problem. In: Digital Publishing, vol. 6076, p. 607609. International Society for Optics and Photonics (2006)
27. O'Donovan, P., Agarwala, A., Hertzmann, A.: Color compatibility from large datasets. ACM Trans. Graph. (TOG) **30**, 63 (2011)
28. Rubner, Y., Tomasi, C.: The earth mover-distance. Perceptual Metrics for Image Database Navigation. The Springer International Series in Engineering and Computer Science (Robotics: Vision, Manipulation and Sensors), vol. 594, pp. 13–28. Springer, Boston (2001). https://doi.org/10.1007/978-1-4757-3343-3_2
29. Rubner, Y., Tomasi, C., Guibas, L.J.: The earth mover's distance as a metric for image retrieval. Int. J. Comput. Vis. **40**(2), 99–121 (2000)
30. Battiato, S., Ciocca, G., Gasparini, F., Puglisi, G., Schettini, R.: Smart photo sticking. In: Boujemaa, N., Detyniecki, M., Nürnberger, A. (eds.) AMR 2007. LNCS, vol. 4918, pp. 211–223. Springer, Heidelberg (2008). https://doi.org/10.1007/978-3-540-79860-6_17
31. Shugrina, M., Kar, A., Singh, K., Fidler, S.: Color sails: discrete-continuous palettes for deep color exploration. arXiv preprint arXiv:1806.02918 (2018)
32. Walch, M., Hope, A.: Living Colors: The Definitive Guide to Color Palettes Through the Ages. Chronicle Books, San Francisco (1995)
33. Wang, B., Yu, Y., Wong, T.T., Chen, C., Xu, Y.O.: Data-driven image color theme enhancement. ACM Trans. Graph. (TOG) **29**, 146 (2010)
34. Weeks, A.R., Hague, G.E.: Color segmentation in the HSI color space using the k-means algorithm. In: Nonlinear Image Processing VIII, vol. 3026, pp. 143–155. International Society for Optics and Photonics (1997)
35. Wong, K.M., Chey, C.H., Liu, T.S., Po, L.M.: Dominant color image retrieval using merged histogram. In: Proceedings of the 2003 International Symposium on Circuits and Systems, 2003 ISCAS 2003, vol. 2, p. II. IEEE (2003)
36. Wyszecki, G., Stiles, W.S.: Color Science, vol. 8. Wiley, New York (1982)

# Long-Term Face Image Analysis Based on Canonical Correlation Analysis on Physical and Psychological Evaluation of Face

Ikumi Nomura[1]($\boxtimes$), Yuri Tatsuzawa[1], Nobutoshi Ojima[2],
Takeo Imai[2], Keiko Ogawa[3], and Norimichi Tsumura[1]

[1] Graduate School of Science and Engineering, Chiba University, Chiba, Japan
`tsumura@faculty.chiba-u.jp`
[2] Skin Care Products Research, Kao Corporation, Kanagawa, Japan
[3] Department of Japanese-Traditional (Kampo) Medicine,
Kanazawa University Hospital, Ishikawa, Japan

**Abstract.** In this paper, we analyze the relationship between impression of facial skin and skin pigmentation distribution by applying Canonical Coefficient Analysis (CCA) to multiple physical and psychological features obtained from facial skin. Based on the acquired relationship expression, we modulate the skin pigment features, and appearances of the face with arbitrary psychological features are reproduced. In our previous work, we applied principal component analysis (PCA) to the melanin pigment variation of the facial skin, and we obtained individual differences in it occurring over seven years. In the previous method, as the factor causing individual difference, we considered the frequency of UV care. However, actual skin appearance is thought to depend not only on melanin but also on several other factors. Therefore, in this study, we photographed the faces of women of various ages for 12 years, and at the same time obtained psychological features of appearance. As physical features, melanin and hemoglobin pigmentation distributions, shading and the frequency of UV care for 12 years were obtained. Subjective evaluation values were acquired as psychological features. As a result of CCA, it was found that the whole face can be made lighter in appearance by using UV protection every day continuously for six years or more.

**Keywords:** Face image · Canonical correlation analysis · UV protection · Skin color · Beauty

## 1 Introduction

Human face is the most watched part in the human body. We obtain many information from face, which are divided into two kinds of feature values. One is called "physical features" such as skin condition or facial structure, and the other is called "psychological features" such as health condition or appearance of age. Facial appearance depends on these two features largely.

---

A part of this paper will be published in Journal of Imaging Science and Technology.

© Springer Nature Switzerland AG 2019
S. Tominaga et al. (Eds.): CCIW 2019, LNCS 11418, pp. 180–194, 2019.
https://doi.org/10.1007/978-3-030-13940-7_14

People, especially, women have a strong interest in their appearance of face or skin. In the beauty industry, therefore, many kinds of cosmetics have been developed for improving appearance, and it is expected to practically predict the effect of cosmetics. For example, we are able to simulate face with makeup by web applications [1]. This system enable to predict the effect of cosmetics anytime, anywhere at low cost and promote sales of cosmetics.

Moreover, there is a lot of research on simulation of facial appearance in recent years. For example, PCA makes it easier to obtain feature values. Lantis *et al.* provided a framework for simulation of aging effects on facial image. By applying PCA to facial landmarks, they simulated facial structure in any age based on classification of age [2]. Suo *et al.* also predicted appearance of face for the long period by changing parts of face for the short period based on result of applying PCA to facial image database divided by parts or ages [3]. However, individual differences were not considered in this method.

As described above, by using PCA, we are able to obtain facial feature values relatively easily from information such as facial structure and skin texture. Most of these researches directly analyze grayscale or RGB images. However, RGB color images don't consider layer structures for skin properly, because color characteristics change depending on the device. For this reason, it is thought that we can analyze for face or skin more effectively by taking into account melanin and hemoglobin colors which is main components of skin color. Tsumura *et al.* proposed the technique to extract pigmentation distribution of melanin and hemoglobin from a single skin color image by applying independent component analysis (ICA) [4, 5]. Melanin and hemoglobin color can be obtained regardless of light sources or characteristics of camera by ICA in their method.

Toyota *et al.* analyzed pigmentation distribution in whole face. Toyota *et al.* obtained feature values of skin pigmentation in whole face by ICA and PCA and simulated appearance of face having arbitrary psychological features [6]. This method can perform to synthesize appearance of face considering the changes of the age. However, as a result of a subjective evaluation experiment by experts, there was large difference between age of synthesized images and evaluated results. For this reason, Hirose *et al.* analyze variation of facial landmarks representing facial structure and surface reflection component representing wrinkles and pores in addition to skin pigmentation distribution by PCA and Multiple Regression Analysis (MRA) [7]. They succeeded to reduce the age difference of synthesized image and real images. Since this simulation is based on changing averaged features in the database with the same age, each synthesized image lost the individual characters. However, the actual aging depends on individuals, and it is expected to predict the appearance of face by considering the individual characters. Therefore, in a previous study, the frequency of UV protection is considered as a factor that causes individual differences in skin color change. [8]. PCA was applied to melanin pigment components extracted from face image changes of same people for 7 years. As a result of comparing melanin principal component score changes of each person, it was found that whole facial skin and skin around cheeks of those who don't use UV protection tend to increase melanin pigment compared with those who use it every day for 7 years. However, it seems that the appearance of the skin is influenced not only by melanin but also by several factors.

In this paper, therefore, CCA is applied to multiple physical and psychological features, and the relationship between skin appearance and facial skin pigment is analyzed. Specifically, first of all, CCA is applied to physical features. In a previous study [8], only melanin pigment was analyzed, but in this study, we perform CCA on the multiple skin pigmentary changes for 12 years and the frequency of UV protection for 12 years. By doing this, we analyze the influence of frequency of UV protection of each year on skin pigment changes for 12 years. Next, in order to realize face simulator, CCA is performed on features of skin pigment which are physical features and the subjective evaluation value of skin which are psychological features. Thus, a relational expression between physical features and psychological features can be derived. By modulating the physical features based on this relational expression, reproductions of facial appearance in arbitrary psychological features are performed.

## 2    Construction of Facial Image Database

The database is consisted of facial images, real age, and the frequency of UV protection. First of all, Japanese women whose age were from 10 s to 80 s are photographed in 2003 and 2015. The number of subjects was 86 in 2003 and 161 in 2015, in total, 247 facial images. Note that 60 women were the same person. Breakdown of the number of subjects and distribution of age in the database are shown in Fig. 1.

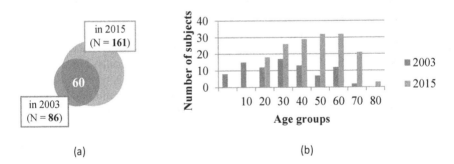

(a)                                         (b)

**Fig. 1.** Breakdown and Distribution of age of the database: (a) Breakdown of the number of subjects, (b) Distribution of age in the database

These photographs were taken in imaging system shown in Fig. 2. This imaging system was surrounded by blackout curtains in order to eliminate the effect of ambient light. As the light source, there were four fluorescent lights so that the lights surrounded the camera as shown in Fig. 2.

 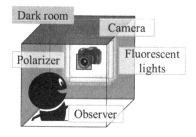

**Fig. 2.** Overview of imaging system

The cameras, NikonD1 and NikonD2H were used; the former was used in 2003 and the latter in 2015. In order to prevent shaking of face, we used the support for neck and head which was fixed on backrest of chair. We obtained facial image without specular reflectance by arranging polarization filters in front of the camera and the light sources mutually perpendicularly. There was difference in color tone between images taken in 2003 and those in 2015 due to using different camera. For this reason, we matched color tone of images taken in 2003 with those in 2015 by MRA.

Figure 3 shows a sample of the captured facial image. These captured facial images were required to be normalized in order to remove influence caused by variation of individual facial shapes on applying PCA accurately to images later.

**Fig. 3.** Sample of captured image

For this reason, we used FUTON (Foolproof UTilities for facial image manipulatiON system), which was facial image synthesis system developed by Mukaida *et al.* [9]. First, we obtained facial landmarks representing facial structure and extracted facial areas from captured facial images. Second, we morphed shape of facial images into an image of an average face which was made from facial images in database. As a result, we obtained normalized facial images while keeping individual skin texture information. The overview of this process is shown in Fig. 4.

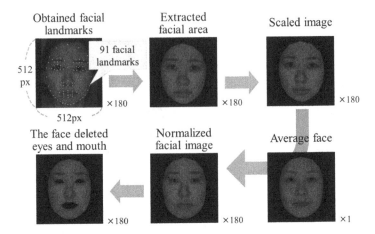

**Fig. 4.** Overview of normalization process for facial images (Each number in the lower right shows the number of images; the average face image is only one).

## 3 Acquisition of Features

This section shows how to acquire both physical and psychological features. In this paper, frequency of UV protection and skin pigmentation distributions are defined as physical features. While a subjective evaluation value for a skin image described later is defined as a psychological features.

### 3.1 Frequency of UV Protection

Frequency of UV protection was obtained by three-tiered evaluation (1: Never, 2: Sometimes, 3: Daily) in winter of 2003 and 2010, and six-tiered evaluation (1: Daily in the last five years, 2: Daily in summer for the last five years, not in winter, 3: Used period is longer than unused period in the last five years, 4: Used period is shorter than unused period in the last five years, 5: Rarely in the last five years, 6: Others) in 2015. Figure 5 shows age distribution of frequency of UV protection in database.

### 3.2 Skin Pigmentation Distribution

#### 3.2.1 Extraction of Skin Pigmentation by ICA

Skin structure can be broadly divided into epidermis where melanin pigment exist and dermis where hemoglobin pigment exist. Assuming that skin color depends on these 2 kinds of pigmentation density, the skin color vector can be represented by three vectors as shown in Fig. 6: melanin, hemoglobin, and shading, by using ICA and modified Lambert-Beer's rule [4, 5].

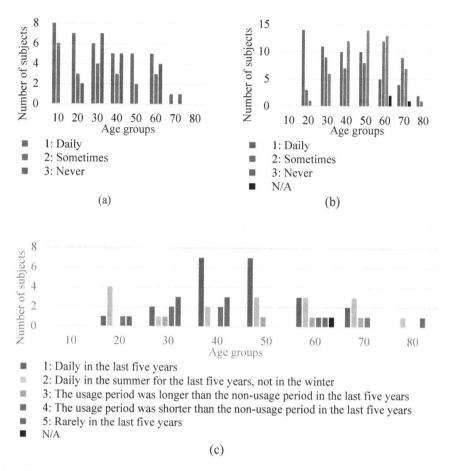

**Fig. 5.** Age distribution of use frequency of UV protection: (a) in 2003, (b) in 2015 (Regrouped), (c) in 2015 (Original)

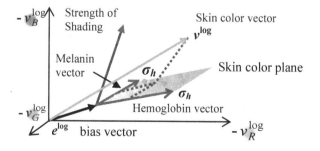

**Fig. 6.** Overview of independent component analysis

Figure 7(a) and (b) show a sample of the extracted melanin and hemoglobin pigmentations, and (c) shows the shading in the whole facial image. As you can see in Fig. 7(a), the mole and pigmented spot can be obtained as melanin component. The redness caused by pimples can be seen in Fig. 7(b), and the shadow caused by uneven facial features can be recognized in Fig. 7(c). In this study, we obtained melanin and hemoglobin pigmentation and shading components of facial skin by this method.

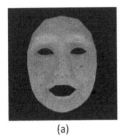 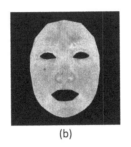 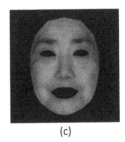

(a)                    (b)                    (c)

**Fig. 7.** The results of independent component analysis for extraction of pigmentation components: (a) melanin, (b) hemoglobin, (c) shading

### 3.2.2 Acquiring Skin Pigmentation Features by PCA

We obtained feature values of uneven pigmentations by applying PCA to melanin, hemoglobin, shading components of 247 facial images extracted in Sect. 3.2.1. PCA is a statistical method to grasp a tendency and features of data by multivariate analysis. This analysis calculates the linear sum of each variable in data group constructed from any variable, and defines a new index as the first component. The second component is defined in such a way that is perpendicular to the first component, and other components are defined similarly. The n-dimensional $l$-th vector in dataset can be represented as the approximated vector as follows:

$$\hat{x}_i\left(x_{i,1}, x_{i,2}, \cdots, x_{i,n}\right) = \sum_{m=1}^{M} w_{i,m} P_m \tag{1}$$

where $n$ is the total number of pixels; $512 \times 512$. $x_i$ means an image represents each pixel as $x_{i,1}, x_{i,2}, \cdots, x_{i,n}$, as shown in Fig. 8. $M$ is the total number of principal components, and the $m$-th principal component vector is defined as $P_m$. The principal component score $w_{i,m}$ is the weight of the $P_m$, in the image $\hat{x}_i$.

We applied PCA to melanin, hemoglobin, shading components whose size were $512 \times 512$ pixels. In this paper, we regarded one pixel as one variable. That is, 247 women's melanin, hemoglobin, shading components existed in $512 \times 512$-dimensional space respectively. As a result of PCA, we obtained 246 principal components for each skin pigmentation components.

For example, if you compare the principal component scores of the same person between 2003 and 2015, you can obtain how the skin pigment components of that person changed in 12 years. Also, by comparing the principal component scores with different people, individual differences in skin pigment components can be obtained. In this study, principal component score were used as physical features representing skin pigment.

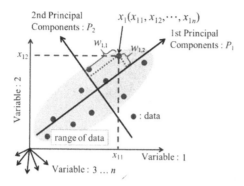

**Fig. 8.** Overview of principal component analysis ($n$ = number of pixels in the image; other variables as defined in the text).

### 3.3 Subjective Evaluation Value of Skin

Subjective evaluation experiments of skin were performed on face images taken in 2015. Three experts determined the evaluation value of the total of 8 items: a kind of spots (on the whole face), 4 kinds of wrinkles (on forehead, corners of the eyes, under the eyes, and nasolabial grooves), and 3 kinds of sagging (on whole face, under the eyes, and corners of mouth). They evaluated the above 8 items in 4 grades for each facial photograph, compared to a photo scale showing stepwise the degree of wrinkles and sagging. In this study, each average values of evaluation values were used for analysis as psychological features.

## 4   CCA for Multiple Features

In this section, we explain the method of CCA and the results of CCA on physical and psychological features.

### 4.1   The Method of CCA

CCA is a method of analyzing the relationship between multivariables by combining variables so that the correlation coefficients between the two variable groups is high. Let us consider the case where there are variable group $X = \{X_1, ..., X_p\}$ and variable group $Y = \{Y_1, ..., Y_q\}$, $(p < q)$. The canonical coefficients $A$ and $B$ which are weights are set and synthesized so that the correlation coefficient $R$ of the weighted linear sum

$U$ of the variable group $X$ and the weighted linear sum $V$ of the variable group $Y$ becomes maximum. Interpretation of a canonical variable is performed by analyzing canonical loading which is a correlation coefficient between each variable constituting a variable group and a canonical variable. The overview of canonical correlation analysis is shown in Fig. 9.

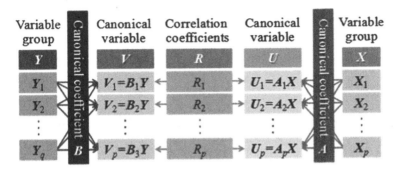

**Fig. 9.** Overview of canonical correlation analysis

### 4.2    CCA on Physical Features

In order to analyze the relationship between multiple skin pigments and frequency of UV protection in each year, CCA was performed among physical features. Specifically, the differences between the principal component scores of 2003 and 2015 of 1st ~ 8th principal components of melanin and 1st ~ 15th principal components of hemoglobin and shading, total of 38 variables were set as the variable group $X$. As the variable group $Y$, frequency of UV protection of 2003, 2010, and 2015, total of 3 variables were set. As a result of CCA on these, the 1st canonical variables $V_1$ and $U_1$ became significant. Here, $V_1$ represents the 1st canonical variable of the variable group $Y$, and $U_1$ represents the 1st canonical variable of the variable group $X$. Tables 1 and 2 shows canonical loadings of $V_1$, $U_1$.

The PC in Table 2 represents the principal component. From Table 1, $V_1$ has the largest negative correlation with the frequency of UV protection of 2003, has the next largest correlation with that of 2010, and has no correlation with that of 2015. That is, $V_1$ is the value that increases as the person who didn't use UV protection in the past. On the other hand, from Table 2, $U_1$ has positive correlation with variation of melanin pigment of whole face, cheeks, and forehead, and hemoglobin pigment of forehead and around eyes. That is, $U_1$ becomes larger as these components increase. Therefore, taken together, it can be said that the less frequencies of UV protection in 2003 and 2015 are, the more increase the amounts of melanin in the whole face, cheeks, and forehead, and hemoglobin of forehead and around eyes in 12 years. Actual 12-year changes of normalized face images whose $V_1$ are smallest and largest are shown in Fig. 10.

**Table 1.** Canonical loading of $V_1$

| Frequency of UV protection | | |
| --- | --- | --- |
| In 2003 | In 2010 | In 2015 |
| −0.855 | −0.694 | 0.005 |

**Table 2.** Canonical loading of $U_1$

| Melanin | | | Hemoglobin |
| --- | --- | --- | --- |
| 1st PC | 2nd PC | 3rd PC | 3rd PC |
| 0.2 | 0.2 | 0.3 | 0.3 |

From Fig. 10(a) and (b), those who had a high frequency of UV protection in 2003 and 2010 could brightened the whole face 12 years later. In contrast, from Fig. 10(c) and (d), those who had low frequency of UV protection in 2003 and 2010, as you can see, the whole face and cheeks had changed darkly in 12 years. Therefore, it seems necessary to use UV protection everyday for more than 6 years in order to keep beautiful skin.

### 4.3 CCA on Physical and Psychological Features

In order to reproduce the appearance of face, CCA was performed on psychological features and physical features. Specifically, subjective evaluation values for 1 spot, 4 wrinkles, 3 sags, 8 variables in total were set as variable group $Y$. As variable group $X$,

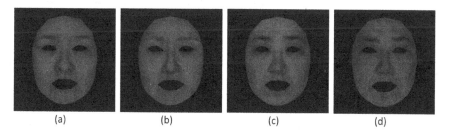

(a)                (b)                (c)                (d)

**Fig. 10.** Actual 12-year changes of normalized face images whose $V_1$ is: (a) smallest (taken in 2003), (b) smallest (taken in 2015), (c) largest (taken in 2003), (d) largest (taken in 2015)

principal component scores in 2015 of 1st ~ 8th principal components of melanin and the 1st ~ 15th principal components of hemoglobin and shading, total of 38 variables were set. As a result of CCA on these, 1st, 2nd and 3rd canonical variables became significant. The canonical correlation coefficients of 1st, 2nd and 3rd canonical variables were 0.93, 0.67 and 0.60. Let V be canonical variable of variable group $Y$, and $U$ canonical variable of variable group $X$. Tables 3 and 4 show particularly large canonical loadings of the 1st canonical variables $V_1$ and $U_1$. From Table 3, $V_1$ has a high positive correlation with spots, wrinkles, and sagging. That is, the more conspicuous a person's spots, wrinkles and sag in her facial skin are, the larger $V_1$ is. On the other hand, from Table 4, $U_1$ has a positive correlation with melanin pigment of cheeks and whole face, and shading of the nasolabial folds. That is, the stronger these pigment components are, the larger $U_1$ is. Canonical correlation coefficient $V_1$ and $U_1$ is 0.93. Therefore, it can be said that melanin of cheeks and shading of whole face and nasolabial lines are darker for people whose spots, wrinkles and sags are conspicuous.

**Table 3.** Canonical loading of $V_1$

| Subjective evaluation value of skin | | |
|---|---|---|
| Age spots on whole face | Sagging on whole face | Wrinkles on the corners of the eyes |
| 0.76 | 0.96 | 0.91 |

**Table 4.** Canonical loading of $U_1$

| Melanin | Shading | |
|---|---|---|
| 2nd PC | 1st PC | 6th PC |
| | | |
| 0.8 | 0.5 | 0.4 |

Next, Tables 5 and 6 show particularly large canonical loadings of the 2nd canonical variables $V_2$ and $U_2$. From Table 5, $V_2$ has a positive correlation with spots on whole face and a negative correlation with sagging on mouth corners. Thus, the more conspicuous a person's spots on whole face are but the less conspicuous a person's sagging of mouth corners are, the larger $V_2$ is, while, the more conspicuous a person's sagging of mouth corners are but the less conspicuous a person's spots on whole face are, the smaller $V_2$ is. On the other hand, from Table 6, $U_2$ has a positive correlation with melanin around eyes, nose ridge and cheeks, and hemoglobin of nose and cheeks. $U_2$ also has a negative correlation with melanin in whole face. This means the stronger melanin pigment around eyes, nose ridge and cheeks, and hemoglobin of nose and cheeks are, the larger $U_2$ is, while the stronger melanin pigment in whole face is, the smaller $U_2$ is. Canonical correlation coefficient of $V_2$ and $U_2$ is 0.67. Therefore, it can be said that people with conspicuous spots have strong melanin around eyes, nose ridge and cheeks, and hemoglobin of nose and cheeks, while people with conspicuous sagging on mouth corners have strong melanin in whole face.

**Table 5.** Canonical loading of $V_2$

| Subjective evaluation value of skin | |
|---|---|
| Age spots on whole face | Sagging on mouth corners |
| 0.62 | −0.30 |

**Table 6.** Canonical loading of $U_2$

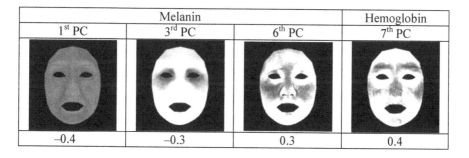

| Melanin | | | Hemoglobin |
|---|---|---|---|
| 1$^{st}$ PC | 3$^{rd}$ PC | 6$^{th}$ PC | 7$^{th}$ PC |
| −0.4 | −0.3 | 0.3 | 0.4 |

Similarly, let us consider the 3rd canonical variables. Tables 7 and 8 show particularly large canonical loadings of the 3rd canonical variables $V_3$ and $U_3$. As shown in Table 7, $V_3$ has a positive correlation with wrinkles on corners of eyes and a negative correlation with sag on mouth corners. On the other hand, from Table 8, $U_3$ has a positive correlation with hemoglobin around nose and cheeks, and shading around eyebrows and eyes, and a negative correlation with melanin of nose ridge. Canonical correlation coefficient of $V_3$ and $U_3$ is 0.60. Therefore, it can be said that people with conspicuous winkles on corners of the eyes have red cheeks and nose and strong shading eyebrows and eyes, while people with conspicuous sagging on mouth corners have strong melanin of nose ridge. In this way, by CCA on physical features and psychological features, skin pigment distribution corresponding to the subjective evaluation value of the skin could be acquired.

**Table 7.** Canonical loading of $V_3$

| Subjective evaluation value of skin | |
|---|---|
| Wrinkles on corners of the eyes | Sagging on corners of mouth |
| 0.38 | −0.21 |

**Table 8.** Canonical loading of $U_3$

| Melanin | Hemoglobin | | Shading |
|---|---|---|---|
| 8th PC | 6th PC | 7th PC | 2nd PC |
| | | | |
| −0.3 | −0.4 | 0.3 | 0.3 |

## 5    Reproduction of Face in Arbitrary Psychological Features

From the results of CCA shown in Sect. 4.3, the following relational expression is established.

$$\left(A^{\mathrm{T}}\right)^+ \cdot diag([R_1, R_2, \cdots, R_7, R_8]) \cdot V^{\mathrm{T}} = X^{\mathrm{T}} \tag{2}$$

Here, $A$ represents canonical coefficient for variable group $X$, $R$ represents canonical correlation coefficient, $V$ represents canonical variable of variable group $Y$, *diag* represents a diagonal matrix, + represents a pseudo inverse matrix, and T represents a transposed matrix. From Eq. (2), we obtained principal component score $X$, and reproduced appearances of face in arbitrary $V_1$, $V_2$, $V_3$. The results reproduced so that $V_1$, $V_2$, and $V_3$ are minimum and maximum are shown in Fig. 11. Reproduced images are emphasized by doubling the actual principal component score change in order to make them easy to see. In Fig. 11(a), color unevenness of the whole face is small, but in Fig. 11(b), cheeks are dark, shadows of the corners of mouth and wrinkles of the corners of the eyes are conspicuous. Also, in Fig. 11(c), cheeks are whitish and there are sag in the corners of mouth, whereas in Fig. 11(d), cheeks are dark and the sagging of the corners of mouth are less noticeable than in Fig. 11(c). From Fig. 11(e), shading of corners of the mouth is dark. While Fig. 11(f) shows darker eyebrows and stronger wrinkles of corner of the eyes than that of Fig. 11(e). From the above, as a result of modulating the pigment distribution based on the results of CCA, we could reproduce the appearance of the skin almost similar to the examination.

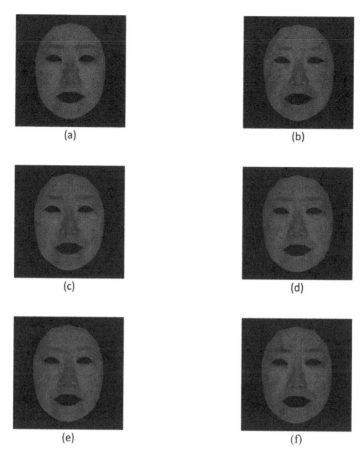

**Fig. 11.** The results of the appearance of a face in arbitrary psychological features: (a) $V_1$ is smallest, (b) $V_1$ is largest, (c) $V_2$ is smallest, (d) $V_2$ is largest, (e) $V_3$ is smallest, (f) $V_3$ is largest

## 6   Conclusion

In this study, CCA was performed on multiple physical and psychological features, and the relation between skin appearance and skin pigment distribution was analyzed. As a result of CCA on physical features, skin pigment distribution affected by frequency of UV protection was acquired. From this, it is thought that beauty of the skin can be maintained by performing UV care everyday continuously for more than 6 years. In addition, as a result of CCA for physical features and psychological features, principal components of skin pigment which greatly affects the appearance of the skin was acquired. Furthermore, based on this result, physical features were modulated, and appearances of the face in arbitrary psychological features were reproduced. In the future, we will examine the estimation formula for reproducing the appearance of the face, and improve reproduction of appearance of the face.

**Acknowledgement.** This research is partly supported by JSPS Grants-in-Aid for Scientific Research (24560040).

# References

1. Application of make-up for smart phone. https://www.perfectcorp.com/app/ymk. Accessed 28 Dec
2. Lantis, A., et al.: Toward automatic simulation of aging effects on face images. IEEE Trans. Patt. Anal. Mach. Intell. **24**(4), 442–455 (2002)
3. Suo, J., Chen, X., et al.: A concatenational graph evolution aging model. IEEE Trans. Patt. Anal. Mach. Intell. **34**(11), 2083–2096 (2012)
4. Tsumura, N., Haneishi, H., Miyake, Y.: Independent component analysis of skin color image. J. Opt. Soc. Am. A **16**(9), 2169–2176 (1999)
5. Tsumura, N., Ojima, N., et al.: Image-based skin color and texture analysis/synthesis by extracting hemoglobin and melanin information in the skin. ACM Trans. Graph. (TOG) **22**, 770–779 (2003)
6. Toyota, S., Fujiwara, I., et al.: Principal component analysis for pigmentation distribution in whole facial image and prediction of the facial image in various ages. In: Color and Imaging Conference, Albuquerque, New Mexico (2013)
7. Hirose, M., Toyota, S., et al.: Principal component analysis for surface reflection components and structure in facial images and synthesis of facial images for various ages. Opt. Rev. **24**(4), 517–528 (2017)
8. Nomura, I., Tatsuzawa, Y., et al.: Analysis of melanin pigment changes in long terms for face of various ages: a case study on the UV care frequency. In: International Conference on Image and Signal Processing, pp. 534–544 (2018)
9. Mukaida, S., Kamachi, M., et al.: Facial image synthesis system: futon - evaluation as tools for cognitive research on face processing. IEICE Trans. Fundam. **J85A**(10), 1126–1137 (2002). (in Japanese)

# A Novel Digital-Camera Characterization Method for Pigment Identification in Cultural Heritage

Emanuela Manfredi[1(✉)], Giovanni Petrillo[1], and Silvana Dellepiane[2]

[1] Department of Chemistry and Industrial Chemistry,
Università degli Studi di Genova, via Dodecaneso 31, 16146 Genoa, Italy
emanuela861@outlook.it, giovanni.petrillo@unige.it
[2] Department of Electrical, Electronics and Telecommunication Engineering
and Naval Architecture, Università degli Studi di Genova,
via All'Opera Pia 11A, 16145 Genoa, Italy
silvana.dellepiane@unige.it

**Abstract.** Color represents a primary feature in the field of Art and Cultural Heritage, which can also be of help in defining the conservation state of an artwork. The color identification by means of a digital camera represents a non-destructive methodology which makes use of a non-expensive and portable device and enables a spatial analysis which is not allowed to a colorimeter. The present study compares an original method for camera characterization with two approaches reported in the literature. The comparison is based on parameters such as the Pearson correlation coefficient and the $\Delta E_{00}$ colorimetric difference, computed according to the CIEDE2000 formula. The data sets used for both the "training" and the "validation" processes are *(a)* the 24 tiles of the Color Checker Passport Photo X-Rite color scale and *(b)* 30 samples of oil painting laid down on a canvas prepared according to the indications of Giorgio Vasari in his renowned "*Le vite*". The data so far available clearly show that our original method leads to results which are similar or better than those furnished by the literature methods.

**Keywords:** Calibration · Camera characterization · Colorimeter ·
Color identification

## 1 Introduction

Color is one of the most important properties of artworks, and color changes provide an indication of an art object's age and conservation state. As a consequence, the monitoring of color changes with time is a useful preventive diagnostic tool for Cultural Heritage preservation. A color change is usually quantified by dedicated color measuring devices, such as colorimeters and spectrophotometers, and analyzed in a device-independent color space as CIE L*a*b* [1,2]. The artwork surface analyzed by common devices is a point area, and thus measurement of heterogeneous and large surfaces provides non-homogeneous values; this limitation can be overcome with the

© Springer Nature Switzerland AG 2019
S. Tominaga et al. (Eds.): CCIW 2019, LNCS 11418, pp. 195–206, 2019.
https://doi.org/10.1007/978-3-030-13940-7_15

use of a digital camera, *i.e.,* a device acquiring color information over a much wider surface, only limited by the illumination area [3]. Moreover, a digital camera is less expensive than a dedicated color-measuring spectrophotometric device.

A major problem when using a digital camera for measuring color is that consumer-level sensors (of either CCD or Cmos type) are typically uncalibrated. As a consequence, even though the raw camera output is declared to be converted in sRGB representation, it is not color-accurate according to sRGB standard definition. In order to face this problem a color calibration algorithm is then required to transform color digital values into L*a*b* values in agreement with spectrophotometric measures.

Leon *et al.* [4] have considered different calibration algorithms, *viz.* *(a)* linear and quadratic models for L*a*b* regression starting from RGB values, and *(b)* a direct model where RGB values are transformed into XYZ values, in turn used to derive L*a*b* values, *(c)* a gamma model which linearizes sRGB data before applying method *b* (transformation into XYZ values and then calculation of L*a*b* values) and *(d)* a "neural network" predicting L*a*b* values from RGB ones. Cheung *et al.* [5] have considered the gamma correction approach to calibrate digital photos, evaluating three different techniques for the linearization of sRGB values: spectral sensitivities, luminance and mean reflectance.

The aim of the present study is to compare the two most effective camera calibration methods among those outlined above (*i.e.,* the regression method and the approach with gamma correction preceding linearization) with an original method we have specifically designed and implemented.

## 2   Materials and Approaches

Three methods have been tested and compared with the purpose of achieving the best calibration of camera pictures, taking colorimetric measurements as reference values.

They are all *supervised* methods, what means that the setting of the calibration parameters is optimized according to a training set, where each digital-camera image is labelled with the reference color parameters obtained with the colorimeter.

Comparison of methods performance is based on the error computed when applying each method to the samples of the training set (to evaluate precision) or to a validation set (to evaluate robustness).

### 2.1   Materials

The *training set* and the *validation set* are made of color samples (see Figs. 1 and 2 below), each measured with both the colorimeter and the camera.

**X-Rite ColorChecker Passport Photo** is a photographic color scale made of 24 tiles for maintaining uniformity and color control in digital photography. Along with color patterns, it also contains gray patches shading from white to black.

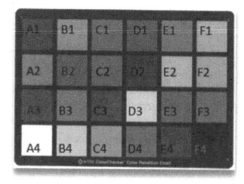

**Fig. 1.** The ColorChecker Passport Photo X-Rite.

**Oil Painting Samples.** A linen canvas has been purposely prepared according to the indications provided by the Italian painter, architect and art historian Giorgio Vasari in his renowned historiographical text *"Le Vite"* [6]. Accordingly, the linen texture was treated with a few layers of rabbit glue, a layer of dough (made of walnut oil and flour), further three layers of rabbit glue, to reach a homogeneous uniform thickness on the linen surface, and finally with the preparatory layer, *i.e.* a mix of linseed oil, white lead [*biacca*: $(PbCO_3)_2 \cdot Pb(OH)_2$] and different ochres [mixed Fe(II) and Fe(III) oxides, generally in presence of Mn(IV), Al(III) and Si(IV) oxides, with different amounts of hydration water molecules]; once the preparatory layer dried, thirty color samples were laid down with the oil painting technique, using different pigments (mainly ochres), each pigment dispersion being prepared in 3 or 4 different w/w compositions. The pigments were: *ombra naturale, ombra bruciata, terra di Siena naturale, terra di Siena bruciata,* white lead, malachite, cinnabar and a pink pigment (obtained by mixing white lead and cinnabar). The color measurements on the paint samples were repeated monthly, with both the spectrophotometer and the camera.

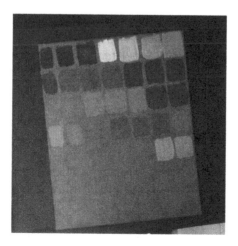

**Fig. 2.** The 30 oil-painting samples on a linen canvas.

## 2.2  Data and Image Acquisition Tools

The data were acquired with both a colorimeter and a digital camera, the Matlab and Excel softwares being used for the mathematical treatment.

**Colorimeter.** Reference measurements were made by the Konica Minolta CM2600d spectrophotometer, a handheld, portable instrument designed to estimate the color parameters. The settings are summarized in Table 1.

**Table 1.**  Colorimeter setup.

| Variable | Value |
|----------|-------|
| Standard observer | 10° |
| Illuminant | D65 |
| Acquisition | SCI |

**Digital Camera.** The digital images were taken with the following image acquisition system:

- A Panasonic Lumix DMC-FZ200 camera was placed vertically at 46.5 cm from the samples. The angle between the axis of the lens and the sources of illumination was approximately 45°.
- Illumination was achieved with 2 OSRAM, Natural Daylight 23 W fluorescent lights, color temperature 6500 K.
- The photos were shot in a dark room.
- The settings of the camera are summarized in Table 2.

**Table 2.**  Camera setup.

| Variable | Value |
|----------|-------|
| Focal distance | 4 mm |
| Flash | Off |
| Iso velocity | 400 |
| White balance | reference D65 |
| Operation mode | Manual |
| Exposure time | 1/60 s |
| Quality | Raw |
| Number f | 3.2 |

## 2.3  Training and Validation Sets

The *training set* consisted of the 24 tiles of the X-Rite ColorChecker Passport Photo, on one side (reference set), and of the 30 painting samples on canvas on the other side; the data (colorimetric measurements and digital-camera acquisitions) were collected in March 2018.

The *validation set* is represented herein by the painting samples on canvas measured with the colorimeter and acquired with the camera in April 2018.

The colorimetric (Konica Minolta CM2600d) value of each painting sample is the average of 5 spot areas and refers to the device-independent L*a*b* space. Likewise, the colorimetric value of each tile of the X-Rite scale is the average of 4 spot areas.

The color measurements taken with the digital camera refer to the sRGB values of the digital image. In this case, the color value of each sample (either the X-Rite tile or the canvas paint samples) is the average of 5 different areas of $16 \times 16$ pixels for each of 9 successive camera acquisitions.

## 3 Calibration Methods

The main purpose of the methods is to estimate the transformation from the camera output given in sRGB space to the L*a*b* space which minimizes the error with respect to the colorimetric L*a*b* values.

### Method 1: Matrix-Based Method Through Polynomial Modelling

According to Hong et al. [7] and to Johnson [8], the most appropriate transformation from the sRGB space to the L*a*b* space requires a polynomial regression with least-squares fitting.

The applied polynomial, $P_{[11]}$, is as follows:

$$P_{[11]} = \begin{bmatrix} R & G & B & RG & RB & GB & R^2 & G^2 & B^2 & RGB & 1 \end{bmatrix}$$

The best matrix is estimated through the pseudo-inverse methodology by using the training set values; R, G, and B refer to the color channels as acquired by the camera on the training set; the target values are the $L_s$, $a_s$, $b_s$ values read by the spectrophotometer on the same training set.

Once the matrix elements are estimated, the transformation is applied independently to the training set and the validation set thus obtaining the calibrated values $L_c$, $a_c$, $b_c$.

### Method 2: Method Based on the Gamma-Correction Technique

This method consists of two parts:

1. estimation of the non-linearity of digital data (gamma correction);
2. application of a polynomial modelling.

The gamma correction was performed through the luminance-based technique as both Valous et al. [9] and Cheung et al. [10] have described.

The gray tiles of the ColorChecker Passport Photo (A4, B4, C4, D4, E4, and F4) were considered to calculate the non-linearity parameter.

The calculated gamma factor was applied to the camera responses for the remaining X-Rite colors so that their sRGB values were corrected for non-linearity. Polynomial modelling was applied to corrected values using the vector $P_{[11]}$ above.

### Method 3: Our Original Approach

An original, alternative approach has been devised and implemented in this study. The initial idea is that a proper calibration must lead to an ideal $y = x$ linear correlation, with unitary slope and without offset between photographic and spectrophotometric data (i.e. null intercept).

Starting from the training set, a general-purpose transform from the sRGB to the L*a*b* space was applied to the digital camera output, thus obtaining $L_p$, $a_p$, $b_p$.

In Figs. 3, 4 and 5, the scatter plots of uncalibrated digital color data *vs.* spectrophotometric values are shown.

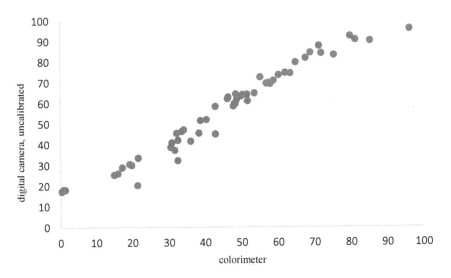

**Fig. 3.** Scatter plot of the L* component: colorimetric values *vs.* uncorrected digital-camera values.

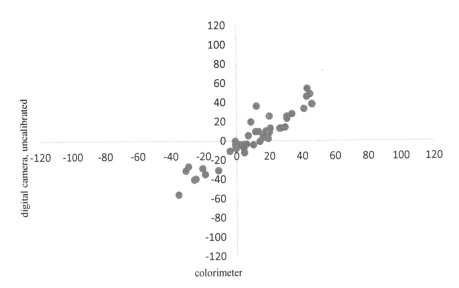

**Fig. 4.** Scatter plot of the a* component: colorimetric values *vs.* uncorrected digital-camera values.

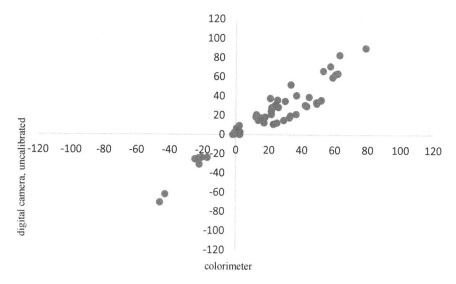

**Fig. 5.** Scatter plot of the b* component: colorimetric values *vs.* uncorrected digital-camera values.

The parameters to be used for camera calibration are then estimated according to the linear regression analysis applied separately to L*, a*, and b* data:

$$L_p = \alpha_L L_s + \beta_L$$

$$a_p = \alpha_a a_s + \beta_a$$

$$b_p = \alpha_b b_s + \beta_b$$

where $(\alpha_L, \beta_L)$, $(\alpha_a, \beta_a)$, and $(\alpha_b, \beta_b)$ are the regression coefficients, the $\beta$'s being the intercepts representing the systematic errors to be corrected by the calibration process.

Since the target is to find calibrated L*, a*, and b* values which better reproduce the colorimeter values it holds that:

$$L_c = L_s$$

$$a_c = a_s$$

$$b_c = b_s$$

Then the proposed transformation is:

$$L_c = \frac{L_p - \beta_L}{\alpha_L}$$
$$a_c = \frac{a_p - \beta_a}{\alpha_a}$$
$$b_c = \frac{b_p - \beta_b}{\alpha_b}$$

As shown in Figs. 3, 4 and 5, the scatter plots displaying the uncalibrated digital color data versus spectrophotometric values show a strong linear correlation: Pearson coefficient are 0.9797, 0.9832, and 0.9596, for L*, a*, and b*, respectively.

In addition, the coefficient of determination is very close to one for L* and a* (0.9675 and 0.9693, respectively) proving that a linear relation exists between uncalibrated and calibrated data.

Indeed, by considering the b* scatterplot and the related coefficient of determination (0.9193), the independent calibration of the b* parameter is expected to be of lower quality. As consequence, a calibration step in the (a, b) space is proposed, by applying the matrix method only to these two chromaticity features. In such a case, the terms of the polynomial $P_{[6]}$ are experimentally proved to be sufficient:

$$P_{[6]} = \begin{bmatrix} a^* & b^* & a^*b^* & a^{*2} & b^{*2} & 1 \end{bmatrix}$$

The mapping can now be represented by:

$$\begin{pmatrix} a^* \\ b^* \end{pmatrix} = \begin{bmatrix} M_{1,1} & M_{1,2} & M_{1,3} & M_{1,4} & M_{1,5} & M_{1,6} \\ M_{2,1} & M_{2,2} & M_{2,3} & M_{2,4} & M_{2,5} & M_{2,6} \end{bmatrix} \begin{pmatrix} a^* \\ b^* \\ a^*b^* \\ a^{*2} \\ b^{*2} \\ 1 \end{pmatrix}$$

## 4  Results

After the analysis of measure reliability through a test-retest evaluation, the three methods have been applied. Their performance evaluation is based on statistical measures (such as correlation coefficients) as well as on color-distance measures.

The analysis of the Pearson coefficients shows a general improvement when comparing the values before and after calibration.

As far as it concerns the training set (reported in Table 3), the best outcome is that achieved by method 2 but is clear how this same method performs very poorly on the validation set (third line in Table 4).

One can also notice that, on the training set, methods 1 and 3 improve or preserve correlation for L* and a*, while b* is less improved by method 3: indeed, on the whole method 1 is better than method 3.

On the contrary, with the validation set the situation is reversed: model 1 improves b* but it gets worse for the other components; model 3 improves b*, preserves the correlation coefficient for L* (as expected by design), and performs better than method 1 on a* component.

What described above is also evident when analyzing the error in L*, a*, and b* components ($\Delta$L*, $\Delta$a*, and $\Delta$b*) between spectrophotometric data and calibrated camera values.

When considering the training set (Table 5), method 2 achieves the smallest error, while method 3 shows the largest ΔL*, Δa*, and Δb* values, confirming its lower accuracy with respect to the other models.

On the other side, when considering the validation set (Table 6), method 2 has the smallest ΔL* and Δa* values, but the b* error is dramatically increased. Method 1 has the largest ΔL* but negligible Δb*. Method 3, performs better than method 1 as dealing with L*, a*, and root-mean-square errors.

**Table 3.** Pearson coefficients on training set.

| Data | r_L* | r_a* | r_b* |
|---|---|---|---|
| Without calibration | 0.9797 | 0.9374 | 0.9454 |
| Method 1 | 0.9912 | 0.9833 | 0.9735 |
| Method 2 | 0.9976 | 0.9895 | 0.9981 |
| Method 3 | 0.9797 | 0.9833 | 0.9596 |

**Table 4.** Pearson coefficients on validation set.

| Data | r_L* | r_a* | r_b* |
|---|---|---|---|
| Without calibration | 0.9752 | 0.9832 | 0.8685 |
| Method 1 | 0.9743 | 0.9651 | 0.9601 |
| Method 2 | 0.9112 | 0.9112 | 0.6464 |
| Method 3 | 0.9752 | 0.9772 | 0.9125 |

**Table 5.** L*, a*, b*, and root-mean-square errors on training set.

| Data | ΔL* | Δa* | Δb* | RMS error |
|---|---|---|---|---|
| Without calibration | 11.243 | 7.335 | 1.289 | 7.786 |
| Method 1 | 2.119 | −6.631 | −1.045 | 4.064 |
| Method 2 | 0.030 | 0.036 | 0.030 | 0.032 |
| Method 3 | 7.407 | −9.013 | 4.802 | 7.284 |

**Table 6.** L*, a*, b*, and root-mean-square errors on validation set.

| Data | ΔL* | Δa* | Δb* | RMS error |
|---|---|---|---|---|
| Without calibration | 5.485 | 12.073 | 3.570 | 7.928 |
| Method 1 | −6.702 | 2.599 | 1.403 | 4.229 |
| Method 2 | 4.966 | 0.722 | 14.091 | 8.636 |
| Method 3 | −6.008 | 2.330 | 2.911 | 4.082 |

When using color metrics, the color distance $\Delta E_{00}$, calculated according to formula CIEDE2000 is applied. The equation used is based on the mathematical observations and implementations analyzed by Sharma *et al.* [11], and the final formula is:

$$\Delta E_{00} = \sqrt{\left(\frac{\Delta L}{K_L \times S_L}\right)^2 + \left(\frac{\Delta C}{K_C \times S_C}\right)^2 + \left(\frac{\Delta H}{K_H \times S_H}\right)^2 + R_t \times \left(\frac{\Delta C}{K_C \times S_C}\right) \times \left(\frac{\Delta H}{K_H \times S_H}\right)}$$

where $\Delta L$, $\Delta C$ and $\Delta H$ are the luminance, chroma and hue difference respectively, $K_L$, $K_C$ and $K_H$ are parametric weighting factors, that we set to unity, while $R_t$, $S_L$, $S_C$ and $S_H$ are terms computed in relation to C and H values.

When referring to the evaluation on the training set, the values reported in Table 7 have been found. The $\Delta E_{00}$ between the reference colorimetric values and the digital data without calibration is 8.8 for X-Rite gray tiles and 13.5 for colored X-Rite tiles and pigments. After applying each of the three methods a smaller distance is achieved, and the improvement is even more evident for the colored tiles.

In general, method 1 achieves a better calibration when compared with method 3. Such a result means that method 1 is very precise and accurate in calibrating the same dataset used for the training phase.

When evaluating performances with the validation set, the values in Table 8 are reported. After acquisition, without any calibration, $\Delta E_{00}$ is close to 13. By applying the calibration methods, the minimum $\Delta E_{00}$ (7.3) is achieved by our model; $\Delta E_{00}$ of model 1 and of method 2 are 7.9 and 9.8, respectively.

Even though results are not yet in line with the recommendation for the Cultural Heritage field, where the accepted limit is $\Delta E_{00} = 3$ [12]), it is interesting to notice how the new method 3 has given positive results as compared to the other two methods.

This result suggests that our method is more robust than method 1 and method 2. Especially, a too large precision of method 1 in the evaluation of the training set should be a symptom of overfitting.

**Table 7.** Performance evaluation on training set.

| Data | $\Delta E_{00}$ (gray tiles) | $\Delta E_{00}$ (non-gray samples) |
|---|---|---|
| Without calibration | 8.8 | 13.5 |
| Model 1 | 6.8 | 3.5 |
| Model 2 | / | 2.2 |
| Model 3 | 8.1 | 4.4 |

**Table 8.** Performance evaluation on validation set.

| Data | $\Delta E_{00}$ |
|---|---|
| Without calibration | 12.8 |
| Model 1 | 7.9 |
| Model 2 | 9.8 |
| Model 3 | 7.3 |

Finally, in Fig. 6 a color display of two data samples is reported, to provide an optical visualization of the comparison of the different methods.

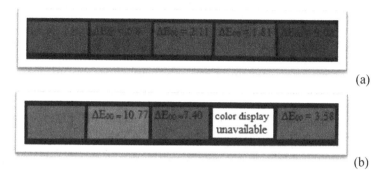

(a)

(b)

**Fig. 6.** Sample color display; from left to right: colorimetric value, uncalibrated camera output, camera output calibrated with method 1, 2, and 3. (**a**) sample within the training set; (**b**) sample within the validation set: in this case the color display calibrated with method 2 is not available because the validation set used for this method is different from that used for the other two methods.

## 5   Conclusions

Despite the intrinsic differences in the samples used in the present work (*i.e.*, the ColorChecker Passport Photo tiles and the paintings on canvas) it has been possible to achieve interesting insights into *supervised* calibration methods and their performances: while method 1 proved to be the most precise and accurate on the same sample set used during the training phase, method 3 proves more effective in the capability to be generalized (robustness).

Robustness is indeed a major desired aspect in a calibration method, especially when it must be applied to cultural heritage problems. In fact, when artistic artworks cannot be measured with a colorimeter, but their image might instead be acquired by a color camera, such an approach could represent a crucial color analytical method if the camera data could be confidently esteemed precise and reliable enough in the identification and characterization of pigments.

Optimization of our method can still be pursued. For example, calibration errors can also be related to the photographic elaboration of reflections on different surfaces. In this context, a database with a larger quantity of samples will be used in future developments, taking surface properties into proper consideration. In order to prove how the proposed approach can be generalized, the results for different cameras will be considered in future works.

# References

1. Sanmartìn, P., Chorro, E., Vàzque-Nion, D., Martìnez-Verdù, F.M., Prieto, B.: Conversion of a digital camera into a non-contact colorimeter for use in stone cultural heritage: the application case to Spanish granites. Measurement **56**, 149–220 (2014)
2. Ibraheem, N.A., Hasam, M.M., Khan, R.Z., Mishra, P.K.: Understanding color models: a review. ARPN J. Sci. **2**, 265–275 (2012)
3. Jackman, P., Sun, D.W., ElMasry, G.: Robust colour calibration of an imaging system using a colour space transform and advanced regression modelling. Meat Sci. **91**, 402–407 (2012)
4. Leòn, K., Mery, D., Pedreschi, F., Leòn, J.: Color measurement in L*a*b* units from RGB digital images. Food Res. Int. **39**, 1084–1091 (2006)
5. Cheung, V., Westland, S., Thomson, M.: Accurate estimation of the nonlinearity of input/output response for color cameras. Color Res. Appl. **29**, 406–412 (2004)
6. Vasari, G.: Le Vite de' più eccellenti pittori, scultori et architettori (often more simply referred to as "Le Vite"), 1st edn. 1550 (Torrentino, Florence), 2nd edn. 1556 (Giunti, Venice)
7. Hong, G., Luo, M.R., Rhodes, P.A.: A study of digital camera colorimetric characterization based on polynomial modelling. Color Res. Appl. **26**, 76–84 (2001)
8. Johnson, T.: Methods for characterizing colour scanners and digital cameras. Displays **16**, 183–191 (1996)
9. Valous, N.A., Mendoza, F., Sun, D.W., Allen, P.: Colour calibration of a laboratory computer vision system for quality evaluation of pre-slides hams. Meat Sci. **81**, 132–141 (2009)
10. Cheung, T.V.L., Westland, S.: Accurate estimation of the non-linearity of input-output response for color digital cameras. In: The Science and Systems of Digital Photography Conference, Rochester, pp. 366–369 (2003)
11. Sharma, G., Wu, W., Dalal, E.N.: The CIEDE2000 color-difference formula: implementation notes, supplementary test data, and mathematical observations. Color Res. Appl. **30**, 21–30 (2004)
12. Barbu, O.H., Zaharide, A.: Noninvasive in situ study of pigments in artworks by means of Vis, IRFC image analysis and X-Ray fluorescence spectrometry. Color Res. Appl. **41**(3), 321–324 (2016)

# Color Image Filtering

# Learning Parametric Functions for Color Image Enhancement

Simone Bianco[1], Claudio Cusano[2], Flavio Piccoli[1(✉)],
and Raimondo Schettini[1]

[1] University of Milano - Bicocca, viale Sarca 336, 20126 Milan, Italy
{simone.bianco,flavio.piccoli,schettini}@disco.unimib.it
[2] University of Pavia, via Ferrata 1, 27100 Pavia, Italy
claudio.cusano@unipv.it

**Abstract.** In this work we propose a novel CNN-based method for image enhancement that simulates an expert retoucher. The method is fast and accurate at the same time thanks to the decoupling between the inference of the parameters and the color transformation. Specifically, the parameters are inferred from a downsampled version of the raw input image and the transformation is applied to the full resolution input. Different variants of the proposed enhancement method can be generated by varying the parametric functions used as color transformations (i.e. polynomial, piecewise, cosine and radial), and by varying how they are applied (i.e. *channelwise* or *full color*). Experimental results show that several variants of the proposed method outperform the state of the art on the MIT-Adobe FiveK dataset.

**Keywords:** Automatic retouching · Image enhancement · Parametric enhancement

## 1 Introduction

The color enhancement of a raw image is a crucial step that significantly affects the quality perceived by the final observer [2]. This enhancement is either done automatically, through a sequence of on-board operations or, when high quality is needed, manually by professional retouchers in post-production. The manual enhancement of an image, in contrast to a pre-determined pipeline of operations, leads to more engaging outcomes because it may reflect the imagination and the creativity of a human being. Manual processing however, requires the retoucher to be skilled in using post-production software and it is a time consuming process. Even if there are several books and manuals describing techniques of photo retouching [10], the decision factors are highly subjective and therefore they cannot be easily replicated in procedural algorithms. For these reasons the emulation of a professional retoucher is a challenging task in computer vision that nowadays resides mostly in the field of machine learning, and in particular in the area of convolutional neural networks.

© Springer Nature Switzerland AG 2019
S. Tominaga et al. (Eds.): CCIW 2019, LNCS 11418, pp. 209–220, 2019.
https://doi.org/10.1007/978-3-030-13940-7_16

In its naive formulation, the color enhancement task can be seen as an *image-to-image transformation* that is learned from a set of raw images and their corresponding retouched versions. Isola et al. [9] propose a generative method that uses an adversarial training schema to learn a mapping between the raw inputs and the manifold of enhanced images. The preservation of the content is ensured by evaluating the raw and its corresponding enhanced image in a pairwise manner. Zhu et al. [12] relax the constraint of having paired samples by ensuring the preservation of the content through the use of cyclic redundancy instead of pair-matching. Those image-to-image transformation algorithms led to important results, but they are very time- and memory-consuming and thus are not easily applicable to high-resolution images. Furthermore, sometimes they produce annoying artifacts that heavily degrade the quality of the output image.

As an evolution of these approaches, Gharbi et al. [6] propose a new pipeline for image enhancement in which the parameters of a color transformation are inferred through a convolutional neural network processing a downsampled version of the input image. The use of a shape-conservative transform and of a fast inference logic, make this method (and all methods following this schema) more suitable for image retouching. Following this approach, Bianco et al. [3] use a polynomial color transformation of degree three, whose inputs are the raw pixels projected into a monomial basis containing the terms of the polynomial expansion. Transforms are inferred in a patchwise manner and then interpolated to have a color transform for each raw pixel. The size of the patch becomes a tunable parameter to move the system toward accuracy or toward speed. Hu et al. [8] use reinforcement learning to define a meaningful sequence of operations to retouch the raw image. In their method, the reward used to promote the enhancement is the expected return over all possible trajectories induced by the policy under evaluation.

In this work, we propose a method that follows the same decoupling between the inference of the parameters and the application of the shape-conservative color transform adopted in the last described methods. We compare four different color transformations (polynomial, piecewise, cosine and radial) applied either *channelwise* or *full color*.

The rest of the paper is organized as follows: Sect. 2 describes the pipeline of the proposed method, the architecture of the CNN used to infer the parameters (Subsect. 2.2) and the parametric functions used as color transforms (Subsect. 2.1). Section 3 assesses the accuracy of the proposed method and all its variants comparing them with the relative state of the art.

## 2    Method

The image enhancement method we propose here is based on a Convolutional Neural Network (CNN) which estimates the parameters of a global image transformation that is then applied to the input image. With respect to a straightforward neural regression, this approach presents two main advantages. The former is that the parametric transformation automatically preserves the content of the images preventing the introduction of artifacts. The latter is that the whole procedure is very fast since the parameters can be estimated from a downsampled version of the image, and only the final transformation needs to be safely applied to the full resolution image. The complete pipeline of the proposed method is depicted in Fig. 1: the input image is downsamopled and fed to a CNN that estimates the coefficients to be applied to the chosen basis function (among polynomial, piecewise, cosine and radial) to obtain the color transformation to be applied to the full resolution input image.

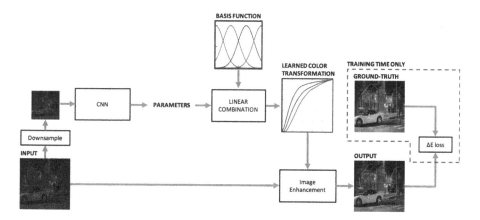

**Fig. 1.** Pipeline of the proposed method. The input image is downsampled and fed to a CNN that estimates the coefficients to be applied to the chosen basis function (among polynomial, piecewise, cosine and radial) to obtain the color transformation to be applied to the full resolution input image.

### 2.1 Architecture of the CNN

The structure of the neural network is that of a typical CNN. It includes a sequence of parametric linear operations (convolutions and linear products) interleaved by non-linear functions (ReLUs and batch normalizations). Due to the limited amount of training data, we had to contain the number of learnable parameters. The final architecture is similar to that used by Bianco et al. [3] to address the problem of artistic photo filter removal. The neural network is relatively small in size, if compared to other popular ones [1].

Given the input image, downsampled to $256 \times 256$ pixels, a sequence of four convolutional blocks extracts a set of local features. Each convolutional block consists of convolution, ReLU activation and batch normalization. Each convolutional block increases the number of channels in the output feature map. All the convolutions have kernel size of $3 \times 3$ and stride of 2, except the first one that has a kernel of $5 \times 5$ pixels with stride 4 (the first convolution differs from the others also because it is not followed by batch normalization). The output of the convolutional blocks is a map of $8 \times 8 \times 64$ local features that are averaged into a single 64-dimensional vector by average pooling. Two linear layers, interleaved by a ReLU activation, compute the parameters of the enhancement transformation. Figure 2 shows a schematic view of the architecture of the network.

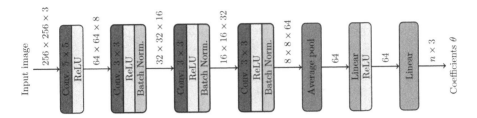

**Fig. 2.** Architecture of the convolutional neural network. The size of the output depends on the dimension $n$ of the functional basis and on the kind of transformation ($n \times 3$ for channelwise, $n \times n \times n \times 3$ for full color transformations).

## 2.2    Image Transformations

We considered two main families of parametric functions: the *channelwise transformations* and the *full color transformations*. Channelwise transformations are defined by a triplet of functions, each one respectively applied to the Red, Green and Blue color channels. Full color transformations are also formed by triplets of functions, but each one considers all the color coordinates of the input pixel in the chosen color space. In both cases the functions are linear combinations of the elements $\phi_1, \phi_2, \ldots \phi_n$ of a $n$-dimensional basis. The coefficients $\theta$ of the linear combination are the output of the neural network. Full color transformations are potentially more powerful as they allow to model more complex operations in the color space. Channelwise transformations are necessarily simpler, since they are forced to modify each channel independently. However, channelwise transformations require a smaller number of parameters and are therefore easier to estimate.

We assume that the values of the color channels of the input pixels are in the $[0, 1]$ range.

In the case of channelwise transformations the color of the input pixel $\mathbf{x} = (x_1, x_2, x_3)$ is transformed into a new color $\mathbf{y} = (y_1, y_2, y_3)$ by applying the equation:

$$y_c = x_c + \sum_{i=1}^{n} \theta_{ic}\phi_i(x_c), \quad c \in \{1, 2, 3\}, \tag{1}$$

where $\boldsymbol{\theta} \in \mathbb{R}^{n \times 3}$ is the output of the CNN. Note that the term $x_c$ outside the summation makes it so we have $\mathbf{x} \simeq \mathbf{y}$ when $\boldsymbol{\theta} \simeq \mathbf{0}$. This detail was inspired by residual networks [7] and allows for an easier initialization of the network parameters that speeds-up the training process.

Full color transformations take into account all the three color channels. Since modeling a generic $\mathbb{R}^3 \to \mathbb{R}^3$ transformation would require a prohibitively large basis, we restricted it to a combination of *separable* multidimensional functions in which each element of the three-dimensional basis is the product of three

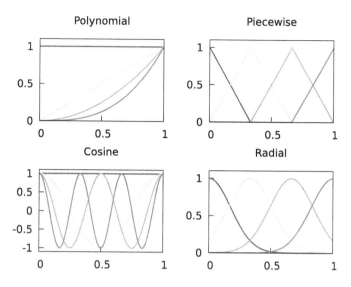

**Fig. 3.** The four function basis used in this work, in the case $n = 4$.

elements in a one-dimensional basis. A full color transformation can be therefore expressed as follows:

$$y_c = x_c + \sum_{i=1}^{n}\sum_{j=1}^{n}\sum_{k=1}^{n}\theta_{ijkc}\phi_i(x_1)\phi_j(x_2)\phi_k(x_3), \quad c \in \{1,2,3\}, \qquad (2)$$

where $\theta \in \mathbb{R}^{n\times n\times n\times 3}$ is the output of the CNN. Note that in this case the number of coefficients grows as the cube of the size $n$ of the one-dimensional function basis.

We experimented with four basis: polynomial, piecewise linear, cosine and radial. See Fig. 3 for their visual representation. The polynomial basis in the variable $x$ is formed by the integer powers of $x$:

$$\phi_i(x) = x^{i-1}, \quad i \in \{1, 2, \ldots n\}. \qquad (3)$$

For the piecewise case, the basis includes triangular functions of unitary height, centered at equispaced nodes in the $[0, 1]$ range:

$$\phi_i(x) = \max\{0, 1 - |(n-1)x - i + 1|\}, \quad i \in \{1, 2, \ldots n\}. \qquad (4)$$

In practice $\phi_i(x)$ is maximal at $(i-1)/(n-1)$ and decreases to zero at $(i-2)/(n-1)$ and $i/(n-1)$. The linear combination of these functions is a continuous piecewise linear function.

The cosine basis is formed by cosinusoidal functions of different angular frequencies:

$$\phi_i(x) = \cos(2\pi(i-1)x), \quad i \in \{1, 2, \ldots n\}. \tag{5}$$

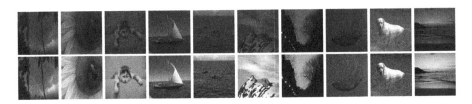

**Fig. 4.** Samples from the FiveK dataset. The top row shows the RAW input images while the bottom row reports their version retouched by Expert C.

The last basis is formed by radial Gaussian functions centered at equispaced nodes in the $[0, 1]$ range:

$$\phi_i(x) = \exp\left(-\frac{(x-(i-1)/(n-1))^2}{\sigma^2}\right), \quad \sigma = \frac{1}{n}, \quad i \in \{1, 2, \ldots n\}. \tag{6}$$

Note that the width of the Gaussians scales with the dimension of the basis.

## 3    Experimental Results

To assess the accuracy of the different variants of proposed method, we took a dataset of manually retouched photographs and we measured the difference between them and the automatically retouched output images. The dataset we considered is the FiveK [4] which consists of 5000 photographs collected by MIT and Adobe for the evaluation of image enhancement algorithms. Each image is given in the RAW, unprocessed format and in five variants manually retouched by five photo editing experts.

We used the procedure described by Hu *et al.* [8] to preprocess the images and to divide them into a training set of 4000 images, and a test set of 1000 images. We followed the common practice to use the third expert (Expert C) as reference, since he is considered the one with the most consistent retouching style. Some images from the dataset are depicted in Fig. 4 together with their versions retouched by Expert C.

As a performance measure we considered the average color difference between the images retouched by the proposed method and by Expert C. Color difference is measured by computing the $\Delta E_{76}$ and the $\Delta E_{94}$ color differences. $\Delta E_{76}$ is defined as the Euclidean distance in the CIELab color space [5]:

$$\Delta E_{76} = \sqrt{(L_1 - L_2)^2 + (a_1 - a_2)^2 + (b_1 - b_2)^2}, \tag{7}$$

where $(L_1, a_1, b_1)$ and $(L_2, a_2, b_2)$ are the coordinates of a pixel in the two images after their conversion from RGB to CIELab. We also considered the more recent $\Delta E_{94}$:

$$\Delta E_{94} = \sqrt{\left(\frac{\Delta L}{K_L S_L}\right)^2 + \left(\frac{\Delta C}{K_C S_C}\right)^2 + \left(\frac{\Delta H}{K_H S_H}\right)^2}, \tag{8}$$

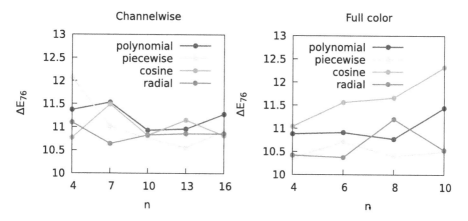

**Fig. 5.** Performance (average $\Delta E_{76}$) obtained with the different function basis varying their dimension $n$.

where $K_L = K_C = K_H = 1$, $\Delta C = C_1 - C_2 = \sqrt{a_1^2 - b_1^2} - \sqrt{a_2^2 - b_2^2}$, $\Delta H = \sqrt{(a_1 - a_2)^2 + (b_1 - b_2)^2 - \Delta C^2}$, $S_L = 1$, $S_C = 1 + K_1 C_1$, $S_H = 1 + K_2 C_1$ with $K_1 = 0.045$ and $K_2 = 0.015$. Finally, we also computed the difference in lightness:

$$\Delta L = |L_1 - L_2|. \tag{9}$$

### 3.1  Basis Function Comparison

As a first experiment, we compared the performance of the proposed method using the two kinds of transformations (channelwise and full color) and the four basis functions (polynomial, piecewise, cosine and radial). We trained the CNN in the configurations considered by using the Adam optimization algorithm [11] using the average $\Delta E_{76}$ between the groundtruth and the color enhanced image as loss function. The training procedure consisted of 40000 iterations with a learning rate of $10^{-4}$, a weight decay of 0.1, and minibatches of 16 samples.

We repeated the experiments multiple times by changing the cardinality $n$ of the basis function. Taking into account that that our training dataset is rather small, for channelwise transformations we limited our investigation to $n \in \{4, 7, 10, 13, 16\}$ while for full color transformations we had to use even smaller values ($n \in \{4, 6, 8, 10\}$) limiting in this way also memory consumption. The results obtained on the test set are summarized in Fig. 5. The plots show different behaviors for the two kinds of transformations: for channelwise transformations increasing the size of the basis tends to improve the accuracy (with the possible exception of polynomials), while for full color transformations small basis seem to perform better.

Table 1 reports in details the performance obtained with the values of $n$ that, on average, have been found to be the best for the two kinds of transformations: $n = 10$ for channelwise and $n = 4$ for full color transformations. For channelwise transformations, it seems that all the basis perform quite similarly. On the other hand, in the case of full color transformations polynomials and cosines are clearly less accurate than piecewise and radial functions. Full color transformations allowed to obtain the best results for all the three performance measures considered.

**Table 1.** Results obtained on the test set by the variations of the proposed method. For each metric, the lowest error is reported in bold.

| Transformation type | Basis | $\Delta E_{76}$ | $\Delta E_{94}$ | $\Delta L$ |
|---|---|---|---|---|
| Channelwise ($n = 10$) | Polynomial | 10.93 | 8.36 | 5.77 |
| | Piecewise | 10.75 | 8.24 | 5.63 |
| | Cosine | 10.82 | 8.14 | 5.58 |
| | Radial | 10.83 | 8.16 | 5.53 |
| Full color ($n = 4$) | Polynomial | 10.88 | 8.33 | 5.79 |
| | Piecewise | **10.36** | 8.02 | 5.48 |
| | Cosine | 11.04 | 8.45 | 5.48 |
| | Radial | 10.42 | **7.99** | **5.47** |

Figure 6 visually compares the results of applying channelwise transformations to a test image. The functions obtained with the piecewise and the radial basis look very smooth. The cosine basis produces a less regular behavior, and the polynomial basis seems unable to keep under control all the color curves.

Figure 7 compares, on the same test image, the behavior of full color transformations. We cannot easily visualize these transformations as simple plots. However, we can notice how a better outcome is obtained for low values of $n$. For large values of $n$ some basis (e.g. cosine) even fail to keep the pixels within the $[0, 1]$ range. This can be noticed in the brightest region of the image, where it causes the introduction of unreasonable colors (we could have clipped these values, but we preferred to make it visible to better show this behavior).

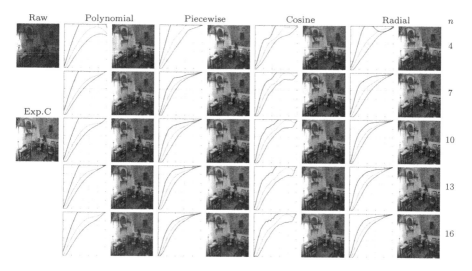

**Fig. 6.** Comparison of channelwise transformations applied to a test image. On the left of each processed image are shown the transformations applied to the three color channels.

**Fig. 7.** Comparison of full color transformations applied to a test image.

## 3.2 Comparison with the State of the Art

As a second experiment we compared the results obtained by the best versions of the proposed method with other recent methods from the state of the art. We included in the comparison methods based on the use of Convolutional

Neural Networks that made publicly available their source code. The methods we considered are:

- Pix2pix [9], that has been proposed by Isola *et al.* for image-to-image translation; even though not specifically proposed for image enhancement, its flexibility make this method suitable for this task as well.
- CycleGAN [12], that is similar to Pix2pix but targeted to the more challenging learning from unpaired examples.
- Exposure [8] is also trained from unpaired examples. It uses reinforcement learning, and has been originally evaluated on the FiveK dataset.
- HDRNet [6], that Gharbi *et al.* designed to make it possible to process high resolution images. Among the others, the authors evaluated it on the FiveK dataset.
- Unfiltering [3], is a method originally proposed for image restoration. However, it was possible to retrain it for image enhancement.

Table 2 reports the results obtained by these methods and compares them with those obtained by the proposed approach. The table includes an example for each type of color transformation. In both cases the piecewise basis is considered with $n = 10$ for the channelwise case and $n = 4$ for the full color transformation. Both variants outperformed all the competing methods in terms of average $\Delta E_{76}$ and $\Delta E_{94}$. Among the other methods Pix2pix was quite close (less than half unit of $\Delta E$) and slightly outperformed the proposed one in terms of $\Delta L$. These results confirm the flexibility of the proposed architecture. HDRNet and Unfiltering also obtained good results. Exposure and cycleGAN, instead, are significantly less accurate than the other methods. This confirms the difficulties in learning from unpaired examples.

**Table 2.** Accuracy in reproducing the test images retouched by expert C by methods in the state of the art.

| Method | $\Delta E_{76}$ | $\Delta E_{94}$ | $\Delta L$ |
|---|---|---|---|
| Exposure [8] | 16.98 | 13.42 | 9.54 |
| CycleGAN [12] | 16.23 | 12.30 | 9.20 |
| Unfiltering [3] | 13.17 | 10.42 | 6.76 |
| HDRNet [6] | 12.14 | 9.63 | 6.27 |
| Pix2pix [9] | 11.13 | 8.53 | 5.55 |
| Channelwise (piecewise $n = 10$) | 10.75 | 8.24 | 5.63 |
| Full color (piecewise $n = 4$) | **10.36** | **8.02** | **5.48** |

Figure 8 shows some test images processed by the methods included in the comparison.

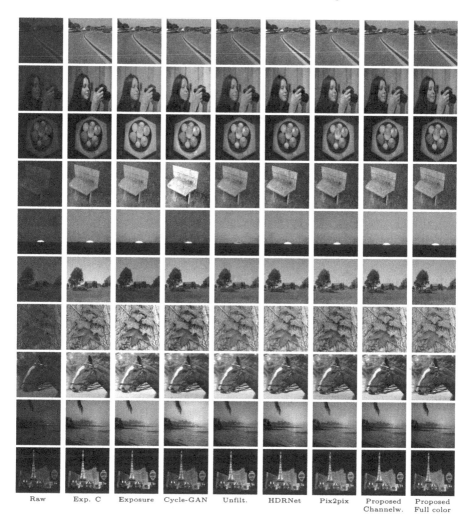

| Raw | Exp. C | Exposure | Cycle-GAN | Unfilt. | HDRNet | Pix2pix | Proposed Channelw. | Proposed Full color |

**Fig. 8.** Results of applying image enhancement methods in the state of the art to some test images. For the proposed method, both variants refer to the piecewise basis ($n = 10$ for the channelwise version, $n = 4$ for the full color transformation).

## 4   Conclusions

In this paper we presented a method for image enhancement of raw images that simulates the ability of an expert retoucher. This method uses a convolutional neural network to infer the parameters of a color transformation on a downsampled version of the input image. In this way, the inference stage becomes faster in test time and less data-hungry in training time while remaining accurate. The main contributions of this paper include:

- a fast end-to-end trainable shape-conservative retouching algorithm able to emulate an expert retoucher;
- the comparison among eight different variants of the method obtained combining four parametric color transformations (i.e. polynomial, piecewise, cosine and radial) and how they are applied (i.e. *channelwise* or *full color*).

The relationship between the cardinality of the basis function and the performance deserve a further investigation. This investigation would need a much larger dataset that we hope to collect in the future. Notwithstanding this, the preliminary results obtained show that the proposed method is able to reproduce with great accuracy a huge variety of retouching styles, outperforming the algorithms that represent the state of the art on the MIT-Adobe FiveK dataset.

# References

1. Bianco, S., Cadene, R., Celona, L., Napoletano, P.: Benchmark analysis of representative deep neural network architectures. IEEE Access **6**, 64270–64277 (2018)
2. Bianco, S., Ciocca, G., Marini, F., Schettini, R.: Image quality assessment by preprocessing and full reference model combination. In: Image Quality and System Performance VI, vol. 7242, p. 72420O. International Society for Optics and Photonics (2009)
3. Bianco, S., Cusano, C., Piccoli, F., Schettini, R.: Artistic photo filter removal using convolutional neural networks. J. Electron. Imaging **27**(1), 011004 (2017)
4. Bychkovsky, V., Paris, S., Chan, E., Durand, F.: Learning photographic global tonal adjustment with a database of input/output image pairs. In: IEEE Conference on Computer Vision and Pattern Recognition (CVPR), pp. 97–104 (2011)
5. Fairchild, M.D.: Color Appearance Models. Wiley, Chichester (2013)
6. Gharbi, M., Chen, J., Barron, J.T., Hasinoff, S.W., Durand, F.: Deep bilateral learning for real-time image enhancement. ACM T. Graphic. (TOG) **36**(4), 118 (2017)
7. He, K., Zhang, X., Ren, S., Sun, J.: Deep residual learning for image recognition. In: IEEE Conference on Computer Vision and Pattern Recognition (CVPR), pp. 770–778 (2016)
8. Hu, Y., He, H., Xu, C., Wang, B., Lin, S.: Exposure: a white-box photo postprocessing framework. ACM T. Graphic. (TOG) **37**(2), 26 (2018)
9. Isola, P., Zhu, J.Y., Zhou, T., Efros, A.A.: Image-to-image translation with conditional adversarial networks. In: IEEE Conference on Computer Vision and Pattern Recognition (CVPR), pp. 5967–5976 (2017)
10. Kee, E., Farid, H.: A perceptual metric for photo retouching. Proc. Nat. Acad. Sci. **108**(50), 19907–19912 (2011)
11. Kingma, D.P., Ba, J.: Adam: a method for stochastic optimization. In: International Conference on Learning Representation (2015)
12. Zhu, J.Y., Park, T., Isola, P., Efros, A.A.: Unpaired image-to-image translation using cycle-consistent adversarial networks. In: IEEE International Conference on Computer Vision (ICCV) (2017)

# Haze Transfer Between Images Based on Dark Channel Prior

Koushirou Maeda[1]([⊠]), Keita Hirai[2]([⊠]) [ID], and Takahiko Horiuchi[2] [ID]

[1] Faculty of Engineering, Chiba University, Chiba, Japan
afsa2528@chia-u.jp
[2] Graduate School of Engineering, Chiba University, Chiba, Japan
hirai@faculty.chiba-u.jp

**Abstract.** This paper presents a method for transferring haze information between the source and target images. First, we applied the dark channel prior method to the input source and target images. The dark channel prior method was proposed for removing haze from an image. By applying the method thereof, an input image can be decomposed to a scene radiance image, global atmospheric color (haze color) vector, and transmission map. Subsequently, for transferring the haze information, we applied the color transfer method to the decomposed information of source and target images. Finally, we reconstructed a haze-transferred image from the decomposed images. Our results indicate that the proposed haze transfer method can reproduce fine haze-transferred appearance, compared with the input source and target images.

**Keywords:** Haze transfer · Dark channel prior · Color transfer

## 1 Introduction

Scene appearance atmospheres such as lighting condition, dominant scene color, and haze information are important factors for determining scene image impressions. Users can obtain more realistic, more dramatic, or more desirable appearance of target images. Image and video editing for addressing such scene appearance atmospheres comprise an interesting topic in image processing, computer vision, and computer graphics [1, 2]. For example, the image editing method for lighting conditions has been studied actively. Zhang et al. decomposed the illumination effects of multiple light sources from a single image [3]. This technique can be applied for editing lighting conditions. Shu et al. transferred the lighting appearance of human faces between the source and target images [4].

In particular, color editing and transferring in images are effective for changing the scene appearance atmospheres [5]. Reinhard et al. proposed a color transfer method between the source and target images [6]. They used averages and standard deviations of input images in the lαβ color space for transferring colors. Their approach can be expressed as a statistical-based method by converting a potentially complex three-dimensional (3D) color space problem into three separate one-dimensional color spaces. Pitie et al. rotated the 3D distributions of the source and target images using a random 3D rotation matrix and projected them to the axes of their new coordinate

© Springer Nature Switzerland AG 2019
S. Tominaga et al. (Eds.): CCIW 2019, LNCS 11418, pp. 221–232, 2019.
https://doi.org/10.1007/978-3-030-13940-7_17

system [7]. Pouli et al. reshaped and matched the two histograms. They applied scale-space approaches for a partial histogram match [8]. Further, several works investigated the performances of different color spaces for color transfer [5, 9].

Similar to color information, haze information is also significant for providing scene appearance atmospheres. Regarding haze images, haze removal (dehazing) methods have been proposed [10]. In particular, a single-image dehazing method is easier to apply in imaging research. Tan proposed a single-image dehazing method to enhance contrast [11]. Fattal presented an image-dehazing method based on a haze-imaging model [12]. He et al. restored the visibility in haze-affected images based on the previously proposed haze-imaging model and used a dark channel prior algorithm [13]. However, no haze transfer methods are available for editing and changing scene appearance atmospheres. By editing the haze in an image, it is possible to change the overall impression evoked by a scene, simulate different lighting environments, or achieve different visual effects.

We herein propose a method of transferring haze information between the source and target images. Hence, we applied the dark channel prior method [13] and Reinhard's color transfer [6]. The dark channel prior method is used for decomposing an input image to a scene radiance image, global atmospheric color (haze color) vector, and transmission map. Subsequently, the color transfer method is applied to the decomposed images for out-haze transfer. Finally, the haze-transferred results are reconstructed from the decomposed images.

This paper is organized as follows: We describe the prosed haze transfer method based on the dark channel prior and color transfer in Sect. 2. Subsequently, we present the experimental results and discussions in Sect. 3. Finally, the conclusions and future research are discussed in Sect. 4.

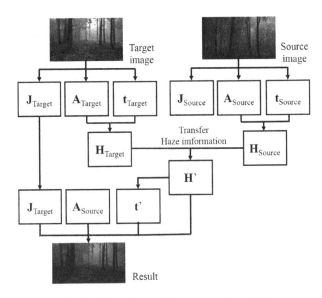

**Fig. 1.** Flow chart of the proposed method.

## 2  Proposed Method

Figure 1 shows the flow chart of our proposed method. First, based on the dark channel method, the haze components are separated from the input source and target images, separately. Next, we transfer the haze information between the images using color transfer. Finally, we reconstruct a haze-transferred image by combining the decomposed images.

### 2.1  Separation of Haze Components

In general, the haze imaging model is given by the following equation:

$$\mathbf{I}(\mathbf{x}) = \mathbf{J}(\mathbf{x})t(\mathbf{x}) + \mathbf{A}(1 - t(\mathbf{x})), \tag{1}$$

where $\mathbf{x}$ is the pixel coordinates in camera image $\mathbf{I}$, $\mathbf{J}$ is the scene radiance, $\mathbf{A}$ is the global atmospheric color, and $t$ is the transmission of the scene radiance. When the atmosphere is homogenous, the transmission value t is defined by

$$t(\mathbf{x}) = \exp(-\beta \cdot d(\mathbf{x})), \tag{2}$$

where $\beta$ is the scattering coefficient of the atmosphere, and $d$ is the distance between the objects and a camera. As shown in Eq. (2), haze is uniformly distributed in the scenes, and depends only on the distances.

He et al. found that at least one of the RGB values in a patch was extremely low (almost zero) when using an image under clear daylight [13]. This statistical observation called the dark channel prior is expressed as follows:

$$\mathbf{J}^{dark}(\mathbf{x}) = \min_{c \in r,g,b} (\min_{\mathbf{y} \in \Omega(\mathbf{x})} J^c(\mathbf{y})) \cong 0, \tag{3}$$

where $\Omega$ is a patch region of a pixel $\mathbf{x}$, and $c$ is an RGB channel. Subsequently, based on Eqs. (1) and (3), a transmission is estimated as follows:

$$\tilde{t}(\mathbf{x}) = 1 - \omega \min_{c \in r,g,b} (\min_{\mathbf{y} \in \Omega(\mathbf{x})} \left( \frac{I^c(\mathbf{y})}{A^c} \right)), \tag{4}$$

where $\omega$ is a parameter for maintaining some amount of haze for far-distant objects.

To estimate the atmospheric color $\mathbf{A}$, it is necessary to obtain a pixel of $t(\mathbf{x}) = 0$. Based on Eq. (2), the transmission value $t(\mathbf{x})$ will be 0 at the pixel of infinite distance $d(\mathbf{x}) = \infty$. Assuming that the distance in the sky area will be infinite, they employed the brightest pixel in an input image as the sky area.

The estimated transmission map $\tilde{t}$ generally contains block noise due to the patch-based processing. After the refinement of noisy transmission map $\tilde{t}$ by soft matting, scene radiance $\mathbf{J}$ is estimated by

$$\mathbf{J}(\mathbf{x}) = \frac{\mathbf{I}(\mathbf{x}) - \mathbf{A}}{\max(t(\mathbf{x}), t_0)} + \mathbf{A}, \tag{5}$$

where $t_0$ is a lower-limit transmission threshold for noise reduction.

Hence, the components of the haze image are separated based on the dark channel prior. Further, we convert Eqs. (1) to (6).

$$\mathbf{I}(x) = \mathbf{J}(x)t(x) + \mathbf{A} - \mathbf{H}(x), \tag{6}$$

where $\mathbf{H}(x)$ indicates the haze information ($\mathbf{H} = \mathbf{A}t(x)$).

## 2.2 Transferring Haze Components

Next, we transfer the estimated atmospheric color $\mathbf{A}$ and transmission $t$ of the source image to the target image using the color transfer method [6]. Because the estimated atmospheric color $\mathbf{A}$ is expressed in a color vector [13], the estimated atmospheric color $\mathbf{A}$ (three-channel vector) or transmission t (monochrome image) of the source image cannot be applied to the color transfer method directly. Therefore, in this study, the color transfer is applied to $\mathbf{H}(x)$.

In the color transfer method of Reinhard et al. [6], they converted the pixel values of the input images to an uncorrelated color space expressed as the $l\alpha\beta$ color space. We obtained the standard deviations and averages for each of l, $\alpha$, and $\beta$. Subsequently, we calculated l', $\alpha'$, and $\beta'$ that are color-transferred values. Finally, the image obtained by transferring the color of the source image to the target image can be generated.

Here, we used another notation for the RGB values of a decomposed image $\mathbf{H}(x)$ as $H_R H_G H_B$. In this study, we chose the conversion matrix of Soo et al.'s for the color transfer; it converts the input RGB values to LMS color spaces [14]. First, we processed a conversion from the $H_R H_G H_B$ to XYZ space and converted the XYZ space to LMS space. Further, the resultant of these two converted matrices between the $H_R H_G H_B$ haze space and LMS cone space can be combined as follows:

$$\begin{bmatrix} L \\ M \\ S \end{bmatrix} = \begin{bmatrix} 0.3811 & 0.5783 & 0.0402 \\ 0.1967 & 0.7244 & 0.0782 \\ 0.0241 & 0.1228 & 0.8444 \end{bmatrix} \begin{bmatrix} H_R \\ H_G \\ H_B \end{bmatrix}, \tag{7}$$

By converting the data to the logarithmic space, a significant amount of skew in the data in this $H_R H_G H_B$ space must be eliminated [15].

$$\mathbf{L} = \log L,$$

$$\mathbf{M} = \log M, \tag{8}$$

$$\mathbf{S} = \log S,$$

Reinhard et al. used the $l\alpha\beta$ color space for each channel maximal uncorrelated by avoiding the unwanted cross effect and treating the three channels separately. Ruderman et al. suggested the following transform [15]:

$$
\begin{bmatrix} 1 \\ \alpha \\ \beta \end{bmatrix} = \begin{bmatrix} \frac{1}{\sqrt{3}} & 0 & 0 \\ 0 & \frac{1}{\sqrt{6}} & 0 \\ 0 & 0 & \frac{1}{\sqrt{2}} \end{bmatrix} \begin{bmatrix} 1 & 1 & 1 \\ 1 & 1 & -2 \\ 1 & -1 & 0 \end{bmatrix} \begin{bmatrix} L \\ M \\ S \end{bmatrix},
\tag{9}
$$

After converting the RGB color space to the uncorrelated color space, the haze components were transferred using Eqs. (10) and (11).

$$
l^* = 1 - \bar{l}
$$

$$
\alpha^* = \alpha - \bar{\alpha}
\tag{10}
$$

$$
\beta^* = \beta - \bar{\beta}
$$

and

$$
l' = \frac{\sigma^l_{Source}}{\sigma^l_{Target}} l^* + \bar{l},
$$

$$
\alpha' = \frac{\sigma^\alpha_{Source}}{\sigma^\alpha_{Target}} \alpha^* + \bar{\alpha},
\tag{11}
$$

$$
\beta' = \frac{\sigma^\beta_{Source}}{\sigma^\beta_{Target}} \beta^* + \bar{\beta},
$$

where $\bar{l}$, $\bar{\alpha}$, and $\bar{\beta}$ are the averages of the quantities, and $\sigma$ represents the standard deviation. Subsequently, the obtained l', $\alpha'$, and $\beta'$ were converted to the original color space as follows:

$$
\begin{bmatrix} H'_R \\ H'_G \\ H'_B \end{bmatrix} = \begin{bmatrix} 0.5773 & 0.2621 & 11.3918 \\ 0.5773 & 0.6071 & -5.0905 \\ 0.5833 & -1.0628 & 0.4152 \end{bmatrix} \begin{bmatrix} l' \\ \alpha' \\ \beta' \end{bmatrix},
\tag{12}
$$

By this conversion, $\mathbf{H}'$ was obtained by transferring the haze information of the source image to the target image.

## 2.3 Reconstructing Haze-Transferred Image

Finally, the haze-transferred image by the proposed method was implemented by Eqs. (13)–(16). In Eq. (14), function $T$ shows the haze component transfer in Sect. 2.2.

$$
\mathbf{I}_{haze\_trans}(x) = \mathbf{J}_{Target}(x)t'(x) + \mathbf{A}' - \mathbf{H}'(x),
\tag{13}
$$

$$
\mathbf{H}'(x) = T\left(\mathbf{H}_{Target}, \mathbf{H}_{Source}\right),
\tag{14}
$$

$$\mathbf{A}' = A_{\text{Source}}, \tag{15}$$

$$\mathbf{t}'(\mathbf{x}) = \frac{\sum_{c=1}^{3} \mathbf{H}'(\mathbf{x})}{\sum_{c=1}^{3} \mathbf{A}'}, \tag{16}$$

where $\mathbf{H}'$ is the haze-transferred component containing the color information of the three channels. Regarding the atmospheric light $\mathbf{A}'$ for an output image, we used the atmospheric light of the source image shown in Eq. (15). The transmission t' for the reconstruction was obtained by converting one channel using Eq. (16). Finally, a haze-transferred image was reconstructed using Eq. (13).

## 3    Results and Discussions

### 3.1    Results of the Proposed Method

In this study, we proposed a method of transferring haze information between images based on the dark channel prior. Figure 2 shows the input source and target images, transmission maps of input images, and estimated transmission maps. These results indicate that transmission can be estimated and haze can be removed by the dark channel prior. Figure 2(g) shows the results of the proposed haze transfer. Figure 2(h) shows the transferred transmission map. We confirmed that the haze concentration in the source image is transferred to the target image. Further, we observed from the reconstructed results that the brightness and appearance of the haze in the source image are transferred properly to the target image, and the appearance atmosphere of the haze can be reproduced similarly.

Next, we adopt an image database called CHIC (Color Hazy Image for Comparison) [16] for evaluating out haze transfer method. This database contains two scenes under controlled environments and nine haze images with different haze density levels. Figure 3 shows the original image. In this database, the higher the value of the level, the thinner the haze in the images. Here, we adopt the original image as a target image and the haze images as source images. Then, we compared the haze appearance between source haze images and haze-transferred images. Figure 4 shows the results of our proposed method. It is confirmed that the haze of the source images is properly transferred to the target image according to the haze level.

Our proposed method can also transfer depth information. As shown in Eq. (2), the estimated transmission contains depth information. The haze of the target image is distributed comprehensively. Meanwhile, the haze distribution of the source image is different between the far and near sides of the image shown in Fig. 2. Owing to the depth information and the transmission map, the haze distribution of the output image is similar to that of the source image.

### 3.2    Differences from Color Transfer

We compared the proposed haze transfer method with the color transfer method. The source and the target images are shown in Fig. 2, and the result by the color transfer method is shown in Fig. 5. Because the color transfer method can consider the color information of the source and the target image, the redness of the ground in the source image is transferred to the whole area in the output images. The color transfer method cannot transfer the appearance atmosphere of haze suitably.

### 3.3   Differences in Image Scenes

We changed the source image for the comparison. Figure 6 shows the input images, transmission maps, and results. The scenes of both input images are completely different. The target image is the forest scene with haze. Meanwhile, the source image is

**Fig. 2.** Our haze-transferred result. Input images; (a) Target image, (b) Source image, the estimated scene radiation; (c) Target image, (d) Source image, transmission of input; (e) Target image, (f) Source image. output images; (g) The proposed haze-transferred image, (h) Transmission map.

**Fig. 3.** Original image (target images)

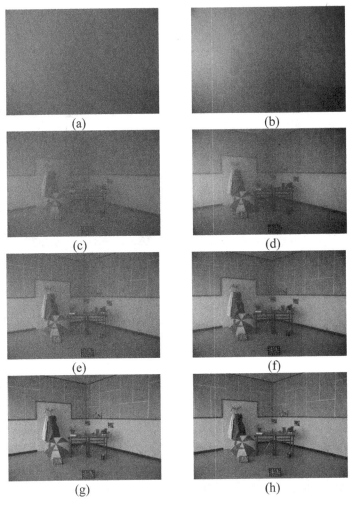

**Fig. 4.** Haze-transferred results using source images with different haze levels. Level 3: (a) Source image, (b) Haze-transferred image from Fig. 3, Level 5: (c) Source image, (d) Haze-transferred image from Fig. 3, Level 7: (e) Source image, (f) Haze-transferred image from Fig. 3, Level 9: (g) Source image, (h) Haze-transferred image from Fig. 3

**Fig. 5.** Color-transferred image.

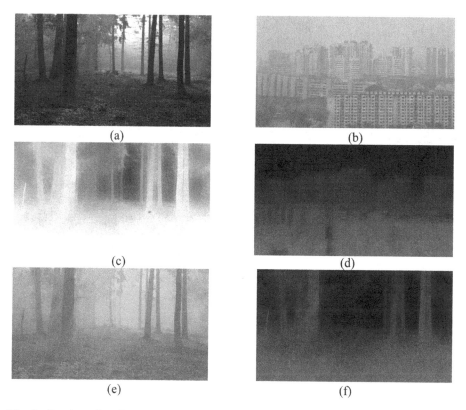

**Fig. 6.** Results using forest and distance view of a city. Input images; (a) Target image, (b) Source image, transmission maps; (c) Target image, (d) Source image, output images; (e) The proposed haze-transferred image, (f) Transmission map of (e)

the building scene with haze. The result images show that the appearance atmosphere of haze is transferred properly. Because our proposed method uses standard deviations and averages of haze information, it does not depend on the target and source scenes.

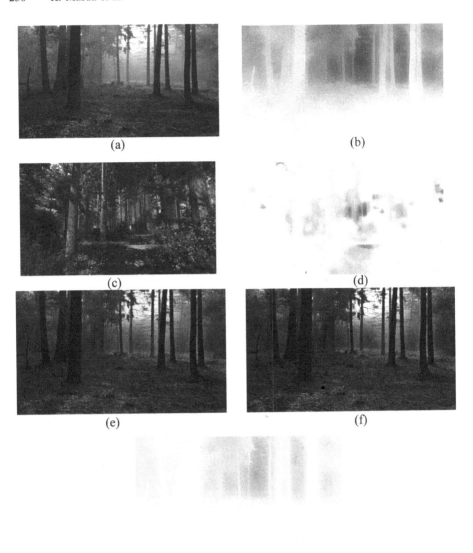

(a)

(b)

(c)

(d)

(e)

(f)

(g)

**Fig. 7.** Results using a hazeless scene as a source image. Input images; (a) Target image, (b) Source image (no haze scene), transmission map; (c) Target image, (d) Source image, result images; (e) Haze-transferred, (f) Scene radiation, (g) Transmission map.

### 3.4   Non-haze Scene

We also changed the source image to the scene without haze. Figure 7 shows the input images, transmission maps, and results. When our proposed method was applied using the source image without haze, the results were similar to those of the image by the haze-removal method based on the dark channel prior. Therefore, we found that our proposed method can be applied to not only haze transfer but also haze reduction.

## 4  Conclusions

In this study, we proposed a method to transfer haze information between two images by decomposing the input images into scene radiation, atmospheric light, and transmission based on the dark channel prior and by adapting the color transfer method. From the experimental results, we confirmed that the haze information of the source image could be transferred to the target image. We also confirmed that the transmission maps were generated successfully.

As future work, we would like to revise the haze transfer model in Eq. (13). As shown in Eqs. (15) and (16), the atmospheric light and the transmission map for the output images were calculated simply. The calculation of these components will be improved. In addition, we will test other color transfer methods. Herein, we used Reinhard's color transfer method. However, numerous other methods are available that could be used to improve our haze transfer method.

## References

1. Faridul, H.S., Pouli, T., Chamaret, C., Stauder, J., Trémeau, A., Reinhard, E.: A survey of color mapping and its applications. In: Eurographics 2014-State of the Art Reports, The Eurographics Association, pp. 43–67. 2 (2014)
2. Bonneel, N., Kovacs, B., Paris, S., Bala, K.: Intrinsic decompositions for image editing. In: Computer Graphics Forum (Eurographics State of the Art Reports 2017), vol. 36, no. 2 (2017)
3. Zhang, L., Yan, Q., Liu, Z., Zou, H., Xiao, C.: Illumination decomposition for photograph with multiple light sources. IEEE Trans. Image Process. 26(06), 4114–4127 (2017)
4. Shu, Z., Hadap, S., Shechtman, E., Sunkavalli, K., Paris, S., Samaras, D.: Portrait lighting transfer using a mass transport approach. ACM Trans. Graph. 37(1), 2:1–2:15 (2017)
5. Fatirul, H.S., Poili, T., Chamaret, C., Stauder, J., Reinhard, E., Kuzovkin, D., Tremeau, A.: Colour mapping: a review of recent methods, extensions, and applications. Comput. Graph. Forum 35, 29 (2015)
6. Reinhard, E., Ashikhmin, M., Gooch, B., Shirley, P.: Color transfer between images. IEEE Comput. Graph. Appl. 21(5), 34–41 (2001)
7. Pitie, F., Kokaram, A., Dahyot, R.: N-Dimensional probability density function transfer and its application to colour transfer. In: International Conference on Computer Vision (ICCV 2005), Beijing (2005)
8. Pouli, T., Reinhard, E.: Progressive color transfer for images of arbitrary dynamic range. Comput. Graph. 35(1), 67–80 (2011)
9. Reinhard, E., Pouli, T.: Colour spaces for colour transfer. In: Schettini, R., Tominaga, S., Trémeau, A. (eds.) CCIW 2011. LNCS, vol. 6626, pp. 1–15. Springer, Heidelberg (2011). https://doi.org/10.1007/978-3-642-20404-3_1
10. Lee, S., Yun, S., Nam, J.-H., Won, C.S., Jung, S.-W.: A review on dark channel prior based image dehazing algorithms. EURASIP J. Image Video Process. 2016(4), 1–23 (2016)

11. Tan, R.T.: Visibility in bad weather from a single image. In: IEEE Conference on Computer Vision and Pattern Recognition, CVPR 2008. IEEE, pp 1–8 (2008)
12. Fattal, R.: Single image dehazing. ACM Trans. Graph. **27**(3), 72 (2008)
13. He, K., Sun, J., Tang, X.: Single image haze removal using dark channel prior. IEEE Trans. Pattern Anal. Machine Intell. **33**(12), 2341–2353 (2011)
14. Pei, S.-C., Lee, T.-Y.: Nighttime haze removal using color transfer pre-processing and dark channel prior. In: IEEE International Conference on Image Processing, Orlando, 30 September–3 October 2012
15. Ruderman, D.L., Cronin, T.W., Chiao, C.C.: Statistics of cone responses to natural images: implications for visual coding. J. Opt. Soc. Am. **15**(8), 2036–2045 (1998)
16. CHIC (Color Hazy Images for Comparison). http://chic.u-bourgogne.fr

# Physically Plausible Dehazing
# for Non-physical Dehazing Algorithms

Javier Vazquez-Corral[1,2]([⊠]), Graham D. Finlayson[1], and Marcelo Bertalmío[2]

[1] School of Computing Sciences, University of East Anglia,
Norwich NR47TJ, UK
{j.vazquez,g.finlayson}@uea.ac.uk
[2] Information and Communication Technologies Department,
Universitat Pompeu Fabra, 08018 Barcelona, Spain
marcelo.bertalmio@upf.edu

**Abstract.** Images affected by haze usually present faded colours and loss of contrast, hindering the precision of methods devised for clear images. For this reason, image dehazing is a crucial pre-processing step for applications such as self-driving vehicles or tracking. Some of the most successful dehazing methods in the literature do not follow any physical model and are just based on either image enhancement or image fusion. In this paper, we present a procedure to allow these methods to accomplish the Koschmieder physical model, i.e., to force them to have a unique transmission for all the channels, instead of the per-channel transmission they obtain. Our method is based on coupling the results obtained for each of the three colour channels. It improves the results of the original methods both quantitatively using image metrics, and subjectively via a psychophysical test. It especially helps in terms of avoiding over-saturation and reducing colour artefacts, which are the most common complications faced by image dehazing methods.

**Keywords:** Image dehazing · Colour image processing · Image post-processing

## 1 Introduction

Images acquired in outdoor scenarios often suffer from the effects of atmospheric phenomena such as fog or haze. The main characteristic of these phenomena is light scatter. The scattering effect distorts contrast and colour in the image, decreasing the visibility of content in the scene and reducing the visual quality.

GF and JVC have received funding from the British Government's EPSRC programme under grant agreement EP/M001768/1. MB and JVC have received funding from the European Union's Horizon 2020 research and innovation programme under grant agreement number 761544 (project HDR4EU) and under grant agreement number 780470 (project SAUCE), and by the Spanish government and FEDER Fund, grant ref. TIN2015-71537-P (MINECO/FEDER,UE).

© Springer Nature Switzerland AG 2019
S. Tominaga et al. (Eds.): CCIW 2019, LNCS 11418, pp. 233–244, 2019.
https://doi.org/10.1007/978-3-030-13940-7_18

**Fig. 1.** Recurring problems of *non-physical based dehazing methods*. From left to right: original image, the solutions of the methods of Galdran *et al.* [11] (top), and Choi *et al.* [6] (bottom), and the result of the post-processing introduced in this paper. We can clearly see the artefacts in the result of Galdran *et al.* and the over-saturation in the result of Choi *et al.* Both problems are solved by the post-processing approach proposed in this paper.

Koschmieder [15] defined a model of how the atmospheric phenomena affects the output images. The model depends on two parameters: a depth-dependent transmission ($t$), and the colour of the airlight ($A$). Mathematically, the model is written as

$$I_{x,\cdot} = t_x \cdot J_{x,\cdot} + (1 - t_x) \cdot A. \tag{1}$$

Here $x$ is a particular image pixel, $J_{x,\cdot}$ is the 1-by-3 vector of the R,G,B values at pixel x of the clear image (i.e., how the image would look without atmospheric scatter) and $I_{x,\cdot}$ is the 1-by-3 vector of the R,G,B values at pixel x of the image presenting the scattering effect. We remark that the transmission $t$ only depends on the depth of the image, and therefore it is supposed to be equal for the three colour channels.

Image dehazing methods -i.e. methods that given a hazy image $I$, obtain a clear image $J$- are becoming crucial for computer vision, because there are several methods -for recognition and classification among other tasks- that are supposed to work in the wild. Some examples are those used for surveillance through CCTV cameras, tracking, or the self-driving of vehicles and drones. However, the vast majority of these methods are devised for clear images, and tend to fail under adverse weather conditions. Image dehazing methods can be roughly divided in two categories: (i) physical-based methods that estimate the transmission of the image and solve for the clear image by inverting Eq. 1 [3, 4, 7, 13, 18, 21, 23, 24, 27], and (ii) image processing methods that directly process the hazy image so as to obtain a dehazed image but without considering the previous equation (from now on, we will call these methods *non-physical dehazing methods*) [2, 6, 10–12, 25, 26].

In this paper we focus on *non-physical dehazing methods*. This type of methods are able to obtain state-of-the-art results, but may sometimes present over-saturated colours and colour artefacts mostly because a different transmission is obtained for each colour channel. An example of the problems just mentioned is shown in Fig. 1 where, from left to right, we show two original images, the results from the methods of Galdran *et al.* [11] (top) and Choi *et al.* [6] (bottom), and the results obtained by using the approach of this paper.

There are very few proven methods that specifically look at reducing the colour artefacts that appear in dehazed images. Matlin and Milanfar [17] proposed an iterative regression method to simultaneously perform denoising and dehazing. Li *et al.* [16] decomposed the image into high and low frequencies, performing the dehazing only in the low frequencies, thus avoiding blocking artifacts. Chen *et al.* [5] applied both a smoothing filter for the refinement of the transmission and an energy minimisation in the recovery phase to avoid the appearance of gradients in the output image that were not presented in the original image.

In this paper we present a post-processing model for *non-physical dehazing methods* that aims at providing an output image that accomplishes the physical constraints given by Eq. 1. Our method is based on a channel-coupling approach, and it is devised to obtain a single transmission for all the different colour channels. Furthermore, our method also improves on the estimation of the airlight colour.

## 2 Imposing a Physically Plausible Dehazing

In this section, we define our approach for the post-processing of *non-physical dehazing methods*. Our main goal is, given an original hazy image and the solution of a non-physical dehazing method, to obtain a single transmission and an airlight that minimise the error of Eq. 1. We can write this minimisation in matrix form as:

$$\{A^{our}, t^{our}\} = argmin_{A^*, t^*} \|(1 - t^*) \cdot A^* - I + T^* \odot J\|. \tag{2}$$

where, $1$ is a $N$-by-1 vector that has a value of 1 in every entry, $t^*$ is a $N$-by-1 vector that represents the transmission, $A^*$ is a 1-by-3 vector that provides us with the airlight, $I$, $J$ are $N$-by-3 matrices representing the input image, and the non-physical dehazing solution, $N$ is the number of pixels, $T^*$ is a $N$-by-3 matrix consisting on the replication of $t^*$ three times, and $\odot$ represents the element-wise multiplication.

It is clear that to solve for this equation, we need to select an input guessing for either $A^{our}$ or $t^{our}$. This is not a problem, since a standard hypothesis used in many image dehazing works is to select $A^{our} = [1,1,1]$. Equation 2 also teaches us that we should perform the minimisation iteratively in two different dimensions. When we look for $t^{our}$ we should perform the minimisation for each pixel $x$ of the image over the three colour channels, while when we look for $A^{our}$ we should perform the minimisation for each colour channel $c$ over all the pixels.

We now detail our iterative minimisation. Let us start by having $I$, $J$, and the initial guessing for $A^{our}$. In this case we can solve for the value of $t^{our}$ at each pixel value $x$ using a least squares minimisation:

$$\forall(x) \; t_x^{our} = argmin_{t_x^*} \|(I_{x,\cdot} - A^{our}) - t_x^* \cdot (J_{x,\cdot} - A^{our})\|_2. \tag{3}$$

As stated in the introduction, $J_{x,\cdot}$ and $I_{x,\cdot}$ are the 1-by-3 colour vectors at pixel $x$. This least squares minimisation has the following solution

$$\forall(x) \; t_x^{our} = (I_{x,\cdot} - A^{our})(J_{x,\cdot} - A^{our})^T((J_{x,\cdot} - A^{our})(J_{x,\cdot} - A^{our})^T)^{-1}. \tag{4}$$

where $T$ denotes the transpose of the vector.

Once we have found the transmission value $t^{our}$, we can refine the value of $A^{our}$ via a least squares approach. In this case, as stated above, we perform the least squares minimisation over the pixels of the image for each of the three colour channels. Mathematically,

$$\forall(c) \; A_c^{our} = argmin_{A_c^*} \|(1 - t^{our}) \cdot A_c^* - I_{\cdot,c} + t^{our} \odot J_{\cdot,c}\|_2. \tag{5}$$

In this case $J_{\cdot,c}$ and $I_{\cdot,c}$ are $N$-by-1 vectors representing each different colour channel of the images -i.e. $c = \{R, G, B\}$-, $N$ is the number of pixels, and $1$ is also a $N$-by-1 vector that has 1 at every entry.

This minimisation leads to

$$\forall(c) \; A_c^{our} = ((1 - t^{our})^T(1 - t^{our}))^{-1}((1 - t^{our})^T(I_{\cdot,c} - t^{our} \odot J_{\cdot,c})) \tag{6}$$

where $T$ denotes the transpose of the vector.

Once this new $A^{our}$ is obtained, we can keep the iterative approach going by further refining the previous $t^{our}$ following again Eq. 3.

Finally, once the desired number of iterations are performed, and given $t^{our}$, $A^{our}$, and the original hazy image $I$, we can obtain our output image $J^{our}$ by solving for Eq. 1:

$$J_{x,\cdot}^{our} = \frac{I_{x,\cdot} - A^{our}}{t_x^{our}} + A^{our}. \tag{7}$$

We want the reader to raise attention to the relation of this approach to the Alternative Least Squares (ALS) method introduced by Finlayson et al. [8]. As in the ALS method, we are following an iterative procedure for the minimisation of a norm-based function.

# 3   Experiments and Results

This section is divided into three parts. First, we show qualitative results for our approach when applied to different *non-physical dehazing methods*. This is followed by a quantitative analysis of our post-processing. The section ends with a subjective evaluation using a preference test. In all our results we have allowed our approach to perform 5 iterations, as we have found experimentally that they are enough to obtain stable results. We have initialised the iterative approach by supposing $A^{our} = [1, 1, 1]$.

## 3.1   Qualitative Evaluation

In all the following figures, we show on the left the original hazy image, on the center the result of the selected dehazing method, and on the right the result obtained by our method.

Figure 2 shows the results for the EVID method [11]. We can see that the original method is inducing an odd increase of contrast in the nearby objects of the image, therefore provoking these objects to look unnatural (e.g. the nearby plants in the top image, and the gravestones in the bottom image). These problems are clearly alleviated in our results.

Figure 3 shows the results for the FVID method [12]. The biggest problem of this image dehazing method is the appearance of artefacts (located in the base of

**Fig. 2.** Results of our post-processing for the EVID method. From left to right: Original hazy image, result of the EVID method, result after our post-processing.

**Fig. 3.** Results of our post-processing for the FVID method. From left to right: Original hazy image, result of the FVID method, result after our post-processing.

**Fig. 4.** Results of our post-processing for the DEFADE method. From left to right: Original hazy image, result of the DEFADE method, result after our post-processing. (Color figure online)

**Fig. 5.** Results of our post-processing for the Wang *et al.* method. From left to right: Original hazy image, result of the Wang *et al.* method, result after our post-processing. (Color figure online)

the bushes in the top image and in the sky in the bottom image). Also, the top image is clearly presenting an excessive unnatural contrast. All these problems are suppressed by our proposed approach.

Figure 4 shows the results for the DEFADE method [6]. This method over-enhances the colours, as it can be clearly seen in the green of the plants in the top image, and in the orange hue of the boy's jacket in the bottom one. Once again, these problems are solved after applying our proposed post-processing.

Finally, Fig. 5 shows the results for the method of Wang *et al.* [26]. In this particular case, images present an unreasonable contrast. This fact provokes the appearance of unrealistic edges and colours (focus on the green of the grass and the closer bushes in the top image, and on the wall of the nearby building in the bottom image). Once again, these problems are mitigated once our method is applied.

## 3.2  Quantitative Evaluation

For this subsection, we have selected six standard hazy images that appear in most of the works dealing with image dehazing. They are shown in Fig. 6. Regarding the *non-physical dehazing methods* to be evaluated, we have selected the following five: the FVID [12], the DEFADE [6], the method of Wang *et al.* [26], and the use of the DehRet method by [10], considering as Retinex the variational approach of SCIE [9] and the Multiscale Retinex (MSCR) method. [22].

We have computed two different image quality metrics in order to evaluate our results: the Naturalness Image Quality Evaluator (NIQE) [20], and the BRISQUE metric [19]. We have selected these metrics as we do not have access to corresponding ground-truth (fog-free) images. Let us note that in the case there are ground-truth images available further metrics can also be considered [14].

**Fig. 6.** Original images used in both the quantitative evaluation and the preference test.

NIQE is an error metric that states how natural an image is (the smaller the number, the higher the naturalness). Table 1 presents the mean and RMS results for this metric. Our method improves in all the cases except for the FVID method. In this last case, the mean for the original dehazing method and the mean for our approach is the same, and the RMS for our approach is slightly worse than the one for the original dehazing.,

BRISQUE is a distortion-based metric that also tries to predict if an image looks natural based on scene statistics (the smaller the value, the better the result). Table 2 presents the results for this metric. In this case, our method outperforms all the others for all the cases.

**Table 1.** Mean and RMS results for the NIQE measure.

|              | Original method | | Our approach | |
|--------------|------|------|------|------|
|              | Mean | RMS  | Mean | RMS  |
| Wang et al.  | 3.89 | 4.00 | **3.45** | **3.51** |
| Defade       | 3.36 | 3.44 | **3.32** | **3.41** |
| FVID         | **3.32** | **3.36** | **3.32** | 3.37 |
| DehRet-MSCR  | 3.83 | 3.91 | **3.46** | **3.49** |
| DehRet-SRIE  | 3.00 | 3.02 | **2.94** | **2.95** |

### 3.3   Preference Test

We have also performed a preference test with the same set of images used in the previous subsection. In total, 7 observers completed the experiment. All observers were tested for normal colour vision. The experiment was conducted

**Table 2.** Mean and RMS results for the BRISQUE measure.

|              | Original method |       | Our approach |       |
|--------------|-----------------|-------|--------------|-------|
|              | Mean            | RMS   | Mean         | RMS   |
| Wang et al.  | 31.58           | 32.33 | **22.44**    | **24.30** |
| Defade       | 21.75           | 22.22 | **20.28**    | **20.85** |
| FVID         | 21.71           | 23.39 | **20.91**    | **22.88** |
| DehRet-MSCR  | 24.81           | 26.34 | **22.97**    | **23.97** |
| DehRet-SRIE  | 25.22           | 25.94 | **24.84**    | **25.73** |

on a NEC SpectraView reference 271 monitor set to 'sRGB' mode. The display was viewed at a distance of approximately 70 cm so that 40 pixels subtended 1° of visual angle. Stimuli were generated running MATLAB (MathWorks) with functions from the Psychtoolbox. The experiment was conducted in a dark room.

Subjects were presented with three images: in the center the original hazy image, and at each side the result of the original dehazing method and the result of our post-processing approach. Let us note that the side for these two images was selected randomly, and therefore varied at each presentation. Subjects were asked to select the preferred dehazed image. The total number of comparisons was 30.

Results have been obtained following the Thurstone Case V Law of Comparative Judgement. Figure 7 shows the results for the whole set of comparisons (i.e., considering the 5 original dehazing methods together). We can clearly see that our method statistically outperforms the original dehazing methods.

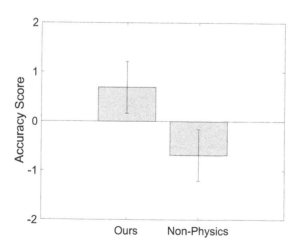

**Fig. 7.** Result of the preference test.

A more detailed analysis that looks individually at each dehazing method is presented in Fig. 8. We can clearly see that our method greatly outperforms the results of the DEFADE, the Wang *et al.*, and the DehRet-MSCR methods. In the case of the FVID and the DehRet-SRIE methods, our method is statistically equivalent to the original method. Let us note that these results are well aligned with those obtained on the previous subsection, as the two methods that are statistically equivalent to our post-processing were also the two methods for which our improvement in the metrics was smaller.

The results shown lead us to conclude that our method is very reliable, both quantitatively and subjectively: It does not output a result that deteriorates from the original dehazing method result. Also, let us note that we can not hypothesise which is the best original method, as no direct subjective comparison among them was performed. However, we can hypothesise that FVID and DehRet-SRIE are closer to follow the physical model as our method does not present a significant improvement over them.

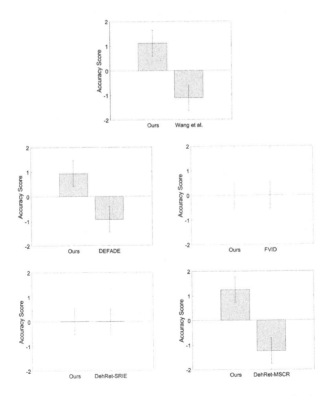

**Fig. 8.** Results of the preference test splited per method.

# 4  Conclusions

We have presented an approach to induce a physical behaviour to *non-physical dehazing methods*. Our approach is based on an iterative coupling of the colour channels, which is inspired by the Alternative Least Squares (ALS) method. Results show that our approach is strikingly promising. As further work, we will perform larger experiments with more images and subjects, will consider other evaluation paradigms (e.g. SIFT-based comparison [1]), and will study the convergence of our iterative scheme.

# References

1. Ancuti, C., Ancuti, C.O.: Effective contrast-based dehazing for robust image matching. IEEE Geosci. Remote Sens. Lett. **11**(11), 1871–1875 (2014). https://doi.org/10.1109/LGRS.2014.2312314
2. Ancuti, C., Ancuti, C.: Single image dehazing by multi-scale fusion. IEEE Trans. Image Process. **22**(8), 3271–3282 (2013)
3. Berman, D., Treibitz, T., Avidan, S.: Non-local image dehazing. In: IEEE Conference on Computer Vision and Pattern Recognition (CVPR) (2016)
4. Cai, B., Xu, X., Jia, K., Qing, C., Tao, D.: DehazeNet: An End-to-End System for Single Image Haze Removal, January 2016. arXiv:1601.07661
5. Chen, C., Do, M.N., Wang, J.: Robust image and video dehazing with visual artifact suppression via gradient residual minimization. In: Leibe, B., Matas, J., Sebe, N., Welling, M. (eds.) ECCV 2016, Part II. LNCS, vol. 9906, pp. 576–591. Springer, Cham (2016). https://doi.org/10.1007/978-3-319-46475-6_36
6. Choi, L.K., You, J., Bovik, A.C.: Referenceless prediction of perceptual fog density and perceptual image defogging. IEEE Trans. Image Process. **24**(11), 3888–3901 (2015)
7. Fattal, R.: Dehazing using color-lines. ACM Trans. Graph. **34**, 1 (2014)
8. Finlayson, G.D., Mohammadzadeh Darrodi, M., Mackiewicz, M.: The alternating least squares technique for nonuniform intensity color correction. Color Res. Appl. **40**(3), 232–242 (2014). https://doi.org/10.1002/col.21889
9. Fu, X., Zeng, D., Huang, Y., Zhang, X.P., Ding, X.: A weighted variational model for simultaneous reflectance and illumination estimation. In: 2016 IEEE Conference on Computer Vision and Pattern Recognition (CVPR), pp. 2782–2790, June 2016. https://doi.org/10.1109/CVPR.2016.304
10. Galdran, A., Alvarez-Gila, A., Bria, A., Vazquez-Corral, J., Bertalmío, M.: On the duality between retinex and image dehazing. In: IEEE Conference on Computer Vision and Pattern Recognition (CVPR) (2018)
11. Galdran, A., Vazquez-Corral, J., Pardo, D., Bertalmío, M.: Enhanced variational image dehazing. SIAM J. Imaging Sci. **8**(3), 1519–1546 (2015)
12. Galdran, A., Vazquez-Corral, J., Pardo, D., Bertalmío, M.: Fusion-based variational image dehazing. IEEE Signal Process. Lett. **24**(2), 151–155 (2017). https://doi.org/10.1109/LSP.2016.2643168
13. He, K., Sun, J., Tang, X.: Single image haze removal using dark channel prior. IEEE Trans. Pattern Anal. Mach. Intell. **33**(12), 2341–2353 (2011)
14. Khoury, J.E., Moan, S.L., Thomas, J., Mansouri, A.: Color and sharpness assessment of single image dehazing. Multimedia Tools Appl. **77**(12), 15409–15430 (2018)

15. Koschmieder, H.: Theorie der horizontalen Sichtweite: Kontrast und Sichtweite. Keim & Nemnich (1925)

16. Li, Y., Guo, F., Tan, R.T., Brown, M.S.: A contrast enhancement framework with JPEG artifacts suppression. In: Fleet, D., Pajdla, T., Schiele, B., Tuytelaars, T. (eds.) ECCV 2014, Part II. LNCS, vol. 8690, pp. 174–188. Springer, Cham (2014). https://doi.org/10.1007/978-3-319-10605-2_12

17. Matlin, E., Milanfar, P.: Removal of haze and noise from a single image. In: Proceedings of SPIE 8296. Computational Imaging X, vol. 8296, pp. 82960T–82960T-12 (2012)

18. Meng, G., Wang, Y., Duan, J., Xiang, S., Pan, C.: Efficient image dehazing with boundary constraint and contextual regularization. In: 2013 IEEE International Conference on Computer Vision (ICCV), pp. 617–624, December 2013

19. Mittal, A., Moorthy, A.K., Bovik, A.: No-reference image quality assessment in the spatial domain. IEEE Trans. Image Process. **21**(12), 4695–4708 (2012). https://doi.org/10.1109/TIP.2012.2214050

20. Mittal, A., Soundararajan, R., Bovik, A.: Making a "completely blind" image quality analyzer. IEEE Signal Process. Lett. **20**, 209–212 (2013)

21. Nishino, K., Kratz, L., Lombardi, S.: Bayesian defogging. Int. J. Comput. Vis. **98**(3), 263–278 (2012)

22. Petro, A.B., Sbert, C., Morel, J.M.: Multiscale retinex. Image Process. On Line, 71–88 (2014). https://doi.org/10.5201/ipol.2014.107

23. Tan, R.: Visibility in bad weather from a single image. In: IEEE Conference on Computer Vision and Pattern Recognition, CVPR 2008, pp. 1–8, June 2008

24. Tarel, J.P., Hautiere, N., Caraffa, L., Cord, A., Halmaoui, H., Gruyer, D.: Vision enhancement in homogeneous and heterogeneous fog. IEEE Intell. Transp. Syst. Mag. **4**(2), 6–20 (2012)

25. Vazquez-Corral, J., Galdran, A., Cyriac, P., Bertalmío, M.: A fast image dehazing method that does not introduce color artifacts. J. Real-Time Image Process., August 2018. https://doi.org/10.1007/s11554-018-0816-6

26. Wang, S., Cho, W., Jang, J., Abidi, M.A., Paik, J.: Contrast-dependent saturation adjustment for outdoor image enhancement. J. Opt. Soc. Am. A **34**(1), 7–17 (2017). https://doi.org/10.1364/JOSAA.34.000007. http://josaa.osa.org/abstract.cfm?URI=josaa-34-1-7

27. Zhang, H., Patel, V.M.: Densely connected pyramid dehazing network. In: IEEE Conference on Computer Vision and Pattern Recognition (CVPR) (2018)

# Color Image Applications

# Evaluating CNN-Based Semantic Food Segmentation Across Illuminants

Gianluigi Ciocca$^{(\boxtimes)}$ (iD), Davide Mazzini (iD), and Raimondo Schettini (iD)

DISCo - Department of Informatics, Systems and Communication,
University of Milano-Bicocca, Viale Sarca 336, 20126 Milan, Italy
{ciocca,mazzini,schettini}@disco.unimib.it

**Abstract.** In this paper we aim to explore the potential of Deep Convolutional Neural Networks (DCNNs) on food image segmentation where semantic segmentation paradigm is used to separate food regions from the non-food regions. Specifically, we are interested in evaluating the performance of an efficient DCNN with respect to variability in illumination conditions that can be found in food images taken in real scenarios. To this end we have designed an experimental setup where the network is trained on images rendered as if they were taken under nine different illuminants. We evaluate the food vs. non-food segmentation performance of the network in terms of standard Intersection over Union (IoU) measure. The results of this experimentation are reported and discussed.

**Keywords:** Semantic segmentation · Food analysis ·
Dietary monitoring · Convolutional Neural Network · Illuminants

## 1 Introduction

The problem of healthy and balanced meal is being seriously tackled by the different health agencies with the aim at reducing obesity and unbalanced nutrition. For example, the Department of Health of the Italian Government promoted an extensive campaign for food and nutrition education[1]. The Department of Health of the Australian Government, compiled a very detailed report with guidelines for healthy foods in school canteens[2]. In Japan, the Ministry of Education, Science and Culture, the Ministry of Health and Welfare, and the Ministry of Agriculture, Forestry and Fisheries developed dietary guidelines with the aim of promoting better dietary patterns[3]. Similar actions can be found across many other countries (e.g. UK[4], USA[5], etc...).

The significant increase rates of obesity and diabetes for both adults and children make it extremely important to devise ways for accurate tracking of

---

[1] http://www.salute.gov.it/imgs/c_17_pubblicazioni_1248_allegato.pdf.
[2] https://education.nt.gov.au/policies/canteen-nutrition-and-healthy-eating.
[3] http://www.maff.go.jp/j/syokuiku/pdf/yo-ryo-.pdf.
[4] http://www.schoolfoodplan.com/actions/school-food-standards/.
[5] http://www.fns.usda.gov/school-meals/child-nutrition-programs.

© Springer Nature Switzerland AG 2019
S. Tominaga et al. (Eds.): CCIW 2019, LNCS 11418, pp. 247–259, 2019.
https://doi.org/10.1007/978-3-030-13940-7_19

nutritional intakes. The conventional way to track food intake has been carried out by exploring manually recorded logs on a daily basis, which is error prone due to delayed reporting, inability to estimate the food type and quantity. More accurate and user-friendly solutions can be achieved by taking advantage of technology, e.g one can simply take a picture of a plate of food using a smartphone and corresponding calorie of the food can be calculated automatically by employing computer vision techniques. In the recent years many research works have demonstrated that machine learning and computer vision techniques can help to build systems to automatically recognize diverse foods and to estimate the food quantity and calories [2, 10, 15, 19, 20, 24, 29, 30].

**Fig. 1.** A general workflow of automatic dietary monitoring.

As shown in Fig. 1, a general work-flow of automatic dietary monitoring a number of computational tasks need to be accomplished. Initially, a given image is segmented in order to locate the boundaries of the food regions (*food segmentation*). Then, each food region is processed to identify the depicted food (*food recognition*). Finally, the quantity of each recognized food is estimated (*quantity estimation*) which paves the way towards calorie measurement. It is undeniable that accurately accomplishing each of these tasks is very important to achieve a well-working dietary monitoring system. In addition, food segmentation has to be used as a pre-processing step for recognition images with multiple food items.

It is clear that any mistakes, e.g under-segmentation or over-segmentation may influence the performance of the other tasks which would inevitably yield to incorrect calorie calculation. Moreover, if the dietary monitoring system is aimed at supporting the user in logging its food consumption in real scenarios, the food segmentation task must be robust to different image acquisition conditions such as changes in illumination, different point of views or different cameras.

Food analysis is a particularly challenging task since food is characterized by an intrinsic high intra-class variability. For instance, the same food can have very diverse visual appearance in the images due to slightly different preparations, presentations, and background. At the same time, we can have a low inter-class variability in the food appearance: different food may have extremely similar visual characteristics that make them difficulty to disambiguate. Figure 2 shows some examples of these two problems.

Due to their robustness with respect to data variability and thanks to their ability to extract and process relevant information within the images, Deep Convolutional Neural Networks (DCNNs) have been effectively used in different computer vision tasks. For these reason, in this paper we aim to explore the potential

**Fig. 2.** Top row: examples of high intra-class variability in visual appearance in food images ("Curry rice"). Bottom row: examples of low inter-class variability ("Fried noodles" vs. "Spaghetti", "Donuts" vs. "Bagel", and "French fries" vs. "Poutine").

of DCNNs on food and non-food image segmentation where semantic segmentation paradigm is used to separate food regions from the non-food regions. The results of this task could be leveraged both for a food recognition task and for a quantity and calories estimation task. Here we are interested in evaluating the performance of an efficient DCNN (GUNet [27,28]) with respect to variability in illumination conditions that can be found in food images taken in real scenarios. We want to investigate if and how we can cope with these variability at training time. To this end we have designed an experimental setup to evaluate a fast DCNN network trained on datasets of images rendered using different illuminants in a similar way as in [7]. We choose GUNet since, differently from other more complex and deep networks, it could be used also in mobile applications.

The paper is organized as follows. In Sect. 2 we briefly revise the state of the art in food segmentation. In Sect. 3, we describe our proposed approach for food segmentation. In Sect. 4 we present the segmentation results on a newly annotated food dataset. Finally, Sect. 5 concludes the paper.

## 2   Related Works

In this Section, we describe recent works dealing with the problem of food segmentation both using conventional approach as well as based on DCNNs.

Among the approaches using conventional image segmentation techniques adopted to food images we can find the work by He et al. [21] which evaluate two segmentation algorithms exploiting normalized cut (NCut) and local variation. Based on the experiments, local variation is found to be more stable among the two algorithms. In [15,16] JSEG segmentation algorithm [18] is used to locate food regions in images acquired in a canteen environment. Coupled with ad-hoc post-processing (given the image domain) of the resulting segmented images it is able to achieve very good performances. In [3], the JSEG-based food segmentation approach is further analyzed with extensive experiments evaluating different color spaces and algorithm's parameters used for the segmentation. Results show that, segmentation results can be improved with respect to the base algorithm.

In order to avoid the high computational cost of normalized cut-based segmentation algorithm in particular when applied per pixel on large images, Wang et al. [32] combine NCut with image superpixels. Superpixels are computed using the SLIC algorithm [1] and rely on color and texture cues. Results obtained on food and non food datasets, show that the proposed method exhibits a fast computation and an efficient use of memory.

Precise automatic food segmentation is a difficult task, in particular if it need to be performed on images acquired in the wild. For this reason, Inunganbi et al. [22] propose an interactive segmentation approach instead. They approach the segmentation task as a two class classification problem (i.e. food vs. non-food). Segmentation is performed using Random Forest ensemble learning, and boundary detection & filling and Gappy Principal Component Analysis methods are applied to refine the initial segmentation result.

The stunning success of DCNNs for image classification, encouraged the use of these techniques for other computer vision tasks as well. In particular they have been successfully employed for the semantic segmentation task where they are able to predict the category label of each image pixel among a set of given ones. However, properties that make DCNNs advantageous for classification tasks, i.e. robustness to spatial transformations and ability to learn increased abstraction of data, impede accuracy of the system for segmentation tasks where precise localization is desired rather than abstraction of spatial details [13]. For this reason, DCNNs that must perform image segmentation need to be designed with operations (i.e. layers) specifically tailored for the segmentation task as in FCN [25], DeepLab [13], SegNet [5] and GUNet [28] networks.

In the context of food segmentation, DCNNs have been used by Dehais et al. [17] to segment the food of already detected dishes in an image. The method combines region growing/merging techniques with a deep CNN-based food border detection to detect food regions outlines.

[30] is the first work accomplishing semantic segmentation specifically for food images by employing DCNNs. Specifically, the network architecture used is based on the earliest version of DeepLab [12]. This model uses a CNN to provide the unary potentials of a CRF, and a fully connected graph to perform edge-sensitive label smoothing (as in bilateral filtering). The network is initialized on ImageNet and fine-tuned on a newly annotated dataset of more than 12,000 images: Food201-segmented.

Bolanos et al. [9] Bolanos et al. employed DCNNs to simultaneously perform food localization and recognition. First, the method produces a food activation map on the input image for generating bounding boxes proposals of food regions. Then, each proposal is processed to recognize food types or food-related objects present in each bounding box. A similar approach is employed by Wang et al. [33]. The segmentation method uses the class activation maps and an adapted VGG-16 architecture to perform weakly supervised learning. The network is trained on food datasets as a top-down saliency model, and a Global Average Max Pooling (GAMP) layer is introduced into the architecture. The activation maps are used as constraints in biased normalized cut. The final segmentation masks are obtained by binarizing the biased normalized cut.

In order to be effective in the context of dietary monitoring in real scenarios (i.e. in the wild), food segmentation algorithms must be robust to changes in illumination conditions. Since the image acquisition environment is mostly uncontrolled we can have large variations in illuminants. A network trained on pristine image datasets could have low performances in real usage. For this reason, large, heterogeneous and representative, for the task at hand, food image datasets are crucial for the design of effective methods for food recognition, segmentation and quantity estimation. One of the largest dataset for food segmentation is Food201-segmented of [30]. Unfortunately the dataset is not publicly available. A smaller but available segmented dataset is, for example, the UNIMIB2015 and UNIMIB2016 datasets [15,16] created collecting tray images in a canteen environment. Finally, if the application require that the processing is to be performed on mobile devices (i.e. acquisition and analysis) in order to reduce the bandwidth consumption, it is essential that the DCNN used for segmentation must be light and thus requiring few operations (see [6] for a benchmark of different DCNN architectures).

## 3 Experimental Setup

For our experiments we adopted the Food50M described in Sect. 3.1. We performed our experiments using an efficient network named GUNet [28] which is presented more in details in Sect. 3.2. Every model is evaluated by means of the pixel-based IoU measure computed as:

$$IoU = \frac{groundtruth \cap prediction}{groundtruth \cup prediction} \tag{1}$$

this formula can be alternatively written as:

$$IoU = \frac{TP}{FP + TP + FN} \tag{2}$$

where TP, FP and FN represent True Positive, False Positive and False Negative pixels respectively. For every experiment we report the IoU measure computed independently for every class. We also report the mean of the food and non-food classes as a more synthetic indicator of the performance of the whole segmentation method.

### 3.1 Food Image Dataset

Available large food image datasets with segmentation information are scarce. The largest dataset in the literature is the one introduced in [30] but unfortunately is not publicly available. Other image datasets are either small of do not have a pixel-based segmentation annotation. For these reason, we decide to use the Food-50 dataset [23] as a base to create our own segmentation datasets. With respect to the available UNIMIB2015 [15] and UNIMIB2016 [16] datasets, Food-50 is large enough to be used for training and validation and is more diverse. Food-50 contains 5,000 images divided into 50 food classes. We manually annotated the regions of all the food items present in the images. This mean that each food belonging to one of the 50 classes as well as any other food found, such as vegetable in side dishes or used for presentation, was annotated as "food". We call this food image dataset *Food50Seg*. Figure 3 shows some examples of images in the dataset with the corresponding pixel-based annotation.

**Fig. 3.** Some segmentation examples of our Food50Seg food image dataset. Top row: "Arepas", "Lobster", and "Popcorn". Bottom row: "Corn", "Fried rice", and "Chocolate".

The images in the Food50 dataset were collected on the Internet from different sources. However, all the images seem to have been acquired using different cameras and mobile devices. They exhibit no evident illuminant cast so we can assume that a form of white balancing has been applied by the imaging devices. Moreover, we can assume the images use the sRGB color space, and thus are rendered under CIE D65 illuminant. To understand the effect of lighting variations in the context of semantic food segmentation, we modified the Food-50 dataset by artificially changing the illumination conditions of the images. In particular we follow a procedure similar to [7] by using nine blackbody radiators with color temperature from 3000 K to 8000 K with step of 1000 K, and with color temperature of 10000 K, 12000 K, and 14000 K. We call this dataset Food50M. Figure 4 shows an image rendered using the nine illuminants considered.

### 3.2    Network Architecture

For our experiments we adopted the GUNet architecture presented for the first time by Mazzini in [27]. In particular we rely on the improved version with the Guided Upsampling Module [28]. This network is designed for real-time applications and thus its main characteristic is the low inference time. The reasons that lead us to employ this architecture are twofold: first, this model can be employed on mobile devices for dietary monitoring applications in real conditions. Second, the architecture is also very fast at train time allowing us to train a relatively high quantity of models for our experiments on a single Titan Xp GPU.

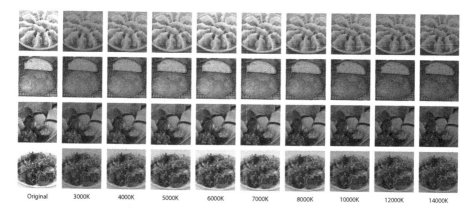

**Fig. 4.** An example of a food image in the Food50M dataset rendered using the nine illuminants considered. From top to bottom: "Dumplings", "Bread", "Sushi", and "Salad".

The network follows an encoder-decoder design. The encoder has a multi-branch structure to encode features at multiple resolutions: the first branch is the deepest one, encoding the most abstract features whereas the second branch is shallower by design in order to encode fine details without being too computational heavy. The first part of the decoder is a Fusion Module. It is composed by a first part where signals are pre-processed independently followed by a second part where signals are jointly processed and information coming from multiple resolution branches is fused together. The Decoder ends with a layer named Guided Upsampling Module that efficiently upsample the feature map. In this way the network is able to produce a semantic segmentation map of the same resolution of the network input.

The network exhibits a total of 19 Millions of parameters and requires 58,7 GFLOP to perform single inference on a $512 \times 1024$ image. Most parameters are in the Encoder part.

### 3.3  Training Recipe

All the network configurations in this paper have been trained with Stochastic Gradient Descent (SGD) plus momentum. Following [28], we set the base learning rate to 0.001 and trained for 150 epochs. We adopted a *fixed step* learning rate policy. The initial value is decreased two times by a order of magnitude (at 100 and 200 epochs).

## 4  Experimental Results

### 4.1  Assessing Robustness to Illuminants

With a first cluster of experiments, we want to assess if our DCNN model trained on Food50 training-set is robust to changes of the illuminant in the scene. The same network, i.e. GUNet [28] described in Sect. 3.2, is trained only once on the original dataset and tested over nine modified versions of the test set with illuminants. Numerical results for this experiment are reported in Table 1 in terms of IoU measure vs illuminant color. The first column reports the network performance on the original test set. It is clearly noticeable a performance degradation on all the modified test sets with respect to the baseline. In particular the IoU levels decay with higher intensity for extreme cast values. The highest IoU values are obtained between 7000 K and 8000 K suggesting that the distribution of illuminants in the original image set is centered on such values (consider that the daylight temperature is 6500 K).

**Table 1.** Results of our DCNN model tested on different illuminants. The first column no-cast reports the results on the original test set.

| Tested on | | | | | | | | | | | |
|---|---|---|---|---|---|---|---|---|---|---|---|
| | | | no-cast | 3000 K | 4000 K | 5000 K | 6000 K | 7000 K | 8000 K | 10000 K | 12000 K | 14000 K |
| Trained on no-cast | IoU(%) | food | 69.9 | 0.5 | 18.8 | 24.7 | 32.0 | 41.0 | 39.3 | 3.8 | 0.3 | 0.1 |
| | | non-food | 87.0 | 87.0 | 74.3 | 71.0 | 73.2 | 74.3 | 75.5 | 77.2 | 77.2 | 71.4 |
| | | mean | 78.5 | 35.7 | 46.0 | 49.5 | 53.7 | 59.0 | 58.2 | 37.6 | 35.6 | 35.6 |

By looking at detailed results (i.e. first two rows) in Table 1 we can observe an interesting detail: IoU values for the non-food class remains quite high for every color cast whereas the real performance decrease is remarkable only for the food class. This might be related to the fact that the non-food images in our test set have been collected "in the wild" and thus they exhibit a wider range of illuminants. The trained model is thus more robust to illuminant changes. In our next experiments we will augment the training set with images with illuminants to measure if the model can acquire a certain degree of robustness to this types of image transformations.

## 4.2  Augmented Training Set

With this set of experiments, we want to assess the behaviour of the DCNN if trained on an augmented training set and observe the difference with the same model trained on the natural dataset. In detail, we want to test if the model benefits from being trained on a dataset with a specific illuminant and compare it with a model which is trained on the union set of all the illuminants. In Table 2 are reported the results for three clusters of experiments: the first three lines represent our baseline from Table 1 (i.e. a single model trained on the original dataset).

The second cluster of experiments is exposed from line 4 to 6. Every column represents the result obtained by training and testing a model on *that* specific illuminant. Notice that the first and the last column are missing because they represent redundant data: the first column represents the model trained and tested on the no-cast dataset, which is shown in the first three rows of the table.

**Table 2.** Results of three different train setups tested against various illuminant casts. First 3 rows: the model is trained on the original test set. Line 4 to 6: the model is trained on the specific illuminant only. Last 3 rows: the training set is augmented with all the illuminants.

| Tested on | | | no-cast | 3000 K | 4000 K | 5000 K | 6000 K | 7000 K | 8000 K | 10000 K | 12000 K | 14000 K | all ill. |
|---|---|---|---|---|---|---|---|---|---|---|---|---|---|
| Trained on | original train set | food | 69.9 | 0.5 | 18.8 | 24.7 | 32.0 | 41.0 | 39.3 | 3.8 | 0.3 | 0.1 | 23.5 |
| | | non-food | 87.0 | 71.0 | 73.2 | 74.3 | 75.5 | 77.2 | 77.2 | 71.4 | 71.0 | 71.1 | 74.3 |
| | | mean | 78.5 | 35.7 | 46.0 | 49.5 | 53.7 | 59.0 | 58.2 | 37.6 | 35.6 | 35.5 | 48.9 |
| | specific illuminant | food | - | 60.5 | 71.0 | 71.0 | 73.4 | 68.4 | 74.0 | 73.1 | 74.2 | 76.1 | - |
| | | non-food | - | 74.2 | 84.0 | 84.2 | 89.2 | 82.7 | 89.2 | 87.8 | 88.0 | 89.0 | - |
| | | mean | - | 67.3 | 77.5 | 77.6 | 81.3 | 75.5 | 81.6 | 80.5 | 81.1 | 82.6 | - |
| | all illuminants | food | 71.9 | 68.3 | 70.8 | 71.2 | 71.2 | 71.1 | 71.1 | 70.7 | 69.8 | 69.5 | 70.5 |
| | | non-food | 86.2 | 83.6 | 85.5 | 85.9 | 85.8 | 85.7 | 85.9 | 85.6 | 85.2 | 85.1 | 85.5 |
| | | mean | 79.0 | 76.0 | 78.2 | 78.5 | 78.5 | 78.4 | 78.5 | 78.2 | 77.5 | 77.3 | 78.0 |

Missing data in the last column represents the model trained and tested on all illuminants, which is presented in the last column. We augmented the original training set with images rendered with that illuminant. The test set, like in all the others experiments, consists of images with a single modified illuminant. The performance raises dramatically with respect to the baseline. Most benefit is relative to the food class.

The last 3 lines of Table 2 represent the results of a single model trained on a set composed of the union set of all the illuminants. Surprisingly, for some illuminants this is the best model outperforming even the models trained on specific illuminants. This suggest that the DCNN model benefits from training on a higher number of images with higher variability. We suppose that the model trained on different illuminants generalize better because it become able to discriminate food from non food areas, abstracting from the type of illuminant in the scene.

In Table 2, the first column indicates tests made on the original test set without any illuminant cast. The last column indicates a test set composed by the union of all the test sets with illuminant casts. The model trained on all the illuminants exhibits an interesting behaviour even in this two cases. With respect to the no-cast set it behaves slightly better than the baseline model, suggesting that this for of data augmentation do not hurt the performance on the original data, i.e. the transformations are balanced and they do not introduce a bias in the data. Concerning the all-illuminant test set it shows a similar performance with respect to the no-cast set. Notice that the performance of the model trained only on the original data are visibly degraded.

In the last cluster of experiments we test the networks trained on specific illuminants against the original test set. With these experiments we want to verify if models trained on those augmented datasets maintain an acceptable segmentation performance even in the original test set not affected by illumination cast. Results are shown in Table 3. For the model trained on the 3000 K

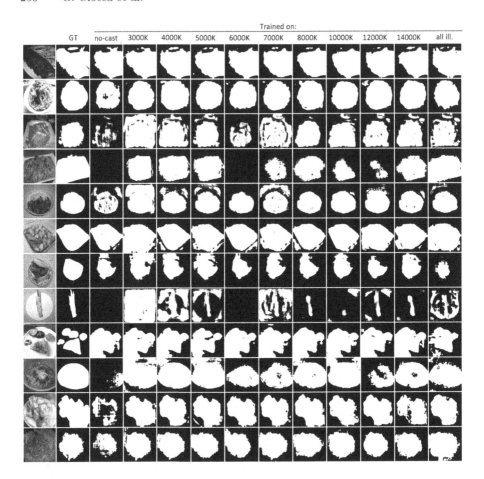

**Fig. 5.** Some segmentation results obtained using the different training strategies. no-cast denotes that the training is performed on the original data. "all ill." denotes that all the illuminants have been used during training. Images have been resized for display.

illuminant the mean IoU si quite lower than the baseline no-cast. This is probably due to the fact that 3000 K is an extreme illuminant color cast and such cast is not present in any of the original test set images. Surprisingly for some other illuminants like 14000 K or 8000 K the specific illuminant train setting is beneficial even when testing on the original set. However these numbers are not significantly higher and could be due the intrinsic randomness when initializing CNN models. As a general consideration we can state that the model do not exhibit evident performance degradation.

Figure 5 shows some visual results obtained using the different training strategies. The no-cast column represents the output of the model trained only on the original data. "all ill." denotes the output of the model trained on the union set

**Table 3.** Results of our DCNN model trained on different illuminants and tested on the original test set. The first column no-cast represents the results of the model trained on the original data.

| | | Trained on | | | | | | | | | | |
|---|---|---|---|---|---|---|---|---|---|---|---|---|
| | | | no-cast | 3000 K | 4000 K | 5000 K | 6000 K | 7000 K | 8000 K | 10000 K | 12000 K | 14000 K | all ill. |
| Tested on no-cast | IoU (%) | food | 69.9 | 60.5 | 71.0 | 71.0 | 73.4 | 68.4 | 74.0 | 73.1 | 74.2 | 76.1 | 71.9 |
| | | non-food | 87.0 | 74.2 | 84.0 | 84.2 | 89.2 | 82.7 | 89.2 | 87.8 | 88.0 | 89.0 | 86.2 |
| | | mean | 78.5 | 67.3 | 77.5 | 77.6 | 81.3 | 75.5 | 81.6 | 80.5 | 81.1 | 82.6 | 79.0 |

of every illuminant cast. The no-cast model clearly produces the worst visual results. In some images (i.e. rows 4,8) it doesn't even detect anything at all. Furthermore the three bottom images are clearly under-segmented. Every other method achieve overall better segmentation results. This is in line with what emerges from Table 3.

## 5 Conclusions

In this work we explored the potential of Deep Convolutional Neural Networks on food image segmentation to discriminate food regions from the background. In particular, we evaluated the performance of an efficient DCNN with respect to the variability in illumination conditions on real scene images. We built a new dataset named Food50M where images from the train and test set have been modified with nine different illuminants. Results show that the network trained on pristine data is not able to cope with strong illuminant shifts. By training and testing the model on a specific illuminant, performance improves with respect to the baseline as expected. Using all illuminants in training we are able to further improve the IoU measure. This demonstrates that we can effectively empower the model robustness exploiting an augmented training set composed by images with simulated illuminants. As future works we plan to evaluate color constancy algorithms or filter removal methods as pre-processing steps during the training phase, both traditional as well as CNN-based such as [8,11,14, 31]. Moreover, our food/non-food segmentation approach can be coupled with a semantic food segmentation technique such as [4,13,26] in order to recognize food-specific regions. This will allow to implement a system able to recognize food and estimate their properties such as quantity, calories, etc...

**Acknowledgements.** We gratefully acknowledge the support of NVIDIA Corporation with the donation of the Titan Xp GPU used for this research. Published in the context of the project FooDesArt: Food Design Arte - L'Arte del Benessere , CUP (Codice Unico Progetto - Unique Project Code): E48I16000350009 - Call "Smart Fashion and Design", cofunded by POR FESR 2014–2020 (Programma Operativo Regionale, Fondo Europeo di Sviluppo Regionale - Regional Operational Programme, European Regional Development Fund).

# References

1. Achanta, R., Shaji, A., Smith, K., Lucchi, A., Fua, P., Süsstrunk, S., et al.: Slic superpixels compared to state-of-the-art superpixel methods. IEEE Trans. Pattern Anal. Mach. Intell. **34**(11), 2274–2282 (2012)
2. Anthimopoulos, M.M., Gianola, L., Scarnato, L., Diem, P., Mougiakakou, S.G.: A food recognition system for diabetic patients based on an optimized bag-of-features model. Biomed. Health Inform. **18**(4), 1261–1271 (2014)
3. Aslan, S., Ciocca, G., Schettini, R.: On comparing color spaces for food segmentation. In: Battiato, S., Farinella, G.M., Leo, M., Gallo, G. (eds.) ICIAP 2017. LNCS, vol. 10590, pp. 435–443. Springer, Cham (2017). https://doi.org/10.1007/978-3-319-70742-6_42
4. Aslan, S., Ciocca, G., Schettini, R.: Semantic food segmentation for automatic dietary monitoring. In: IEEE 8th International Conference on Consumer Electronics, Berlin (ICCE-Berlin), pp. 1–6 (2018)
5. Badrinarayanan, V., Kendall, A., Cipolla, R.: Segnet: a deep convolutional encoder-decoder architecture for image segmentation. IEEE Trans. Pattern Anal. Mach. Intell. **39**(12), 2481–2495 (2017)
6. Bianco, S., Cadene, R., Celona, L., Napoletano, P.: Benchmark analysis of representative deep neural network architectures. IEEE Access **6**, 64270–64277 (2018)
7. Bianco, S., Cusano, C., Napoletano, P., Schettini, R.: On the robustness of color texture descriptors across illuminants. In: Petrosino, A. (ed.) ICIAP 2013, Part II. LNCS, vol. 8157, pp. 652–662. Springer, Heidelberg (2013). https://doi.org/10.1007/978-3-642-41184-7_66
8. Bianco, S., Cusano, C., Piccoli, F., Schettini, R.: Artistic photo filter removal using convolutional neural networks. J. Electron. Imaging **27**(1), 011004 (2017)
9. Bolanos, M., Radeva, P.: Simultaneous food localization and recognition. In: 23rd IEEE International Conference on Pattern Recognition (ICPR), pp. 3140–3145 (2016)
10. Bosch, M., Zhu, F., Khanna, N., Boushey, C., Delp, E.: Combining global and local features for food identification in dietary assessment. In: 18th IEEE International Conference on Image Processing (ICIP), pp. 1789–1792 (2011)
11. Buzzelli, M., van de Weijer, J., Schettini, R.: Learning illuminant estimation from object recognition. In: 25th IEEE International Conference on Image Processing (ICIP), pp. 3234–3238 (2018)
12. Chen, L.C., Papandreou, G., Kokkinos, I., Murphy, K., Yuille, A.: Semantic image segmentation with deep convolutional nets and fully connected crfs. In: International Conference on Learning Representations (2015)
13. Chen, L.C., Papandreou, G., Kokkinos, I., Murphy, K., Yuille, A.: Deeplab: semantic image segmentation with deep convolutional nets, atrous convolution, and fully connected crfs. IEEE Trans. Pattern Anal. Mach. Intell. **40**(4), 834–848 (2017)
14. Ciocca, G., Marini, D., Rizzi, A., Schettini, R., Zuffi, S.: Retinex preprocessing of uncalibrated images for color-based image retrieval. J. Electron. Imaging **12**(1), 161–172 (2003)
15. Ciocca, G., Napoletano, P., Schettini, R.: Food recognition and leftover estimation for daily diet monitoring. In: Murino, V., Puppo, E., Sona, D., Cristani, M., Sansone, C. (eds.) ICIAP 2015. LNCS, vol. 9281, pp. 334–341. Springer, Cham (2015). https://doi.org/10.1007/978-3-319-23222-5_41
16. Ciocca, G., Napoletano, P., Schettini, R.: Food recognition: a new dataset, experiments and results. IEEE J. Biomed. Health Inform. **21**(3), 588–598 (2017)

17. Dehais, J., Anthimopoulos, M., Mougiakakou, S.: Food image segmentation for dietary assessment. In: Proceedings of the 2nd International Workshop on Multimedia Assisted Dietary Management, pp. 23–28. ACM (2016)

18. Deng, Y., Manjunath, B.: Unsupervised segmentation of color-texture regions in images and video. IEEE Trans. Pattern Anal. Mach. Intell. **23**(8), 800–810 (2001)

19. Ege, T., Yanai, K.: Simultaneous estimation of food categories and calories with multi-task CNN. In: Fifteenth IAPR International Conference on Machine Vision Applications (MVA), pp. 198–201. IEEE (2017)

20. Ege, T., Yanai, K.: Multi-task learning of dish detection and calorie estimation. In: Proceedings of the Joint Workshop on Multimedia for Cooking and Eating Activities and Multimedia Assisted Dietary Management, pp. 53–58. ACM (2018)

21. He, Y., Khanna, N., Boushey, C.J., Delp, E.J.: Image segmentation for image-based dietary assessment: a comparative study. In: IEEE International Symposium on Signals, Circuits and Systems (ISSCS), pp. 1–4 (2013)

22. Inunganbi, S., Seal, A., Khanna, P.: Classification of food images through interactive image segmentation. In: Nguyen, N.T., Hoang, D.H., Hong, T.-P., Pham, H., Trawiński, B. (eds.) ACIIDS 2018, Part II. LNCS (LNAI), vol. 10752, pp. 519–528. Springer, Cham (2018). https://doi.org/10.1007/978-3-319-75420-8_49

23. Joutou, T., Yanai, K.: A food image recognition system with multiple kernel learning. In: 16th IEEE International Conference on Image Processing (ICIP), pp. 285–288. IEEE (2009)

24. Kawano, Y., Yanai, K.: Foodcam: a real-time food recognition system on a smartphone. Multimed. Tools Appl. **74**(14), 5263–5287 (2015)

25. Long, J., Shelhamer, E., Darrell, T.: Fully convolutional networks for semantic segmentation. In: IEEE Conference on Computer Vision and Pattern Recognition, pp. 3431–3440 (2015)

26. Long, J., Shelhamer, E., Darrell, T.: Fully convolutional networks for semantic segmentation. In: Proceedings of the IEEE conference on computer vision and pattern recognition. pp. 3431–3440 (2015)

27. Mazzini, D., Buzzelli, M., Pau, D.P., Schettini, R.: A CNN architecture for efficient semantic segmentation of street scenes. In: IEEE 8th International Conference on Consumer Electronics, Berlin (ICCE-Berlin), pp. 1–6 (2018)

28. Mazzini, D.: Guided upsampling network for real-time semantic segmentation. In: British Machine Vision Conference, BMVC 2018, Northumbria University, Newcastle, 3–6 September 2018, p. 117 (2018)

29. Mezgec, S., Koroušić Seljak, B.: Nutrinet: a deep learning food and drink image recognition system for dietary assessment. Nutrients **9**(7), 657 (2017)

30. Myers, A., et al.: Im2calories: towards an automated mobile vision food diary. In: IEEE International Conference on Computer Vision (ICCV), pp. 1233–1241 (2015)

31. Rizzi, A., Gatta, C., Slanzi, C., Ciocca, G., Schettini, R.: Unsupervised color film restoration using adaptive color equalization. In: Bres, S., Laurini, R. (eds.) VISUAL 2005. LNCS, vol. 3736, pp. 1–12. Springer, Heidelberg (2006). https://doi.org/10.1007/11590064_1

32. Wang, Y., Liu, C., Zhu, F., Boushey, C.J., Delp, E.J.: Efficient superpixel based segmentation for food image analysis. In: IEEE International Conference on Image Processing (ICIP), pp. 2544–2548. IEEE (2016)

33. Wang, Y., Zhu, F., Boushey, C.J., Delp, E.J.: Weakly supervised food image segmentation using class activation maps. In: IEEE International Conference on Image Processing (ICIP), pp. 1277–1281. IEEE (2017)

# Color-Base Damage Feature Enhanced Support Vector Classifier for Monitoring Quake Image

Takato Yasuno[✉], Masazumi Amakata, Junichiro Fujii, and Yuri Shimamoto

Research Institute for Infrastructure Paradigm Shift,
Yachiyo Engineering Co., Ltd., CS-Tower, 5-20-8 Asakusabashi,
Taito-ku, Tokyo 111-8648, Japan
{tk-yasuno, amakata, jn-fujii,
yr-shimamoto}@yachiyo-eng.co.jp

**Abstract.** In recent times, significant natural disasters have affected our city lives. This includes the occurrence of large earthquakes that have devastated the city's infrastructure. During such times of crisis, it is important that emergency response times be as quick as possible to mitigate harm and loss. To achieve this, priority must be given to the various types of initial emergency response. Color image monitoring has the potential to prioritize responses. It uses multimode data resources such as openly sourced photos on social media, smartphone cameras, CCTV, and so forth. This paper presents a method to enhance the damaged color features extracted based on a pre-trained deep architecture DenseNet-201 in order to classify damage caused by several earthquakes, whose classifiers are Bayesian optimized to minimize the loss function with cross-validation. This method is applied to a case study of an earthquake image dataset. The study incorporates five target categories, namely bridge collapse, initial smoke and fire, road damage with accident risk to expand secondary loss for relevant users, tsunami damage, and non-disaster. Some advantages have been found when using color feature extraction for monitoring quake damage and further opportunities are remarked (189 words).

**Keywords:** Quake image monitoring · Color-base augmentation ·
DenseNet-201 · Damage feature enhancement · Support vector classifier

## 1 Introduction

### 1.1 Related Papers and Damage Color Imaging

#### Disaster Damage Monitoring and Color Image Sources

Manzhu et al. [1] reviewed the major sources of big data, the associated achievements in disaster management phases to monitor and detect natural hazards, methods to mitigate against disaster-related damage, and the recovery and reconstruction processes. This study focuses on the urgent response phase after an earthquake, which monitors and detects damage and allows for make decisions in order to address initial

S. Tominaga et al. (Eds.): CCIW 2019, LNCS 11418, pp. 260–275, 2019.
https://doi.org/10.1007/978-3-030-13940-7_20

rapid actions regarding high-priority infrastructures such as roads, intersections, bridges, river gates, and public facilities. Between 2014 and 2016, several data sources were observed in articles, during a time when big data was a popular topic in disaster management. These data sources included satellite, social media, crowd-base data source, sensor web and IoT, mobile GPS, simulation, unmanned aerial vehicles (UAVs), light detection and ranging (LiDAR). Among these digital data sources, satellite imagery [2, 3] and social media [4, 5] data serve as the most popular type of data for disaster management.

However, satellites used for remote sensing travel at slow speeds and contain an interval gap in the data spanning from the previous flyover to the subsequent flyover. These photographs are not sequential causing delay when trying to recognize features of an earthquake disaster. Through the use of social media, spatial temporal sentiment analysis is possible. However, this is prone to inaccuracies because users of social media do not always monitor the disaster damage consistently. Witnesses to a natural disaster will prioritize their well-being and seek safety and shelter after an earthquake resulting in inconsistent data. Messaging is found to occasionally lack essential signals owing to noise, resulting in misinformation. This study focuses on the damaged color image source for monitoring the disaster damage of critical infrastructures to efficiently decide which high-priority responses to undertake them.

## Color-Base Segmentation and Color Feature Augmentation

Regarding color-based image segmentation using K-means clustering, many proposals and experimental results have been reported. Chitade [6] presented an image segmentation for satellite imagery based on color features in two stages where enhancement of color separation used decorrelation stretching and then grouped the regions into five classes using the K-means clustering algorithm to convert image from RGB to L*a*b* color space. The source claimed that it is possible to reduce the computational cost avoiding feature calculation for every pixel in the image. However, the source focused only on the satellite imagery for mapping the changes of color-base land cover to classify land use pattern. Shmmala [7] compared three versions of K-means clustering algorithms for biological images and ordinary full-colored images under RGB and L*a*b* spaces. Hassan et al. [8] attempted to find the optimal parameter K automatically, and therefore created segmentation without any human supervision to the algorithm. Then, they applied the algorithm to several types of images including flowers, birds, fruits, and games having funs. They presented the combined segmentation of RGB and HSV color spaces, which yielded more accurate results compared to that of a single color space. This combined case had the disadvantage of requiring twice the calculation costs; further, both color spaces are device-dependent.

However, there is currently no approach that is focused on using images of disasters for monitoring damage, and a method of damage color segmentation has not yet been reported to be used as an input for the enhancement of damage feature extraction. Adding the original images with such damage feature extraction using color-based segmentation could enhance the damage features, thereby improving the accuracy of classifier incorporating with color-base saliency enhancement more than that of classifier using the original images. This paper presents a method to enhance the damaged color-base feature extracted based on a pre-trained deep architecture in order to classify several types of damage after a disaster event, whose classifiers are Bayesian optimized to minimize the loss function with cross-validation. This method is applied to a case study of an earthquake image dataset. Five target classes, namely bridge collapse, initial smoke and fire, road damage with accident risk to expand secondary loss for relevant users, tsunami damage, and non-disaster are incorporated.

## 2 Damage Color Imaging Application

### 2.1 Earthquake Damage Image Dataset

With regard to disaster image datasets, the NOAA [9] provides a natural hazard image database with 1,163 photo images of 67 events of earthquakes that have occurred in the past 100 years from 1915 to 2015. It provides a gallery view of images of each earthquake event. The database includes earthquake disaster images from the USA, Mexico, Guatemala, Colombia, Nicaragua, Peru, Chile, Haiti, Ecuador, Russia, Iran, Turkey, Pakistan, Algeria, Romania, Italy, Papua New Guinea, Australia, New Zealand, Samoa, China, Indonesia, Taiwan, and Japan. However, the quality of the image differs for instances where low-resolution satellite images are used, airplane flight downward view is used, the angle of some photos is on the outdoor and indoor and front of the crushed house. Their region of interests and angles are different and the almost private historical photo collected wisdom without any unified rule. Each earthquake event has limited images; these ones consist of only few disaster images at each earthquake events on that database. Almost all these images are recorded after the earthquakes have occurred, when it has taken more than one week for an international academic survey to obtain relevant lesson historically. We attempted to collect openly source web pages from where the earthquake damage images could be downloaded.

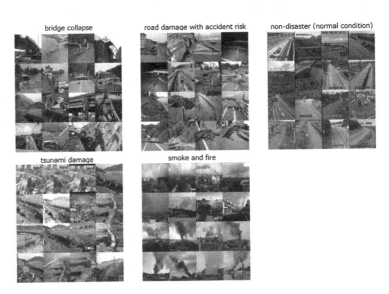

**Fig. 1.** Thumbnail of disaster color image: QuakeV dataset with 16 chosen examples.

This paper highlights the five features of earthquake disasters, namely tsunami damage, bridge collapse, road damage with accident risk, initial smoke and fire, and non-disaster. The authors collected a total number of 1,117 earthquake disaster feature images featured in the datasets. Herein, we focus on earthquake damage features among the color images, and we propose a dataset called QuakeV. Figure 1 shows the thumbnail of the earthquake damage image dataset with validation data that comprised 16 chosen images of each class: tsunami damage, bridge collapse, road damage with accident risk, initial smoke and fire, and non-damage.

## 2.2    Damage Color Feature Extraction

### L*a*b* Color Space Transformation from RGB

Several color spaces exist for color image representations; some spaces are device-dependent and the other spaces are device-independent. The former includes the RGB, NTSC, YCbCr, HSV, CMY, CMYK, and HSI spaces; these spaces represent color information in ways that are more intuitive or suitable for a particular application. For example, the appearance of RGB colors varies with display and scanner characteristics, and CMYK colors vary with printer, ink, and paper characteristics [10]. These device-dependent color spaces are not the preferred choice for disaster monitoring. This is because the color imaging system does not achieve a sufficient consistency in pre-trained detectors or classifiers required to predict target images. In contrast, one of the

**Fig. 2.** Thresholding three components to mask the background based on RGB (top) and L*a*b* (bottom), photo of the Great Hanshin Awaji Earthquake using the Kobe open data.

most widely used device-independent color spaces is the 1931 CIE XYZ color space developed by Commission Internationale de l'Eclairage (CIE). The CIE has developed additional color space specifications that are better suited to some purposes than XYZ. For example, these include the xyY, uvL, L*a*b*, and L*ch, and sRGB spaces. These device-independent color spaces are supported by the Image Processing Toolbox [11]. The L*a*b* color space was introduced in 1976, and is widely used in color science as well as the design of color devices such as printers, cameras, and scanners. The L*a*b color space provides two key advantages over XYZ as a working space. First, L*a*b* more clearly separates gray-scale information represented as L* values from color information represented using a* and b* values. Second, the L*a*b* was designed so the Euclidean distance in this space corresponds reasonably well with perceived differences between colors. Because of this property, the L*a*b* color space is perceptually uniform. As a corollary, L* values relate linearly to human perception of brightness [11].

The device-independent color space is suited to disaster monitoring. This study uses the L*a*b* color space to take advantage of this trait. Figure 2 shows the thresholding three components on two color spaces such as RGB (top) and L*a*b* (bottom), photo of the Great Hanshin Awaji Earthquake [12]. In the RGB color space, each component has a similarly distributed histogram. Thresholding R, G, and B components, the sky background is masked and the targets such as bridge and road pavement are focused, although trees and grass remain. In the L*a*b* color space, L* represents the brightness information of gray scale, and a*b* components represent the color information. The L*a*b* color space more flexibly achieved to mask sky, trees, and grass. This paper proposes a damage color segmentation based on the L*a*b* values to localize the target features such as infrastructures and damage for disaster monitoring (Fig. 3).

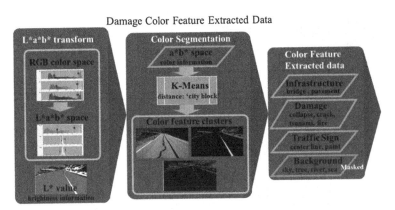

**Fig. 3.** Damage color segmentation based on the a*b* space using K-means clustering.

## Color-Base Augmentation Using Color Segmentation K-Means Clustering

This paper presents a color-base augmentation using damage color segmentation, where the original images are transformed from the RGB to L*a*b* color space to take advantage of the fact that L*a*b* is one example of a device-independent color space. The L* value can represent the brightness with gray-scale information. The a*b* space can represent the color information. These values can act as the input for the K-means clustering algorithm for color-based segmentation. We can calculate these distances with color space similarity on neighbor pixels selecting whether the Euclidean or city block. In the case using the Euclidean distance to minimize a cost function, there were many calculation results that did not converge in the disaster image dataset. This paper proposes to use the city block distance between the center and any nearby points.

## Color-Base Damage Feature Categorization for Quake Disaster Monitoring

The color-base region of interest (ROI) monitoring a disaster image is divided into four categories, namely (1) damaged infrastructure with earthquake disaster or (2) health infrastructure without disaster, (3) traffic sign, and (4) background. For example, the color-base ROI of health infrastructure is represented by bridge with concrete white color and road pavement is denoted by blue-colored asphalt (fresh pitch stone - rekisei) and faded into gray-colored. In detail, damaged infrastructure with disaster features are divided into two patterns, at first, the same color with disaster specific-shape (collapse, crack, curve like wave, break, and interruption). Second, the specific-color with damaged parts of infrastructure (road crack showing stratum underground with brown-color) and the background disaster-change (gray and black smoke, orange fire, tsunami black sea). The color-base ROI of traffic sign is denoted by the center line with orange-color, and the side line with white-color. That of background contains sky with light blue or cloudy white color, tree with green and brown-color, and river with blue and green-color, and ground with brown-color, these color corresponds to the temperature and time-range. Several color clusters (K = 2, 3, 4, 5) are segmented; these categorized images are used as an input of color feature extracted data for learning a damage classifier. In contrast, the parts of the background category are masked. These background color segmented images are not added to the original images as an input of a damage classifier, because the background color is not damaged signal but noise without enhancement.

### 2.3   Support Vector Damage Classifier

### Damage Feature Extraction using Pre-trained Deep Network: DenseNet-201

Feature extraction is commonly used in machine learning applications. We can consider a pre-trained network and use it as an input feature to learn a classification task. Image classification using feature extraction is generally much faster and less computationally strenuous than the transfer learning process tuning weights and biases at deep layers. We can rapidly construct a classifier to a new task using an extracted feature at the concatenated layer as a training column vector [13]. This paper proposes a support vector classification model using a single layer from the concatenated feature extraction. Furthermore, we provide the classification model using multiple layers from several feature extractions at significant concatenated points. We can load pre-trained networks such as AlexNet [14], GoogleNet [15], VGG16 and VGG19 [16], ResNet18, ResNet50 and ResNet101 [17], Inception v3 [18], Inception-ResNet-v2 [19], Squee-zeNet [20] and DenseNet-201 [21]. Yasuno et al. have already compared feature extracted support vector classifiers based on above ten pre-trained architectures, where they found that DenseNet-201 based support vector classifiers had the best accuracy among the 10 models toward the disaster image dataset [22]. This paper proposes that the damage feature extraction using DenseNet-201 whose features under "conv5_block32_concat" concatenated layer are used as an input of the support vector classification model.

**Color-Base Damage Feature Enhanced Support Vector Classifier**
Let us suppose multiple disaster feature classes for a support vector classification model. In multiple classification models of more than two classes, we use a voting strategy [23–25]: each binary classification is considered to be a vote where votes can be for all data points in the end. The point is designated to be in a class with the maximum number of votes. The rapid library, LIBSVM, implements the one-against-one approach for multi-class classification. Many other methods are available for the multi-class support vector classification [23–25]. This study uses the kernel of a radial basis function with parameter gamma. In the case of image classifications, the number of extracted features is always a large number. In this study, there is a maximum instance whose number of disaster feature column vectors is 89,736 elements. In the case of an earthquake damage dataset we used, the support vector classification method confirmed the preferred advantage concerning both faster and accurate computation compared with other classification methods such as k-nearest neighbors, decision trees, random forests, and boosting methods. This study constructs a support vector classifier using damage color extracted features based on DenseNet-201 pre-trained networks (Fig. 4).

Color Feature Extracted Damage Classifier

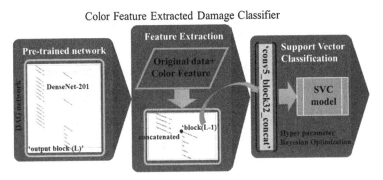

**Fig. 4.** Feature extraction enhanced with damage color and support vector classifier optimization.

**Hyper Parameter Bayesian Optimization Method for Damage Classifier**
There exists automated machine learning methods that use Bayesian optimization to tune hyper parameters of the machine learning pipeline. We can implement some libraries such as Auto-WEKA, auto-sklearn, and Auto-Model [26–28]. Grid search and

randomized search do not use the information produced from previous training runs; this is a disadvantage not encountered with Bayesian-based optimization methods. Bayesian-based optimization methods leverage the information of previous training runs to determine the hyper parameter values for the next training run and navigate through the hyper parameter space in a more efficient manner. The basic idea of warm start is to use the information gained from previous training runs to identify smarter starting points for the next training run. When building machine learning models, a loss function helps in minimizing the prediction error during the training phase. This paper proposes a Bayesian optimization method whose objective function is a loss function from five-fold cross validation to minimize the classification error using a support vector classifier that contains input of extracted features based on a pre-trained network. As a standard setting, we propose that the support vector classification model is based on a radial basis kernel function with two hyper parameters such as a box constraint C and kernel scale gamma [23, 24]. This study attempts to find as many hyper parameters as possible as we can minimize the cross-validation loss function with 30 iterations using the Bayesian optimization method.

**Table 1.** Quake image original/augmented dataset and number of images within each class.

| Earthquake damage class | Number of original images | Number of color-base augmented images | Number of combined both images |
|---|---|---|---|
| Tsunami damage | 40 | 51 | 91 |
| Bridge collapse | 40 | 42 | 82 |
| Road damage with accident risk | 40 | 70 | 110 |
| Initial smoke and fire | 40 | 46 | 86 |
| Non-disaster | 40 | 43 | 83 |
| **Sum of five classes** | **200** | **252** | **452** |

## 3   Applied Results

### 3.1   Quake Disaster Image Dataset

We attempted to collect open source data from web pages where images of earthquake were available. The collective area made up of high-resolution earthquake disaster images is primarily based on large Japanese earthquake experiences such as the Great Hanshin Earthquake (1995 Jan 17) and the Great East Japan Earthquake (2011 Mar 11). However, these areas are not limited only to Japan but areas whose images can be used worldwide. This paper highlights the four earthquake disaster features consisting of tsunami damage, bridge collapse, road damage with accident risk, and initial smoke and fire. Table 1 shows that the number of original images for each category is 40, resulting in a total dataset containing 200 earthquake disaster feature images. After damage color segmentation without background clusters such as sky, trees, and rivers, the number of each target color extracted cluster image is 51, 42, 70, 46, 43, such that the total number of images within the color extracted features dataset is 252. Therefore, the number of each target damage feature image is 91, 82, 110, 86, 83, resulting in a total usable dataset of 452 images. The total images are partitioned into training dataset and test dataset with rate 7 and 3, respectively. In order to compare the original data and the damage color added data, a test dataset consisting of 60 images is used for both cases, which is calculated as 30% of the original dataset. The number of training data with the original data is 140 images; this number is 70% of 200. Meanwhile, the total number of training data with added color extracted data with the original data is 316 images; this number is 70% of 452.

## 3.2   Color-Base Augmentation Using Damage Feature Extraction

In the following, the quake image dataset is applied to the color segmentation method using the K-means clustering algorithm. We indicated some color cluster images corresponding to each category such as background, infrastructure, road damage, smoke and fire, and tsunami on the following images.

### Background Color Feature Extraction
*Sky, Tree, River Feature* (Fig. 5).

**Fig. 5.**  Background color segmentation K-means clustering results.

### Health Infrastructure Color Feature Extraction (Non-disaster)
*Road Pavement, Bridge Feature* (Fig. 6).

**Fig. 6.**  Infrastructure color segmentation K-means clustering results.

## Traffic Sign Color Feature Extraction

*Center line, Sidewalk line* (Fig. 7).

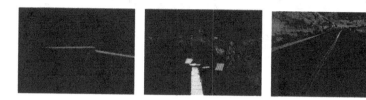

**Fig. 7.** Broken and curved traffic sign color segmentation K-means clustering results.

## Damaged Infrastructure Color Feature Extraction

*Bridge Collapse Feature* (Fig. 8).

**Fig. 8.** Bridge collapse and interruption color segmentation K-means clustering results.

*Road Damage Color Feature* (Fig. 9).

**Fig. 9.** Crack and stratum color segmentation K-means clustering results.

*Smoke and Fire Color Feature* (Fig. 10).

**Fig. 10.** Smoke and fire color segmentation K-means clustering results.

*Tsunami Color Feature* (Fig. 11).

**Fig. 11.** Wave with splash color segmentation K-means clustering results.

## 3.3   Quake Damage Classifier Prediction Results

### Classification Results Using Color-Base Augmentation

On the first row of Table 2, we show a result where input features with 89,736 values were extracted based on DenseNet-201 under "conv5_block32_concat." The feature inputs are computed to optimize hyper parameters for support vector classifiers, resulting in an accuracy improvement of 96.67%. The minimum objective function value is 0.0429. The process had a duration of 16 min 17 s during five-fold cross-validation iterations. On the second row of Table 2, we show a result where input features were extracted based on DenseNet-201 under the same concatenated layer, and the feature inputs are computed to optimize hyper parameters for support vector classifiers, resulting in an accuracy improvement of 98.68% more than previous original case. The minimum objective function value is 0.0568. The process has a duration of 16 min 50 s during five-fold cross-validation iterations. Thus, the color-base augmentation enhanced damage features is possible to improve the accuracy of the hyper parameter optimized support vector classifier using an earthquake damage dataset.

**Table 2.** Hyper parameter optimized results of support vector classifiers under an input of extracted features using pre-trained DenseNet-201.

| Input data | Feature extraction under pre-trained network | Hyper parameter optimized classifier |
|---|---|---|
| Original images #200 | DenseNet-201 "conv5_block32": #89,736 | Objective function: **0.0429** Box constraint C: 0.0010 Rbf kernel scale: 0.0190 Training run time: 16 min 17 s **96.67%** |
| Color-base augmentation added damage feature extracted images #452 | DenseNet-201 "conv5_block32": #89,736 | Objective function: **0.0568** Box constraint C: 0.0298 Rbf kernel scale: 0.0112 Training run time: 16 min 50 s **98.68%** |

Note: The objective function denotes the five-fold cross validation function value.

Figure 12 shows a hyper parameter optimization process of support vector classifier based on DenseNet-201 extracted single feature "conv5_block32_concat" layer. After three iterations, the loss function minimized at the stable level around 0.042.

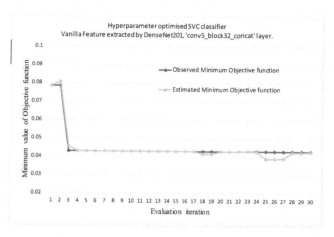

**Fig. 12.** Original image dataset (#200): hyper parameter optimization process of support vector classifier based on DenseNet-201 extracted single feature "conv5_block32_concat" layer.

Figure 13 shows a hyper parameter optimization process of support vector classifier based on DenseNet-201 extracted single feature "conv5_block32_concat" layer. After two iterations, the loss function minimized at the stable level around 0.056.

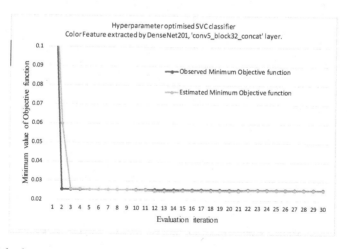

**Fig. 13.** Color-base augmentation added with original image dataset (#452): hyper parameter optimization process of support vector classifier based on DenseNet-201 extracted above layer.

Figure 14 shows the estimated minimum objective function value at the hyper parameter optimization process of support vector classifier. Although the minimized value under the original data (green line) warm starts, but after two iterations, the objective function value under the color-base augmentation (red line) maintains smaller level than the original one. Thus, this indicates that color-base augmentation has advantages with regard to accuracy and fast minimization for hyper parameter optimization.

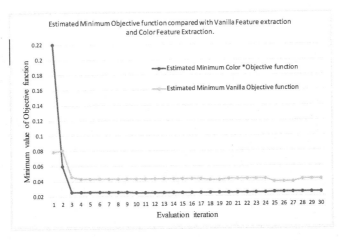

**Fig. 14.** Comparison of estimated objective functions of the original image data and the color image enhanced with the original image dataset: hyper parameter optimization process of support vector classifier based on DenseNet-201 (Color figure online)

## Confusion Matrix Under Damage Color Classifier

Table 3 shows the confusion matrix of a hyper parameter optimized support vector classifier extracted feature "conv5_block32_concat" layer based on DenseNet-201.

**Table 3.** Confusion matrix of hyper parameter optimized support vector classifier extracted feature based on DenseNet-201; the original data training (left), and the damage color feature added with original data (right).

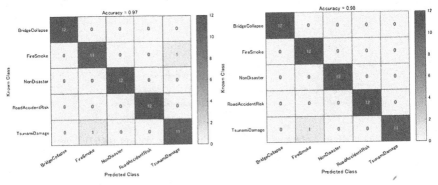

# 4 Concluding Remarks

## 4.1 Color Imaging Applications for Quake Disaster Monitoring

This paper presented a method to enhance the damage color feature extracted based on an object suited deep architecture DenseNet-201 in order to classify five classes of quake damage: tsunami, bridge collapse, road crack with accident risk, and smoke and fire. The training data were based on original images combined with added damage color features to incorporate the enhancement of several target features without other masked regions such as the sky, trees, and rivers. This support vector classifier containing a radial basis kernel function, the image classification model were Bayesian optimized to minimize the loss function with five-fold cross-validation. This method was applied to a case study of an earthquake image dataset whose total number was 452 examples with 89,736 color features. The first study using the original images were carried out with an accuracy of 96.67%, whereas the second study using the original and damage color extracted images achieved a more accurate rate of 98.68%. The loss function was also minimized faster and at a stable level. Therefore, it can be concluded that damage color extraction has advantages with regard to accuracy and fast minimization for hyper parameter optimization.

## 4.2 Future Works for Disaster Color Monitoring

The earthquake image dataset has 1,117 examples; therefore, we will attempt to apply this proposed method with color enhancement. Here, it is important to automate the hyper parameter K based on K-means clustering and an autonomous color segmentation; i.e., whether each color cluster corresponds to a damage class or not. We will tackle the problem thresholding color components under the a*b*space. We will investigate further opportunities regarding disaster damage classification for not only earthquake damage features but also other disaster features such as strong winds [31], building break down [32], traffic signal black out, and heavy rain and flood [33]. Disasters such as fire and flood are likely to occur more frequently when compared to earthquakes. This proposed color enhanced classifier could enable targeted disaster surveillance within each region, learning thousands of damage color features. It would take considerable time to collect newly damaged color data. We will continue to collect video data after the occurrence of any large earthquake worldwide to incorporate novel damage color variations not yet experienced. Such data mining of damage colors could contribute to better decision-making and prioritization of deploying an initial response to damaged infrastructure.

**Acknowledgements.** We wish to thank the CCIW committee and referees for their thoughtful comments. We would like to thank Fukumoto Takuji and Kuramoto Shinichi (MathWorks Japan) for providing us useful information on the MATLAB resources: the Image Processing, Machine Learning, and Parallel Computing. We also wish to thank Yachiyo Engineering Co., Ltd. for various supports.

# References

1. Manzhu, Y., Chaowei, Y., Yun, L.: Big data in natural disaster management: a review. Geosciences **8**, 165 (2018)
2. Michel, U., Thunig, H., Reinartz, P.: Rapid change detection algorithm for disaster management. ISPRS Ann. Photogramm. Remote Sens. Spat. Inf. Sci. **1–4** (2012)
3. Singh, A.: Review article digital change detection techniques using remotely-sensed data. Int. J. Remote Sens. **10**(6), 989–1003 (1989)
4. Saptarsi, G., Sanjay, C., Sanhita, G., et al.: A review on application on data mining techniques to combat natural disasters. Ain Shams Eng. J. **9**(3), 365–378 (2018)
5. Sakaki, T., Okazaki, M., Matsuo, Y.: Earthquake shakes Twitter users: real-time event detection by social sensors. In: Proceedings of 19th International Conference on World Wide Web. ACM (2010)
6. Chitade, A., Katiyar, S.K.: Color based image segmentation using K-means clustering. Int. J. Eng. Sci. Technol. **2**(10), 5319–5325 (2010)
7. Shmmala, F., Ashour, W.: Color based image segmentation using different versions of K-means in two spaces. Glob. Adv. Res. J. Eng. Technol. Innov. **1**(9), 30–41 (2013)
8. Hassan, R., Ema, R., Islam, T.: Color image segmentation using automated K-means clustering with RGB and HSV color spaces. Glob. J. Comput. Sci. Technol. F Graph. Vis. **17** (2) (2017)
9. National Oceanic and Atmospheric Administration (NOAA) Homepage, Natural Hazards Image Database, Events contains Earthquake, Tsunami, Volcano, and Geology. https://www.ngdc.noaa.gov/hazardimages/earthquake. Accessed 17 Sept 2018
10. Sharma, G.: Digital Color Imaging Handbook. CRC Press, Boca Raton (2003)
11. Gonzalez, R., Woods, R., Eddins, S.: Digital Image Processing Using MATLAB, 2nd edn. McGrawHill Education, New York (2015)
12. The Great Hanshin Awaji Earthquake 1.17 Records, Kobe City Homepage, open photo data. http://kobe117shinsai.jp/. Accessed 27 Oct 2018
13. Aurelien, G.: Hands-On Machine Learning with Scikit-Learn and TensorFlow: Concepts, Tools, and Techniques to Build Intelligent Systems. O'Reilly Media Inc., Sebastopol (2017)
14. Krizhevsky, A., Ilya, S., Hinton, G.E.: ImageNet classification with deep convolutional neural networks. In: Advances in Neural Information Processing Systems (2012)
15. Szegedy, C., Wei, L., Yangqing, J., et al.: Going deeper with convolutions. In: Proceedings of the IEEE Conference on Computer Vision and Pattern Recognition, pp. 1–9 (2015)
16. Simoniyan, K., Zisserman, A.: Very deep convolutional networks for large-scale image recognition. In: ICLR. VGG model, the Visual Geometry Group at University of Oxford (2015)
17. Kaiming, H., Xiangyu, Z., Shaoqing, R., et al.: Deep residual learning for image recognition. ResNet model. arXiv:1512.03385v1 (2015)
18. Szegedy, C., Vincent, V., Sergey, I., et al.: Rethinking the inception architecture for computer vision. In: CVPR, pp. 2818–2826. Inception v3 model (2015)
19. Szegedy, C., Sergey, I., Vincent, V., et al.: Inception-v4, Inception-ResNet impact of residual connections on learning. Inception-ResNet-v2 model. arXiv:1602.07261v2 (2016)
20. Forrest, N.I., Song, H., Matthew, W., et al.: SqueezeNet: AlexNet-level accuracy with 50x fewer parameters and < 0.5 MB model size. In: ICLR (2017)
21. Huang, H., Liu, Z., Maaten, L., et al.: Densely connected convolutional networks. In: CVPR (2017). DenseNet model

22. Yasuno, T., Amakata, M., Fujii, J., Shimamoto, Y.: Disaster initial response mining damages using feature extraction and bayesian optimised support vector classifier. In: 3rd International Conference on Data Mining & Knowledge Management, Dubai (2018)
23. Scholkopf, B., Smola, A.J.: Learning with Kernels: Support Vector Machines, Regularization, Optimization, and Beyond. MIT Press, Cambridge (2002)
24. Hsu, C.-W., Chang, C.-C., Lin, C.-J.: A practical guide to support vector classification. Technical report, Department of Computer Science, National Taiwan University (2003)
25. Chan, C.-C., Lin, C.-J.: LIBSVM: a library for support vector machines, pp. 29–30 (2013). Initial version 2001, Multi-class classification
26. Feurer, M., Klein, A., Eggensperger, K.: Efficient and robust automated machine learning. In: Neural Information Processing Systems Conference (NIPS) (2015)
27. Sergios, T.: Machine Learning: A Bayesian and Optimization Perspective. Academic Press, Cambridge (2015)
28. Sibanjan, D., Cakmak, U.M.: Hands-On Automated Machine Learning, Packt (2018)
29. Prince, S.: Computer Vision Models, Learning, and Inference. Cambridge University Press, Cambridge (2017)
30. Rajalingappaa, S.: Deep Learning for Computer Vision, Packt (2018)
31. Yasuno, T.: Estimating occurrence probability and loss index to manage the social risk of storing-winds. In: International Symposium Society for Social Management Systems (SSMS) (2009)
32. Yasuno, T.: Daily interaction behavior, urgent support network on Tohoku Tsunami 2011, Tottori Quake 2000, Social Capital and Development Trends in Rural Areas, vol. 8, Chap. 12 (2012)
33. Takato, Y.: Dam inflow time series regression models minimising loss of hydropower opportunities. In: Ganji, M., Rashidi, L., Fung, B.C.M., Wang, C. (eds.) PAKDD 2018. LNCS (LNAI), vol. 11154, pp. 357–367. Springer, Cham (2018). https://doi.org/10.1007/978-3-030-04503-6_34

# Colorization of High-Frame-Rate Monochrome Videos Using Synchronized Low-Frame-Rate Color Data

Ching-Fan Chiang, Yang-Ming Yeh, Chi-Yun Yang, and Yi-Chang Lu[✉]

Graduate Institute of Electronics Engineering,
National Taiwan University, Taipei, Taiwan
{r01943001,d05943006,r03943126,yiclu}@ntu.edu.tw

**Abstract.** The frame rate of a color camera is usually limited by its maximum data bandwidth. To obtain high-frame-rate color videos, we propose to colorize high-frame-rate monochrome videos using data from a system composed of one high-frame-rate monochrome camera and two low-frame-rate color cameras. The cameras are synchronized by external triggering signals. With stereo matching and motion estimation algorithms, colorization of high-frame-rate monochrome videos can be realized. The system is very cost-effective, and the processing steps can be fully automated as demonstrated in the paper.

**Keywords:** Colorization · Multiple-camera systems · High-frame-rate video

## 1 Introduction

High-speed cameras are able to acquire videos at very high frame rates. These high-speed videos are very important in various fields such as scientific research and television production. However, there are some known disadvantages and limitations in high-speed cameras. For instance, a high-speed camera is often much more expensive than a low-frame-rate camera. Also, with a very high frame rate, the exposure time of each frame can be extremely short. Therefore, monochrome high-speed cameras are frequently used because of their stability in low light conditions. In addition, monochrome cameras provide the benefits of higher resolution since no demosaicing of color patterns is needed. Unfortunately, in most applications users favor color videos than monochrome videos. There are many studies to address general colorization issues. For example, the authors in [1] proposed to combine the methods of color transfer in [2] and feature mapping in [3] to transfer color characteristics from one color image to a greyscale image.

---

This work is partially supported by Ministry of Science and Technology, Taiwan, under Grant numbers MOST 106-2221-E-002-055, 107-2221-E-002-123-MY2 and 107-2622-8-002-009-TA.

S. Tominaga et al. (Eds.): CCIW 2019, LNCS 11418, pp. 276–285, 2019.
https://doi.org/10.1007/978-3-030-13940-7_21

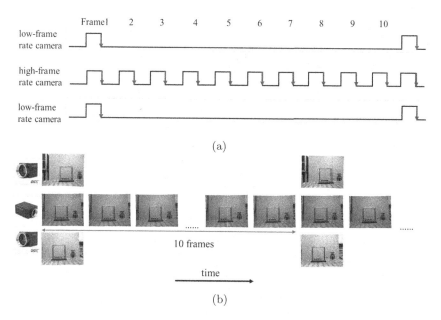

**Fig. 1.** (a) Triggering signals for cameras. (b) The captured image sequences.

On the other hand, some researchers [4,5] suggested using iterative methods with initial color annotation of a small portion within the image. Recently, deep learning networks are also applied to the field of colorization [6].

In this paper, to put emphasis on high-frame-rate applications, we set up a high-frame-rate monochrome video colorization system. We apply stereo matching and motion estimation techniques to colorize high-frame-rate monochrome videos using color information from nearby low-frame-rate color videos. The proposed system is capable of generating high-frame-rate colors video at a more affordable price while preserving the advantages of monochrome cameras.

## 2   Monochrome Video Colorization System

### 2.1   System Overview

The proposed system setup is illustrated in Fig. 1. Two Point Gray Flea3 low-frame-rate color cameras are used to provide color references. One Point Gray Gazelle high-frame-rate monochrome camera gives the complete image sequence.

To precisely control the triggering time of three cameras, we use FPGA to provide the triggers to three cameras. We set the triggering rate at 10 Hz for color cameras and 100 Hz for the monochrome camera. It means the FPS (frame per second) of the monochrome camera is ten times faster than that of color cameras. After rectification, two color cameras will provide color information to the high-speed camera. In the cross-camera colorization stage, we colorize every

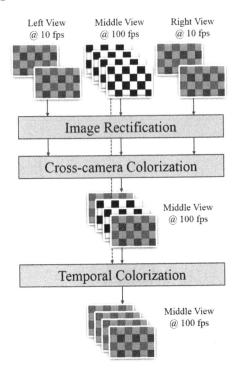

**Fig. 2.** The flow chart of our colorization system.

tenth monochrome image using the color information which captured at the same moment. In the temporal colorization stage, we used the colorized images in the monochrome sequence as the guide to generate the final high-speed color sequence. The flow chart is shown in Fig. 2.

## 2.2   Image Rectification Stage

Since our cameras are a set of stereo vision cameras, we should first calibrate three cameras and rectify each captured image. Secondly, we change the color domain of each color image from RGB to YCbCr since we prefer not modifying the luminance of monochrome images after colorization. The occlusion problem happens when using a two-camera stereo system. It means that, for certain parts of some objects in one view, we may not be able to find the corresponding pixels in the other view. To prevent this problem, we use three cameras to avoid this problem. For example, the insufficient information of occlusion regions between the left and middle views can be provided by the right view.

## 2.3   Cross-Camera Colorization

Since sensors of cameras are not totally identical, the luminance values captured are not the same even the same camera setting is used. If the luminance informa-tion differs between images, the result of stereo matching is not convincing. Thus,

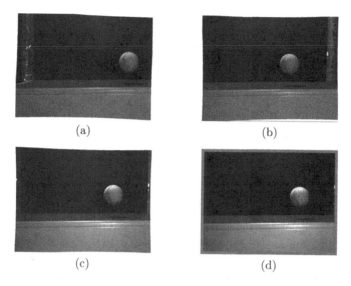

(a)                                          (b)

(c)                                          (d)

**Fig. 3.** (a) Left view, (b) right view, (c) middle view, and (d) the colorized image after applying cross-camera colorization.

before implementing stereo matching, we need to adjust the luminance of two low-frame-rate color images, to make their luminance similar to the one in the high-frame-rate monochrome image, using the transformation proposed by [3]:

$$C'(p) = \frac{\sigma_G}{\sigma_C}(C(p) - \mu_C) + \mu_G. \tag{1}$$

$C(p)$ and $C'(p)$ stand for the original and calibrated luminance in the low-frame-rate color image, respectively. $\mu_C$ and $\sigma_C$ are the mean and standard deviation in the color image, while $\mu_G$ and $\sigma_G$ are the mean and standard deviation in the monochrome image. This equation brings the mean and standard deviation of the color image to the same as those in the monochrome image.

After adjusting the luminance for two color images, we utilize a stereo matching algorithm to find the matching point for each pixel in the monochrome image. By creating a block of $17 \times 17$ pixels for each pixel in the monochrome image, we generate blocks of the same size along the corresponding 1-D search line in the two reference color images. Then, we perform the Sum of Absolute Difference (SAD) similarity check between these blocks with every possible horizontal shift which depends on the maximum disparity of the objects in the scene. Finally, we choose the best matching point from two color images and use its Cb, Cr as the color information for the current monochrome pixel. After matching all color information for each pixel in the monochrome image, one-tenth of the monochrome images are colorized. Then, we move to the next step to colorize other high-frame-rate monochrome images using colorized monochrome images obtained.

**Fig. 4.** The scheme of temporal colorization.

## 2.4  Temporal Colorization

In this step, we want to colorize the monochrome images which do not have corresponding color information from the low-frame-rate images. We use the colorized high-frame-rate monochrome images to colorize other monochrome images by finding motion vectors using motion estimation algorithm.

We treat the colorized monochrome images as the reference frames and the current monochrome image as the target frame to be processed. We first divide the current frame into macro blocks. Each macro block is $6 \times 6$ pixels, and its corresponding search region on the reference frame is $15 \times 15$ pixels. Then we compute the similarity between the current block and each candidate block in the search region. When the best match has been found, we record this motion vector as the spatial offset between the two blocks, which also means that the color information is copied from the best matched block on the reference frame. In our proposed system, we use full search method for motion estimation algorithm. Although larger block size is preferred for SAD, the colorization results would be discontinuous at the edges of blocks. Thus, we propose to use two different types of blocks. The macro block mentioned above is Matching block, and the other type is called Painting block. We should keep the size of Painting block small ($2 \times 2$ pixels) enough to minimize the blocking effect of colorization results. On the other hand, we use a larger Matching block when computing the similarity to ensure the accuracy. The reason that we do not use a single pixel as Painting block is a result of the trade-off between image quality and computing time, since the 2-D search region in this stage contains far more candidates than the ones in the previous stage. Figure 4 shows the procedure to propagate the color information in the temporal colorization step. Each colorized middle frame obtained from the cross-camera colorization step provides color information to its previous four monochrome frames and the latter five monochrome frames as indicated by the red and blue arrows shown in Fig. 4, respectively.

## 3  Experimental Results

Since the images are directly obtained from the prototype system we built, there is no ground truth of color high-frame-rate images available to calculate PSNR and SSIM metrics. Nevertheless, we show the qualitative results of three sequences to demonstrate the feasibility of the system. The first and eleventh images are the colorized results from cross-camera colorization.

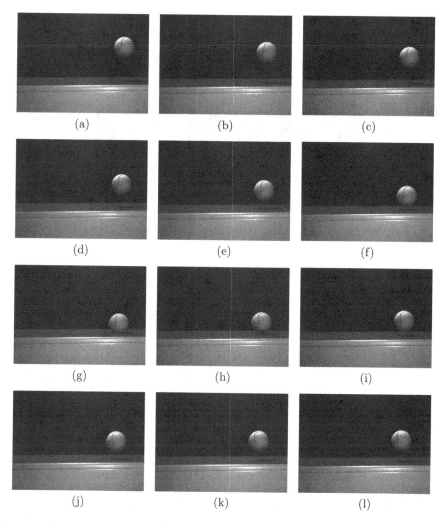

**Fig. 5.** Scene with an object in rigid motion: (a) and (k) are the colorized images after applying cross-camera colorization. The rest images are the colorized results after temporal colorization.

The rest images are the colorized results after temporal colorization. Since the frames are obtained directly from the monochrome camera, the information of the luminance channel is always correct. Combining with the fact that chrominance information is less sensitive to human eyes, the flaws of the colorized video are very difficult to be spotted.

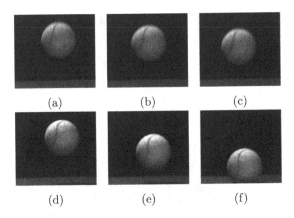

(a)          (b)          (c)

(d)          (e)          (f)

**Fig. 6.** (a)–(c) are from a sequence generated by interpolation of two adjacent frames from a low-speed-color camera. (d)–(f) are colorized frames using the proposed pipeline.

### 3.1   Scene with Objects in Rigid Motion

In the first experiment, we record the bouncing behavior of a tennis ball. The input images for cross-camera colorization are shown earlier in Fig. 3. The edges and patterns in Fig. 3(d) are clearer than those in the images from the left and right color cameras because the intensity information that comes from the middle camera has a very short exposure time. Since the trajectory of the ball is not linear, if an ordinary interpolation method is used, the interpolated frames could not look natural. In this work, with the high-frame-rate data, we are able to retain the real temporal information. Figure 5 shows the sequence after our temporal colorization flow. The non-linear motion, especially at the moment of impact, is well-preserved and colorized. Figure 6 compares the sequences obtained from the interpolation method and the proposed approach. The results in the first row of Fig. 6 are interpolated from the two adjacent frames captured by a low-speed color camera. Therefore, the results look blurred. When compared with our method, we can see that interpolation method could not generate the correct trace of the tennis ball.

The second experiment is to make the background more complicated. Besides, each ball in the Newton's cradle is not completely still. If we zoom in to a small region of Fig. 7, we can find some defects in the colorization results. Since we hold the intensity of high-frame-rate video constant, the impact of colorization errors are difficult to be discovered unless the video is played at a very low speed on a large screen.

### 3.2   Scene with an Object in Non-rigid Motion

Here we conduct another experiment, a scene with an object in non-rigid motion, which is considered harder to estimate the motion vectors due to the deformation of the object between frames. However, we can still obtain the colorized video frames as shown in Fig. 8. We can see that the colorized water balloon looks very realistic. We also try to increase the deformation level by dropping the water balloon from a higher place. In that case, the water balloon would form larger deformation within a shorter time period. Figure 9 shows the zoomed-in images of our colorized results of the case with larger deformation. Although there are some errors due to large deformation as highlighted in Fig. 9(c), the flaws in video are not obvious to human eyes.

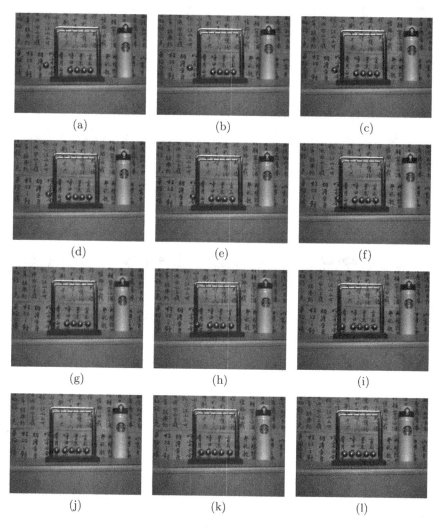

**Fig. 7.** Scene with objects in rigid motion: (a) and (k) are the colorized images after applying cross-camera colorization. The rest images are the colorized results after temporal colorization.

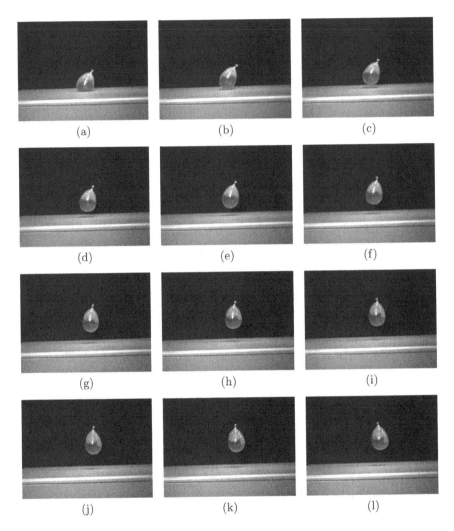

**Fig. 8.** Scene with an object in non-rigid motion: (a) and (k) are the colorized images after applying cross-camera colorization. The rest images are the colorized results after temporal colorization.

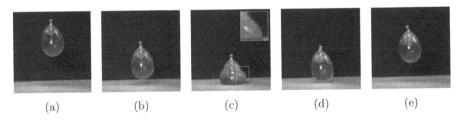

**Fig. 9.** The zoomed-in results, (a)–(e), are from the five consecutive frames of the case with larger deformation.

## 4   Conclusion

In this paper, we propose a high-frame-rate monochrome video colorization system which is composed of one high-frame-rate monochrome camera and two low-frame-rate color cameras. The three cameras are synchronized by external triggering signals. With stereo matching and motion estimation algorithms, colorization of high-frame-rate monochrome video can be realized using the proposed system. As demonstrated in the paper, the image quality is good and the process can be fully automated.

## References

1. Welsh, T., Ashikhmin, M., Mueller, K.: Transferring color to greyscale images. ACM Trans. Graph. **21**(3), 277–280 (2002)
2. Reinhard, E., Adhikhmin, M., Gooch, B., Shirley, P.: Color transfer between images. IEEE Comput. Graph. Appl. **21**(5), 34–41 (2001)
3. Hertzmann, A., Jacobs, C.E., Oliver, N., Curless, B., Salesin, D.H.: Image analogies. In: Proceedings of the 28th Annual Conference on Computer Graphics and Interactive Techniques, pp. 327–340 (2001)
4. Levin, A., Lischinski, D., Weiss, Y.: Colorization using optimization. ACM Trans. Graph. **23**(3), 689–694 (2004)
5. Nie, D., Ma, Q., Ma, L., Xiao, S.: Optimization based grayscale image colorization. Pattern Recogn. Lett. **28**(12), 1445–1451 (2007)
6. Cheng, Z., Yang, Q., Sheng, B.: Deep colorization. In: Proceedings of the 2015 IEEE International Conference on Computer Vision (ICCV), pp. 415–423 (2015)

# Color Imaging for Material Appearance

# Reflectance Computation for a Specular Only V-Cavity

Dorian Saint-Pierre[1](✉), Lionel Simonot[1,2], and Mathieu Hébert[1]

[1] Université de Lyon, UJM-Saint-Etienne, CNRS, Institut D'Optique Graduate School, Laboratoire Hubert Curien UMR 5516, Saint-Etienne, France
dorian.saint.pierre@univ-st-etienne.fr
[2] Université de Poitiers, Institut Prime UPR CNRS 3346,
Futuroscope Chasseneuil, Poitiers, France

**Abstract.** The color of a surface structured at the mesoscopic scale differs from the one of a flat surface of the same material because of the light interreflections taking place in the concavities of the surface, as well as the shadowing effect. The color variation depends not only on the surface topology but also on the spectral reflectance of the material, its matte or glossy finishing, and the angular distribution of the incident light. For an accurate prediction of the radiance perceived from each point of the object by an observer or a camera, we must take into account comprehensively the multiple paths of light which can be reflected, scattered or absorbed by the material and its surface. In this paper, we focus on the light reflection component due to the material-air interface, in the special case of a surface structured with parallel, periodical, specular V-shaped ridges, illuminated either by collimated light from any direction of the hemisphere, or by diffuse light. Thanks to an analytical model, we compute the radiance reflected in every direction of the hemisphere by accounting for the different interreflections, according to the angular reflectance of the panels and the aperture angle of the cavity. We can then deduce the apparent reflectance of the cavity when viewed from a large distance.

**Keywords:** Surface reflection · Light interreflections · Reflectance model

## 1 Introduction

It is well known that the structure of surfaces and materials has a crucial influence on the way they reflect light, thereby on their appearance. A same material structured in different ways can yield very different appearance attributes, from bright to dark, glossy to matte or transparent to opaque.

The influence of the material structure on appearance is mainly related to concept of light scattering, a concept which covers a wide variety of optical principles according to the size of the material structures and their periodicity. Regular or periodical structures whose characteristic size is comparable to the wavelength of light generate interferences or diffraction, and consequently colorations which are often called structural colors [1]. These effects have been widely explored in optics for more than one century, even though pseudo-periodical structures are still an active subject of investigation [see

© Springer Nature Switzerland AG 2019
S. Tominaga et al. (Eds.): CCIW 2019, LNCS 11418, pp. 289–303, 2019.
https://doi.org/10.1007/978-3-030-13940-7_22

for example Ref. 2]. In opposition, irregular structures can generate both coherent and incoherent light scattering which mainly results in a reorientation of light in space and depolarization. For these randomly microstructured materials, many models have also been proposed in the last century to predict their reflection and transmission properties according to the wavelength, polarization, orientation and position of light. Among the most famous theories for the light scattering by volumes, we can mention the Kubelka-Munk model initially introduced for paints [3], the Melamed model for pigments powders and slurries [4], the radiative transfer theory by Chandrasekhar [5], the multi-flux theory, the Van de Hulst works for scattering by particles [6], etc. We can also evocate famous models for the scattering of light by surfaces with a random roughness, from Beckman and Spizzichino [7] who modelled diffraction by such surfaces, through Torrance and Sparrow [8] who modelled incoherent reflection by randomly organized microfacets, to the most advanced models which also take into account the multiple scattering between different facets [9–11]. All these models form a large prediction toolbox for many visual attributes (color, translucency and opacity, gloss and matt aspect), applicable to a wide range of materials according to their optical properties (refractive indices, scattering and absorption coefficients...) and structural properties (surface roughness, particle size and concentration, layer thickness...), provided the material can be considered as homogeneous at the macro- or mesoscopic scale.

However, for many kinds of surfaces or objects, the multiscale structure of the matter do have to be taken into account in order to obtain accurate optical models and appearance predictions. Describing scattering at multiple scales is generally done by combining different models. The classical literature in physics shows various examples. Mie scattering model is used to describe the light scattering by one particle, and a radiative transfer model is then used to describe the light transport through a piece of medium with particles. For stacks of diffusing layers, the Kubelka-Munk model describes the light scattering at the microscopic scale within each layer and predicts its reflectance and transmittance, then the Kubelka layering model [12] or more advanced models describe the flux transfers at the mesoscopic scale between the different layers with their respective interfaces [13, 14]. For halftone prints, the optical properties of the paper and the inks can be both modeled by the Kubelka-Munk theory [15], then the scattering properties of the set of ink dots on top of the paper can be predicted by a number of models describing the flux transfers between the different inked and non-inked areas [16–19]. But models are still missing for a volume made of an alternation of mesoscopic bricks of materials and the 3D flux transfers taking place between them, as we can find in 3D inkjet printing, and for a surface whose shape has been given a mesoscopic, possibly periodical structure.

In the latter case on which the present paper is focused, the multiple reflections between the different areas of the non-flat surface, also called interreflections, give to the object specific reflection properties according to the illumination conditions that the models mentioned above cannot render properly. As shown in recent studies dedicated to ridged Lambertian materials (ridges with V-profile) [20, 21], the presence of periodical ridges modifies the color of the material in comparison to the color of the flat surface, in different ways according to the ridge aperture and the illumination conditions: the color of the ridge surface is brighter and more saturated than the one of the flat surface under frontal collimated illumination, but it is darker and less saturated under diffuse illumination. Interreflection models taking explicitly into consideration the microscopic optical properties of the material and the mesoscopic structure of the surface are capable to predict these color variations, thus also allowing the prediction of the irradiance repartition at these two scales. The present paper follows this investigation on materials with periodical V-shaped ridges under different illumination conditions, by considering this time a nonscattering material and describing the multiple specular reflections undergone by each ray between faces of the structure, behaving like mirrors. As for the model dedicated to Lambertian materials, we adopt a radiometric approach, yielding analytical expressions for the angular and bi-hemispherical reflectance of the structured surface, as a function of the material refractive index and the ridge aperture $\alpha$ (see Fig. 1).

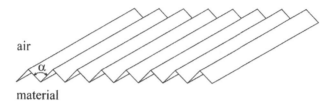

**Fig. 1.** Structured surface with parallel and periodical V-shaped ridges of aperture angle $\alpha$.

The paper is structured as follows: we first present the useful concepts for describing our model, to then introduce the formalization of multiple light reflections happening in a V-cavity, with specular surfaces as pannels. After this we move on to the fourth section where we present the results obtained by using the presented model, and we end with our conclusions.

## 2  Reflectance

The fraction of light reflected by the structured surface is characterized by the *reflectance* concept, which is defined for an area of the surface much larger than the width of the cavities. This concept relies on radiometric quantities related to the amount of incident and reflected light, recalled below, which can also be used to describe the multiple reflection process within each cavity.

The light power, or flux, denoted as $F$, can be regarded as a collection of light rays propagating from the source to the objects, then from areas of the objects to other areas, then from the objects to the observer. The distribution of the light flux over a given surface is described by the concept of *irradiance* (for incoming light) or *exitance* (for outgoing light), defined as the density of received or emitted flux $dF$ per elementary area $dA$:

$$E = \frac{dF}{dA} \tag{1}$$

Radiance, denoted as $L$, is defined by the density of light power (or flux) $d^2F$ per elementary geometrical extent $d^2G$:

$$L = \frac{d^2F}{d^2G} \tag{2}$$

where the geometrical extent defines the flux transfer volume between the two elementary areas.

*Reflectance* denotes any ratio of reflected flux to incident flux relative to the same surface element, defined for a given illumination and observation geometry. In this paper, reflectance is generically denoted as $R$. In the special case of air-medium interfaces, the angular reflectance is denoted as $R_{01}(\theta)$ for collimated light coming from medium 0 (in our case, it is air, of refractive index $n_0 = 1$) at the interface with medium 1 (of refractive index $n_1$, which can be either real or complex), with an angle of incidence $\theta$. The term $n$ denotes the relative optical index of the interface, i.e., the ratio of the refractive indices as follows:

$$n = \frac{n_1}{n_0} \tag{3}$$

When a light ray with radiance $L_i$ is reflected on a flat interface, the reflected radiance $L_r$ is simply given by:

$$L_r = R_{01}(\theta)L_i \tag{4}$$

where $\theta$ is the angle between the incident radiance and the normal of the interface.

# 3    Multiple Reflections of a Light Ray in a Specular Cavity

We can notice from Fig. 1 that a light ray entering into one cavity is reflected, possibly multiple times, in this cavity only. Therefore, we can focus on the reflection of light by one cavity, and consider that all cavities reflect light in the same way. In this section, we propose to present the analytical model permitting to accurately predict the amount and directions of light reflected by the cavity. The model is based on geometrical optics, with an approach comparable to ray tracing. It describes the path of the light after the different reflections across the structure, and takes into account the precise number of bounces that the light undergoes on the panels.

## 3.1    Geometry of the Cavity

Each cavity is formed by two specular panels of infinite length along the $x$ axis of the 3D Cartesian space (Fig. 2). The width of both panels is set to unity (it could be equivalently any other value: the width has no impact on the interreflection phenomenon as shown in [18] and on the computation of the specular radiance that we want to perform here). The angle between the two panels, also called "aperture of the

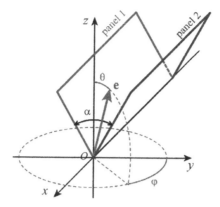

**Fig. 2.** 3D geometry of one cavity, and vector **e** representing the direction of illumination.

cavity", is denoted as $\alpha$. Hence, each panel forms a dihedral angle $\alpha/2$ with the $(xOz)$-plane, where the $z$ axis corresponds to the normal of the average structured surface.

The normal of panels 1 and 2 are respectively:

$$\mathbf{N_1} = \begin{pmatrix} 0 \\ \cos(\alpha/2) \\ \sin(\alpha/2) \end{pmatrix} \quad \text{and} \quad \mathbf{N_2} = \begin{pmatrix} 0 \\ -\cos(\alpha/2) \\ \sin(\alpha/2) \end{pmatrix} \tag{5}$$

The incident light ray is characterized by unit radiance, and a unit vector **e** with spherical coordinates $(\theta, \varphi)$ represented in Fig. 2. In this Cartesian coordinate system, the vector **e** is given by:

$$e = \begin{pmatrix} \sin\theta \sin\varphi \\ \sin\theta \cos\varphi \\ \cos\theta \end{pmatrix} \tag{6}$$

### 3.2 Multiple Reflections in a Cavity

Once a light ray enters into a cavity, it may undergo one or several successive reflections on the panels. After each reflection, the direction of the ray is modified according to Snell's laws. However, in geometrical optics, it is classical to represent the image of the ray reflected by a mirror which is aligned with the incident ray, as shown on the left of Fig. 3 through the example of two rays. By using this representation for the cavity, we can draw a straight line aligned with the incident ray, crossing the successive images of the panels: after a reflection on panel 1, the ray reaches the image of panel 2 (which forms an angle $\alpha$ with panel 1), then the image of panel 1 (which also forms an angle $\alpha$ with the image of panel 2, and so on).

The number of reflections depends on both orientation and position of the ray. This is visible in Fig. 3 where the two rays are parallel (thus characterized by the same

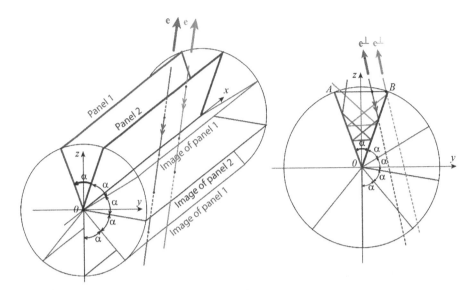

**Fig. 3.** Left: 3D representation of two parallel light rays oriented according to a same vector **e** striking the cavity in different positions on panel 2. Right: 2D representation of the two same light rays projected onto the $(yOz)$ vertical plane. The light path can be represented by a straight line meeting the successive images of the panels from each other. The projection of real light paths in broken straight lines is also represented on the figure (left).

vector **e**) and strike panel 2 in different positions: one ray (represented in red) undergoes 4 reflections, whereas the other ray undergoes 3 reflections. The ray light paths in broken straight lines are featured on the right of the figure, in a projection onto the $(yOz)$ plane of the 3D scene represented on the left of the figure. In this plane, the projection of vector **e**, denoted as $\mathbf{e}^{\perp}$, is:

$$\mathbf{e}^{\perp} = \begin{pmatrix} \sin \theta' \\ \cos \theta' \end{pmatrix}$$

with

$$\theta' = \arctan(\tan \theta \cos \varphi) \tag{7}$$

### 3.3   Number of Reflections

The number of reflections according to the orientation and position of the ray is computed according to the following geometrical considerations, in the $(yOz)$ plane.

The orientation of the ray is denoted by the angle $\theta'$ given by Eq. (7). Its position is described by the point $P$ where the ray meets the line $(AB)$ which joins the extremities of the panels in the $(yOz)$ plane, drawn in Fig. 4. This point $P$ has the coordinates

$P = (y_P, \cos(\alpha/2))$. The ray meets the unit circle centered in point $O = (0,0)$ in two points: first in point $G = (\sin \beta_G, \cos \beta_G)$, then in point $H = (\sin \beta_H, \cos \beta_H)$.

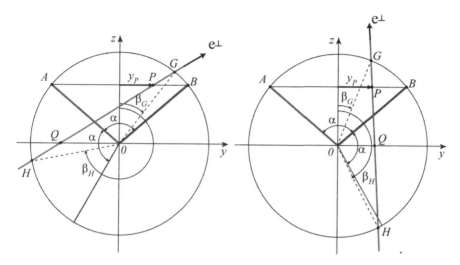

**Fig. 4.** Geometry for the calculation of the number of reflections, for a same position $y_P$ of the ray, and two different orientations.

Figure 4 shows two examples for the same position $y_P$ but two different orientations of the ray. On the left of the figure, the ray strikes first panel 1, on the right of the figure, it strikes first panel 2. The panel first met is determined by the following condition: if the meeting point $Q = (y_q, 0)$ of the ray and the y-axis has a negative abscissa $y_q$, panel 1 is met first, otherwise, panel 2 is met first. With some geometrical calculation, we find that abscissa $y_q$ is given by

$$y_q = \frac{\sin(\beta_H - \beta_G)}{\cos \beta_G - \cos \beta_H} \tag{8}$$

where the angles $\beta_G$ and $\beta_H$ are computed as follows.

Since $\overrightarrow{PG} = \left(\sin \beta_G - y_P, \cos \beta_G - \cos\left(\frac{\alpha}{2}\right)\right)$ and $\mathbf{e}^\perp$ are collinear, we have:

$$\det \begin{pmatrix} \sin \beta_G - y_P & \sin \theta' \\ \cos \beta_G - \cos\left(\frac{\alpha}{2}\right) & \cos \theta' \end{pmatrix} = 0 \tag{9}$$

After some calculation, Eq. (9) can be written

$$\sin(\beta_G - \theta') = y_P \cos \theta' - \cos\left(\frac{\alpha}{2}\right) \sin \theta' \tag{10}$$

and by noticing that $\beta_G - \theta' < \pi/2$, we obtain

$$\beta_G = \theta' + \arcsin\left[y_P \cos \theta' - \cos\left(\frac{\alpha}{2}\right) \sin \theta'\right] \tag{11}$$

Likewise $\overrightarrow{PH}$ and $\mathbf{e}^\perp$ are collinear, and by following similar reasoning as above with point $H$ in place of point $G$, therefore with angle $\beta_H$ in place of $\beta_G$, we obtain

$$\sin(\beta_H - \theta') = y_P \cos \theta' - \cos\left(\frac{\alpha}{2}\right) \sin \theta' \tag{12}$$

This time, we can notice that $\beta_H - \theta' > \pi/2$, therefore we have:

$$\beta_H = \theta' + \pi - \arcsin\left[y_P \cos \theta' - \cos\left(\frac{\alpha}{2}\right) \sin \theta'\right] \tag{13}$$

Figure 4 illustrates the fact that $\beta_H$ is a reflex angle, i.e., higher than $\pi$, when the ray strikes first panel 1 ($y_q < 0$), and a salient angle, i.e., lower than $\pi$, when it strikes first panel 2 ($y_q > 0$). We may prefer using the angle $\gamma_H$, obtuse in any case, defined as:

$$\gamma_H = \begin{cases} 2\pi - \beta_H & \text{when } y_q < 0 \\ \beta_H & \text{when } y_q > 0 \end{cases} \tag{14}$$

Finally, the number of reflections occurring after the first reflection of the first panel met is the number of times angle $\gamma_H - \alpha/2$ contains $\alpha$. Hence, the total number of reflections is given by

$$m = \text{floor}\left[\frac{\gamma_H}{\alpha} - \frac{1}{2}\right] + 1 \tag{15}$$

where symbol floor[.] gives the integral part of the number in argument.

### 3.4   Radiance Attenuation for One Ray

Now that the number of light reflections has been determined, we can express the global attenuation undergone by the radiance, by multiplying the successive Fresnel reflectances $R_{12}(\theta_i)$ corresponding to the different reflections. For each reflection, we need to compute the local incidence angle $\theta_i$. This local incidence angle can be easily obtained through the dot product between vector $\mathbf{e}$, which describes the direction of the ray, and the normal of the panel, or image of panel, on which the considered reflection occurs.

The panels have the normal vectors $\mathbf{N}_1$ and $\mathbf{N}_2$ given by Eq. (5). The local incident angle for the first reflection depends on whether the ray first meets panel 1 or panel 2, therefore on the sign of the parameter $y_q$ defined by Eq. (8):

$$\theta_i = \begin{cases} \arccos(\mathbf{e} \cdot \mathbf{N}_1) & \text{if } y_q < 0 \\ \arccos(\mathbf{e} \cdot \mathbf{N}_2) & \text{if } y_q > 0 \end{cases} \tag{16}$$

where the symbol "·" denotes the dot product

The following reflections, if any, occur on images of panels whose normal vector denoted as $N_1^{(j)}$ or $N_2^{(j)}$ if the first reflection occurs on panel 1, respectively on panel 2. These normal vectors, for $j = 2$ to the number of reflections $m$ given by Eq. (15), are defined as

$$N_1^{(j)} = \begin{pmatrix} 0 \\ \cos(\alpha/2 + (j-1)\alpha) \\ \sin(\alpha/2 + (j-1)\alpha) \end{pmatrix} \quad \text{and} \quad N_2^{(j)} = \begin{pmatrix} 0 \\ -\cos(\alpha/2 + (j-1)\alpha) \\ \sin(\alpha/2 + (j-1)\alpha) \end{pmatrix} \quad (17)$$

and the local incident angle is given by

$$\theta_i^{(j)} = \begin{cases} \arccos\left(e \cdot N_1^{(j)}\right) & \text{if } y_q < 0 \\ \arccos\left(e \cdot N_2^{(j)}\right) & \text{if } y_q > 0 \end{cases} \quad (18)$$

Finally, the global attenuation of the radiance according to its position $y_P$ between $-\sin(\alpha/2)$ and $\sin(\alpha/2)$ and its orientation $(\theta, \varphi)$, is given by the reflectance:

$$R(\theta, \varphi, y_P) = \prod_{j=1}^{m} R_{01}\left[\theta_i^{(j)}\right] \quad (19)$$

where $\theta_i^{(1)}$ denotes the local angle $\theta_i$ for the first reflection given by Eq. (16).

Notice that according to the Helmholtz reciprocity principle, a ray following the same path within the cavity but in opposite direction would undergo exactly the same attenuation. Hence, $R(\theta, \varphi, y_P)$ can denote the attenuation for the ray coming or exiting the cavity at the angle $(\theta, \varphi)$ through the position $y_P$.

## 4   Reflectance of the Structured Surface

From the reflectance attached to each incident ray within the cavity, we can derive the reflectance of the structured surface for a Lambertian illumination. It can be a hemispherical-directional reflectance, also called angular reflectance, being a function of the observation direction. Another interesting type is the bi-hemispherical reflectance. It is also possible to compute directional-hemispherical reflectance, equivalent to the hemispherical directional reflectance in this case, thanks to the reversibility of light principle.

### 4.1   Angular Reflectance

Let us consider that the cavity is illuminated over a band of width $\Delta x$ along the $x$ axis, perpendicular to the cavity, i.e. illuminated along the $y$ axis, by collimated light from a direction $(\theta, \varphi)$. The illumination is uniform, i.e., same radiance $L_i$ arrives in each point of the band, which receives a uniform irradiance

$$E_i = L_i \cos \theta_i \Delta \omega_i \quad (20)$$

where $\Delta\omega_i$ denotes the small solid angle of illumination. Since the illuminated area is $2\sin(\alpha/2)\Delta x$, the incident flux on the band is $F_i = 2\sin(\alpha/2)\Delta x E_i$. On each elementary area within the band, centered around the position and of size $\Delta x dy_P$, the elementary flux is $dF_i = \Delta x dy_P E_i$.

The different elementary fluxes are reflected in various directions according to the panel that each one meets first and the number of reflections. By collecting the whole reflected flux, in practice with a measurement device equipped with an integrating sphere, the captured flux $F_R$ is given by

$$F_r = \Delta x E_i \int_{y_P=-\sin(\alpha/2)}^{\sin(\alpha/2)} R(\theta, \varphi, y) dy_P \tag{21}$$

The directional-hemispherical reflectance of the band, and by extension to the whole structured surface, associated with this orientation of the incident light, is therefore:

$$R(\theta, \varphi) = \frac{F_r}{F_i} = \frac{1}{2\sin(\alpha/2)} \int_{y_P=-\sin(\alpha/2)}^{\sin(\alpha/2)} R(\theta, \varphi, y) dy_P \tag{22}$$

Again, according to the Helmholtz reciprocity principle, the angular function $R(\theta, \varphi)$ given by Eq. (22) also corresponds to the hemispherical-directional reflectance function of the structured surface when it is illuminated by Lambertian light over the hemisphere (same radiance $L_i$ comes from every direction) and observed in the direction $(\theta, \varphi)$.

Notice that since the specular reflections on the panels do not modify the geometrical extent of the rays, the radiance $L_r$ perceived in one direction $(\theta_r, \varphi_r)$ is:

$$L_r(\theta_r, \varphi_r) = R(\theta_r, \varphi_r) L_i \tag{23}$$

It is possible to display the reflectance given by Eq. (22) according to the observation direction on a 2D map thanks to the Lambert azimuthal equal area projection. To every direction $(\theta, \varphi)$ corresponds a point $(u, v)$ within a disk of radius $\sqrt{2}$ whose coordinates are given by:

$$\begin{cases} u = 2\sin(\theta/2)\cos\varphi \\ v = 2\sin(\theta/2)\sin\varphi \end{cases} \tag{24}$$

The advantage of this transformation is that it conserves the areas by mapping a portion of the hemisphere of a given area, into a portion of the disk with same area.

In Fig. 5, we present the results given by Eq. (22) for two different materials, for aperture angle values of 45, 60, 90, 120, 150° and 180°. One material is dielectric, with a refraction index of 1.5. Its spectral reflectances are converted first in CIE 1931 XYZ tristimulus values then into L*a*b* color values, for a better visualization. The other one is made of copper, with tabulated values for the refractive index in the visible spectrum of light (400–700 nm), the spectral reflectances being converted in CIE 1931 XYZ tristimulus values, and then into sRGB color values.

For the dielectric material, we can see that the reflectance is globally very weak, except at high incidence angles (periphery of the graphs) when the cavity aperture angle is large. This is coherent with the angular variations of the Fresnel formulae. The highest angular reflectances peaks are located near the zones where the azimuthal angle $\varphi = \pi/2$, i.e. when the incident plane contains the $x$-axis. We can also see that the

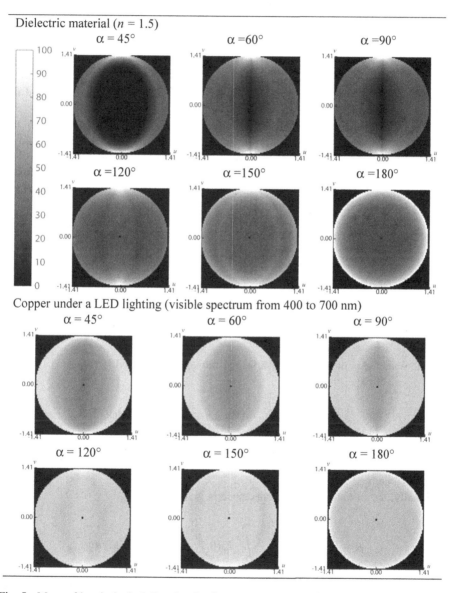

**Fig. 5.** Maps of hemispherical-directional reflectance (in %) for cavities of dielectric material, and color maps for cavities of copper, obtained with different aperture angles of cavities, represented with the Lambert azimuthal equal area projection.

radiance gradients have some discontinuities, which correspond to the directions at which the number of reflections within the cavity is incremented by one. For example, on the map attached to an aperture of 120°, a central area is lighter than the rest of the graph: it corresponds to rays undergoing one reflection, whereas in the rest of the graphs, rays undergo two reflections.

It is even more visible in the case of the copper. This material being more reflective, the reflected light appears more sliced into specific areas. It is also important to notice the saturation of the color increasing when the aperture angle decreases, as also shown in the case of diffusing surfaces in [20].

## 4.2   Bi-Hemispherical Reflectance

Now, we want to investigate the bi-hemispherical reflectance of the V-cavity and the influence of the surface structure (aperture angle $\alpha$).

The bi-hemispherical reflectance corresponds to a uniform illumination over the hemisphere (Lambertian illumination, characterized by a constant radiance $L_i$ from every direction), and a capture of the whole reflected light over the hemisphere. It is obtained by integrating over the hemisphere the angular reflectance studied previously, as follows.

The irradiance on the structured surface is related to the radiance $L_i$ by:

$$E_i = \int_{\theta=0}^{\pi/2} \int_{\varphi=0}^{2\pi} L_i \cos\theta \sin\theta d\theta d\varphi = \pi L_i \tag{25}$$

and the incident flux on a band of the $2\sin(\alpha/2)\Delta x$ area cavity is:

$$F_i = 2\sin(\alpha/2)\Delta x E_i \tag{26}$$

The exitance is the sum of the reflected radiances expressed by Eq. (23):

$$M = \int_{\theta_r=0}^{\pi/2} \int_{\varphi_r=0}^{2\pi} L_r(\theta_r, \varphi_r) \cos\theta_r \sin\theta_r d\theta_r d\varphi_r \tag{27}$$

where $L_r = R(\theta_r, \varphi_r)L_i$ is the radiance reflected by the cavity according to the reflectance defined by Eq. (22).

Finally, the bi-hemispherical reflectance is given by:

$$R = \frac{M}{E_i} = \frac{1}{\pi L_i} \int_{\theta_r=0}^{\pi/2} \int_{\varphi_r=0}^{2\pi} L_r(\theta_r, \varphi_r) \cos\theta_r \sin\theta_r d\theta_r d\varphi_r \tag{28}$$

which yields, according to Eqs. (20) and (21),

$$R = \frac{1}{2\pi \sin(\alpha/2)} \int\limits_{\theta_r=0}^{\pi/2} \int\limits_{\varphi_r=0}^{2\pi} \int\limits_{y_p=-\sin(\alpha/2)}^{\sin(\alpha/2)} R(\theta_r, \varphi_r, y) dy_P \cos\theta_r \sin\theta_r d\theta_r d\varphi_r \quad (29)$$

Using Eq. (29), we computed the bi-hemispherical reflectances for various aperture angles of the specular V-cavity, for the dielectric material previously studied, and for a cavity of silver at 550 nm ($n = 0.1249 + i3.3391$). The values are presented in Table 1.

**Table 1.** Bi-hemispherical reflectances for various cavity aperture angles.

| Aperture angle | 45° | 60° | 90° | 120° | 150° | 180° |
|---|---|---|---|---|---|---|
| Silver | 0.87 | 0.91 | 0.94 | 0.95 | 0.96 | 0.97 |
| Dielectric ($n = 1.5$) | 0.01 | 0.02 | 0.04 | 0.05 | 0.08 | 0.09 |

The bi-hemispherical values in Table 1 confirm the tendencies drawn by the angular reflectance maps. As the aperture angle gets smaller, the reflectance is lower and the structured surface has a darker appearance, which is due to the increase of the number of light reflections in the cavities, each reflection introducing a radiance attenuation. It is illustrated by Table 2, where we computed, in the case of a cavity of silver at 550 nm ($n = 0.1249 + i3.3391$) with an aperture of 45°, the bi-hemispherical reflectance by taking into account only 1 light reflections, then adding the paths of the light where a second reflection happens, then a third one, up to the maximum number of 4 light reflections possible in this structure.

**Table 2.** Bi-hemispherical reflectance of a 45° V-cavity made of silver at 550 nm

| Maximal number of light reflections | Bi-hemispherical reflectance |
|---|---|
| 1 | 0.14 |
| 2 | 0.40 |
| 3 | 0.70 |
| 4 | 0.97 |

We observe from these results that if we take into account only one or two light reflections, as it is often done in light scattering models by rough metallic surfaces, we underestimate the reflectance. The error is sensible in the case of media with high refractive index, like metals. It is also visible through Fig. 6, where the angular reflectance for silver at 550 nm with an aperture of 45° is represented in the cases where we only consider one reflection of the light, or all the possible reflections.

In order to obtain a more precise prediction of the appearance, especially in the case of a small aperture angle in the concavities of the surface topography, it is necessary to compute it with a sufficient number of light reflections, as also shown recently in the domain of computer graphics [10, 11].

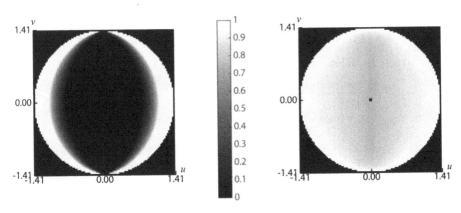

**Fig. 6.** Maps of angular reflectance for a 45° V-cavity made of silver, at 550 nm ($n = 0.1249 + i3.3391$), represented with the Lambert azimuthal equal area projection, where only one reflection (left) and all the possible reflections (right) of rays in the cavity are rendered.

## 5   Conclusions

In this paper, we analyzed the interreflections happening in a structured surface made of parallel, specular V-cavities under a Lambertian illumination. We proposed a model taking into account the exact number of light reflections occurring in the structures, in order to accurately predict the reflectance according to the observation angle. We saw that the material and the angle of the cavity have a strong impact on the interreflections and the reflectance of the concave surfaces, in particular because of the number of light reflections. We also showed that it is crucial to model correctly the number of light reflections happening in surfaces presenting concavities with small aperture angle, as it has a great influence on the final visual appearance. This constitutes an extension for the modelization of the light being reflected by complex surfaces, to better predict the visual appearance of given surfaces. It could be combined in the future with a model predicting the interreflections in similar cavities made of a Lambertian material, in order to predict the appearance of a diffusing material presenting a structured interface with air.

# References

1. Kinoshita, S., Yoshioka, S., Miyazaki, J.: Physics of structural colors. Rep. Prog. Phys. **71**, 076401 (2008)
2. Charrière, R., Lacaille, G., Pedeferri, M., Faucheu, J., Delafosse, D.: Characterization of the gonioapparent character of colored anodized titanium surfaces. Color Res. Appl. **40**(5), 483–490 (2015)
3. Kubelka, P.: New contributions to the optics of intensely light-scattering material. Part I. J. Opt. Soc. Am. A **38**, 448–457 (1948)
4. Melamed, N.T.: Optical properties of powders: Part I. optical absorption coefficients and the absolute value of the diffuse reflectance. J. Appl. Phys. **34**, 560–570 (1963)
5. Chandrasekhar, S.: Radiative Transfer. Dover, Illinois (1960)
6. van de Hulst, H.C.: Light Scattering by Small Particles, pp. 200–227. Dover, Illinois (1981)
7. Beckmann, P., Spizzichino, A.: The Scattering of Electromagnetic Waves from Rough Surfaces, pp. 70–98. MA Artech House Inc, Norwood (1963)
8. Torrance, K.E., Sparrow, E.M.: Theory for off-specular reflection from roughened surfaces. J. Opt. Soc. Am. **57**(9), 1105–1114 (1967)
9. Heitz, E., Hanika, J., d'Eon, E., Dachsbacher, C.: Multiple-scattering microfacet BSDFs with the Smith model. ACM Trans. Graph. **35**(4) (2016). Proceedings of the SIGGRAPH 2016. Article 58
10. Lee, J.H., Jarabo, A., Jeon, D.S., Gutierrez, D., Kim, M.H.: Practical multiple scattering for rough surfaces. In: SIGGRAPH Asia 2018 Technical Papers, p. 275. ACM (2018)
11. Xie, F., Hanrahan, P.: Multiple scattering from distributions of specular v-grooves. In: ACM SIGGRAPH Asia, p. 276 (2018)
12. Kubelka, P.: New contributions to the optics of intensely light-scattering materials. Part II: non homogeneous layers. J. Opt. Soc. Am. A **44**, 330–335 (1954)
13. Simonot, L., Hébert, M., Hersch, R.D.: Extension of the Williams-Clapper model to stacked nondiffusing colored coatings with different refractive indices. J. Opt. Soc. Am. A **23**, 1432–1441 (2006)
14. Hébert, M., Hersch, R.D., Becker, J.-M.: Compositional reflectance and transmittance model for multilayer specimens. J. Opt. Soc. Am. A **24**, 2628–2644 (2007)
15. Emmel, P., Hersch, R.D.: A unified model for color prediction of halftoned prints. J. Im. Sci. Technol. **44**(4), 351–359 (2000)
16. Clapper, F.R., Yule, J.A.C.: The effect of multiple internal reflections on the densities of halftone prints on paper. J. Opt. Soc. Am. **43**, 600–603 (1953)
17. Yule, J.A.C., Nielsen, W.J.: The penetration of light into paper and its effect on halftone reproductions. In: Proceedings of the TAGA, vol. 3, pp. 65–76 (1951)
18. Rogers, G.: Effect of light scatter on halftone color. J. Opt. Soc. Am. A **15**, 1813–1821 (1998)
19. Rogers, G.: A generalized clapper-yule model of halftone reflectance. Color Res. Appl. **25**, 402–407 (2000)
20. Saint-Pierre, D., Deeb, R., Muselet, D., Simonot, L., Hébert,M.: Light interreflections and shadowing effects in a Lambertian V-cavity under diffuse illumination. In: IS&T Electronic Imaging Symposium, Material Appearance, Burlingame, USA, 29 January–2 February 2018
21. Deeb, R., Muselet, D., Hebert, M., Trémeau, A.: Spectral reflectance estimation from one RGB image using self-interreflections in a concave object. Appl. Opt. **57**(17), 4918–4929 (2018)

# Makeup Skin Appearance Reproduction by Spectral Projection Mapping

Hiroki Shirasawa[1]([✉]), Keita Hirai[2] [iD], and Takahiko Horiuchi[2] [iD]

[1] Graduate School of Science and Engineering, Chiba University, Chiba, Japan
aema2587@chiba-u.jp
[2] Graduate School of Engineering, Chiba University, Chiba, Japan

**Abstract.** Projection mapping can control object surface appearances without painting or finishing. An existing problem in projection mapping is the control of skin appearances. This paper presents a spectral projection mapping method to reproduce makeup skin appearances. Spectral information is significant for the physically accurate reproduction of human skin. First, we propose a spectral projection mapping model for computing the projection spectra and controlling skin appearance. Subsequently, we developed a spectral projection mapping system for realizing skin appearance control. For projecting spatially varying spectra, we used spectral basis functions by non-negative matrix factorization. In our experiment, actual makeup skins and projection-mapped skins were compared spectrally. The results indicated that our method could reproduce makeup skins with good accuracy.

**Keywords:** Projection mapping · Skin appearance · Spectral reproduction · Spectral measurement · Non-negative Matrix Factorization (NMF)

## 1 Introduction

Projection mapping enables the control of an object's surface appearance without painting and finishing. It has been applied to a wide range of specialized fields such as entertainment, and simulations of product development. Raskar and Bimber studied surface control techniques using a projector-camera (procam) system and contributed significantly to the technical development of projection mapping [1]. In particular, Rasker et al. developed shader lamps that project textures and animations on white mock-ups. Shader lamps have enabled the control of surface appearance using multiple projectors. They managed to defy the principles of projection mapping techniques and procam systems [2]. In addition, several researchers are addressing high-order visual information on surface appearances by advanced projection mapping techniques. For examples, Bimber et al. extended the dynamic ranges of reflective media by superimposing images [3]. Amano et al. proposed a method for controlling the glossiness and transparency of object surfaces using a procam system [4].

Recently, projection mapping has been applied to control facial expressions. For example, Team WOW developed a dynamic projection mapping system by attaching physical tracking markers on a face [5]. In addition, Bermano et al. developed the

S. Tominaga et al. (Eds.): CCIW 2019, LNCS 11418, pp. 304–317, 2019.
https://doi.org/10.1007/978-3-030-13940-7_23

*makeup lamps* that performs markerless dynamic projection mapping for facial expression control using expression trackers with infrared illumination [6].

Although dynamic projection mapping systems have been developed actively for real-time facial appearance controls, studies on projection mapping for reproducing skin appearances spectrally are non-existent. As is known, skin colorimetry and human perceived colors are different. Yoshikawa et al. investigated the relationships among the perceived whiteness and the metric lightness/chroma/hue angle of the facial skin color of Japanese females. They demonstrated that, in regard to the facial skin color of Japanese females, the metric lightness disagrees with the perceived whiteness or brightness in a narrow lightness range [7]. Hamada et al. suggested that the discrimination ability for skin images tended to be higher than that of uniform color stimuli [8]. As shown in the skin investigations above, colorimetric (photometric) approaches are often insufficient for skin color control. Spectral (radiometric) approaches are more accurate and useful for skin appearance control. A spectral skin appearance control technique can manipulate and reproduce the complicated optical characteristics of human skins. In addition, spectral simulations of makeup skin appearance are important for the cosmetic industry. As an example, Doi et al. developed a spectral skin simulation method using the Kubelka-Munk theory [9]. Therefore, a spectral projection mapping for makeup skin simulation is important in the skin and cosmetic studies. However, studies on such projection mappings are non-existent.

In this study, we propose a method to reproduce the appearance of makeup skins by a spectral projection mapping that combines spatial appearance manipulation by projection mapping with spectral appearance manipulation by spectral lighting. Hence we first develop a spectral model for spectral projection mapping. Subsequently, we build a system for realizing the proposed method. Finally, we conduct experiments for validating the proposed system.

This paper is organized as follows: We describe the spectral projection mapping model to control the appearance of the makeup skin in Sect. 2. Subsequently, we propose a system based on the proposed model in Sect. 3. In Sect. 4, we present the experimental results and discussions. Finally, conclusions and future research are discussed in Sect. 5.

## 2  Proposed Model

Figure 1 shows the comparison of the real appearance of makeup skin with the augmented appearance of makeup skin by spectral projection mapping. Humans perceive reflected light from skins under an environmental lighting condition. The reproduced model of makeup skin by spectral projection mapping is as follows:

$$E_{env}(\lambda)S_{make}(\lambda) = \big(E_{pro}(\lambda) + E_{env}(\lambda)\big)S_{skin}(\lambda), \tag{1}$$

where $E_{env}(\lambda)$ is the spectral distribution of uniform environmental illumination, $S_{make}(\lambda)$ is the spectral reflectance of makeup skin, $E_{pro}(\lambda)$ is the spectral distribution of projected light, and $S_{skin}(\lambda)$ is the spectral reflectance of the target non-makeup skin.

$\lambda$ comprises a visible wavelength range from 400 nm to 700 nm. From Eq. (1), the spectral distribution of the projection light source is calculated as follows:

$$E_{pro}(\lambda) = \left(\frac{S_{make}(\lambda)}{S_{skin}(\lambda)} - 1\right)E_{env}(\lambda). \tag{2}$$

The equation above is a case of controlling one local point on the skin surface. However, in the projection mapping, the spatial control of skin is necessary, calculated as follows:

$$E_{pro}(x, y, \lambda) = \left(\frac{S_{make}(\lambda)}{S_{skin}(x, y, \lambda)} - 1\right)E_{env}(\lambda), \tag{3}$$

where $(x, y)$ are the pixel positions of the non-makeup skin. As shown in Eq. (3), the spectral reflectance of non-makeup skin depends on the spatial position. Meanwhile, we assumed that one of the makeup skins do not depend on the spatial position, because the makeup skin appears uniform.

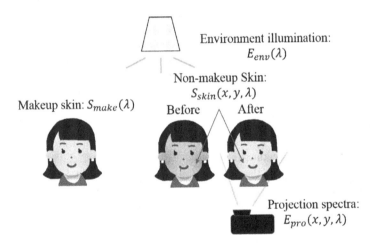

**Fig. 1.** Illustration of real makeup skin and spectral-projection-mapped skin

## 3   System Overview

Figure 2 shows an overview of the proposed system. Prior to spectral projection mapping, spectral reflectances of reference makeup skins were measured at five places using a spectrodensitometer (KONICA MINOLTA FD-7, which measurement aperture is 3.5 mm). The spectral distribution of the environmental light source was measured using a spectroradiometer (KONICA MINOLTA CS2000). These two parameters were obtained in advance. Subsequently, the processing flow of the projection mapping is as follows:

1. The spectral reflectance of a target non-makeup skin was measured using the spectral reflectance estimation system developed by Hirai et al. [10] (See Sect. 3.2)
2. Based on these measured information, the projection spectra were calculated based on the proposed model. (See Sect. 2)
3. The spatially-varying spectra for spectral projection mapping were represented by spectral basis functions and spatial weight images. We used non-negative matrix factorization (NMF) to obtain the basis functions. (See Sect. 3.3)
4. Spatial weight images with spectral basis functions were projected on the target non-makeup skin.

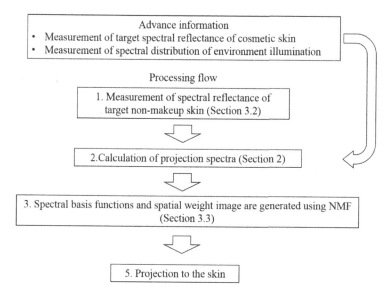

**Fig. 2.** Flowchart of the spectral projection mapping system.

### 3.1 System Configuration

In this study, we developed a spectral projection mapping system using a multi-primary image projector [11]. This multi-primary projector can reproduce not only wide gamut images but also spectral images. The projector has been applied to computer vision problems such as photometric and geometric image calibration, and spectral three-dimensional (3D) measurements [10, 12].

The multi-primary image projector was configured primarily with a light source component and an image projection component (Fig. 3). The light source component of the projector consists of OL490 (Optronic Laboratories), which is programmable using a computer. It is composed of a xenon lamp source, grating, a DMD chip, and a liquid light guide. The wavelength resolution was in the range of 380–780 nm. In this study, the sampling pitch of the projection light source was set to a 4 nm interval. The image projection component is based on the DLP Lightcrafter (Texas Instruments). The original LED-based RGB primary colors were replaced with the spectral light source above. This system used a DMD chip with a resolution of 608 × 684 pixels for image projection. In summary, the grating and DMD in the light source of the projector produced the spectra, whereas the DMD in image projection reproduced a monochromatic image with each light source spectrum. The light source and the image projection components were both controlled by a computer to project image sequences synchronously. A trigger signal was sent from the image projection component to the light source.

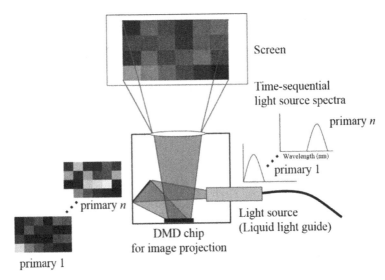

**Fig. 3.** Configuration and projection principle of the multi-primary image projector.

## 3.2    Spectral Reflectance Estimation Measurement System

For the spectral reflectance measurement of the target non-makeup skins, we used the spectral reflectance measurement system [10]. This system measures the spectral reflectances using a multi-primary image projector and a high-speed monochrome camera system (Fig. 4). The projector and camera are synchronized by a trigger signal. The projector reproduces the spectral distributions of nine basis functions for estimating the spectral reflectance.

An algorithm for the spectral reflectance measurement is described. This involves a set of orthonormal basis functions $\psi_m(\lambda)$ to represent the surface spectral reflectance [13]. The surface spectral reflectance $S(\lambda)$ can be expressed as follows:

$$S(\lambda) = \sum_{m=1}^{M} w_m \psi_m(\lambda) \ (m = 1, 2, \cdots, M), \tag{4}$$

where $M$ is the number of orthonormal basis functions, $w_m$ are the weights of the functions, and $M$ indicates the wavelength. In this study, we selected five spectral basis functions, i.e., $M = 5$. The basis functions were computed by the principal component analysis (PCA) of a spectral reflectance database with 507 samples. If we irradiate an object surface with spectrum $E_m(\lambda)$ of the orthonormal basis functions divided by the camera sensitivity $R(\lambda)$, the camera output $O_m$ can be modeled as follows:

$$
\begin{aligned}
O_m &= \int E_m(\lambda) R(\lambda) S(\lambda) \\
&= \int (\psi_m(\lambda)/R(\lambda)) R(\lambda) \sum_{m=1}^{M} w_m \psi_m(\lambda) d\lambda \\
&= w_m.
\end{aligned}
\tag{5}
$$

As shown in Eq. (5), we can obtain the weights $w_m$ directly from the camera outputs that are obtained by the projections based on the orthonormal basis functions. In the actual case, we could not irradiate an object surface with the spectral basis functions based on PCA, because the orthonormal basis functions included negative values. In this study, we decompose the orthonormal basis functions into positive and negative functions. Subsequently, the absolute values of the decomposed negative functions were used as the projected illumination. Finally, we estimated the surface spectral reflectance using the following values:

$$\psi_m(\lambda) = \psi_m^+(\lambda) - \psi_m^-(\lambda), \ w_m = O_m^+ - O_m^-. \tag{6}$$

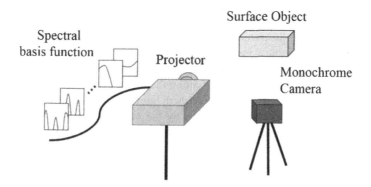

**Fig. 4.** Overview of the spectral measurement system.

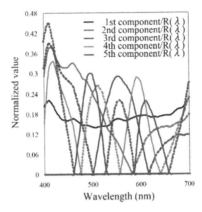

**Fig. 5.** Projected waveforms of orthonormal basis functions. (Solid line: Waveforms obtained by dividing the camera sensitivity are the positive values of the principal component. Dashed line: Waveforms divided by the camera sensitivity are the inverted negative values of the primary component).

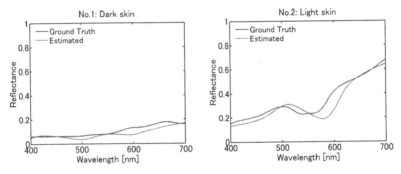

**Fig. 6.** Estimated spectral reflectances: (left) reflectance of ColorChecker No.1 (RMSE = 0.028, $\Delta E_{ab}^* = 8.83$), and (right) reflectance of ColorChecker No.2 (RMSE = 0.055, $\Delta E_{ab}^* = 11.14$).

Figure 5 shows the projected spectra designed for estimating the spectral reflectance. The figure shows the waveforms of nine orthonormal basis functions with the negative values inverted and divided by the camera spectral sensitivity $R(\lambda)$. The solid lines are the waveforms calculated by dividing the positive original orthonormal bases by the camera spectral sensitivity: the dashed lines are the waveforms obtained by dividing the reversed negative components by the camera sensitivity. The second to fifth principal components include negative values and require the illumination of two sources each. Subsequently, nine waveforms are projected for spectral reflectance estimation.

Figure 6 shows examples of the spectral reflectance estimation accuracy of this system. We used an X-Rite Mini ColorChecker. The average root mean square error (RMSE) and color difference $\Delta E_{ab}^*$ of 24 colors are 0.063 and 7.14.

### 3.3   Spectral Basis Functions and Spatial Weight Images Using NMF

The number of projections from the proposed system is defined as $N$. If the spectral control of each spatial point on the skin surface is required, the brute-force spectral projection for a target skin can be applied. In this case, the number of projections becomes $N = X \times Y$, where $X$ is the number of horizontal pixels, and $Y$ is that of vertical pixels. However, the number of projections is too large to realize spectral projection mapping. Subsequently, we applied the NMF technique to reduce the number of projections.

NMF is an algorithm that decomposes a non-negative matrix into two non-negative value matrices. NMF is often used in the research fields of image processing and computer vision. Lee and Seung extracted facial parts from facial images using NMF [14]. Akaishi et al. proposed a method for separating reflection components in a single image based on the dichromatic reflection model [15]. Their method is based on a modified version of sparse NMF. In this study, the projection spectra of Eq. (3) is decomposed by NMF as follows:

$$E \approx WH, \tag{7}$$

where $E$ is the projection spectra matrix of size $N \times 76$ ($N = X \times Y$ pixels and 76 dimensions of 400 nm to 700 nm). $W$ is a basis function matrix of size $76 \times I$, where $I$ is the number of spectral basis functions. $H$ is a weight image matrix with the size of $I \times N$. Subsequently, each row of $H$ corresponds to each grayscale weight image.

The projection spectra can be represented by the basis functions above. In other words, as shown in Eq. (3), we are to calculate only the basis functions from the spectral reflectance of the non-makeup skins. In this study, $W$ is determined from the measured spectral reflectances of a target non-makeup skin. Finally, we rewrite Eq. (3) using the basis functions as follows

$$E_{pro}(x, y, \lambda) = \sum_{i=1}^{I} E_i(x, y, \lambda) = \sum_{i=1}^{I} \left( \frac{S_{make}(\lambda)}{W_i(x, y) S_i(\lambda)} - 1 \right) E_{env}(\lambda), \tag{8}$$

where $S_i$ is the $i$-th basis function and $W_i$ is the $i$-th weight image corresponding to the $i$-th basis function.

## 4   Validation Experiment

In the validation experiment, the feasibility of the proposed method was verified by comparing the reference makeup skin with augmented makeup skin by spectral projection mapping.

## 4.1 Experimental Setups

Figure 7 shows the experimental conditions. The experiment was conducted under the following conditions: The reference makeup skins were produced using powder foundations: CEZANNE Cream-Beige and Dark-Ocher. The powder foundations were applied to the back of the right hand. The experimental environment was established using the spot lighting of a xenon lamp. Figure 8 shows the spectral reflectance of the target non-makeup skin measured by the reflectance estimation method in Sect. 3.2. Figures 9, 10, and 11 show the calculation results of four basis functions of Fig. 7 using NMF, that of the basis functions for reproducing augmented makeup skin spectra, and the close-ups of projected weight images corresponding to the projection basis spectra, respectively.

**Fig. 7.** Experimental condition.

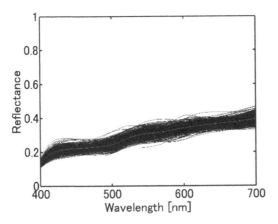

**Fig. 8.** Spectral reflectance of measured non-makeup skin. The white line is the average of the total spectral reflectances.

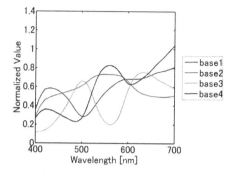

**Fig. 9.** Spectral basis functions of Fig. 6 using NMF.

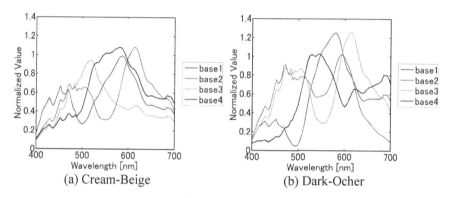

(a) Cream-Beige                    (b) Dark-Ocher

**Fig. 10.** Spectral basis functions for reproducing augmented makeup skin based on NMF: (a) Spectral basis functions for Cream-Beige, (b) Spectral basis functions for Dark-Ocher.

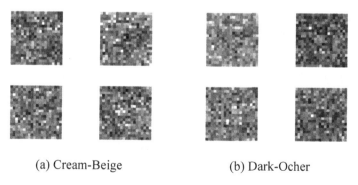

(a) Cream-Beige                    (b) Dark-Ocher

**Fig. 11.** Close-ups of projected weight images: (a) Close-ups of projected images for Cream-Beige, (b) Close-ups of projected images for Dark-Ocher. Each close-up images corresponds to the spectral basis functions in Fig. 8 (Top left: Base 1, top right: Base 2, bottom left: Base 3, and bottom right: Base 4).

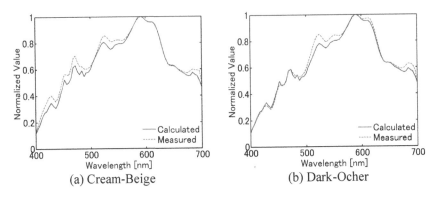

**Fig. 12.** Simulation result of superimpose-projected weight image with the spectral basis function. (Blue line: calculated spectral basis function, red line: measured spectral basis function) (Color figure online)

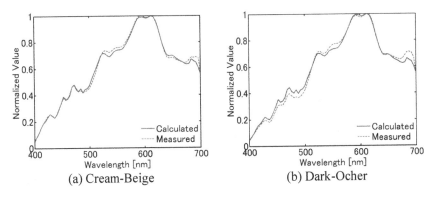

**Fig. 13.** Simulation result of the weight image with the spectral basis function superimpose-projected to non-makeup skin reflectance (Fig. 8). (Blue line: calculated spectral basis function, red line: measured spectral basis function) (Color figure online)

## 4.2    Results and Discussion

Figure 12 shows the experimental results of the calculated and measured projection spectra shown in Eq. (8). The results are averaged spatially. Figure 13 shows the results of multiplying the results of Fig. 12 by the average spectral reflectance of the target non-makeup skin (Fig. 6). As shown in Figs. 12 and 13, the projected spectra and augmented reflectance were reproduced accurately. By projecting the spatial weight images with the measured spectral basis functions onto the target non-makeup skins, an augmented makeup skin appearance that is similar to the reference makeup skin can be reproduced.

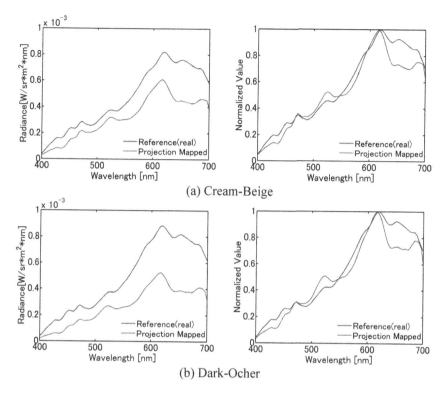

(a) Cream-Beige

(b) Dark-Ocher

**Fig. 14.** Spectral distribution of reference makeup skin (Blue line) and augmented skin (Red line) and the result of normalizing each right figure with the maximum value: (a) spectral of distribution of Cream-Beige (RMSE = $1.79 \times 10^{-4}$, GFC = 0.9944, $\Delta E_{ab}^{*}$ = 7.97), and (b) spectral distribution of Dark-Ocher (RMSE = $2.22 \times 10^{-4}$, GFC = 0.9940, $\Delta E_{ab}^{*}$ = 9.83). (Color figure online)

Figure 14 shows the spectral reflectance of the reference makeup skin and augmented skin. In this case, we projected and measured the actual target skin by spectral projection mapping. The RMSE of the Cream-Beige makeup skin and the Dark-Ocher makeup skin are $1.79 \times 10^{-4}$, and $2.22 \times 10^{-4}$, respectively. Those GFC (goodness-of-fit coefficient) [16] are 0.9944 and 0.9940, respectively. In addition $\Delta E_{ab}^{*}$ are 7.97 and 9.83, respectively. The spectral forms between the reference and augmented spectral reflectance of the makeup skins were similar. However, the augmented makeup skin was darker than the reference skin. There are two primary concerns on the accuracy. One is the alignment problem. The accuracy deteriorates owing to the misalignment between the measured and projected spatial positions by the spectral reflectance estimation system and the spectral projection mapping. Because the proposed projection spectra were controlled pixel-by-pixel, it was difficult to accurately project the weight images on precise positions on a target skin. Furthermore, the 3D shape on the target hand may differ between the measurement and the projection. This system is not compatible with the projection mapping of 3D shapes. The other problem is that the proposed model cannot fully consider the optical properties of the skin. The actual makeup skin was divided into a two-layer structure of foundation and skin. The internally scattered light and the surface reflected light within the two layers caused spectral distributions such as sub-surface scattering. However, the current spectral projection mapping considers only surface reflected lights.

## 5 Conclusion

We herein proposed a method to reproduce the appearance of makeup skin by applying spectral projection mapping to non-makeup skins. First, we modeled the spectral projection mapping to calculate the projected spectra. Subsequently, we developed a spectral projection mapping system using a multi-primary image projector. For realizing spectral projection mapping, we applied NMF to calculate spectral basis functions and spatial weight images. From the experimental results, we confirmed the feasibility of the proposed method that exhibited good accuracy.

In our study, the spectral reflectance of the makeup skin could be reproduced exactly. However, the actual use for the skin appearance reproduction is still insufficient. Alignment is a problem. It is necessary to develop a spatial alignment technique to address the spatially varying reflectance of skin surfaces. Additionally, the subsurface scattering characteristics in skins are important for realistic skin appearance reproduction. It is necessary to improve such optical characteristics by the spectral projection mapping.

**Acknowledgment.** This work was supported by JSPS KAKENHI Grant Number JP15H05926 (Grant-in-Aid for Scientific Research on Innovative Areas "Innovative SHITSUKAN Science and Technology") and JSPS KAKENHI Grant Number JP18K11347 (Grant-in-Aid for Scientific Research(C)).

## References

1. Bimber, O., Rasker, R.: Spatial Augmented Reality: Merging Real and Virtual Worlds. A K Peters Ltd., Natick (2015)
2. Raskar, R., Welch, G., Low, K. L., Bandyopadhyay, D.: Shader Lamps: Animating Real Objects with Image-Based Illumination. EGWRS (2001)
3. Bimber, O., Iwai, D.: Superimposing dynamic range. ACM Trans. Graph. (Proc. SIGGRAPH Asia), 27(5) (2008). Article No. 150
4. Amano, T., Komura, K., Sasabuchi, T., Nakano, S., Yamashita, S.: The appearance control for the human material perception manipulation. In: 21st International Conference on Pattern Recognition, pp. 13–16. IEEE, Tsukuba (2012)
5. OMOTE: OMOTE – real-time face tracking & projection mapping. https://vimeo.com/103425574.3. Accessed July 2017
6. Bermano, A., Billeter, M., Iwai, D., Grundhöfer, A.: Makeup lamps: live augmentation of human faces via projection. Comput. Graph. Forum 36(2), 311–323 (2017)
7. Yoshikawa, H., Kikuchi, K., Yamaguchi, H., Mizokami, Y., Takata, S.: Effect of chromatic components on facial skin whiteness. Color Res. Appl. 37(4), 281–291 (2012)

8. Hamada, K., Mizokami, Y., Kikuchi, K., Yaguchi, H.: Discrimination thresholds for skin image and uniform color stimulus. In: The 13th International AIC Congress, PS03-74, Jeju, pp. 1–4 (2017)

9. Doi, M., Ohtsuki, R., Tominaga, S.: Spectral estimation of skin color with foundation makeup. In: Kalviainen, H., Parkkinen, J., Kaarna, A. (eds.) SCIA 2005. LNCS, vol. 3540, pp. 95–104. Springer, Heidelberg (2005). https://doi.org/10.1007/11499145_11

10. Hirai, K., Nakahata, R., Horiuchi, T.: Measuring spectral reflectance and 3D shape using multi-primary image projector. In: Mansouri, A., Nouboud, F., Chalifour, A., Mammass, D., Meunier, J., ElMoataz, A. (eds.) ICISP 2016. LNCS, vol. 9680, pp. 137–147. Springer, Cham (2016). https://doi.org/10.1007/978-3-319-33618-3_15

11. Hirai, K., Irie, D., Horiuchi, T.: Multi-primary image projector using programmable spectral light source. J. Soc. Inf. Disp. 24(3), 144–153 (2016)

12. Hirai, K., Irie, D., Horiuchi, T.: Photometric and geometric measurements based on multi-primary image projector. In: The Colour and Visual Computing Symposium (CVCS2015), Article No. 2, pp. 1–5. IEEE, Gjovik (2015)

13. Tominaga, S., Horiuchi, T.: Spectral imaging by synchronizing capture and illumination. J. Opt. Soc. Am. A 29(9), 1764–1775 (2012)

14. Lee, D., Seung, H.: Learning the parts of objects by non-negative matrix factorization. Nature 401(6755), 788–791 (1999)

15. Akashi, Y., Okatani, T.: Separation of reflection components by sparse non-negative matrix factorization. Comput. Vis. Image Underst. 146, 77–85 (2016)

16. Romero, J., García-Beltrán, A., Hernández-Andrés, A.: Linear basis for representation of natural and artificial illuminants. J. Opt. Soc. Am. A 14(5), 1007–1014 (1997)

# Evaluating the Material Appearance of Objects Under Different Lighting Distributions Against Natural Illumination

Takashi Yamazoe[1][✉], Tomohiro Funaki[2], Yuki Kiyasu[2],
and Yoko Mizokami[3]

[1] Institute for Global Prominent Research, Chiba University, 1-33, Yayoicho,
Inage Ward, Chiba-shi, Chiba 263-8522, Japan
yamazoe@chiba-u.jp
[2] Department of Imaging Sciences,
Graduate School of Science and Engineering, Chiba University, 1-33, Yayoicho,
Inage Ward, Chiba-shi, Chiba 263-8522, Japan
[3] Graduate School of Engineering, Chiba University,
1-33, Yayoicho, Inage Ward, Chiba-shi, Chiba 263-8522, Japan

**Abstract.** The recent development of new solid-state lamps including OLED lighting offered a wide variety of lighting conditions through controlling the spectral power distribution and the spatial distribution of light. The appearance of an object surface is largely influenced by lighting conditions and object materials. Variable control of lighting condition would be useful to offer an optimal material impression. We have investigated the possibility whether the subjective evaluation, comparing material appearance under different lighting distribution with that under natural illumination, is able to determine a lighting condition for an appropriate material appearance. We tested viewing condition consisted of three spotlight sizes and three illuminance levels. Participants chose one viewing condition in which the material appearance of fruits and vegetable food samples was closest to those impression learned from observing and holding freely in a reference natural illumination. In addition, they evaluated impressions of stimuli in each condition by the twelve questionnaires of seven-point scales. The result showed higher tendencies to select the wide spotlight size condition with higher diffuseness of illumination rather than narrower spotlight conditions, suggesting that diffuseness of illumination influences object material appearance. Results of seven-point scales showed differences between samples, but little differences among lighting distribution. It was thus suggested the possibility to provide an optimal lighting condition to offer material appearance similar to material impression learned with visual and tactile information in natural illumination.

**Keywords:** Material perception · Material appearance · Lighting distribution · Illumination diffuseness

© Springer Nature Switzerland AG 2019
S. Tominaga et al. (Eds.): CCIW 2019, LNCS 11418, pp. 318–333, 2019.
https://doi.org/10.1007/978-3-030-13940-7_24

# 1   Introduction

The recent development of new solid-state lamps including OLED lighting offered a wide variety of lighting conditions through controlling the spectral power distribution and the spatial distribution of light. Especially, OLED lighting would give a surface light source with strong diffuseness. There are also other various ways of changing lighting distributions such as spotlights, which change the size of a lighting area through the changing the distance of a lens and a lamp. This kind of variation in lighting distribution also give rise to the changes of the lighting conditions such as the state of shadow and diffuseness.

The appearance of an object surface is mainly influenced by lighting conditions and object materials. Considerable amounts of researches have been done on the color rendering of lighting and the influence of lighting on color appearance. The technical Report on new color fidelity index for accurate scientific use" has been published recently and other evaluation methods are also under consideration in the CIE [1]. It has, however, not been systematically studied how the diffuseness of lighting influences material appearance.

The material and texture of objects is one of the major information to determine object impression. Material perception can be mainly classified into the visual and the tactile sensation. The object impression is consisted of the combination of these information. Besides, we normally have quite good material perception through visual observation without touching. However, this perception is not perfect and could vary under different lighting conditions. It is important to offer desirable material impression under artificial lighting. One important citation to give desirable material impression would be the fidelity of material appearance which is similar to color fidelity, namely the evaluation of color appearance under artificial lighting to give close enough to that under natural illumination. Variable control of lighting condition would be useful to offer an optimal material appearance.

The perception of an object surface is influenced by color (including hue, value, and chroma), material properties (including diffuse and specular reflection, scattering, and transparency) and the surface roughness of the object [2]. The random subsurface scattering of light and the emerging light rays distributed in a wide range of directions, give the surface a matte appearance [3]. The previous study of computer-generated graphics clarified that appearances depend on a viewpoint, illumination and a scale at which the texture is observed [4]. It suggests illumination, viewpoint and surface condition are important factors for material perception. It was shown that both lightness and glossiness ratings were well correlated with the skewness of the luminance histogram. It indicates optical conditions are corresponding surface physical properties [5]. The histogram of gloss surface has a positive skewness, while that of matte surface has a negative skewness. There are interactions between illumination and material perception [6]. In the cases where the correct perception of the light field is important, more emphasis should be put on the realism of the global properties of the light field such as direction and diffuseness. In the perception of computer-generated graphics, the global properties of the light field such as the mean direction and directedness (or diffuseness) would be the most important for light field perception [6]. The texture perception of roughness or smoothness is correlated with the global properties of the light field. It was also reported that the diffusivity of lighting influenced the appearance of an object surface such as glossiness and roughness [7], but the color appearance was stable [8]. These researches suggest that the distribution and diffuseness of lighting can be a strong factor of material perception. It was reported that an effect of material constancy appeared among different distribution of specular and diffuse reflection, but no obvious gloss constancy when observing only the distribution of specular reflection since the shape and size of light source give a great influence to the gloss perception in the research using printed paper object [9]. Previous research suggests that texture perception is generated by the interaction between the optical condition of an object surface and a lighting environment. However, it was suggested that the estimation of surface reflectance does not require the knowledge of the specific conditions of illumination [10]. Thus, the influence of illumination would be one of the key factors of material perception and the appearance of objects should be investigated further. However, it is not clear what kind of lighting conditions are adequate to realize the appropriate appearance reproduction of materials.

In the present study, we have investigated the possibility whether the subjective evaluation, comparing material appearance under different lighting distribution with that under natural illumination, is able to determine a lighting condition for an appropriate material appearance by comparing subjective evaluations under different lighting distribution with those under natural illumination. There are varieties of lighting conditions changing light field and diffuseness. Thus, it is difficult to test all conditions. Here, we focus on the effect of lighting with the different size of spotlights for the appearance of vegetable and fruits. We often encounter these kinds of lighting conditions in shops, home and restaurants in our daily life, and their appearances and impression are sometimes not identical or quite different from what we expect or prefer. It would be useful to examine whether we actually can evaluate the difference in naturalness or impression of objects under those lighting and decide a preferable lighting condition giving the natural appearance.

## 2  Experiment

Spot light size and intensity were controlled by an LED lighting system. It was constructed for evaluating the influence of lighting distribution to material appearance. We tested how the appearance of fruit and vegetable food samples under different lighting conditions was close to the impression of those objects constructed by viewing and touching under natural light. In a reference phase, participants held and observed stimulus objects under natural illumination and evaluated the impression of objects' appearance. Then, the participants evaluated the appearance of objects under nine viewing conditions (three spotlight conditions and three illuminance conditions) against the material impression of the objects under natural illumination.

### 2.1  Apparatus and Stimuli

A viewing booth was placed in a dark room. An LED lighting control system was set on the ceiling of the viewing booth as shown in Fig. 1. A participant viewed food samples in the booth through a window and observed only illuminated stimulus. An LED lighting system blind from participant.

The LED lighting control system consisted of an LED bulb, a Fresnel lens, diaphragm rings, slide rails, and a flexible duct. An LED bulb (Panasonic LDA7DHEW2, 6500 K, Ra 80) used as a light source. Fresnel lens and slide rail were used for spotlight control. The four slide rails guided the Fresnel lens to move up and down. The slide rails were able to change the distance between the Fresnel lens and the LED bulb. The spotlight size was controlled by changing their distance. The diaphragm rings managed illuminance.

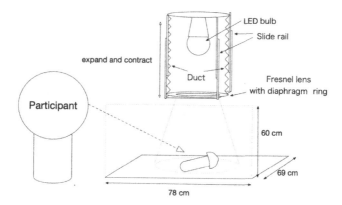

**Fig. 1.** Arrangement of an experimental booth with an LED lighting system and a stimulus.

We tested three levels of spotlight size; narrow, middle, and wide. The change of spotlight size corresponded to the change in the diffuseness of lighting. Thus, we measured the diffuseness of the illumination at the position of a stimulus was measured by a cubic illuminance measurement [11]. The illuminance of six directions (tilt angle +35° with rotate angle 0° ($E_{(u+)}$), 120° ($E_{(v+)}$), 240° ($E_{(w+)}$) and tilt angle −35° with rotate angle 60° ($E_{(w-)}$), 180° ($E_{(u-)}$), 300° ($E_{(v-)}$) were measured to calculate cylindrical illuminance ($E_{cl}$) and horizontal working plane illuminance ($E_{wp}$). Diffuseness ($E_{cl}/E_{wp}$) can be specified from cylindrical illuminance and working plane illuminance. The diffuseness was 0.16 for wide spot, 0.12 for middle spot, and 0.06 for narrow spot size condition as shown in Table 1. The relation between spotlight size and the skewness of luminance histogram are shown in Fig. 2.

Three illuminance levels (800 lx, 600 lx, and 400 lx) were tested also to examine the influence of the overall lighting level to the material impression of objects. We used the appearance of stimuli under natural illumination as a reference in fidelity evaluation, but our lighting system was difficult to realize such a high illuminance environment (>1990 lx). We tested three illuminance levels to examine the influence of illuminance on the fidelity evaluation and to confirm that the result was not determined solely by illuminance difference between the test and reference environments.

Four kinds of food samples included Orange, Apple, Eryngii, and Paprika were used for stimuli. These stimuli were selected by the combination of matte-gloss (micro texture) and smooth-rough (macro texture) surface. Orange had gloss and rough surface. Apple had a matte and smooth surface. Eryngii had a matte and rough surface. Paprika had a gloss and smooth surface. Stimuli under the different size of spotlight were shown in Fig. 3. Three spotlight sizes and three illuminances conditions were combined to establish nine viewing conditions.

Natural illumination condition (Fig. 4) was used for a reference phase to establish the criterion of the objects' material appearance. Any standard illumination condition for material evaluation has not been established like the color fidelity evaluation using blackbody and daylight color as references. Therefore, we decided to use a condition with free observation under natural illumination from a north window as a reference since we normally use visual factors and tactile sensation to establish a solid impression for materials and natural illumination would be natural and easy to recognize objects in the same way as color evaluation. We chose natural illumination condition which illuminance and geometry largely change since we usually establish "stable and acculate object recognition" not by observing in one particular viewing condition but by observing and touching under the variation of viewing conditions. Participants were able to hold and rotate food samples to see them from different angles. The diffuseness ($E_{cl}/E_{wp}$) of natural illumination varied from 0.542 to 0.674 which are relatively high diffuseness and the illuminance varied from 1990 lx to 7010 lx. Natural illumination illuminance was fluctuated by weather at observation with tac-tile. However, in present study, no significant difference was detected in subjective evaluation results under natural illumination ($P > .05$).

**Table 1.** Viewing conditions of illuminance, spotlight size and diffuseness.

| Illuminance (lx) | 800 | 600 | 400 | 800 | 600 | 400 | 800 | 600 | 400 |
|---|---|---|---|---|---|---|---|---|---|
| Spotlight size | Wide | Wide | Wide | Middle | Middle | Middle | Narrow | Narrow | Narrow |
| Diffuseness ($E_{cl}/E_{wp}$) | 0.166 | 0.163 | 0.168 | 0.119 | 0.118 | 0.119 | 0.057 | 0.054 | 0.055 |

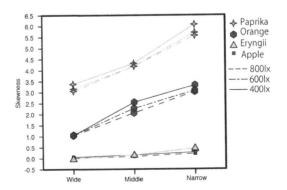

**Fig. 2.** Relation of skewness and spotlight size.

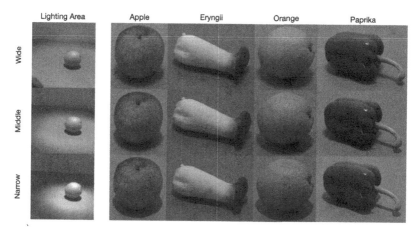

**Fig. 3.** Spotlight size and each stimulus.

**Fig. 4.** Natural illumination condition (by a north window).

## 2.2 Subjective Evaluation

Participants answered a viewing condition which the material appearance of a stimulus was the closest to the reference condition from nine viewing conditions. The evaluation for the impression of the stimuli was also conducted in each viewing condition including the reference condition with natural illumination. Participants answered twelve questionnaires using a seven-point scale (Fig. 5). The questionnaires included following items; bright-dark (brightness), vivid-dull (chroma), gloss-matte (glossiness), smooth-rough (smoothness), transparent-opaque (transparency), fresh-bad (freshness), delicious-awful (taste), sharp-blunt (sharpness), light-heavy (weight), distinct-indistinct (distinction), hard-soft (stiffness) and natural-unnatural (naturalness) [7, 12]. After finishing all trials, we took participant's direct reports and their implications.

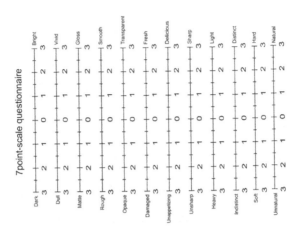

**Fig. 5.** Twelve questionnaires of seven-point scale evaluation sheet.

## 2.3  Procedure

First, a participant held and observed stimulus under natural illumination condition for 10 min in a reference phase. The participant observed stimuli from various angles by rotating them by their hands with memorized the material appearance of stimulus. After the observation, participant evaluated the impressions of stimulus using a seven-point scale. A rest time was set for making form a firm object impression, and the test phase started 30 min after the reference phase. The participant sat in front of the viewing booth. Viewing distance to a stimulus was about 60 cm. The participant observed the stimulus and evaluated its impressions by seven-point scale questionnaires in one of nine viewing conditions. Then participant repeated evaluations for nine viewing conditions in random order. After nine trials finished, participants selected a condition which the appearance of a stimulus was closest to that in the reference condition. One session consisted by the evaluation of impression in nine conditions and the fidelity judgment. Three sessions were executed for each of four stimuli and twelve sessions were executed in total. Participant gave direct reports and their implications after all sessions finished.

## 2.4  Participant

Two males and four females participated. The range of their age was 22 to 25 years old (the average was 23.0 years old). All participants had normal visual acuity (binocular vision was 1.0 or better) either naturally or with correction and normal color vision which was confirmed by Ishihara color vision test plate and Anomaloscope (OT-II, Neitz). A thorough explanation regarding the purpose and the method of experiment was provided to participants, and their consents were obtained before the experiment.

## 2.5   Analysis

Two-way ANOVA was used to compare the average frequency of fidelity selection as well as the reference condition and test conditions on seven-scale questionnaires. Multiple comparisons of the Tukey-Kramer test were used to compare each factor of spot light size, illuminance, stimulus and participant. Two-way ANOVA compared the differences between the reference condition and test conditions on seven-point scale questionnaires.

# 3   Result

The result of the fidelity selection is shown in Fig. 6. The selection of a stimulus closest to the appearance of the reference is examined. The horizontal axis represents nine viewing conditions and the vertical axis represents a frequency that each condition was chosen. Each bar corresponds to the average value of all participants and food samples. Error bars show the standard deviations. The wide spotlight condition at 800 lx was chosen most frequently, followed by those at 600 lx and 400 lx, the middle size spotlight condition at 800 lx, 600 lx and 400 lx, then the narrow spotlight condition at 800 lx, 600 lx and 400 lx. Significant differences are detected between the wide and narrow spotlight conditions ($p < .001$), and between wide and middle condition ($p < .001$) ($F = 16.61$). There are also significant differences between wide and narrow ($p < .05$) spotlight conditions at 800 lx, wide and narrow ($p < .001$), wide and middle ($p < .05$) at 600 lx, wide and narrow ($p < .001$), at 400 lx. No significant differences were detected between illuminance levels ($F = 0.439$). These results suggested that the illuminance levels does not influence the material appearance, but a large impact was observed on spotlight size causing the light with different diffuseness.

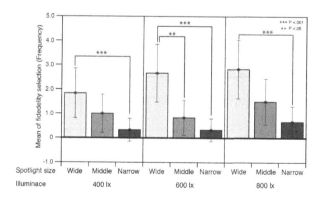

**Fig. 6.**  Result of the fidelity selection of each diffuseness and illuminance conditions.

We compared the results of food sample stimuli (Fig. 7). The horizontal axis represents spotlight size conditions for each stimulus and the vertical axis represents the frequency of fidelity selection. Each bar corresponds to the average of all participants and all illuminance levels. Error bars show the standard deviations. The wide spotlight conditions are chosen more frequently than the narrow spotlight conditions for Apple (p < .05), Orange (p < .001), and Paprika (p < .001). There is also a significant difference between middle and narrow condition (p < .05) for Paprika. No significant differences were detected for Eryngii.

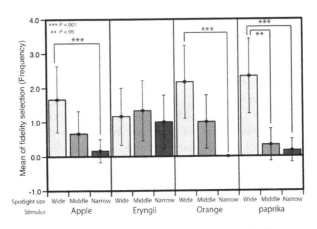

**Fig. 7.** Result of fidelity selection for each stimulus.

Next, we compared the results of the individual participant (Fig. 8). The horizontal axis represents spotlight size conditions for each participant and the vertical axis represents the frequency of fidelity selection. Each bar corresponds to the average of all stimuli and all illuminance levels. All participants chose the wide spotlight condition the most. There were significant differences between the wide and narrow conditions for participant B, D, E, and F (p < .05), and between wide and middle conditions for participant C and F (p < .05).

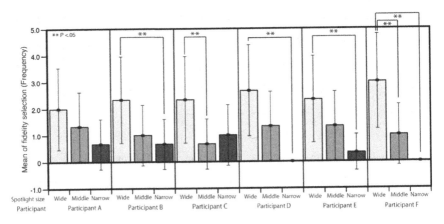

**Fig. 8.** Result of fidelity selection for each participant.

The result of fidelity selection for each spotlight sizes is shown in Fig. 9. They are the average results of all illuminance levels, stimuli, and participants. There are some individual differences between participants. The appearance of material is closest to the reference condition in the wide spotlight size condition in general.

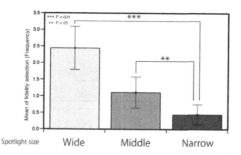

**Fig. 9.** Result of fidelity selection for each spotlight size conditions.

No significant differences were detected among spotlight size conditions on the result of seven-point scale questionnaires. Differences were observed among stimuli such as questionnaires of gloss-matte (glossiness), light-heavy (weight), and natural-unnatural (naturalness).

The score of glossiness is shown in Fig. 10. The vertical axis represents the difference of the score from that in a reference condition. Each bar corresponds to the average result of all participants and illuminance levels. Error bars show the standard deviations. Orange and Eryngii appeared glossier than Apple and Paprika (p < .05) in all spotlight conditions. The score for Eryngii was not stable and had large standard deviations. There are significant differences between glossiness for Eryngii and Paprika (p < .001), Orange and Paprika in wide (p < .001), Apple and Eryngii (p < .001), Eryngii and Paprika (p < .001), Orange and Paprika (p < .05) in middle, and Orange and Paprika in narrow (p < .05) spotlight conditions (F = 14.53).

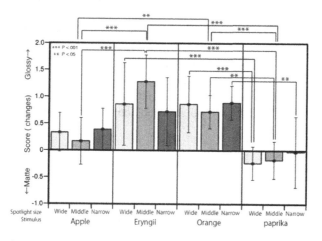

**Fig. 10.** Glossiness changes from that in the reference condition.

As shown in Fig. 11, Apple appeared heavier, and Eryngii, Orange and Paprika appeared lighter in all spotlight conditions. There are significant differences between weight score for Apple and Eryngii (p < .001), Apple and Orange (p < .001), Apple and Paprika (p < .001) in wide, Apple and Eryngii (p < .05), Apple and Orange (p < .001), Apple and Paprika (p < .001) in middle spotlight conditions (F = 17.84). Differences in score among stimuli become a little bit smaller in the narrow spotlight condition.

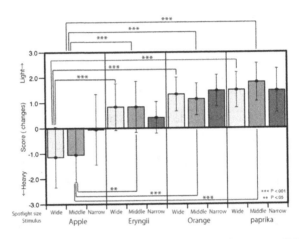

**Fig. 11.** Weight score changes from that in the reference condition.

As shown in Fig. 12, Orange and Paprika showed little changes their appearance of naturalness. On the other hand, Apple appeared more natural and Eryngii appeared less natural. There are significant differences between naturalness for Apple and Eryngii (p < .001), in wide (p < .05) and middle spotlight (p < .05) conditions (F = 6.263). Apple appeared most natural and Eryngii appeared most unnatural There are significant difference between Apple and Eryngii in wide (p < .05) and middle spotlight (p < .05) conditions (F = 8.01). However, differences in stimuli become smaller in the narrow spotlight condition. These trends imply that the impression of object material become similar in the narrow spotlight with low diffuseness.

As the results of direct reports, participants did not recognize the difference in illuminance conditions, but they were able to distinguish the change in spotlight size. All participants felt that narrow spotlight condition gave strong shade and shadow to the observed scene.

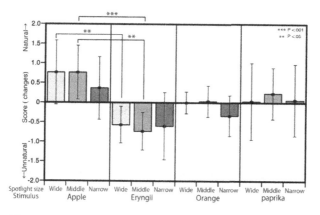

**Fig. 12.** Naturalness score changes from that in the reference condition.

## 4 Discussion

The present study examined the material perception under different lighting distributions. Results showed that the appearance under the wide spotlight was closest to that in a reference condition under natural illumination. The present results also suggest that change in the diffuseness of lighting due to the spotlight size influence a material perception. In addition, the frequency of fidelity selection is correlated with diffuseness at Pearson's rank correlation. ($r = 0.577$) (Fig. 13). Our results are consistent with previous studies which showed a relationship between object surface perception and diffuseness of illumination [6, 7]. Moreover, a material appearance would be more natural and appropriate under diffused light at least in the ranges we tested. It is interesting that the participant was able to do fidelity selection task even through the illuminance levels and various diffuseness of lighting in the viewing conditions we tested were far from those of reference illumination. The present results suggest a possibility to create an indoor lighting environment to offer an accurate reproduction of material appearance under natural illumination.

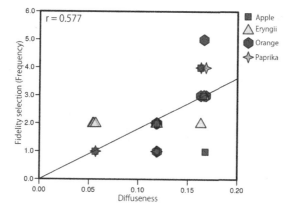

**Fig. 13.** Correlation of diffuseness and fidelity selection (each observed condition).

The results of illuminance level (Fig. 6) suggests that the material appearance is significantly influenced by the spot size and diffuseness of lighting, rather than illuminance. In the post interview, participants also reported that they barely noticed the illuminance difference. However, the higher frequency of fidelity selection in 800 lx would be because that condition was closer to the illuminance level of the reference illumination.

We used different kind of fruit and vegetables to test the influence of stimuli surface; Apple with a matte and smooth surface, Eryngii with a matte and rough surface, Orange with a gloss and rough surface, and Paprika with a gloss and smooth surface. The influence of spotlight size is different in stimuli. For example, the glossiness score was higher than that in the reference condition for Orange, Apple, and Eryngii, which is expected because the diffuseness of spotlights was much higher than the reference illumination. However, there was no difference for Paprika. This result may suggest that the Paprika with gloss and smooth surface appeared glossy enough under natural illumination and its impression did not change by adding spotlight, but the glossiness of other stimuli was enhanced by the spotlights. The fidelity selection for Eryngii did not show systematic difference among spotlight size, but the results of impression score showed glossier, lighter, and less natural than the impression in the reference condition. This suggests that the appearance of Eryngii with a matte and rough surface is changed by spotlight in comparison with the reference condition, but the difference in spotlight size did not have a large influence. These differences in stimuli suggest that the influence of lighting distribution differ among object materials and surface properties, and thus we have to consider object property in cases that we need to choose an appropriate lighting condition.

We have found the influence of spotlight size for the fidelity selection in the present study. Participants successfully selected the viewing condition, in which the material perception closest to that in the reference condition. However, the results of seven-point scale questionnaires showed no difference in the present study. Seven-point scale questionnaires include twelve questionnaires, but they may not sensitive enough to show the difference in viewing conditions.

To see if any trends revealed by an analysis using the relationship between scores and image statistics, we took the Pearson's rank correlation of each score and the skewness of luminance histogram of stimuli. They suggest that skewness does not correlate with glossiness, weight or naturalness questionnaires (Figs. 14, 15 and 16). Stimuli were used the combination of matte-gloss (micro smoothness) and smooth-rough (macro smoothness).

In the present study, we have used the viewing conditions with the definite ranges of lighting distribution and diffuseness. Further studies will be necessary to use more wider range of lighting distribution and diffuseness to find a lighting condition for accurate material impression. The method of impression evaluation should be improved to be able to extract the differences among lighting conditions.

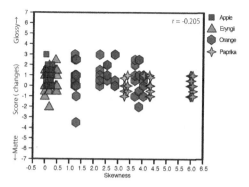

**Fig. 14.** The relationship between the skewness of luminance histogram and glossiness.

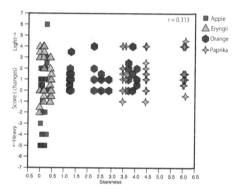

**Fig. 15.** The relationship between the skewness of luminance histogram and weight.

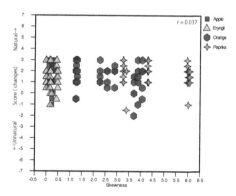

**Fig. 16.** The relationship between the skewness of luminance histogram and naturalness.

## 5  Conclusion

We investigated whether it is possible to determine a lighting condition to show an appropriate material appearance by comparing material appearance under different lighting distribution with that under natural illumination by subjective evaluation. We tested viewing condition consisting three spotlight sizes and three illuminance levels by the fidelity selection and the impression evaluations of stimuli. The result shows the wide spotlight size condition with higher diffuseness of lighting is more selected than narrower spotlight conditions. It suggests that the diffuseness of illumination influences object material appearance and a wider and more diffused spotlight would be more appropriate to show the impression under natural illumination. The results of seven-point scales show differences between samples, but little differences among lighting distribution. It was suggested that it would be possible to set a lighting condition to realize an appropriate material appearance.

**Acknowledgment.** This work was partially supported by Next Generation Research Incubator project "the Creation of Imaging Science and Technology for Material Appearance" in the Institute for Global Prominent Research (Chiba University), JSPS KAKENHI JP16K00368, and the Konica Minolta Imaging Science Encouragement Award.

## References

1. [CIE] Commission Internationale de l'Eclairage: colour fidelity index for accurate scientific use. CIE, Vienna, Austria (2017)
2. Nayar, S.K., Oren, M.: Visual appearance of matte surfaces. Science **267**(5201), 1153–1156 (1995)
3. Dana, K.J., Van Ginneken, B., Nayar, S.K., Koenderink, J.J.: Reflectance and texture of real-world surfaces. ACM Trans. Graph. (TOG) **18**(1), 1–34 (1999)
4. Pont, S.C., Koenderink, J.J.: Bidirectional reflectance distribution function of specular surfaces with hemispherical pits. JOSA A **19**(12), 2456–2466 (2002)
5. Motoyoshi, I., Nishida, S.Y., Sharan, L., Adelson, E.H.: Image statistics and the perception of surface qualities. Nature **447**(7141), 206 (2007)
6. te Pas, S.F., Pont, S.C.: A comparison of material and illumination discrimination performance for real rough, real smooth and computer generated smooth spheres. In: Proceedings of the 2nd Symposium on Applied Perception in Graphics and Visualization, pp. 75–81. ACM (2005)
7. Kiyasu, Y., Mizokami, Y., Yaguchi, H.: Influence of changes in diffusivity of lighting on appearance of object surface. In: ICVS 2017 Abstract Book, p. 77 (2017)
8. Mizokami, Y., Nozaki, W., Yaguchi, H.: Stable colour appearance among change in the diffuseness of illumination, In: Proceedings of CIE 2018 "Topical Conference on Smart Lighting" (CIE x045:2018), pp. 50–54. CIE, Taipei (2018)
9. Maki, M., Domon, R., Yamamoto, S., Tsumura, N.: Gloss and material constancy in the change of light source size. In: Color and Imaging Conference, vol. 2015, no. 1, pp. 191–195. Society for Imaging Science and Technology (2015)

10. Fleming, R.W., Dror, R.O., Adelson, E.H.: Real-world illumination and the per-ception of surface reflectance properties. J. Vis. **3**(5), 3 (2003)
11. Cuttle, C.: Research note: a practical approach to cubic illuminance measurement. Light. Res. Technol. **46**(1), 31–34 (2014)
12. Yamazoe, T., Gouma, Y., Azuma, Y.: Evaluation of connectives between color and typical adjective metaphor in Japanese language. In: Proceedings of the 2nd International Conference on Culture Technology, pp. 150–152 (2017)

# Material Appearance Transfer with Visual Cortex Image

Hiroaki Kotera[✉]

Kotera Imaging Laboratory, Chiba 266-0032, Japan
hiroimage@asahi.email.ne.jp

**Abstract.** Material perception is a current hot topic. Recently a basic research on SHITSUKAN (material perception) has advanced under MEXT (Ministry of Education, Culture, Sports, Science and Technology) in Japan. It is expected to bring innovation for not only traditional craft, ceramic or plastic arts but also more realistic picture displays on 4K/8K HD TVs and VR/CG world. The material perception is said as a phenomenon that our brain feels from retinal images. Now, the analysis is progressing what features of optical images are more strongly related to the stimulus inside the visual cortex of V1–V5.

BRDF model describes the Specular and Diffusion components of optical surface reflection which carry "gloss" and "texture" appearance and used to adjust or modify material appearances.

Different from BRDF or other models, this paper tries to transfer a material color appearance from one to another images. First, the retinal image is converted to visual cortex image based on LPT (Log-Polar Transform). Since LPT samples the retinal image higher rate at the fovea but lower rate at the peripherals, the color information gathers to central areas in the visual cortex. After the LPT, PCM (Principal Component Matching) is applied to make the color matching between source and target images. Using the joint LPT-PCM model, a material color appearance of target image is transferred to source image without any priori informations on the target.

**Keywords:** Material appearance · Color transfer · Visual cortex · Principal component

## 1 Background

Human observers can recognize material property at a glance through our sensory organ. Without touching materials, we can tell whether they would feel hard or soft, rough or smooth, wet or dry.

The material perception is said as a perceptual phenomenon of feeling or sensation that our brain perceives from optical image projected onto retina. Though, it's hard to untangle what information of the retinal image stimulates the visual cortex and how it induces the material feeling in our brain. The mechanism of INNER VSION in brain is still a black box at present [1].

As a framework for material perception, Tsumura initiated the skin color appearance and proposed the concept of appearance delivering system [2].

© Springer Nature Switzerland AG 2019
S. Tominaga et al. (Eds.): CCIW 2019, LNCS 11418, pp. 334–348, 2019.
https://doi.org/10.1007/978-3-030-13940-7_25

In Brain Information Science research on *SHITSUKAN* by *MEXT* in Japan, the first stage (2010–2014, led by Dr. H. Komatsu) has just finished and the second stage (2015–2019 led by Dr. S. Nishida) stepped forward into "multi-dimensional" material perception and now is approaching to the final goal.

In spite of the complexity in material appearance mechanism, human sensations such as "gloss/mat", "transparent/translucent", "metal/cloth" are controllable by an intuitive but a smart technique.

For instance, Motoyoshi and Nishida et al. [3] noticed the *"gloss"* perception appears when the luminance histogram is skewed. If it's stretched smoothly to the higher luminance, the object looks "glossy" but looks *"mat"*, if compressed to the lower.

Sawayama and Nishida [4] developed *"wet"* filter by a combination of exponent-shaped TRC and boosted color saturation. It's very interesting any *"skew"* in the image features induces a sensational material perception. The finding of *"skew"* effect seems *heuristic* and *intuitive*. However, the mechanism why and how such sensations as *"gloss"* or *"wet"* are activated by the *"skew"* effect in INNER VISION is not still untangled yet.

On the other hand, many R&D for practical applications are making steady progresses in private enterprises. As a typical successful example, a specular reflection control algorithm based on BRDF (Bidirectional Reflectance Distribution Function) is implemented in LSI chip and mounted on next generation 4K HD TV "REGZA" [5].

## 2   Color Transfer Model Between Images

Since the material perceptions such as *gloss* or *clarity* are related to a variety of factors [6], it's hard to specify the cause of perceptual feeling to a single factor. Nevertheless, trials on material or textual appearances transfer between CG images [7] or 3D objects [8] are reported. Especially, color appearance plays an important role in the material perception. The color transfer model [9] tried to change the color atmosphere of source scene A into that of target scene B, where the clustered color distribution of A is roughly matched with that of B. There, the use of vision-based $l\alpha\beta$ color space [10] attracted interest.

### 2.1   $l\alpha\beta$ Color Transfer Model

The $l\alpha\beta$ is known as an orthogonal *luminance-chrominance* color space simply transformed from *RGB* by the following **Step1** and **Step2** and the color distribution of source image is changed to match with that of target (reference) image by the scaling process in **Step3** and the color atmosphere of target is transferred to the source via the inverse transform in **Step4** as follows

**Step1:** RGB to LMS cone response transform

$$\begin{bmatrix} L \\ M \\ S \end{bmatrix} = \begin{bmatrix} 0.381 & 0.578 & 0.040 \\ 0.197 & 0.724 & 0.078 \\ 0.024 & 0.129 & 0.844 \end{bmatrix} \begin{bmatrix} R \\ G \\ B \end{bmatrix} \tag{1}$$

**Step2:** *LMS to lαβ transform with orthogonal luminance l and* chrominance αβ

$$\begin{bmatrix} l \\ \alpha \\ \beta \end{bmatrix} = \begin{bmatrix} 1/\sqrt{3} & 0 & 0 \\ 0 & 1/\sqrt{6} & 0 \\ 0 & 0 & 1/\sqrt{2} \end{bmatrix} \begin{bmatrix} 1 & 1 & 1 \\ 1 & 1 & -2 \\ 1 & -1 & 0 \end{bmatrix} \begin{bmatrix} \log L \\ \log M \\ \log S \end{bmatrix} \tag{2}$$

**Step3:** *Scaling of lαβ around the mean values $\{\bar{l}\,\bar{\alpha}\,\bar{\beta}\}$ by the ratio of standarddeviation to make match the color distributions between source and target images.*

$$\begin{aligned} l' &= (\sigma^l_{DST}/\sigma^l_{ORG})(l - \bar{l}) \\ \alpha' &= (\sigma^\alpha_{DST}/\sigma^\alpha_{ORG})(\alpha - \bar{\alpha}) \\ \beta' &= (\sigma^\beta_{DST}/\sigma^\beta_{ORG})(\beta - \bar{\beta}) \end{aligned} \tag{3}$$

*Where, $\sigma^l_{ORG}$ and $\sigma^\alpha_{DST}$ denote the standard deviation of luminance l for the source image and that of chrominance α for the target image, and so on.*
**Step4:** *Inverse transform $[l'\alpha'\beta'] \Rightarrow [L'M'S'] \Rightarrow [R'G'B']$.*
*Finally, the scaled $l'\alpha'\beta'$ source image with the color distribution matched to the target image is displayed on sRGB monitor.*

## 2.2  PCM Color Transfer Model

Prior to *lαβ* model, the author et al. developed PCM (Principal Component Matchng) method [11, 12] for transferring the color atmosphere from one scene to another as illustrated in Fig. 1. The *lαβ* model works well between the scenes with color similarity but not for the scenes with color dissimilarity and often fails. While, PCM model works almost stable between the scenes with color dissimilarities and advanced toward automatic scene color interchange [13–15].

In our basic object-to-object PCM model a vector $X$ in a color cluster is projected onto a vector $Y$ in PC space by Hotelling Transform as

$$Y = A(X - \mu) \tag{4}$$

Where, $\mu$ denotes the mean vector and the matrix $A$ is formed by the set of eigen vectors $\{e_1\,e_2\,e_3\}$ of covariance matrix $\Sigma_X$ as

$$A = [e_1\,e_2\,e_3] \tag{5}$$

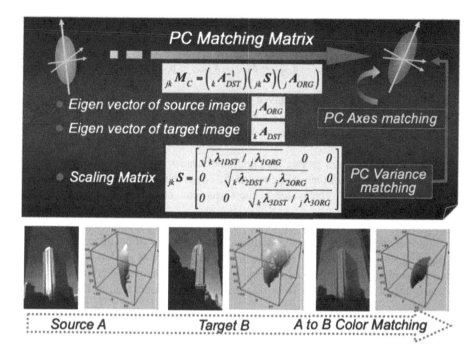

**Fig. 1.** Concept of PCM color transfer model between images

The covariance matrix $\Sigma_Y$ of $\{Y\}$ is diagonalized in terms of $A$ and $\Sigma_X$ with the elements composed of the eigen values $\{\lambda_1\ \lambda_2\ \lambda_3\}$ of $\Sigma_X$ as

$$\Sigma_Y = A(\Sigma_X)A^t = \begin{bmatrix} \lambda_1 & 0 & 0 \\ 0 & \lambda_2 & 0 \\ 0 & 0 & \lambda_3 \end{bmatrix} \tag{6}$$

Thus the color vectors in source and target images are mapped to the same *PC* space and the following equations are formed to make match a *source* vector $Y_{ORG}$ to a *target* vector $Y_{DST}$ through the scaling matrix $S$ as follows.

$$Y_{DST} = A_{DST}(X_{DST} - \mu_{DST}) \text{ and } Y_{ORG} = A_{ORG}(X_{ORG} - \mu_{ORG}) \tag{7}$$

$$Y_{DST} = S \cdot Y_{ORG} \tag{8}$$

$$S = \begin{bmatrix} \sqrt{\lambda_{1DST}/\lambda_{1ORG}} & 0 & 0 \\ 0 & \sqrt{\lambda_{2DST}/\lambda_{2ORG}} & 0 \\ 0 & 0 & \sqrt{\lambda_{3DST}/\lambda_{3ORG}} \end{bmatrix} \tag{9}$$

Solving (7) and (8), we get the following relation between a source color $X_{ORG}$ and a target color $X_{DST}$ to be transferred and matched.

$$X_{DST} - \mu_{DST} = M_{PCM}(X_{ORG} - \mu_{ORG}) \tag{10}$$

The matching matrix $M_{PCM}$ is given by

$$M_{PCM} = \left(A_{DST}^{-1}\right)(S)(A_{ORG}) \tag{11}$$

Where, $A_{ORG}$ and $A_{DST}$ denote the eigen matrices for the *source* color cluster and the *target* color cluster. In the scaling matrix $S$, $\lambda_{1ORG}$ means the 1st eigenvalue of the source and $\lambda_{2DST}$ the 2nd eigenvalue of the target, etc. These are obtained from each covariance matrix.

In general, the PCM model works better than $l\alpha\beta$ even for the scenes with color dissimilarities, because of using the statistical characteristics of covariance matrix.

Figure 2 shows a successful example in both $l\alpha\beta$ and PCM models for the images with color similarity. While, in case of Fig. 3, $l\alpha\beta$ fails to change the color atmosphere of A into that of B due to their color dissimilarities, but works well in PCM.

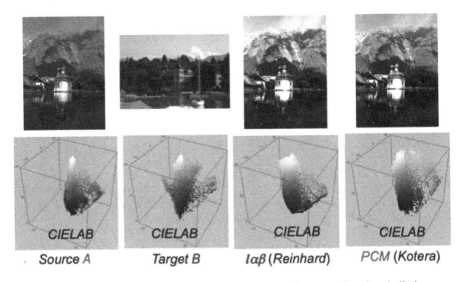

**Fig. 2.** Successful example in color transfer between images with color similarity

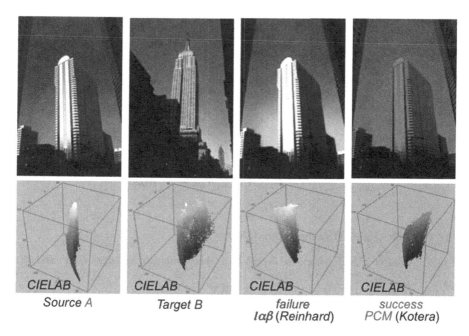

Source A | Target B | failure<br>*Iαβ (Reinhard)* | success<br>*PCM (Kotera)*

**Fig. 3.** Comparison in $I\alpha\beta$ vs. PCM models for images with color dissimilarity

## 3  Color Transfer by Spectral Decomposition of Covariance

Following the $I\alpha\beta$ model, a variety of improved or alternative color transfer models have been reported. As a basic drawback in $I\alpha\beta$ model, Pitié et al. [16] pointed out that it's not based on the statistical covariance but only on the mean values and variances in the major $I\alpha\beta$ axes. Hence PCM model is better than $I\alpha\beta$ because of using the statistical covariance matrix $\Sigma_X$ with the Hotelling transform onto the PC space. At the same time, Pitie suggested to make use of orthogonal spectral decomposition paying the attention to the Hermitian (Self adjoint) property of symmetric matrix $\Sigma_X$ with real eigenvalues.

### 3.1  Eigen Value Decomposition (EVD) of Covariance

In general, the covariance matrix $\Sigma$ in a clustered color distribution of image is a real symmetric matrix. The square root of $\Sigma$ for source and target images is decomposed by eigenvalues as

$$\Sigma_{ORG}^{1/2} = A_{ORG}^{-1}D_{ORG}^{1/2}A_{ORG} \text{ and } \Sigma_{DST}^{1/2} = A_{DST}^{-1}D_{DST}^{1/2}A_{DST} \qquad (12)$$

$A_{ORG}$ and $A_{DST}$ denote the eigen matrices for source and target images. $D_{ORG}$ and $D_{DST}$ are given by the diagonal matrices with the entries of their eigen values respectively.

$$D_{ORG} = \begin{bmatrix} \lambda_{1ORG} & 0 & 0 \\ 0 & \lambda_{2ORG} & 0 \\ 0 & 0 & \lambda_{3ORG} \end{bmatrix}, D_{DST} = \begin{bmatrix} \lambda_{1DST} & 0 & 0 \\ 0 & \lambda_{2DST} & 0 \\ 0 & 0 & \lambda_{3DST} \end{bmatrix} \quad (13)$$

Now, the color matching matrix $M_{Eigen}$ corresponding to Eq. (11) is given by

$$\begin{aligned} M_{Eigen} &= \Sigma_{DST}^{1/2} \Sigma_{ORG}^{-1/2} \\ &= \left( A_{DST}^{-1} D_{DST}^{1/2} A_{DST} \right) \left( A_{ORG}^{-1} D_{ORG}^{1/2} A_{ORG} \right)^{-1} \\ &= \left( A_{DST}^{-1} D_{DST}^{1/2} A_{DST} \right) \left( A_{ORG}^{-1} D_{ORG}^{-1/2} A_{ORG} \right) \end{aligned} \quad (14)$$

### 3.2   Singular Value Decomposition (SVD)

A m $\times$ n Matrix $\Sigma$ is decomposed by **SVD** as the product of matrices $U$, $V$, and $W$

$$\Sigma = UWV \quad (15)$$

Where, $U$ and $V$ are m $\times$ m and n $\times$ n orthogonal matrices. If $\Sigma$ is a m $\times$ n rectangular matrix of rank-r, matrix $W$ is composed of r $\times$ r diagonal matrix with the singular values as its entries and the remaining small null matrices.

Because the covariance $\Sigma$ is a 3 $\times$ 3 real symmetric matrix, the singular values equal to the eigenvalues and **SVD** equals **EVD** in Eq. (12).

### 3.3   Cholesky Decomposition

Cholesky, a compact spectral decomposition method, decomposes the covariance $\Sigma$ as a simple product of lower triangular matrix and its transpose as follows.

$$\begin{aligned} \Sigma_{ORG} &= L_{ORG} L_{ORG}^T \ for \ L_{ORG} = Chol[\Sigma_{ORG}]^T : T = transpose \\ \Sigma_{DST} &= L_{DST} L_{DST}^T \ for \ L_{DST} = Chol[\Sigma_{DST}]^T \end{aligned} \quad (16)$$

Where, $Chol[*]$ denotes the Cholesky decomposition. The lower triangular matrix $L$ is obtained by the iteration just like as Gaussian elimination method (details omitted).

The color matching matrix $M_{Chol}$ to transfer the color atmosphere of target image into the source is given by

$$M_{Chol} = L_{DST}(L_{ORG})^{-1} \quad (17)$$

# 4   Color Transfer by PCM After Mapping to Visual Cortex

## 4.1   Retina to Visual Cortex Mapping by Log Polar Transform

The PCM model works well to transfer the color atmosphere between the images even with color dissimilarities. However, any human visual characteristic has not been taken into account. In this paper, a striking feature in the spatial color distributions in our visual cortex image is introduced to improve the performance in PCM.

The mapping to visual cortex from retina is mathematically described by Schwartz's complex Logarithmic Polar Transform (LPT) [17].

The complex vector $z$ pointing a pixel located at $(x, y)$ in the retina is transformed to a new vector $log\,(z)$ by LPT as follows.

$$z = x + jy = \rho e^{j\theta} \,;\, \rho = |z|\; and\; \theta = tan^{-1}(y/x)$$
$$log(z) = u + jv = log(\rho) + j\,\theta\,;\, j = \sqrt{-1} \tag{18}$$

The retinal image is sampled at spatially-variant resolution on the polar coordinate $(\rho, \theta)$, that is, in the radial direction, fine in the fovea but coarser towards peripheral according to the *logarithm of $\rho$,* while in the angle direction, at a constant pitch $\varDelta\theta$ and stored to the coordinate $(u, v)$ in the striate cortex V1. Figure 4 illustrates a sketch how the retinal image is sampled, stored in the striate cortex, and played back to retina.

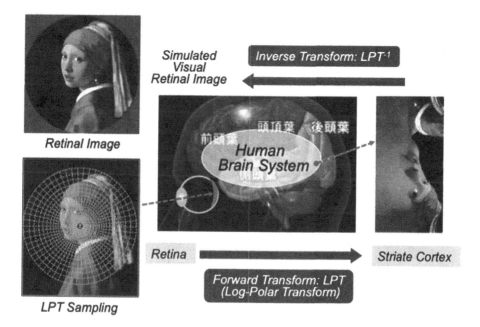

**Fig. 4.** Outline of Spatially-variant Mapping to Visual Cortex from Retina

## 4.2   Discrete Log Polar Transform

In the discrete LPT system, $(\rho, \theta)$ is digitized to $R$ number of rings and $S$ number of sectors. The striate cortex image is stored in the new Cartesian coordinates $(u, v)$ as

$$(u, v) \underline{\underline{\Delta}} \{\rho(u), \theta(v)\}$$
$$\rho(u) = \rho_0 a^u \ for \ \rho \geq \rho_0, u = 1, 2, \cdots, R$$
$$a = exp[log(\rho_{max}/\rho_0)/R]$$
$$\theta(v) = v\Delta\theta = (2\pi/S)v \ for \ v = 1, 2, \cdots, S$$

(19)

$\rho_0$ denotes the radius of blind spot and $\rho \geq \rho_0$ prevents for the points near origin not to be mapped to the negative infinite-point. This regulation is called CBS (Central Blind Spot) model. Figure 5 illustrates how the image "sunflower" is sampled in LPT lattice and transformed to striate cortex image, then stored in the coordinates $(u, v)$.

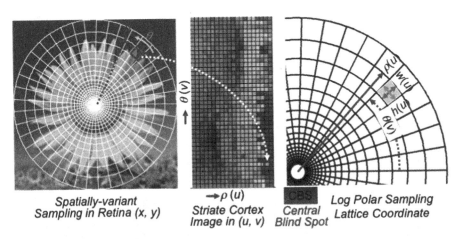

Spatially-variant Sampling in Retina (x, y)      Striate Cortex Image in (u, v)   Central Blind Spot   Log Polar Sampling Lattice Coordinate

**Fig. 5.** Image "sunflower" sampled in LPT lattice, transformed and stored in Striate Cortex

The height $h(u)$ and width $w(u)$ of an unit cell between $u + 1$ and $u$ are given by the following equations. Hence the area $\alpha(u)$ of unit cell increases exponentially with $u$.

$$h(u) = \rho(u + 1) - \rho(u) = \rho_0(a - 1)a^u$$
$$w(u) = \frac{1}{2}(2\pi/S)\{\rho(u + 1) + \rho(u)\} = (\pi/S)(1 + a)a^u \rho_0$$
$$\alpha(u) = h(u)w(u) = \pi\rho_0^2(a^2 - 1)a^{2u}S^{-1}$$

(20)

As sensed in Fig. 5, the color is sampled finer in the center but coarser towards peripheral. The pixels in the yellow petals occupy larger area than peripheral. This spatially-variant characteristics to collect the color information on the viewpoint must be reflected in the population density in the color distribution of striate cortex image.

Figure 6 is another example for a pink rose *"cherry shell"*. It shows how the color distribution is concentrated on the pinkish petal area around at the central viewpoint in the striate cortex image. Hence it'll be better for applying PCM not on the original but on the striate cortex image after LPT to perform the color matching more effective for the object of attention.

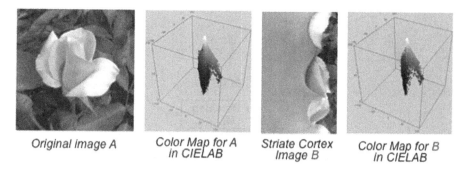

Original image A     Color Map for A
in CIELAB     Striate Cortex
Image B     Color Map for B
in CIELAB

**Fig. 6.** Spatially-variant color concentration effect in striate cortex image by LPT

Now the basic PCM matrix $M_{PCM}$ in Eq. (11) is applied to the covariance after LPT and we get newly the following color transfer matrix.

$$M_{LPTPCM} = \left(_{LPT}A_{DST}^{-1}\right)\left(_{LPT}S\right)\left(_{LPT}A_{ORG}\right)$$

$$_{LPT}S = \begin{bmatrix} \sqrt{_{LPT}\lambda_{1DST}/_{LPT}\lambda_{1ORG}} & 0 & 0 \\ 0 & \sqrt{_{LPT}\lambda_{2DST}/_{LPT}\lambda_{2ORG}} & 0 \\ 0 & 0 & \sqrt{_{LPT}\lambda_{3DST}/_{LPT}\lambda_{3ORG}} \end{bmatrix}$$

$$(21)$$

Figure 7 illustrates the color transfer process in LPTPCM model. In this sample, both the source image A and target image B are first transformed to the visual cortex images by LPT, then the clustered color distribution in cortex image A is transformed to match with that of cortex image by PCM. As a result, the material appearance of greenish transparent wine glass B looks to be transferred to that of gold mask image A.

Since the original images A and B have color dissimilarity, it's a hard to make the color matching only by the single use of basic PCM. While, by just placing LPT before PCM, the feeling of greenish wine glass B is well conveyed to that of gold mask A.

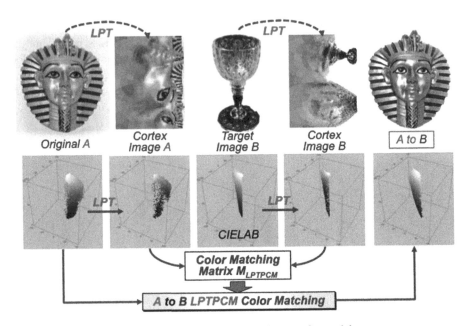

**Fig. 7.** Improved LPTPCM color transfer model

## 5 Experimental Results and Discussions

The performance of proposed LPTPCM model is compared with the other methods mentioned in Sect. 3. Figure 8 shows the results for the same images used in Fig. 7. The $l\alpha\beta$ model fails for such images with color dissimilarity. The source image colors remain almost unchanged. Eigenvalue and Cholesky decomposition methods reflect the greenish target colors a little bit, but look unnatural. In the basic PCM model, the black in eyes and the green in mask face seem to have replaced unnatural. Any mismatches in the directions of PC axes might occur. While, LPTPCM model worked successful for transferring the color atmosphere of wine glass to that of gold mask.

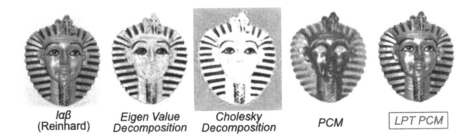

**Fig. 8.** Performance of LPTPCM model in comparison with other methods

Figure 9 shows another example for color transfer between three glass vases with different patterns. As well, $l\alpha\beta$ was hardly function remaining the source colors almost unchanged. Though Eigenvalue and Cholesky decomposition methods showed certain effects, a partial color mixing happened between the source B and target A as shown in B to A color matching. PCM and LPTPCM looks like a neck and neck. But looking carefully, LPTPCM gives a little bit better impression than PCM due to conveying the clean textures in the target.

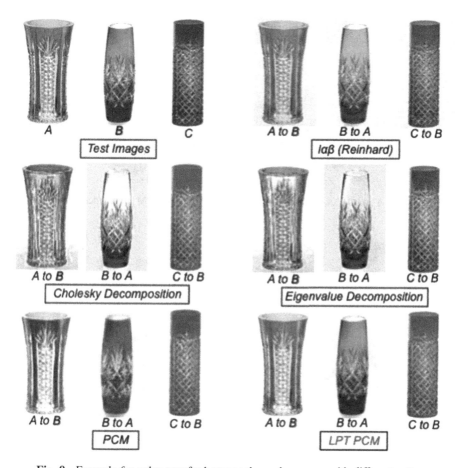

**Fig. 9.** Example for color transfer between three glass vases with different patterns

Figure 10 is a comparison in PCM and LPTPCM for handcraft pots. Both achieved the expected results. It's hard to tell which is better. How to make a quantitative evaluation is left behind as a future challenge.

On the other hand, Fig. 11 shows a result for color transfer between the images with heterogeneous textures. (a) tried to transfer the color atmosphere of *"greenish wine glass"* to that of *"reddish Porsche"*, where only LPTPCM was successful.

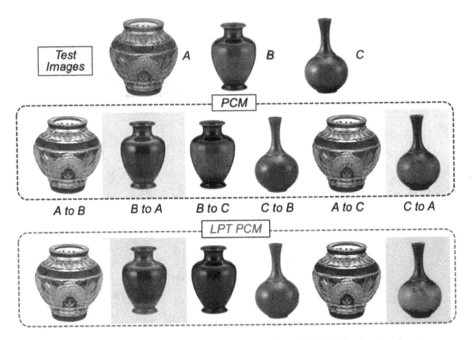

**Fig. 10.** Almost neck and neck results in PCM vs. LPCPCM for handcraft pots

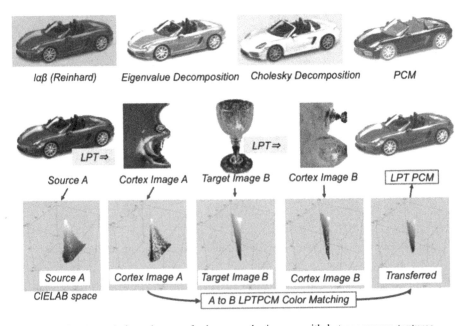

**Fig. 11.** A result for color transfer between the images with heterogeneous textures

Figure 12 shows the performance between PCM vs. LPTPCM in case of changing the target image B to the gold mask or handcraft pot B. In the upper case of gold mask target, LPTPCM clearly reflects the feeling of the target, but in the lower case of green pot target, it's hard to tell which is better, maybe, depending on personal preference.

**Fig. 12.** Comparisons in PCM vs. LPTPCM for changing the target images

For the sake of simplicity, the basic PCM is applied assuming a single clustered image. In the case of multi-clustered image, any segmentation is needed for separeting the colored objects to each cluster then the oblect-to-object PCM is performed. But, it's hard to find the corresponding pair of objects particularly in the case of dissimilar color images [12–14]. Hence, the proposed model is not universal but limited to the images handled as a single cluster. Also, it should be noted on the margin of image background. Figure 13 shows how the results in PCM differes by the margin of background, because the white margins influence on the image color clusters. As clearly seen, LPTPCM is insensitive to the margins and robust than PCM. The reason why comes from that LPT mimics the retina to/from cortex imaging called *Foveation*.

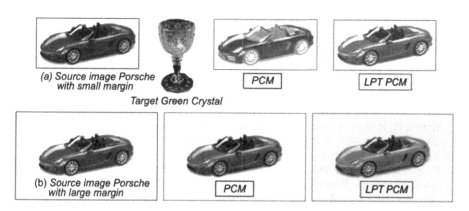

**Fig. 13.** Comparisons in PCM vs. LPTPCM for the different margin of image background

# 6  Conclusions

This paper challenged to apply the scene color transfer methods to the material appearance transfer. The proposed LPTPCM model is a joint LPT-PCM algorithm. Prior to PCM (Principal Component Matching), the source A and Target B retinal images are transformed to striate cortex images by LPT (Log-Polar-Transform). The key is to make use of color concentration characteristics on the central viewpoint of striate cortex by LPT. The performance of conventional PCM is significantly enhanced by the cooperation with LPT. The proposed model transfers the color atmosphere of target image B to that of source image A without any a priori information or optical measurement for the material properties. The question is how to evaluate the transformed image is perceptually acceptable or not. Any quantitative quality measure is hoped to be developed and is left behind as a future work.

# References

1. Zeki, S.: Inner Vision: An Exploration of Art and the Brain. Oxford University Press, Oxford (1999)
2. Tsumura, N., et al.: Estimating reflectance property from refocused images and its application to auto material appearance balancing. JIST **59**(3), 30501-1–30501-6 (2015)
3. Motoyoshi, I., Nishida, S., Sharan, L., Adelson, E.H.: Image statistics and the perception of surface qualities. Nature **447**, 206–209 (2007)
4. Sawayama, M., Nishida, S.: Visual perception of surface wetness. J. Vis. **15**(12), 937 (2015)
5. Kobiki, H., et al.: Specular reflection control technology to increase glossiness of images. Toshiba Rev. **68**(9), 38–41 (2013)
6. Fleming, R.W.: Visual perception of materials and their properties. Vis. Res. **94**, 62–75 (2014)
7. Mihálik, A., Durikovi£, R.: Material appearance transfer between images. In: SCCG 2009, Proceedings of the 2009 Spring Conference, CG, pp. 55–58 (2009)
8. Nguyen, C.H., et al.: 3D material style transfer. In: Proceedings of the EUROGRAPHICS, vol. 31, no. 2 (2012)
9. Reinhard, E., et al.: Color transfer between images. IEEE CG Appl. **21**, 34–40 (2001)
10. Ruderman, D.L., et al.: Statistics of cone responses to natural images: implications for visual coding. JOSA **A-15**(8), 2036–2045 (1998)
11. Kotera, H., et al.: Object-oriented color matching by image clustering. In: Proceedings of the CIC6, pp. 154–158 (1998)
12. Kotera, H., et al.: Object-to-object color mapping by image segmentation. J. Electron. Imaging **10**(4)/1, 977–987 (2001)
13. Kotera, H., Horiuchi, T.: Automatic interchange in scene colors by image segmentation. In: Proceedings of the CIC12, pp. 93–99 (2004)
14. Kotera, H., et al.: Automatic color interchange between images. In: Proceedings of the AIC 2005, pp. 1019–1022 (2015)
15. Kotera, H.: Intelligent image processing. J. SID **14**(9), 745–754 (2006)
16. Pitié, F., Kokaram, A.: The linear Monge-Kantorovitch colour mapping for example-based colour transfer. In: Proceedings of the IET CVMP, pp. 23–31 (2007)
17. Schwartz, E.L.: Spatial mapping in the primate sensory projection: analytic structure and relevance to perception. Biol. Cybern. **25**, 181–194 (1977)

# Author Index

Printed in the United States
By Bookmasters